T0387034

Access your online resources

Working with Adults with Communication Difficulties in the Criminal Justice System is accompanied by a number of printable online materials, designed to ensure this resource best supports your professional needs.

Go to https://resourcecentre.routledge.com/speechmark and click on the cover of this book.

Answer the question prompt using your copy of the book to gain access to the online content.

Working with Adults with Communication Difficulties in the Criminal Justice System

This book offers guidance for speech and language therapists and other professionals who are working in a criminal justice setting or who are interested to know more about this dynamic and rewarding client group.

The criminal justice system (CJS) includes police custody, community services, secure hospitals and prisons. Although each setting has its differences, there are overarching areas associated with speech, language and communication needs (SLCN) within the population who find themselves coming into contact with the CJS.

These needs are many and varied: from social deprivation and developmental language disorder, to head injury, substance misuse and ADHD. The variety is both stimulating and challenging, and this book provides the reader with a range of resources to use with such a complex client base. Key features include:

- academic evidence about SLCN in the CJS
- accessible visuals explaining the systems pathways
- resources to support assessment and intervention
- information to support individuals with a range of overlapping needs.

Aimed primarily at speech and language therapists, the book also includes useful content for students, academics and professionals who wish to know more about SLCN within the CJS. As well as being full of useful infographics, this book includes a vast appendix of online material that can be downloaded and printed for use in practice.

Jacqui Learoyd is a speech and language therapist with experience of working with adults in secure hospitals and prisons. Jacqui works across all ages from 18 to end of life, trying to support the communication needs of this marginalised group at all stages of their criminal justice journey. She has specific interests in de-escalating tense situations via communication, supporting competence in social communication and helping everyone to understand that just because a person can talk, it doesn't mean that they are skilled in understanding and expression.

Karen Bryan is a professor and Vice-Chancellor at York St John University. She previously worked as a consultant speech and language therapist in a high-secure setting for 15 years. Her research interests are in communication difficulties in young offenders and in forensic populations, as well as the impact of communication difficulties on access to health care.

The *Working With* Series

The *Working With* series provides speech and language therapists with a range of 'go-to' resources, full of well-sourced, up-to-date information regarding specific disorders. Underpinned by robust theoretical foundations and supported by intervention options and exercises, every book ensures that the reader has access to the latest thinking regarding diagnosis, management and treatment options.

Written in a fully accessible style, each book bridges theory and practice and offers ready-to-use and well-rehearsed practical material, including guidance on interventions, management advice and therapeutic resources for the client, parent or carer. The series is an invaluable resource for practitioners, whether speech and language therapy students or more experienced clinicians.

Books in the series include:

Working with Solution Focused Brief Therapy in Healthcare Settings
Kidge Burns and Sarah Northcott
2022 / pb: 9780367435097

Working with Children Experiencing Speech and Language Disorders in a Bilingual Context
Sean Pert
2022 / pb: 9780367646301

Working with Global Aphasia
Sharon Adjei-Nicol
2023 / pb: 9781032019437

Working with Trans Voice
Matthew Mills and Sean Pert
2023 / pb: 9781032012605

Working with Autistic Children and Young People
Sally Mordi
2023 / pb: 9780367723149

Working with Adults with Communication Difficulties in the Criminal Justice System
Jacqui Learoyd and Karen Bryan
2023 / pb: 9781032265322

Working With Adults with Communication Difficulties in the Criminal Justice System

A Practical Guide for Speech and Language Therapists

Jacqui Learoyd and Karen Bryan

Routledge
Taylor & Francis Group

LONDON AND NEW YORK

Designed cover image: © Getty Images

First published 2024
by Routledge
4 Park Square, Milton Park, Abingdon, Oxon OX14 4RN

and by Routledge
605 Third Avenue, New York, NY 10158

Routledge is an imprint of the Taylor & Francis Group, an informa business

© 2024 Jacqui Learoyd and Karen Bryan

British Library Cataloguing-in-Publication Data
A catalogue record for this book is available from the British Library

Library of Congress Cataloging-in-Publication Data
Names: Learoyd, Jacqui, author. | Bryan, Karen, author.
Title: Working with adults with communication difficulties in the criminal justice system: a practical guide for speech and language therapists/ Jacqui Learoyd and Karen Bryan.
Description: New York, NY: Routledge, 2023. |
Series: Working with | Includes bibliographical references and index. |
Summary: – Provided by publisher.
Identifiers: LCCN 2023000972 (print) | LCCN 2023000973 (ebook) |
ISBN 9781032265315 (hbk) | ISBN 9781032265322 (pbk) |
ISBN 9781003288701 (ebk)
Subjects: LCSH: Prisoners with disabilities. | Special needs offenders. |
People with disabilities-Means of communication. |
Communicative disorders. | Speech therapists.
Classification: LCC HV1568.4 .W67 2023 (print) | LCC HV1568.4 (ebook) |
DDC 362.4/048-dc23/eng/20230328
LC record available at https://lccn.loc.gov/2023000972
LC ebook record available at https://lccn.loc.gov/2023000973

ISBN: 978-1-032-26531-5 (hbk)
ISBN: 978-1-032-26532-2 (pbk)
ISBN: 978-1-003-28870-1 (ebk)

DOI: 10.4324/9781003288701

Typeset in Interstate
by Deanta Global Publishing Services, Chennai, India

Access the companion website: https://resourcecentre.routledge.com/speechmark

Contents

Foreword

As Chief Inspector of Prisons, I commissioned a systematic review of the treatment of young prisoners. I thought that it would be a pity if we did not include how young people were managed in other parts of the United Kingdom, and I met Dan Gunn. the Governor of Polmont Prison in Scotland.

While we were walking around his prison, Dan Gunn surprised me by saying, apropos of nothing, that if, by any mischance, he were ordered to dismiss all his staff, the last one out of the gate would be his speech and language therapist. Never having come across such an appointment in England, I was keen to learn more.

So we went to see Shirley Johnson, the admirable woman who was conducting the speech and language therapy, who told me that the boys could not communicate because they did not communicate during normal family life. Unless they could communicate with staff, staff did not know how they should deal with them.

I asked who was the best speech and language therapist in England, to which she replied at once that Karen Bryan was, who was at that time at University College London. So I rang her up and asked her to an inspection of HMYOI Stoke Heath, where I knew there was a very good governor, who had been in post for several years, and where Karen's task as a researcher was to put 10% of the boys through a standardised speech and language therapy assessment.

I cannot remember all the things she found, but the fact that always remains in my memory is that 100% of the boys assessed would benefit from speech and language therapy. Armed with this fact, I went to see Jack Straw, at that time Home Secretary and responsible for prisons, to ask him for £30,000, every year, to provide an SLT for each young offender institution (YOI). Despite giving my reasoning, he refused point blank.

But I still had one arrow left up my sleeve. Lady Hamlyn said that she was willing to provide the funds to pay for an evaluated experiment to provide evidence to support something truly worthwhile, which providing an SLT in every YOI obviously was. I proposed setting up two SLTs for two years in each of two YOIs, the whole thing being academically led by Professor Karen Bryan. Thus, SLTs were appointed to HMYOI Werrington and HMYOI Brinsford, with the governors of each contacting me within a month to say that they did not know how they managed without an SLT for so long.

I went to HMYOI Brinsford where a hard-bitten senior officer – and within the YOI system they don't come more hard-bitten than that – admitted to me that until Cheryl (naming the SLT) came along, they had probably damaged some boys through punishment, when all that they needed was therapy.

Successive Home Secretaries turned the obvious and, by now, academically researched proposal down. By then, more international evidence was emerging and the issue of young offenders with low levels of language ability was highlighted in the Bercow report in 2008.

I have been a strong advocate for SLT in YOIs and prisons ever since, and it is very positive to see the progress made. In this very readable book, Jacqui Learoyd and Karen Bryan continue to make the case for SLT, which is all the stronger for the evidence and resources included.

Lord David Ramsbotham
HMCIP 1995-2001
November 2022

Abbreviations

ABA	applied behaviour analysis
ABI	acquired brain injury
ACCT	Assessment, Care in Custody and Teamwork
ACE	adverse childhood experience
ADD	attention deficit disorder
ADHD	attention deficit hyperactivity disorder
ADL	activities of daily living
AHP	allied health professional
ASC	autism spectrum conditions
ASOTP	Adapted Sex Offender Treatment Programmes
AVOTP	Adapted Violent Offender Treatment Programmes
BAME	Black, Asian and Minority Ethnic
BBV	blood-borne virus
BPVS III	British Picture Vocabulary Scale: 3rd Edition
CAI	court-appointed intermediary
CAT	Comprehensive Aphasia Test
CC-A	Communication Checklist – Adult
CELF-5 UK	Clinical Evaluation of Language Fundamentals Fifth Edition
CHAT	Comprehensive Health Assessment Tool
CJLDS	Criminal Justice Liaison and Diversion Services
CJS	criminal justice system
COM	community offender manager
COPD	chronic obstructive pulmonary disease
CPA	Care Programme Approach
CPS	Crown Prosecution Service
CSEW	Crime Survey for England and Wales
CSIP	Challenge, Support and Intervention Plan
CSRA	Cell Sharing Risk Assessment

CVA	cerebrovascular accident
DCD	developmental coordination disorder
DBS	Disclosure and Barring Service
DLD	developmental language disorder
EMS	Everyday Memory Survey
EVT-3	Expressive Vocabulary Test Third Edition
FOLS	Forensic Outreach Liaison Services
FPN	fixed penalty notice
GMC	General Medical Council
HCPC	Health and Care Professions Council
HMIP	His Majesty's Inspectorate of Prisons
HMPPS	His Majesty's Prison and Probation Services
IFL	identity-first language
IMCA	independent mental capacity advocate
IMHA	independent mental health advocate
IPP	Imprisonment for Public Protection
LA	local authority
LDDS	learning difficulties and disabilities
MDT	multi-disciplinary team
MHA	Mental Health Act (1983)
MI	motivational interviewing
MOJ	Ministry of Justice
NFA	no further action or no fixed abode
NMC	Nursing and Midwifery Council
NOMIS	National Offender Management Information System
NPS	National Probation Service
NQP	newly qualified practitioner
OM	offender manager
OT	occupational therapist
PACE	Police and Criminal Evidence
PACT	Prison Advice and Care Trust
PBS	positive behaviour support
PER	Person Escort Record
PFL	person-first language
PIPE	psychologically informed planned environment
POM	prison offender manager
PTSD	post-traumatic stress disorder

QAB	Quick Aphasia Battery
RC	responsible clinician
RCSLT	Royal College of Speech and Language Therapists
RI	registered intermediary
RN	registered nurse
SCFT	specialist community forensic team
SCH	secure children's home
SLCN	speech, language and communication need(s)
SLT	speech and language therapist/therapy
SOTP	Sex Offender Treatment Programmes
STC	secure training centre
TC	therapeutic community
TCSEW	Telephone-operated Crime Survey for England and Wales
TEA	Test of Everyday Attention
TOAL-4	Test of Adolescent and Adult Language Fourth Edition
TOMS	therapy outcome measures
TROG-2	Test for Reception of Grammar
VOTP	Violent Offender Treatment Programmes
WAIS	Wechsler Adult Intelligence Scale
WHO	World Health Organization
YJB	Youth Justice Board
YOI	young offender institution
YOT	youth offending team

Figures

Tables

INTRODUCTION

DOI: 10.4324/9781003288701-1

History of forensic SLT services

Working with people who are in contact with criminal justice services is a relatively new area of professional development for speech and language therapy (SLT). In the early 1990s, two of the three high-secure hospitals in England and Wales had an SLT service. These services reflected the dedication and determination of inspired and forward-thinking speech and language therapists (SLTs) Jenny France and Karen Elliot. In each hospital, the service was established and then evolved, with Rampton eventually having a national high-secure role for people with deafness and people with learning difficulties. At Broadmoor, the early focus was on facilitating psychotherapy in people with significant language limitations, later evolving into a service more orientated to enabling those with speech, language and communication difficulties to thrive within the hospital and to benefit from verbally mediated interventions. So it is interesting to note that the origins of forensic SLT practice are with adults who are held in an institution for the protection of themselves or the public.

Around the same time, the first SLT service for young offenders was established at Polmont in Scotland, again with a pioneering individual involved – Shirley Johnson. The governor at Polmont, Dan Gunn, was one of the first individuals in the prison service to raise the issue of communication difficulties in young offenders. When Lord David Ramsbotham, HM Chief Inspector of Prisons, was conducting a review of conditions and treatment of young offenders, he visited Polmont; during his tour, the governor remarked that if he had to get rid of any of his staff, his speech and language therapist would be the last to go. Lord Ramsbotham had never encountered such a professional and asked why. The governor stated: 'because the young people cannot communicate, with each other or with us, and until and unless they can, we do not know what we could be doing to help them. A trained therapist (SLT) is the only person capable of unlocking them for us' (Ramsbotham, 2012).

Lord Ramsbotham asked Shirley Johnson about her work and asked who would be the right person to undertake a research assignment for the Inspectorate on communication skills in young offenders. I was then fortunate enough to join an inspection in 2000, with an agreement to assess a random sample of 10% of the population. The results showed that over 60% of young offenders had significant speech, language and communication needs (SLCN) (Bryan, 2004). Lord Ramsbotham used the results to call for a full-time speech and language therapist in every young offender institution (YOI). In 2008, the Royal College of Speech and Language Therapists (RCSLT) proposed a service model for those at risk of offending or reoffending (Bryan and MacKenzie, 2008). However, it was to be some time before access to SLT was more routinely achieved. A Youth Justice Board survey in 2014, found that about half of the youth justice practitioners responding were screening young people for SLCN.

Policy developments recognising communication difficulties

A number of policy developments contributed to gradual awareness of the significance of speech, language and communication difficulties across youth justice services. A development that helped to highlight the negative impact of communication difficulties on a person's journey through the criminal justice system was the Registered Intermediary Service. In 1999, the registered intermediary role was introduced by section 29 of the Youth Justice and Criminal Evidence Act 1999 (YJCEA), which provides for the examination of a witness in criminal proceedings (other than a defendant) to be conducted through an intermediary if:

- they are under the age of 18 at the time of the hearing; or
- if the court considers that the quality of evidence given by the witness is likely to be diminished by: a mental disorder (within the meaning of the 1983 Mental Health Act); a significant impairment of intelligence and social functioning; or a physical disability or physical disorder.

Registered intermediaries (RI) are appointed for their ability to assess and diagnose communication difficulties and to support others, such as the police and court officials, to achieve effective communication so that the person can tell their story and give the best possible evidence that they can (Ministry of Justice, 2011). The service was piloted in England from 2004 and implemented fully in 2008. The scheme is now supporting nearly 7,000 vulnerable victims and witnesses with communication difficulties a year (Ministry of Justice, 2020) (see Chapter 3 for more information on the work of RIs).

Section 33BA of the Youth Justice and Criminal Evidence Act (1999) extends such support to defendants who qualify for intermediary special measures. However, this provision has not yet been implemented and is therefore not yet routinely available unless a judge determines that a trial cannot continue without RI support for the defendant.

However, the initial use of RIs was very limited, and a number of reports in the late 2000s highlighted the injustices of not supporting the communication needs of young people in touch with criminal justice services. In 2008, the *Bercow Report* highlighted that young people in youth justice settings with communication difficulties often experienced difficulties in responding to interventions as being 'sufficient to affect their ability to communicate with staff on a day-to-day basis, to prevent them from benefiting from verbally mediated interventions such as education and offender behaviour work and, if not addressed, to contribute to reoffending' (Bercow, 2008, p.41).

A criminal justice joint inspection thematic report of youth alcohol misuse and offending (Care Quality Commission et al., 2010) highlighted the variation among youth offending services in relation to how they assess communication difficulties. The report noted that there tended to be an assumption that any specific needs in this area would previously have been identified in an educational setting. However, a study of SLCN services in Milton Keynes Youth Offending Team (YOT) suggested that children are often misdiagnosed as having a behavioural problem or conduct disorder when in fact they have undiagnosed SLCN (Lanz, 2009).

Gradually, the need to support young people with communication difficulties within the criminal justice system became more compelling. In 2014, the *Asset Plus* speech, language, communication and neuro-disability screening tool based on the RCSLT screening tool (with broader elements to include neuro-disability) (Youth Justice Board of England and Wales, 2014) was included in the Comprehensive Health Assessment Tool (CHAT) (Offender Health Research Network, 2013). This was a significant step in that for the first time every young person entering a community youth justice service or a custodial environment would have systematic assessment including speech, language and communication assessment. However, the assessments are often undertaken by staff who are not trained (or supported) to conduct the assessments, and concerns have been raised by studies that compare CHAT results with more systematic assessment (Hughes et al., 2017).

The Youth Justice Board (YJB) continues to highlight the need to ensure that young people receive support to achieve effective communication. For example, the *Case Management Guidance: Work in Court*, first issued in 2014 and then updated in 2019, outlines the following YOT responsibilities in court to:

- help children and young people understand the requirements of their court order
- give initial appointments to assist and enable compliance
- ensure the safety and well-being of children and young people in court
- ensure that they receive the support they need to understand and engage in the court processes.

The latter may involve ensuring that special measures such as a registered intermediary being used. In 2015, the YJB and the RCSLT issued *Practice Advice: Speech, Language and Communication Needs in the Youth Justice System.*

The Children and Families Act (2014) extended significant responsibilities to local authorities (LA) and other services in relation to children and young people who are detained in custody. The provisions commenced in April 2015. The main principles are:

- the home local authority's continued engagement and responsibility for arranging a child or young person's special educational provision while they are in custody
- the child or young person receives appropriate special educational provision and health provision in custody
- identifying need and ensuring that provision continues on release will help a child or young person's resettlement
- making a request and getting an assessment underway in custody will be a good use of time.

The provisions apply to:

- children and young people aged 18 and under (i.e. up to their 19th birthday)
- children and young people who have been sentenced or remanded by the courts to an under-18 young offender institution, a secure training centre or a secure children's home in England
- children voluntarily detained in a secure children's home.

While some YOTs have speech and language therapists embedded within their organisations, this is not consistent. Data from the RCSLT, highlighted in the Communication Trust report of the proceedings of a round table on SLCN, found that funding and recruitment of speech and language therapists to support children and young people in the youth justice sector had increased, both in YOTs and youth accommodation (Communication Trust, 2015).

The Domestic Abuse Act (2021) states that victims of domestic abuse will automatically be eligible for special measures on the grounds of fear or distress. However, whether any special measures are ultimately provided in a particular case will still depend on whether the court considers they would be likely to improve the quality of the witness's evidence (taking into account the witness's wishes and the ability of parties to effectively test the evidence).

In 2017, the government announced a reform of the Mental Health Act (MHA) (1983). The proposed reforms include:

- ensuring that care and treatment are of the highest quality and promote recovery
- detention only when appropriate and there is demonstrable therapeutic benefit
- improving patient's choice and experience
- improving how MHA works for people with a learning disability and autistic people
- enabling patients to access safeguards earlier and more often
- reducing racial disparities under the MHA.

Understanding and being understood are central to the reforms proposed. However, choice and autonomy can only be achieved if the person can make their needs known and understand the issues being discussed. In terms of achieving therapeutic benefit, SLTs must be a core part of the multi-disciplinary team in all mental health services in order to:

- support identification of communication and swallowing needs
- provide SLT for those who need it
- provide training of the wider mental health workforce.

In addition, to achieve least restriction, service users need to be able to tell their story and give evidence in court, and may need SLT to enable engagement with other services and group interventions – for example, risk assessment or treatments to reduce violence such as anger management.

It is hoped that the White Paper and the guidance for implementing it will highlight the need for SLT expertise to ensure that patients can genuinely influence their care and make their needs known within the reformed Mental Health Act.

Many studies of the challenges that people with communication difficulties are likely to experience when navigating the communication demands of the justice system suggest various guidance for reducing the demands. However, Sowerbutts et al. (2021) question whether actions such as rephrasing language are either practical or sufficiently effective without specialist support such as that provided by RIs and suggest that broader changes to the communication environment are required.

Research into communication difficulties in young offenders

Since 2004, most of the research and service development for speech and language therapy involving people in contact with criminal justice services took place with young people in community settings – see reviews in Snow (2019) and Snow and Bryan (2018). These reviews outline the high proportion of young people in contact with criminal justice services who have speech, language and communication difficulties. In this volume, we do not describe such people as offenders because, in the UK, youth justice services take prevention referrals as well as deal with those who have offended. Similarly, in many adult prisons, there are people on remand for a crime (i.e. awaiting trial to determine guilt or otherwise), as well as those actually convicted of a crime.

The research that has been conducted with young offenders demonstrates:

- SLT services can be delivered effectively in criminal justice settings (Bryan, Freer and Furlong, 2007; Gregory and Bryan, 2011; Snow and Woodward, 2017).
- Improvements in language functioning are detectable on standardised tests when SLT provision is added to the support package available to young people (Gregory and Bryan, 2011).
- A phase one clinical trial of one-to-one SLT intervention delivered in a custodial setting showed that intervention was effective, and the young people engaged well. However, the trial also illustrated the complexities of service delivery and sudden changes to routine that make such research pragmatically complex to deliver (Snow and Woodward, 2017).
- Staff perceive a benefit to the wider delivery of justice services when they have access to training and support to manage communication difficulties given by a speech and language therapist (Bryan and Gregory, 2013).

Winstanley, Webb and Conti-Ramsden (2018) found that individuals with identified developmental language difficulties (DLD) reported less contact with the local police service than age-matched peers, although they did show significantly higher aggression scores. The authors suggest that early identification of language difficulties and opportunities for intervention are vital in preventing offending. In 2021, Winstanley and colleagues examined reoffending rates and demonstrated that 60% of a sample of 145 young offenders had DLD. None had previously been diagnosed or received SLT intervention. Of the young people with DLD, 62% reoffended compared to 25% of young people without DLD. The study also showed that DLD was a much stronger predictor of reoffending than other factors. This study again illustrates the need for systematic assessment of SLCN in young people who come into contact with criminal justice services.

Research on young offenders is relevant to the adult prison population in the UK because a significant proportion of young offenders will continue to offend and will transfer to the adult estate. Bryan (2021) suggested that extrapolating from the 2018 population size, and with a reoffending rate of 39.3% (Ministry of Justice, 2019), around 415 young offenders with significant speech and language difficulties will enter the adult estate each year.

Clearly, systematic studies of speech, language and communication skills are needed in adults who enter prison to confirm such figures.

Further evidence base for SLT in criminal justice settings

Alongside the development of an evidence base demonstrating the value of SLT assessment and intervention for young people in contact with criminal justice services, two other coalescing strands of evidence contribute to demonstrating the value of the SLT role with adults in prison. One is the recognition over the last ten years of the impact of communication difficulties on mental health and the impact of mental health conditions such as depression and schizophrenia on the ability to communicate (Jagoe and Walsh, 2020). Many people held in custodial settings are known to experience mental health problems which can impact on their communication, thus highlighting the need for communication support. Alongside this runs the ongoing development of the evidence base for SLT intervention with specific disorders (Cummings, 2013; Dobinson and Wren, 2019; Jagoe and Walsh, 2020). This evidence base is well established and evolving all the time. This evidence base is applicable to conditions such as DLD and stammering found in people who are in criminal justice services, but further studies are needed to test the delivery of SLT interventions within prison environments.

Adults with mental health difficulties (Fazel and Seewald, 2012), deafness (Williamson and Grub, 2015), learning difficulties (Jones and Talbot, 2010) and autistic spectrum disorders (Young et al., 2018) are over-represented in the prison population (see Bryan, 2021 for an overview). Many of these adults will have speech, language and communication difficulties associated with those conditions. When working with adults who are in prison, it is important to ascertain:

- whether their speech, language and communication developed normally or whether it was impacted by a pre-existing disorder such as learning difficulties or a stammer
- whether there is an acquired disorder such as stroke, head injury, hearing loss, early dementia or depression
- whether there are side effects of treatment such as excess saliva or swallowing difficulties caused by certain antipsychotic medications.

Challenges of working in criminal justice settings

There is an added challenge in trying to understand the speech, language and communication profile of an adult prisoner, because often there are few records available in relation to previous episodes of healthcare, any diagnostic tests or access to health and educational services. So the person's story has to be gradually elicited, with careful checking of information, reconciling information offered with assessment outcomes, piecing together findings from the multi-disciplinary team and gradually gaining an understanding of the person's journey to prison, their thinking processes and their interests and motivations (see Chapter 5 for more detailed discussion).

Within this profile, any communication difficulties will affect the person's engagement with the regime in many ways:

- Initially understanding a wealth of information on rules and procedures.
- Getting to know fellow prison residents and building up a support network.
- Benefiting from any type of buddying scheme – these vary from informal pairings suggested by wing staff to formal 'trustee' buddying schemes where experienced prison residents who are deemed reliable are linked with new prisoners as part of a formal support scheme.
- Participating meaningfully in assessment, much of which is verbally mediated (i.e. the person is asked questions and is expected to give a verbal response).
- Achieving a reliable risk assessment. Risk assessments are largely verbally mediated processes, which will be more challenging for a person with speech, language and communication difficulties. Effective risk assessment requires a detailed understanding of how a person thinks and reacts as well as what motivates them. Where communication difficulties compromise risk assessment, risk will tend to be deemed to be higher. Being deemed higher risk will limit the person's activities and contacts with others, potentially further adding to the person's isolation. Similarly, a higher-risk categorisation may lead to care within a more restrictive part of the prison, which increases the cost of care.
- Interacting with staff and accessing services within the prison.
- Engagement in education or skills provision and in activities designed to prevent reoffending.

Enabling staff to understand the full impact of communication difficulties is important, but it should be noted that prison officers receive minimal training with regard to communication difficulties or the impact of communication difficulties on everyday functioning. One of the most persistent misperceptions among prison staff is that a person who can physically speak cannot possibly have communication difficulty. 'Why are you seeing him? He can talk' is a frequent (and very genuine) question from staff. If that 'talk' is largely unhelpful, such as 'not interested', 'no' or 'not me', staff may feel very frustrated by the person. Such responses are often produced by people in prison as a means of reducing engagement with others in order to try to hide or avoid the fact that communication is difficult.

Models of SLT provision within custodial environments

A further challenge for a speech and language therapist working in an adult custodial setting is that models of SLT provision may vary. This could be:

- A service set within a multi-disciplinary team (MDT) ideally with several SLTs and capacity to take students to ensure that future generations of SLTs are attracted to working in forensic settings. This is probably the most familiar model as it is similar to teams within hospitals, community settings and specialist facilities within health delivery services such as the National Health Service in the UK.
- As above but with a single SLT in the team.
- A regular sessional service where it is more difficult to establish SLT as a core part of the MDT. In this circumstance, establishing key contact links with health, education, work areas and residential blocks (usually called wings) is very helpful to the SLT.
- A consultancy model where there is usually an agreement with another SLT service to meet referrals on an 'as and when' basis. This can be more challenging as largely the SLT's contact is with the referring agent. However, where these referrals link to patient pathways such as transfer from high-secure forensic settings to medium-secure, the SLT's knowledge of the person's profile may be very helpful. Where the referrals are for unknown clients, these are often 'desperation referrals' where communication is highly compromised so that verbally mediated processes for assessment, risk profiling, etc. cannot be undertaken. The team then reaches a point where their management of the client cannot progress. This is an opportunity for the SLT to 'unlock' understanding of the client, train staff to achieve the most effective communication possible with the person, and enable information about the client to guide the team. Gaining insight into a person's wishes, fears and motivations can be helpful to the team in determining the best way to manage a client with significant communication difficulties. In this scenario, the SLT as 'superhero' can be motivating, but the lack of longer-term monitoring of the client, or follow-up as the person progresses, can lead to SLTs feeling demotivated and questioning the value of this type of input.

It is important that SLTs working in single-practitioner or consultancy-type services are realistic about what can be achieved and negotiate what the service provider is willing to fund (whether directly to the SLT or via some form of service-level agreement), and that expectations are managed around what can be delivered within time or funding constraints.

We hope that this volume will give SLTs and students insight and enthusiasm for a fascinating and rewarding branch of speech and language therapy. We aim to demonstrate how tried and tested SLT techniques can be adapted for use within criminal justice settings, and also to show that SLTs have the necessary skills to work in criminal justice settings once the contextual factors are understood.

References

Bercow, J. (2008) *The Bercow Report: A Review of Services for Children and Young People (0-19) with Speech, Language and Communication Needs*. Nottingham: DCSF Publications.

Bryan, K. (2004) Preliminary study of the prevalence of speech and language difficulties in young offenders. *International Journal of Language and Communication Disorders*, 39, 391-400.

Bryan, K. (2021) Adults in the Prison Population. In L. Cummings (ed.) *Pragmatic Language Disorders: Complex and Underserved Populations*. New York: Springer.

Bryan, K. and Gregory, J. (2013) Perceptions of staff on embedding speech and language therapy within a youth offending team. *Child Language Teaching and Therapy*, 29(3), 359-371.

Bryan, K. and Mackenzie, J. (2008) *Meeting the Speech, Language and Communication Needs of Vulnerable Young People. Model of Service Delivery for Those at Risk of Offending and Re-offending*. London: Royal College of Speech and Language Therapists.

Bryan, K., Freer, J. and Furlong, C. (2007) Language and communication difficulties in juvenile offenders. *International Journal of Language and Communication Disorders*, 42(5), 505-520.

Care Quality Commission, HMI of Probation, Healthcare Inspectorate Wales and Estyn (2010) *Message in a Bottle: A Joint Inspection of Youth Alcohol Misuse and Offending*. Manchester: HM Inspectorate of Probation.

Communication Trust (2015) *Doing Justice to Speech, Language and Communication Needs*. London: Communication Trust.

Cummings, L. (ed.) (2013) *The Cambridge Handbook of Communication Disorders*. Cambridge: Cambridge University Press.

Dobinson, C. and Wren, Y. (eds) (2019) *Creating Practice-Based Evidence: A Guide for SLTs* (2nd edn). Guildford: J&R Press.

Fazel, S. and Seewald, K. (2012) Severe mental illness in 33,588 prisoners worldwide: Systematic review and meta-regression analysis. *British Journal of Psychiatry*, 200(5), 364-373.

Gregory, J. and Bryan, K. (2011) Speech and language therapy intervention with a group of persistent and prolific young offenders in a non-custodial setting with previously un-diagnosed speech, language and communication difficulties. *International Journal of Language and Communication Disorders*, 46(2), 202-215.

Hughes, N., Chitabesan, P., Bryan, K., Borschmann, R., Swain, N., Lennox, C. and Shaw, J. (2017) Language impairment and comorbid vulnerabilities among young people in custody. *Journal of Child Psychology and Psychiatry*, 58(10), 1106-1113.

Jagoe, C. and Walsh, I.P. (eds) (2020) *Communication and Mental Health Disorders*. Guildford: J & R Press.

Jones, G. and Talbot, J. (2010) No one knows: The bewildering passage of offenders with learning disability and learning difficulty through the criminal justice system. *Criminal Behaviour and Mental Health*, 20(1), 1-7.

Lanz, R. (2009) *Speech and Language Therapy within Milton Keynes Youth Offending Team. A Four-Month Pilot Project*. Milton Keynes: Youth Offending Team.

Ministry of Justice (2011) *Achieving Best Evidence in Criminal Proceedings*. London: Ministry of Justice.

Ministry of Justice (2019) *Proven Re-offending Statistics Quarterly Bulletin, January 2017 to March 2017*. London: Ministry of Justice.

Ministry of Justice (2020) *The Witness Intermediary Scheme Annual Report 2019/20*. London: Ministry of Justice.

Offender Health Research Network (2013) *The Comprehensive Health Assessment Tool (CHAT): Young People in the Secure Estate*. Manchester: University of Manchester.

Ramsbotham, D. (2012) Speech and Language Therapy with Young Offenders. In *Nurturing Innovation: The First 10 Years of the Helen Hamlyn Trust* (pp.56-57). London: Helen Hamlyn Trust.

Snow, P.C. (2019) Speech-language pathology and the youth offender: Epidemiological overview and roadmap for future speech-language pathology research and scope of practice. *Language, Speech, and Hearing Services in Schools*, 50(2), 324-339.

Snow, P.C. and Bryan, K. (2018) Supporting young adults with language impairments in the youth justice system. In S. Spencer (ed.) *Supporting Adolescents with Language Disorders* (pp.73–92). Chichester: J & R Press.

Snow, P.C. and Woodward, M.N. (2017) Intervening to address communication difficulties in incarcerated youth: A phase 1 clinical trial. *International Journal of Speech-Language Pathology*, 19, 392–406.

Sowerbutts, A., Eaton-Rosen, E., Bryan, K. and Beeke, S. (2021) Supporting young offenders to communicate in the youth justice system: A scoping review. Speech, *Language and Hearing*, 24, 87–104.

The Mental Health Act (1983). London: HM Government.

The Children and Families Act (2014). London: HM Government.

The Youth Justice and Criminal Evidence Act (1999). London: HM Government.

The Domestic Abuse Act (2021). London: HM Government.

Williamson, L.H. and Grubb, A.R. (2015) An analysis of the relationship between being deaf and sexual offending. *Journal of Sexual Aggression*, 21(2), 224–243.

Winstanley, M., Webb, R.T. and Conti-Ramsden, G. (2018) More or less likely to offend? Young adults with a history of identified developmental language disorders. *International Journal of Language and Communication Disorders*, 53, 256–270.

Winstanley, M., Webb, R.T. and Conti-Ramsden, G. (2021) Developmental language disorders and risk of recidivism among young offenders. *The Journal of Child Psychology and Psychiatry*, 62, 396–403.

Young, S., González, R.A., Mullens, H., Mutch, L., Malet-Lambert, I. and Gudjonsson, G.H. (2018) Neurodevelopmental disorders in prison inmates: Comorbidity and combined associations with psychiatric symptoms and behavioural disturbance. *Psychiatry Research*, 261, 109–115.

Youth Justice Board of England and Wales (2014) *Asset Plus*. London: YJB.

Youth Justice Board (2019) *Case Management Guidance: Work in Court*. London: YJB.

1

CRIME AND WHO COMMITS CRIME

DOI: 10.4324/9781003288701-2

One of the most compelling questions for people who work in or alongside the criminal justice system (CJS) is 'Why do people commit crimes?'

If professionals can better understand why people commit crimes, then perhaps this can inform policy and practice at all levels, with the hope of positively impacting the incidence of crime and recidivism (reoffending). However, understanding why people commit crimes remains complex and multi-faceted. This introductory chapter aims to give an overview of the reasons that people might become involved in crime.

How is 'crime' defined?

Before considering why people commit crimes, a definition of 'crime' should be articulated. Crime is understood to be the intentional commission of an act which is usually deemed socially harmful or dangerous and which is specifically defined, prohibited and punishable under criminal law. What is considered to be a 'crime' is different in different parts of the world. For example, in some countries, adultery remains punishable by death; in others, assisted suicide is legal, as is the possession of certain drugs.

Within the UK, and the rest of the world, what constitutes a crime has changed over time. This largely reflects changes in attitude which lead to an issue no longer being in the public interest to prosecute. Examples of historical criminal offences include: herding cows along streets between 10am and 7pm (Metropolitan Streets Act, 1867) and ringing someone's doorbell before running away (Metropolitan Police Act, 1829).

There are also 'crimes' which change with societal opinion over time, which is vividly exemplified by the criminalisation of homosexuality in the UK over hundreds of years. The first act of parliament addressing this topic was the Buggery Act (1533) which made homosexuality punishable by death. Since this, amendments to this law have been made. The Offences Against the Person Act (1861), the Sexual Offences Act (1967) and the more recent Marriage (Same Sex Couples) Act (2013) alongside the Equality Act (2010), which legalised the rights of homosexual people in the UK to marry and to be protected from discrimination, are good examples of change in societal opinion that changed laws and therefore the definition of 'crime' within the UK. However, in contrast, homosexuality remains a crime in many countries across the globe (Human Dignity Trust, 2023).

Crime is therefore not a fixed construct but one that is time and location bound. Throughout history and across cultures, when a person is exhibiting a behaviour that gives others 'a cause for concern', the people who represent 'society' put pressure on government to have the behaviour forbidden by deeming it against the law and therefore illegal (Hostettler, 2009). In addition, governments try to develop a deterrent to the targeted behaviour by defining a range of punishments. Thus a 'crime' is created (Tierney and O'Neill, 2013).

The study of criminology suggests that once a crime is created, crime statistics increase, which makes 'society' perceive that there is increased crime and additional criminals. As a result, members of society put further pressure on their governing body to eradicate the crime or behaviour that causes concern by increasing the punishment available to courts of law. A vicious circle is constructed. This helps us to understand that a crime is 'an action forbidden by law and liable to attract punishment' (Canton, 2016). It also helps us understand that crime is socially constructed, based on the values of the society that judges a behaviour to be unacceptable.

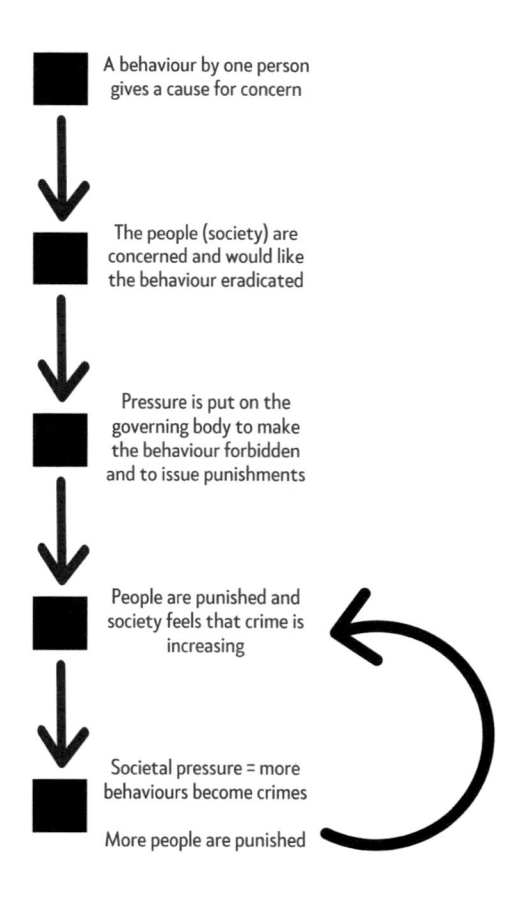

A behaviour by one person gives a cause for concern

The people (society) are concerned and would like the behaviour eradicated

Pressure is put on the governing body to make the behaviour forbidden and to issue punishments

People are punished and society feels that crime is increasing

Societal pressure = more behaviours become crimes

More people are punished

Adapted from Tierney and O'Neill (2013)

FIGURE 1.1 A cycle of crime, social pressure and criminality

General crime statistics

Analysing crime statistics for a particular country gives a snapshot in time of the societal culture which predominates. The statistics illustrate that perceptions of crime may not align with facts and that societal circumstances can significantly impact on crime statistics.

Taking the crime figures for England and Wales for the year ending June 2021 (Office for National Statistics, 2021), we can see that patterns of crime have been significantly affected by the coronavirus (COVID-19) pandemic, government instructions to limit social contact and changing attitudes towards reporting sexual crimes. Periods of national lockdown in the UK saw decreases in the incidence of many types of crime, followed by a return towards previous incidence levels once lockdowns ended.

The Crime Survey for England and Wales (2022) estimates provide the best indicator of long-term trends. Estimates from the Telephone-operated Crime Survey for England and Wales (Crime Survey for England and Wales, 2022) for the year ending June 2021 compared with the pre-COVID year ending June 2019 show:

- An increase in total crime by 12%. When the total crime increase is considered in more detail, there was a 43% increase in fraud and computer misuse with a 32% increase in occasions of fraud. This was largely because of substantial increases in both 'consumer and retail fraud' and 'advance fee fraud'. There was an 85% increase in computer misuse incidents which were attributed to an increase in 'unauthorised access to personal information including hacking'.
- There was an 18% decrease in theft offences.
- There were minimal changes in the total number of incidents of violence towards an individual but a 27% decrease in the number of victims of violent crime. This shows reduced violence between unknown parties and reflects the closure of the night-time economy in the UK during the pandemic.

Police-recorded crime data (Home Office, 2022) shows a similar pattern to the Crime Survey for England and Wales (2022). The Home Office (2022) reported overall reductions in the reporting and recording of many types of crime during periods of pandemic lockdown. These data show:

- decreased number of homicides by 11% compared to the previous year
- decreased number of police-recorded offences involving firearms by 6%

- decreased occurrences of offences involving knives or sharp instruments (knife-enabled crime) by 8%.

Sexual offences recorded by the Home Office (2022) present a more complicated picture:

- Sexual offences reported to the police were lower during periods of pandemic lockdown in both spring 2020 and winter 2020.
- When COVID-19 restrictions were eased in March 2021, there was a change to the reporting of sexual offences. The number of sexual offences reached its highest-ever quarterly level between April and June 2021.

Caution is needed when interpreting the level of police-recorded sexual offences because they may be influenced by the impact of high-profile cases and campaigns aimed at increasing the public's willingness to report sexual assault (Ministry of Justice, 2021a).

With respect to sexual offences, police-recorded crime data for the year ending June 2021 (Home Office, 2022) shows:

- the highest number of rape offences (a total of 61,158) recorded in a 12-month period with the highest quarterly figure (17,285) between April and June 2021
- the second highest number of sexual offences which are not recorded as rape but which remain sexual assault (a total of 164,763) recorded in a 12-month period, with the highest quarterly figure (48,553) between April and June 2021.

An overview of the adult prison population

Having considered the crime statistics for England and Wales, it is helpful to take a snapshot of the adult prison population so that we can contextualise theoretical models of crime.

The Prison Reform Trust produces a regular Bromley Briefing that describes the prison population. The briefing from summer 2021 (Prison Reform Trust, 2021) showed that 78,037 adults were in prison on 21st June 2021. This is an upward trend over the last 30 years of 74%. It is also interesting to note that England, Wales and Scotland have the highest imprisonment rates in Western Europe (World Prison Brief, 2021).

In England and Wales, the picture of adult incarceration has the following breakdown (Ministry of Justice, 2021b):

- 40,000 people were sent to prison with 63% committing a non-violent crime and 44% sentenced to serve six months or less.
- The data also shows that 48% of adults are reconvicted within one year of release.
- People are spending longer in prison with three times as many people sentenced to ten years or more in 2019 compared to 2008.
- People serving mandatory life sentences are spending an average of 17 years in custody (an increase from 13 years in 2001).
- Over a quarter of the prison population are from minority ethnic groups (Black or Black British 13%; Asian or Asian British 8%; Mixed Heritage 5%; and other ethnic groups 1%).
- Of those incarcerated, 5% of men and 7% of women identify as Gypsy, Roma or Traveller compared to 0.1% of the general population in England.
- Foreign nationals make up 13% of the prison population in England and Wales. This includes refugees, asylum seekers, people who have entered the UK illegally, as well as second-generation immigrants. Of those, 265 (26%) have committed drug-related offences, with 24% committing violence against another person.

This breakdown of the incarceration data gives a picture of an increased number of individuals being sentenced to short custodial imprisonment for non-violent crime such as shoplifting. Such sentencing practices result in the individuals losing their employment or housing, so they leave prison facing increased barriers to lawfulness. These circumstances link to the potential for reoffending and reconviction as the unemployed homeless person seeks illegal means to meet their needs.

In respect of those sentenced to longer periods in custody, such as life-sentenced prisoners, the length of stay in prison has increased over the last 20 years so that it is currently 30% longer.

Age of people in prison

Age-related data from the Ministry of Justice (2021c) reports:

- People aged 60 and over are the fastest-growing age group with 17% (13,038) of the population over the age of 50. Of these, 3,281 are in their 60s and 1,638 are 70 or older.
- In September 2020, 315 people in prison were over 80 (311 men and four women).

Reasons for the ageing of the prison population are the increased use of longer custodial sentences by the courts (so that people grow old in prison) and forensic improvements that make historic offences possible to solve long after the offence occurred (so that people who committed crimes are convicted later in life).

There has been a change in the reporting of historic sexual offences since Operation Yewtree, which was a police investigation into sexual abuse allegations, predominantly the abuse of children, against the late Jimmy Savile and other high-profile persons of the same era (Gray and Watt, 2013). It is understood that the increased reporting of historic sexual offences is because of media coverage and increased confidence of victims that they will be believed. The events of the past ten years have resulted in the conviction and incarceration of people over the age of 50 with 44% of the over-50s convicted of sexual offences (Ministry of Justice, 2021c).

Gender of people in prison

In 2020, convicted women accounted for 4% of the prison population. Despite a recent decline in this percentage figure, there are still twice as many women in prison today as there were 27 years ago (Ministry of Justice, 2021c). Data relating to females is as follows:

- Women tend to commit less serious offences, with 72% committing a non-violent offence.
- 58% of sentenced females served a sentence of less than six months.
- 71% of women in prison reported mental health needs compared to 47% of men (Ministry of Justice, 2020a).
- 36% of women in the year to March 2021 left prison without settled accommodation, with 18% homeless and 4% sleeping rough on release (Ministry of Justice, 2020b).
- 9% of women in prison are foreign nationals and some are known to have been coerced or trafficked into offending (Hales and Gelsthorpe, 2012).

People with a disability in prison

People with a learning disability are over-represented within the CJS:

- 34% of people assessed in prison in 2017-18 reported that they had a learning disability or difficulty (Skills Funding Agency, 2018).
- 7% of people in contact with wider criminal justice services have a learning disability compared to only 2% of the general population (NHS England, 2016).
- Four-fifths of prisoners with learning disabilities or difficulties report problems with reading prison information, expressing themselves and understanding certain words (Talbot, 2008).

The take-home message from the above description is that many adults in prison have a troubled and complex background, with multiple disadvantages contributing to their offending. With this in mind, we will consider theoretical models of crime.

Theoretical models of crime

Our academic understanding of crime is based on theoretical models and research conducted with people who have been convicted of crimes. This provides us with a methodological issue in understanding what crime is – because the models are theoretical and are tested on people who are already convicted. The models are not tested on those who commit crimes but are not convicted (because they would not participate) or on those who think about crimes but do not commit them.

Classicism and positivism were early theoretical models of crime, and these models continue to underpin more contemporary theories. Classicism refers to the balance between 'desired outcome' and punishment. This theory assumes that a person committing a crime is a rational being, capable of accurately weighing up the potential gain and the potential punishment. This assertion leads to a need to impose the least restriction on society, but to use deterrent (i.e. punishment) to prevent crime. Positivism theories aim to understand the genetically determined psychological characteristics such as 'feeble-mindedness' and 'moral degeneracy' (Tierney and O'Neill, 2013).

Twin studies in the 1970s showed high rates of criminal concordance for identical twins at 26% compared to 12% for non-identical twins (Christiansen, 1977). However, the author was clear that it was impossible to separate hereditary causes from the effects of a shared environment. In more recent thinking, biology and the environment are understood to interact. Ainsworth (2000) suggests that some types of personality may have a genetic predisposition to criminality, but this will only become a reality under certain social and environmental circumstances.

This is manifested in the study of conditions such as attention deficit hyperactivity disorder (ADHD) and other forms of 'soft' neurological signs. Unever, Cullen and Pratt (2003) found that ADHD was associated with conduct disorders, lower IQ and parents with criminal histories, but that patterns of involvement in criminal activity varied widely across individuals. Hollin (1992) states that a substantial body of work suggests that some criminals have central nervous system impairment or dysfunction; other research suggesting that these individual factors are strongly mediated by social influences (Piquero, Farrington and Blumstein, 2007). These include complications in pregnancy, early maternal rejection, nutrition, social and environmental factors (Brennan, Grekin and Mednick, 1999).

The same issues emerge in studies of brain damage in offenders. Miller (1999) found that offenders were more likely to have suffered head injuries than non-offenders, but questioned whether the injury leads to the offending or the offending to the injury.

Howitt (2002) posits a number of methodological difficulties related to such research, thereby questioning 'causal' relationships. People with a history of violence are more likely to get into fights and suffer brain damage; research may focus on higher levels of disadvantage explaining the disproportionate levels of offending; and pre- and post-injury studies tend to focus on more severely injured people and may therefore be unrepresentative.

Akers (2011) has proposed a social learning and social structure model of crime. This acknowledges the role of social structures mediated by social learning processes in determining criminal behaviour or conforming behaviour. Variables such as social organisation, location in the social (or family) structure, age, gender, race, class, along with theoretically defined variables such as social disorganisation and family, peer, school and other relationships, all influence whether circumstances and decisions lead to offending behaviour. We therefore see a complex interplay of factors that determine, across a lifespan, whether a person turns to crime and subsequently whether they go on to become a career criminal or can be diverted from this back to conformity.

Psychological models of crime

The notion that a person's reasoning and actions are based on their 'thinking' patterns is the basic tenet of cognitive behavioural psychological models of offending (Palmer, 2013). These models suggest that a person has risk factors for criminality in their lived experience. Some of the risks are static and stem from past experiences such as being subject to childhood trauma. Other risks are dynamic, in that they change depending on what is happening to the person. Dynamic risks are usually more in the present day such as homelessness or debt.

How the individual tolerates the risks is based on their skills associated with thinking, feeling and behaviour. A person with a childhood trauma of violent assault may find themselves homeless and feel intense emotions of fear associated with this. Cognitive behavioural psychological models would suggest that the feeling of fear induces a person to flight (run), freeze (remain still) or fight (violence).

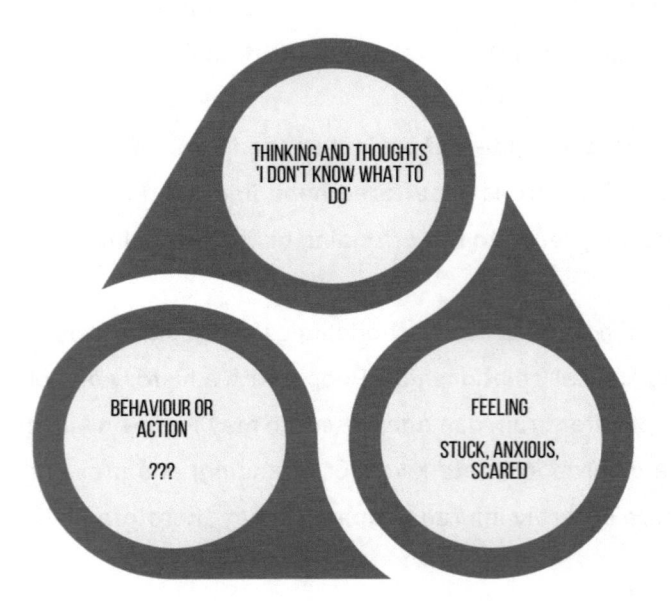

FIGURE 1.2 Individual tolerance of risk based on cognitive behavioural models

In this scenario, the static risk is the childhood trauma, and the dynamic risk is the home-lessness. These combine to create a situation where a person might be violent to resolve their problem, such as attempting to steal from a petrol station while carrying an object which could become a weapon if fear increases. Other risks will also determine whether a crime occurs. If the person has a previous conviction, this is factored into the risks and increases the likelihood that the person is assessed as 'at risk of committing a crime'. If a person's reasoning is impacted or impaired – for example, being under the influence of a substance or having a brain injury or learning disability – then their risk increases further.

This model of understanding why crime is committed suggests that the higher the risks, the higher the need for 'supervision' (Clear and Latessa, 1993). Supervision in this scenario can be:

- having a case worker whom the convicted person meets regularly for support
- being under the supervision of the probation service who expect you to follow a set of rules such as where you can go
- having a home detention curfew which is monitored via an electronic tag
- living in a forensic supported living setting
- residing in a secure hospital
- being incarcerated in prison.

The psychological model of crime most appropriately fits with crimes that are influenced by intense emotions such as violence.

Social models of crime

A social model of crime would posit that social factors and personality influence the person's motivation to commit crime (Gudjonsson and Sigurdsson, 2007). This is based on the concept that there is a tension between the individual's aspiration at any given time and the reality, and how they tolerate this based on their personality.

A person might aspire to own a car, while having their ability to seek a job adversely affected by a lack of public transport. This may provide a justification for stealing a car. However, the decision will also be mediated by multiple other factors including family codes of conduct, peer opinions, media information, personality, religion and culture. Some factors such as media information may be either positive or negative (e.g. 'I deserve a car as everyone has one, and garages make a lot of money so theft is justified' vs 'If I steal, I am likely to get found out and be punished'). Temporary changes to cognitive state, such as being under the influence of drugs or poor stress management, may also impact on the final decision.

These theories assume that a person has individual agency which concerns their thinking skills, their ability to make decisions and their understanding of cause and effect. In addition, the person's thinking will be influenced by the norms, values and expectations placed on them. The social model of crime most appropriately fits with acquisition crime such as theft (Canton, 2016).

The social model goes on to offer a cycle to understand reoffending as illustrated below (Grimwood and Berman, 2012).

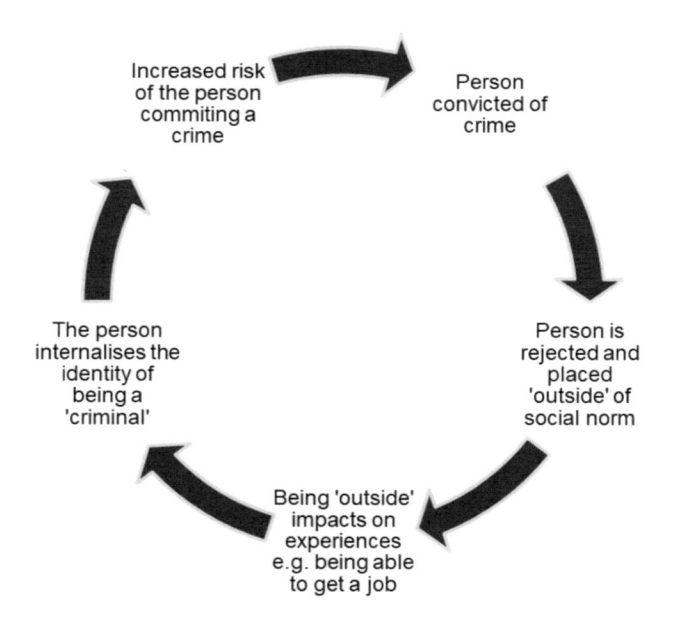

FIGURE 1.3 A cycle of reoffending

In this cycle, the person is labelled as a criminal – that is, a 'bad' person, one who cannot be trusted and who needs to be excluded from society. That exclusion changes the person's individual agency and social structure, which results in them developing new understandings of the world and new values. This further impacts on self-identity and propagates the cycle anew. The conclusion of this model is that stigmatising people reduces choice and increases risk (Canton, 2016).

Internal justification theory

The internal justification theory suggests that an individual can justify any temptation to commit a criminal act (Berman, 2003). This theory advocates that a person can enact a cost-benefit analysis of a situation and use this information to make an informed choice. An example could return us to the quandary of owning a car. An individual might justify stealing a car based on their need to travel to gain work and therefore support a family. In the context of having stolen several cars before and evaded punishment, they might view the risk of punishment as low.

If a person planned to commit a crime such as bank robbery, they would consider the cost (i.e. going to prison or living 'on the run' and away from their family) against the potential benefit (i.e. substantial financial gain). This cost-benefit analysis is dependent on the person's skills in judging cause and effect, weighing options and having a way to operationalise risk.

The ability to justify committing the criminal act comes when:

- internal inhibitors indicate that the cost is too great to be worth the potential risk
- the person's internal narrative creates cognitive dissonance such as a version of events where what they are considering is acceptable (e.g. it's fine to live on the run because my family will be well provided for).

In this situation, the internal narrative accepts the societal label of being a 'bad person' and creates a version where the self-image is not damaged (e.g. it's okay to rob a bank because the bank is insured, and they are a faceless corporation where no individual is perceived to be impacted).

These thinking processes enable justification of a crime and suppression of inhibitors that normally encourage an individual to not violate the law. Finkelhor, Cuevas and Drawbridge (2017) use these principles in their precondition model which resembles a staircase to committing crime (adapted from Duff and Willis, 2006) (see Figure 1.4 overleaf).

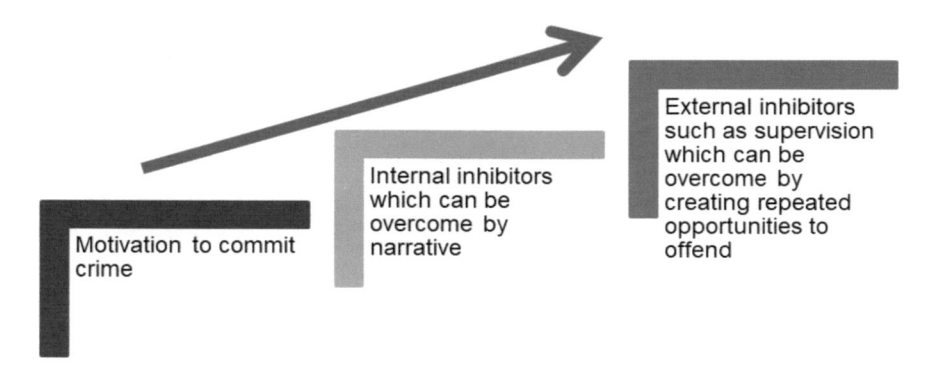

FIGURE 1.4 The staircase model of justification of a crime and suppression of inhibitors

These models suggest that interventions can be devised to modify internal justifications. For example, interventions for internal justification would include attempting to change the person's motivations, attempting to change their internal narratives which neutralise inhibition, and strengthening inhibitors with strategies such as victim awareness or more intensive supervision.

Control theory of conformity

Control theory is grounded in the notion that if certain factors are met, a person is less likely to engage in criminal acts because they are compelled to conform to social norms (Costello and Hope, 2016). The four factors are:

- The individual must feel an attachment to their family, community, culture or society, and the strength of the attachment protects the person from criminality because their fear of rejection is too great.
- The individual must have personal ambitions that they are strongly committed to, which protect the person from criminality because they value the ambitions so highly that they would not jeopardise them.
- The individual must have an embedded daily routine that is satisfying and involves them to an extent whereby the thought of criminality would not be considered. In these circumstances, the person would not countenance crime as a solution to any problem.
- An individual must have beliefs, morals and values that are so intense that the idea of violating them would be abhorrent.

Within this theoretical approach, a person is considered 'safe' from the motivation for crime because each of the four protective factors is experienced to a high degree. The converse is that if protective factors start to erode, then the risk for offending increases.

Control theory links well to the Good Lives model of offender rehabilitation (Ward, 2002; Loney and Harkins, 2018) which aims to increase these four factors via analysis and planning. The model is represented by a circle divided into 11 sections.

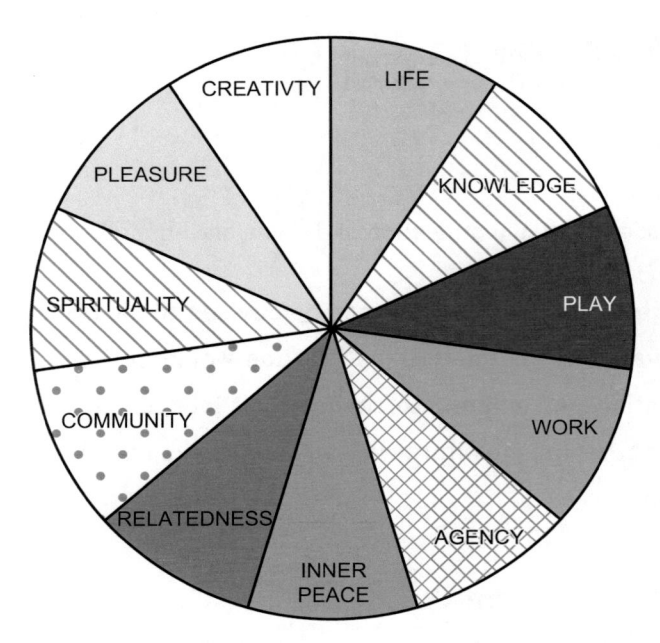

FIGURE 1.5 The Good Lives model of offender rehabilitation represented as a subdivided circle

Each section represents an area of life as follows:

- life (including healthy living, disability, medication and functioning)
- knowledge (how well informed one feels about things that are important to them)
- excellence in play (hobbies and recreational pursuits)
- excellence in work (including mastery of experiences)
- excellence in agency (autonomy, power and self-directedness)
- inner peace (freedom from emotional turmoil and stress)
- relatedness (including intimate, romantic and familial relationships)
- community (connection to wider social groups)
- spirituality (in the broad sense of finding meaning and purpose in life)
- pleasure (feeling good in the here and now)
- creativity (expressing oneself through alternative forms).

The individual is asked to reflect on their life and place 'goods' in each section of the circle. This can be as simple as drawing an asterisk or colouring in part of the section. Ideally, a person would have 'goods' in all sections.

For a person with a reduced set of factors who would be at risk of committing a crime, a profile such as that in Figure 1.6 (below) might be seen.

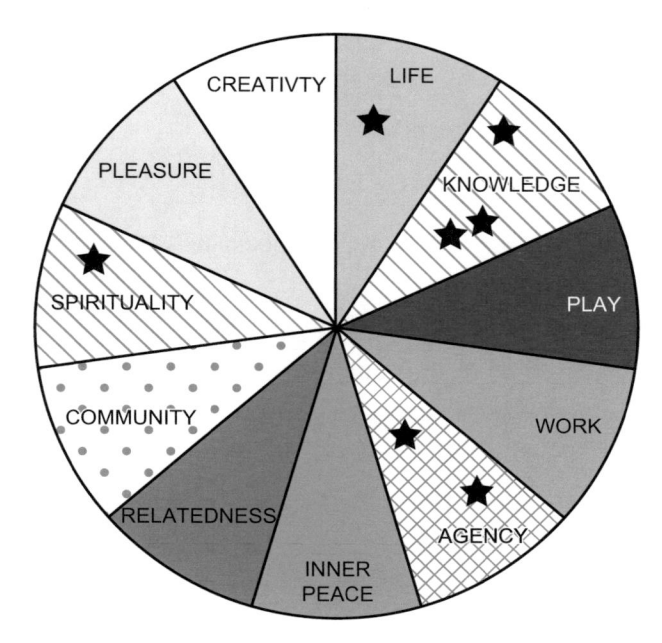

FIGURE 1.6 An example profile using the Good Lives model

There are goods in only four sections (life, knowledge, agency and spirituality).

The person is asked to think of ways to obtain goods in other sections and a plan is drawn up to achieve this. The model is reviewed and goods are added as they are achieved. This analysis and planning enable the person to place emphasis on their strengths and gain insight into their areas of need.

Similar tools such as the Individual Recovery Outcomes Counter (Kelly, 2019) and the Outcomes Star (Triangle, 2021) have also been published.

Integrated systems theory

The final theory to be considered is the integrated systems theory (Robinson, 2014). This model suggests that there is no single cause of crime, but that there are multiple factors, both micro and macro, that influence outcomes. The model has been developed into a diagram to aid understanding (see Figure 1.7 overleaf).

FIGURE 1.7 The integrated systems theory relating to causality of crime in pyramid form

While this pyramid model might look familiar to scholars of biological models of crime, in this model each level contributes to the complex factors that influence a person's decision making in respect to crime or lawbreaking. Each level is explained below.

TABLE 1.1 Each systemic level contributes to the functioning of the individual in respect of their decision making relating to crime

Level	Contribution to functioning
Cellular	Conditions that affect decision making because of changes at a cellular level such as the protein TAU in dementia (Guo et al. 2020) which affects emotion regulation, impulse control and cognition.
Organ	Conditions affecting organs which impact on functioning. For example, a brain tumour can cause frontal lobe changes and disinhibition (Ron 1989) which may present as a personality change, inability to recognise the impact on others and reduced problem-solving skills.
Organism	At organism level, various internal and external factors contribute, such as: psychosis as a condition that is an interplay of genetics and environment; choices such as abusing substances that impact on decision making when taken in excess, such as alcohol, and the interplay of this with the environment that the person is in. The internal and external factors impact on thinking skills, understanding of risk and perception of situations.
Social group	The immediate group of those who contribute via behaviour modelling, expectations placed, holding group members accountable for decisions and offering care/learning/support with daily living.
Social community	The wider group such as town, workplace, school or religious institution. The wider group models values and culture and modifies the actions of group members via feedback (positive or negative) and co-production of group norms. Principles that influence decision making are reviewed as part of the group narrative.
Wider society	The wider society represents government, societal frameworks, political contexts and global affairs. This is where top-down decisions such as laws are shaped, but also bottom-up decisions such as democratic voting for a preferred representative. Wider society influences via national or global movements which may impact on decisions of individuals when they are functioning in a large group such as school strikes for climate change (Boulianne, Lalancette and Ilkiw, 2020).

Robinson (2014) asserts that although people have a choice in respect of decision making and crime, the choice is influenced by factors that are sometimes out of their control.

Indeed, they may be outside of a person's control as well as their awareness, particularly at a cellular, organ or organism level where cognition, reasoning and insight are altered.

The model complements the other theories discussed so far, in that it suggests that factors at each level might be increasing risk or offering protection from risk. The integrated system also concludes that a person does not exist as a vacuum outside of their internal and external modifiers. What we can be certain of from more recent methodological approaches to crime is that there is not a single cause of criminality, but multiple causes with complex associated and interacting factors.

For a more detailed account and critique of theories of crime, see Newburn (2017) and Cullen, Agnew and Wilcox (2018).

The individual's life course

Now that we have explored what crime is and why people may find themselves in a situation whereby they encounter the criminal justice system, let us now explore some additional, useful information which we hope will add to an understanding of the issues more widely.

Adverse childhood experiences

The lived experience of an individual is fundamentally important to their prospects (Bellis et al., 2017). There is a well-researched body of evidence that explains adverse childhood experiences (ACEs) and the causal link between these experiences and poor outcomes in: socio-economic status, education, employment and health, both in the UK and across developed countries (British Psychological Association, 2019).

Adverse childhood experiences are traumatic events, particularly those in early childhood, which significantly affect the health and well-being of people. These experiences range from suffering verbal, mental, sexual and physical abuse, to being raised in a household where domestic violence, alcohol abuse, parental separation or drug abuse is present (Ace Aware Wales, 2021).

The event may be a single event that causes significant psychological trauma or a series of different events over a prolonged period. The psychological impact of the event varies from person to person due to their resilience, so while some young people may tolerate their parents' divorce with no concerns, others can find a similar experience very hard to manage.

As well as specific events that may happen within the individual's immediate surroundings, the community environment also plays a part. While ACEs are being experienced, the social environment can support or negatively affect the individual's resilience (see Figure 1.8 below).

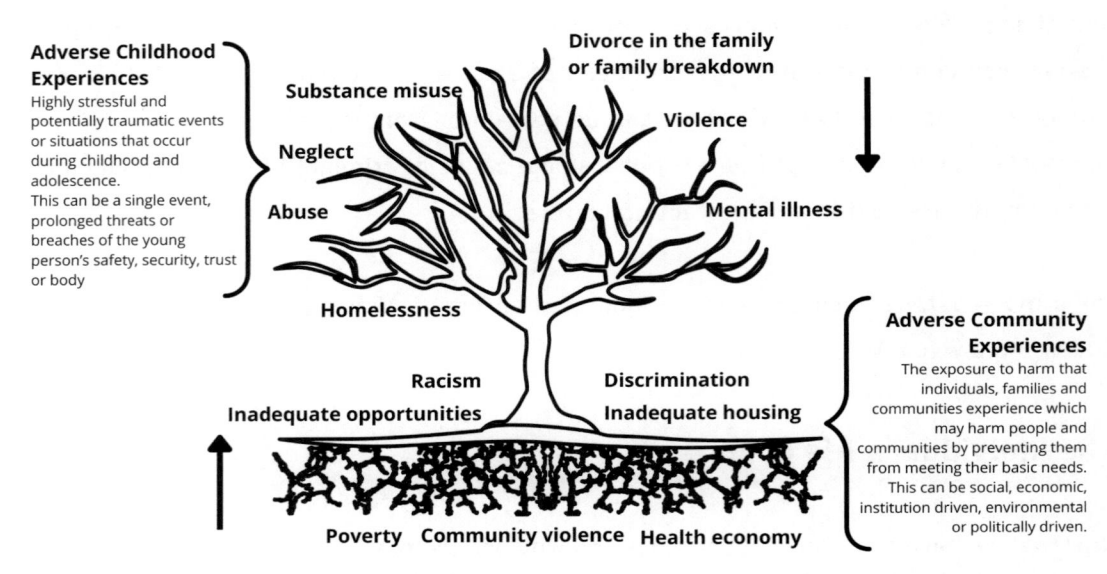

FIGURE 1.8 Adverse childhood experiences and adverse community experiences which impact on individual health and well-being

The more adversity that a child faces in their formative years, the greater the potential for them to (Ace Aware Wales, 2021):

- be affected psychologically in respect of attachment difficulties
- fail to thrive in their daily routine in respect of food, sleep and basic care
- have chaotic school attendance and start to fall behind their peers in the classroom
- miss healthcare appointments, potentially failing to take advantage of important health information and advice that would support their development – it is a sad fact that many adults with ACEs have undiagnosed neurodevelopmental disorders
- experience increased stress and anxiety which impacts on neurological development.

Table 1.2 (overleaf) is adapted from the work completed by the Center for Disease Control and Prevention (2021) at the US Department of Health and Human Services. The table locates the impacts of ACEs over a person's lifespan as they move into teenage years and illustrates the fact that the implications of ACEs can lead to other adverse circumstances.

The take-home message is that experiencing ACEs is a risk factor for poor outcomes. The interplay of ACEs and personal resilience should be considered when thinking about the needs of an individual.

TABLE 1.2 The impact of adverse childhood experiences in different health and well-being domains

Life course	Example consequence (these are to illustrate and are not an exhaustive list)
Adverse childhood experiences	- attachment difficulties - failure to thrive - reduced school attendance and affected academic progress - barriers to attending healthcare appointments - higher risk of being the victim of abuse - witness to violence - exposure to substance misuse
Disrupted or impaired neurological development	- toxic stress impacting on neurological development
Social, emotional and cognitive impairment/disorder or delay	- poor emotion recognition or regulation - issues with attention and listening - finds the classroom hard to tolerate - poor literacy and numeracy - speech, language and communication needs - executive functioning issues - hypervigilance
Development of behaviours which are a risk to health or well-being	- isolating self or joining a gang - poor sleep and food routines - increase risky activities such as mild antisocial activities - drinking, smoking, use of substances
Disease, disability, socio-economic problems	- unemployment - issues with housing/homelessness - debt - unplanned/early pregnancy - sexually transmitted diseases - poor mental health
Overall poor outcomes	- family relationship breakdown - addiction - homelessness - criminal justice system contact

Prisoner adverse childhood experiences

As the realisation increased that ACEs impact on life course, research was conducted to try to understand the frequency and intensity of ACEs experienced by those incarcerated within the criminal justice system (Ford et al., 2019).

Research studies have demonstrated that half of all adults in some regional areas of the UK have suffered at least one ACE in childhood, while in excess of 10% of all adults in some regional areas of the UK experienced four or more (Bellis et al., 2016; Hughes et al., 2018). The same studies found that people who had experienced four or more ACEs were 20 times more likely to have been in prison at some point in their lives (Bellis et al., 2016).

Alongside this, research conducted within the prison population over the last ten years found that individuals in the criminal justice system report higher levels of childhood adversity than those within the general population, and that ACEs are associated with more serious offending and the potential to reoffend (Godet-Mardirossian, Jehel and Falissard, 2011; Naramore et al., 2017; Ramirez et al., 2015). This profile is borne out in the description of people found within the prison service at any one time given earlier in this chapter.

Ford et al. (2019) developed this research further and more comprehensively by completing work in Wales, UK, using a survey with men in prison. The study demonstrated the following:

- One in three men in the criminal justice system in Wales have no formal qualifications (suggesting incomplete education).
- 90% of men in prison in Wales had at least one adverse childhood experience, while 60% had four or more.
- Males with multiple ACEs were more likely to spend time in young offender institutions.
- Men with ACEs were more likely to be involved in violent crime.

To conclude, it is vitally important that those working within the criminal justice system understand ACEs and have an awareness of trauma-informed care. Trauma-informed care will be explored in detail in Chapters 5 and 6 of this book.

Contact with the criminal justice system by demographic categories

As with much of the research that interrogates crime and the causes of crime, various demographic categories have been explored linking to the overview of crime statistics outlined above. These will be explored in this section. It is important to note that data on those who commit crime is complex, difficult to interpret and collected by many different stakeholders. As the data is explored, it becomes apparent that:

- Trends are generally applicable to most countries in the global majority.
- There is data bias and/or errors whereby the information gathered is not consistently inclusive of all members of society so may result in false conclusions (Maguire and McVie, 2017).
- The full gender spectrum is not properly differentiated in official statistics (Jans et al. 2018).
- Data gathered by government departments is reported by the same departments potentially leading to a conflict of interest (Georgiou, 2018).

To be motivated to commit crime, the individual must have the following drivers (Cornish, 2017) (see Figure 1.9 overleaf):

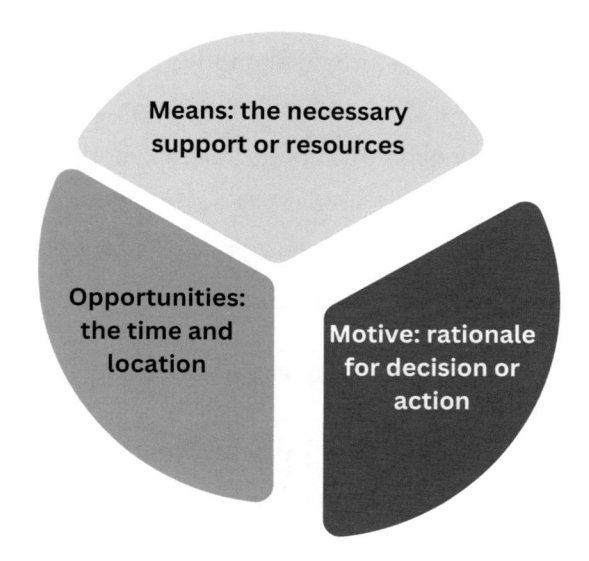

FIGURE 1.9 Drivers that motivate criminal acts within the individual

These drivers will be linked to the demographic categories to support an inclusive understanding.

Age, gender and socio-economic background

Age is an important consideration for the potential to commit crime. Younger people are more likely to engage in criminal activity than older people, and the nature of the crime varies with age. Neurological maturity is an important area to consider in this clinical field and will be fully explored in Chapter 7.

Gender plays a part in frequency and types of crime. Socio-economic background is also relevant. If you have read the earlier parts of this chapter, you may already be linking these pieces of information to the frameworks provided.

The age and gender facts (Office for National Statistics, 2021):

- People aged 14 to 25 are the most likely age group to be involved in crime.
- Males aged 14 to 25 are more likely to engage in criminal acts than females of the same age. This may be because males have more social 'freedom' offered by their families (opportunity), or it may be the influence of male peer groups (means and motive) (Skrzypiec, 2013).
- Males aged 14 to 25 are most likely to be involved in violent crimes in public locations which are unplanned and more likely to be witnessed/reported.

- Males aged 14 to 25 are most likely to use alcohol or substances in social groups which impact on their internal inhibitors (providing motive and opportunity).
- Females are more likely to be involved in non-violent crime under the influence of men/ male partners such as receiving stolen goods (means, motive and opportunity).
- Older people are more likely to commit a crime against their employer such as theft or fraud (opportunity), especially if they are in a position of middle management and have access to resources or knowledge (means).

The socio-economic picture (Office for National Statistics, 2021):

- People living in urban places are more likely to commit crimes due to the increased opportunities offered by local access to homes/shops/vehicles (opportunity).
- People who are not in education, employment or training are more likely to commit crime due to lack of routine (opportunity).
- Unemployed people are more likely to commit crimes due to reduced income (motive) and time to prepare/enact the offence (opportunity).
- People with low socio-economic status can commit a crime for financial gain, social standing or excitement (motive).

Ethnicity - arrests and sentencing

Ethnicity among people involved with criminal justice services is a major societal issue. The UK Home Office (2020) provides data on arrests by age and ethnicity. In summary, males from Black and Asian heritage are more likely to be arrested compared to Caucasian males. This has been a trend over many years and has been explored in relation to the notorious murder of Stephen Lawrence and the part that bias plays in police arrests (Macpherson, 1999). A full discussion of institutionalised racism is outside the scope of this book, but there are many sources of quality information available online (see Chapter 8 for a starting point).

After arrest, a person can be charged with a crime, and this may progress to court. This will be discussed and explained in later chapters of this book.

At this stage, all the reader is required to know is that if a case is brought to court and the person is found guilty, they will be sentenced. The sentence may be a fine, a community-based sentence, a custodial sentence or another type of disposal (an order by the judge for something else to happen such as the person going to hospital) (Sentencing Council, 2021).

The Ministry of Justice (2020c) provides data on crime, ethnicity and sentencing for those cases which have been presented in court. The Ministry of Justice (2020c) offers the following summaries with respect to sentencing and ethnicity:

- The Black ethnic group had the highest percentage of individuals sent to a young offender's institution, suggesting that teenagers from this group are more likely to attract a custodial sentence compared to other groups who attract fines or community orders.
- The White ethnic group had the highest number of individuals sent to the adult estate (prison) for the most serious crimes (indictable offences). This percentage has increased since 2009.
- People from the Black ethnic group had the highest custody rates for possession of weapons (37.9%) and violence against another person (51.3%), while people from the White ethnic group had the highest custody rate for public order offences (30.3%), robbery (79.1%) and sexual offences (60.9%). There is a tangible difference in the types of crime conducted by different ethnic groups.

Conclusion

As professionals working in health, education or social care, we need to be mindful that many people have contact with the criminal justice system. This may not have been as a person who has committed a crime; the person you meet might be a victim of crime, a witness to crime or the family member of someone who has been found guilty of a crime. Luckily, we are skilled in sensitively managing difficult topics with professionalism. As a reminder of these skills, here are some tips for working with people who have been directly in contact with the criminal justice system:

- Ensure the person is at the centre of all decisions and processes, and empowered to be engaged throughout.
- Make sure the person's identity is recognised and respected – be respectful of the diversity of those you will encounter.
- Offer a bespoke approach to each task within your role.
- Try to understand the social circumstances which led to this point for this person.

Specifically, for those who are in contact with the criminal justice system because they have been convicted of a crime:

- Help the person to learn, think and reflect via multimodal means such as total communication strategies and other tools that you will discover in this book.

- Work as part of the multi-disciplinary team.

- Use a biopsychosocial model of care because criminality is not caused by a single factor.

- Model pro-social skills such as relationship building or motivation with goals.

References

Ace Aware Wales (2021) A short guide to understanding Adverse Childhood Experiences and a Trauma and ACE (TrACE) informed approach. Available at https://acehubwales.com/resources/a-short-guide-to-understanding-adverse-childhood-experiences-and-a-trauma-and-ace-trace-informed-approach [accessed 28th February 2023]

Ainsworth, P.B. (2000) *Psychology and Crime: Myths and Reality*. Harlow: Longman.

Akers, R.L. (2011) *Social learning and social structure: A general theory of crime and deviance*. Transaction Publishers.

Bellis, M.A., Ashton, K., Hughes, K., Ford, K.J., Bishop, J. and Paranjothy, S. (2016) *Adverse Childhood Experiences and Their Impact on health-harming behaviours in the Welsh Adult Population*. Public Health Wales NHS Trust.

Bellis, M., Hughes, K., Hardcastle, K., Ashton, K., Ford, K., Quigg, Z. and Davies, A. (2017) The impact of adverse childhood experiences on health service use across the life course using a retrospective cohort study. *Journal of Health Services Research & Policy*, 22(3), 168–177.

Berman, M.N. (2003) Justification and excuse, law and morality. *Duke Law Journal*, 53(1), 1–77.

Boulianne, S., Lalancette, M. and Ilkiw, D. (2020) 'School Strike 4 Climate': Social media and the international youth protest on climate change. *Media and Communication*, 8(2), 208–218.

Brennan, P., Grekin, E. and Mednick, S. (1999) Maternal smoking during pregnancy and adult male criminal outcomes. *Archives of General Psychiatry*, 56, 216–219.

British Psychological Association (2019) Evidence Briefing: Adverse Childhood Experiences. Available at https://cms.bps.org.uk/sites/default/files/2022-06/Briefing%20Paper%20-%20Adverse%20Childhood%20Experiences_0.pdf [accessed 28th February 2023]

Canton, R. (2016) Why Do People Commit Crimes? In F. McNeill, F. I. Durnescu and R. Butter (eds) *Probation* (pp.9–34). London: Palgrave Macmillan.

Center for Disease Control and Prevention (2021) About the CDC-Kaiser ACE Study. Available at www.cdc.gov/violenceprevention/aces/about.html?CDC_AA_refVal=https%3A%2F%2Fwww.cdc.gov%2Fviolenceprevention%2Facestudy%2Fabout.html [accessed 28th February 2023]

Christiansen, K.O. (1977) A Preliminary Study of Criminality among Twins. In S.A. Mednick and K.O. Christiansen (eds) *Biosocial Bases of Criminal Behavior* (pp.89–108). Washington, DC: Gardner Press.

Clear, T.R. and Latessa, E.J. (1993) Probation officers' roles in intensive supervision: Surveillance versus treatment. *Justice Quarterly*, 10(3), 441–462.

Cornish, D. (2017) Theories of Action in Criminology: Learning Theory and Rational Choice Approaches. In R.V. Clarke and M. Felson (eds) *Routine Activity and Rational Choice* (pp.351–382). New York: Routledge.

Costello, B.J. and Hope, T.L. (2016) *Peer Pressure, Peer Prevention: The Role of Friends in Crime and Conformity*. New York: Routledge.

Crime Survey for England and Wales (2022) Crime in England and Wales: Year ending December 2021. Available at www.ons.gov.uk/peoplepopulationandcommunity/crimeandjustice/bulletins/crimein englandandwales/yearendingdecember2021 [accessed 28th February 2023]

Cullen, F.T., Agnew, R. and Wilcox, P. (2018) *Criminological Theory: Past to Present*. New York: Oxford University Press.

Duff, S. and Willis, A. (2006) At the precipice: Assessing a non-offending client's potential to sexually offend. *Journal of Sexual Aggression*, 12, 43–51.

Finkelhor, D., Cuevas, C.A. and Drawbridge, D., (2017) The Four Preconditions Model: An Assessment. In D.P. Boer, A.R. Beech, T. Ward, L.A. Craig, M. Rettenberger, L.E. Marshall, and W.L. Marshall (eds) *The Wiley Handbook on the Theories, Assessment, and Treatment of Sexual Offending* (pp.25–51). Washington, DC: Wiley Blackwell.

Ford, K., Barton, E., Newbury, A., Hughes, K., Bezeczky, Z., Roderick, J. and Bellis, M. (2019) *Understanding the Prevalence of Adverse Childhood Experiences (ACEs) in a Male Offender Population in Wales: The Prisoner ACE Survey*. Public Health Wales NHS Trust and Bangor University.

Georgiou, A.V. (2018) The production of official statistics needs to be a separate branch of government. *Statistical Journal of the IAOS*, 34(2), 149–160.

Godet-Mardirossian, H., Jehel, L. and Falissard, B. (2011) Suicidality in male prisoners: Influence of childhood adversity mediated by dimensions of personality. *Journal of Forensic Science*, 56(4), 942–949.

Gray, D. and Watt, P. (2013) *'Giving Victims a Voice': A joint MPS and NSPCC Report into Allegations of Sexual Abuse Made Against Jimmy Savile under Operation Yewtree*. London: Metropolitan Police.

Grimwood, G.G. and Berman, G. (2012) Reducing reoffending: The 'what works' debate. *Economic Indicators*, 6, 12.

Gudjonsson, G.H. and Sigurdsson, J.F. (2007) Motivation for offending and personality: A study among young offenders on probation. *Personality and Individual Differences*, 42(7), 1243–1253.

Guo, T., Zhang, D., Zeng, Y., Huang, T.Y., Xu, H. and Zhao, Y. (2020) Molecular and cellular mechanisms underlying the pathogenesis of Alzheimer's disease. *Molecular Neurodegeneration*, 15, 40.

Hales, L. and Gelsthorpe, L. (2012) *The Criminalisation of Migrant Women*. Cambridge: University of Cambridge.

Hollin, C.R. (1992) *Criminal Behaviour: A Psychological Approach to Explanation and Prevention*. London: Falmer Press.

Home Office (2020) *Criminal Justice and the Law: Arrests*. Available at www.ethnicity-facts-figures .service.gov.uk/crime-justice-and-the-law/policing/number-of-arrests/latest [accessed 4th October 2021]

Home Office (2022) Police recorded crime and outcomes open data tables, available at www.gov.uk/ government/statistics/police-recorded-crime-open-data-tables [accessed 28th February 2023]

Hostettler, J., (2009) *A History of Criminal Justice in England and Wales*. Waterside Press.

Howitt, D. (2002) *Forensic and Criminal Psychology*. Harlow: Longman.

Hughes, K., Ford, K., Davies, A.R., Homolova, L. and Bellis, M.A. (2018) *Sources of Resilience and Their Moderating Relationships with Harms from Adverse Childhood Experiences*. Cardiff: Public Health Wales.

Human Dignity Trust (2023) Map of countries that criminalise LGBT people. Available at www .humandignitytrust.org/lgbt-the-law/map-of-criminalisation [accessed 28th February 2023]

Jans, M., Wilson, B.D. and Herman, J.L. (2018) Measuring aspects of sexuality and gender: A sexual human rights challenge for science and official statistics. *CHANCE*, 31(1), 12–20.

Kelly, M.J. (2019) Recovery monitoring and goal development using the Individual Recovery Outcomes Counter (I. ROC) and the Home, Opportunity, People, Empowerment (HOPE) toolkit. Doctoral dissertation, Rutgers University, School of Nursing, RBHS.

Loney, D.M. and Harkins, L. (2018) Examining the Good Lives model and antisocial behaviour. *Psychology, Crime & Law*, 24(1), 38–51.

Macpherson, W. (1999) *The Stephen Lawrence Inquiry: Report of an Inquiry*. Parliamentary papers, Cm 4262. London: Stationery Office.

Maguire, M. and McVie, S. (2017) *Crime Data and Criminal Statistics: A Critical Reflection* (Vol. 1, pp.163–189). Oxford: Oxford University Press.

Miller, E. (1999) The neuropsychology of offending. *Psychology, Crime and Law*, 5, 515–536.

Ministry of Justice (2020a) *Safety in Custody Statistics: Quarterly to June 2020*. London: Ministry of Justice.

Ministry of Justice (2020b) *Community Performance Quarterly MI, Update to March 2020*, London: Ministry of Justice.

Ministry of Justice (2020c) *Crime, Justice and the Law: Sentences and Custody*. Available at www.ethnicity-facts-figures.service.gov.uk/crime-justice-and-the-law/courts-sentencing-and -tribunals/sentences-and-custody/latest#by-ethnicity-of-offender-all-types-of-sentences [accessed 28th February 2023]

Ministry of Justice (2021a) Press release: Extra £40m to help victims during pandemic and beyond. Available at www.gov.uk/government/news/extra-40m-to-help-victims-during-pandemic-and -beyond [accessed 28th February 2023]

Ministry of Justice (2021b) *Offender Management Statistics: Prison Receptions 2020* (Table A2.7 and A2.9i). London: Ministry of Justice.

Ministry of Justice (2021c) *Offender Management Statistics Quarterly: October to December 2020*. London: Ministry of Justice.

Naramore, R., Bright, M.A., Epps, N. and Hardt, N.S. (2017) Youth arrested for trading sex have the highest rates of childhood adversity: A statewide study of juvenile offenders. *Sexual Abuse*, 29(4), 396–410.

Newburn, T. (2017) *Criminology*. Abingdon: Routledge.

NHS England (2016) *Strategic Direction for Health Services in the justice system: 2016-2020.* London: NHS England.

Office for National Statistics (2021) All data related to crime and justice. Available at www.ons.gov.uk/peoplepopulationandcommunity/crimeandjustice/datalist [accessed 28th February 2023]

Palmer, E.J. (2013) *Offending Behaviour.* Abingdon: Routledge.

Piquero, A., Farrington, D. and Blumstein, A. (2007) *Key Issues in Criminal Career Research.* Cambridge: Cambridge University Press.

Prison Reform Trust (2021) *Bromley Briefing: Summer.* London: Prison Reform Trust.

Ramirez, A.M., Andretta, J.R., Barnes, M.E. and Woodland, M.H. (2015) Recidivism and Psychiatric Symptom Outcomes in a Juvenile Mental Health Court. *Juvenile and Family Court Journal*, 66(1), 31-46.

Robinson, M. (2014) Why Do People Commit Crime? An Integrated Systems Perspective. In A. Pycroft and C. Bartollas (eds), *Applying Complexity Theory: Whole Systems Approaches to Criminal Justice and Social Work* (pp.59-77). Bristol: Policy Press.

Ron, M.A. (1989) Psychiatric manifestations of frontal lobe tumours. *The British Journal of Psychiatry*, 155(6), 735-738

Sentencing Council (2021) Types of sentence. Available at www.sentencingcouncil.org.uk/sentencing-and-the-council/types-of-sentence [accessed 28th February 2023]

Skills Funding Agency (2018) *OLASS English and Maths Assessments by Ethnicity and Learners with Learning Difficulties or Disabilities: Participation 2014/15 to 2017/18.* London: SFA.

Skrzypiec, G. (2013) Adolescents' beliefs about why young people commit crime. *Australian Journal of Guidance and Counselling*, 23(2), 185-200. doi:10.1017/jgc.2013.16

Talbot, J. (2008) *Prisoners' Voices: Experiences of the Criminal Justice System by Prisoners with Learning Disabilities and Difficulties.* London: Prison Reform Trust.

The Buggery Act (1533). Available at www.bl.uk/collection-items/the-buggery-act-1533 [accessed 28th February 2023]

The Offences Against the Person Act (1861). Available at www.legislation.gov.uk/ukpga/Vict/24-25/100/section/20 [accessed 28th February 2023]

The Metropolitan Streets Act, Amendment Act (1867): street traders within special limits of Metropolitan Police District Liability to proceedings for causing obstruction of the highway. Available at https://discovery.nationalarchives.gov.uk/details/r/C3330427 [accessed 28th February 2023]

The Metropolitan Police Act (1829). In: Lyman, J. (1964) *Journal of Criminal Law and Criminology*, 55(1), 18.

The Sexual Offences Act (1967). Available at www.legislation.gov.uk/ukpga/1967/60/data.htm?timeline=false [accessed 28th February 2023]

The Equality Act (2010). Available at www.legislation.gov.uk/ukpga/2010/15/contents [accessed 28th February 2023]

The Marriage (Same Sex Couples) Act (2013). Available at https://bills.parliament.uk/bills/1135 [accessed 28th February 2023]

Tierney, J. and O'Neill, M. (2013) *Criminology: Theory and context.* Routledge.

Triangle. (2021) The Outcomes Star. Available at www.outcomesstar.org.uk [accessed 28th February 2023]

Unever, J., Cullen. F. and Pratt, T. (2003) Parental management, ADHD and delinquent involvement: Reassessing Gottfredson and Hirchi's general theory. *Justice Quarterly*, 20(3), 471-500.

Ward, T. (2002) Good lives and the rehabilitation of offenders: Promises and problems. *Aggression and Violent Behavior*, 7(5), 513-528.

World Prison Brief (2021) World Prison Brief data. Available at www.prisonstudies.org/world-prison-brief-data [accessed 28th March 2023]

HOW DOES THE CRIMINAL JUSTICE SYSTEM WORK?

DOI: 10.4324/9781003288701-3

The legal and criminal justice system in the UK is a complex beast. While there are text books which give a detailed and full account of all aspects (Davies, Croall and Tyrer, 2009), this chapter aims to give the reader some background insight into:

- how the criminal justice system evolved over time until it developed into the processes which we have in place today
- what the processes are that we have today including different roles and settings
- where speech and language therapy fits into these processes.

The evolution of justice

In this section, the reader is offered selected information to enable an understanding of the current legal system in England and Wales. For more detailed information on the history of the UK legal system, see *Slapper and Kelly's English Legal System* (Kelly, 2020).

This chapter refers to the evolution of the justice system in England and Wales, and does not seek to cover justice systems in other countries.

The justice system in place in England and Wales began its evolution a thousand years ago in the eleventh century. Prior to this date, there was no formal and universal system – local customs dictated sanctions if a person digressed from the social norm. Indeed, England was a territory which was governed by leaders from Anglo-Saxon, Norse and Norman cultures – each with separate ideas on justice.

In 1066, William the Conquer ascended to the English throne, finally uniting England under one government. The system of justice put in place offered 'local' courts which were overseen by lords and the 'King's Court' which was overseen by William himself. Examples of the processes used for legal decision making at this time included:

- Trial by Ordeal, which involved a physical task as part of the judgement of guilt. For example, having to remove a stone from a boiling pot of water – if the accused was able to remove the stone and had no wound after three days, God was with them and they were innocent of the accusation. Trial by Ordeal was made famous by the witch trials during this era.
- Trial by Combat, whereby a fight or dual would decide the outcome. This process was also less than ideal – the accused did not have to be involved in the combat if they could persuade or hire a person with combat skills to represent them.

During this phase of justice, the role of the judge was not the same as we understand it today. Judges were either clergy or knights who acted as court officials and advised the lords and the King on 'legal' decision making. They were very different from today's judges in that bribery and corruption were common within their trade. They were unpopular with the general population and had a reputation for oppression and bias based on their own motivations.

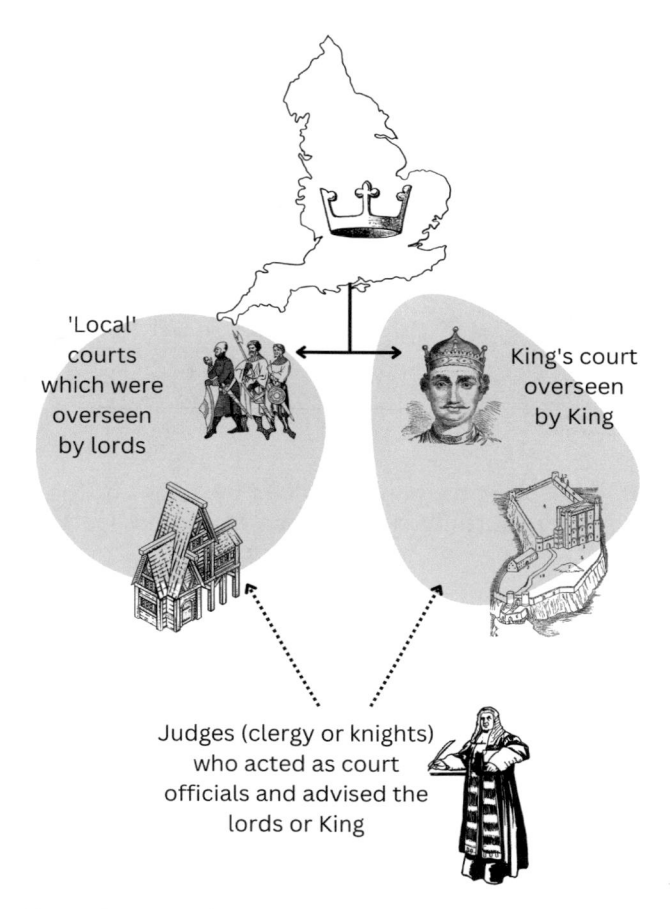

'Local' courts which were overseen by lords

King's court overseen by King

Judges (clergy or knights) who acted as court officials and advised the lords or King

FIGURE 2.1 The eleventh-century English and Welsh legal system was arranged into local courts and the King's Court

The local courts were nomadic, with lords travelling and the court session being held in various locations and at various times.

A hundred years after the establishment of local and King's courts, the next important changes occurred in 1166–1187. The then King, Henry II, put in place some changes in an attempt to improve fairness and the application of justice. The local courts became the Court of Common Pleas. These courts were fixed in set locations, sat at set times and aimed to address legal matters between people without the involvement of the King.

FIGURE 2.2   While two differing courts continued, chaired by judges or the King, the local courts became the regional Courts of the Common Pleas and operated at set locations on fixed days

As well as the court becoming 'fixed' in location and time, Henry II changed the role of judges. Judges moved from being court officials to deciding on cases by replacing the lords and sitting on the bench. The country was divided into regions, called assizes, and the judges travelled to different assizes passing judgements based on their expertise in certain areas of legal decision making. This constituted the establishment of circuit courts.

Alongside circuit courts, Henry II retained the King's Court, renaming it the Court of the King's Bench, and created the precursor of the jury by establishing a group of 12 knights to attend the court and offer opinion. While this is a long way from a jury of our peers as we know it today, the building blocks of a legal system were starting to be put in place.

Henry II also reformed the law. He provided a 'National Law' which was applied by the judges across the land. This came to be called the 'Common Law' due to its application to everyone. This is a term still employed today to describe laws across England.

Despite these changes, there were still significant problems with the application of fairness and justice, so in the thirteenth century the judges were reformed further. Previously, the judges had been either clergy or knights of the realm, leading to issues with corruption as these professions could be against the application of the law due to conflicts of interest. In the thirteenth century, judges started to be chosen from a pool of advocates who were employed in the Court of the Common Pleas.

This change had numerous benefits:

- It helped the role of judge to become a profession in its own right.
- It ensured that the person entering the role had experience of courts prior to sitting on the bench.
- It reduced conflicts of interest associated with other organisations (such as the Church) or influential sponsors (such as members of the royal circle).

The judges were charged by the King to 'keep the peace of the land', and this resulted in the coining of the term Justice of the Peace. However, these changes did not fully resolve all of the conflicts of interest that surrounded the position of judge. Shortly after this development, in the fourteenth century, the Court of the King's Bench also saw some changes, with the addition of some specialist courts with specific functions. England now had the two original courts:

- the Court of the Common Pleas overseen by judges (Justice of the Peace) for criminal matters between people in fixed locations and at fixed times
- the Court of the King's Bench overseen by the King and moving from location to location as the King moved. This court considered matters of legislation, security or diplomacy with the 12 knights advising the King.

With the addition of:

- the Court of the Exchequer for royal financial matters
- the Court of the Chancery overseen by the Lord Chancellor and concerned with fairness and justice matters which developed equity law
- the High Court of Admiralty concerned with occurrences at sea such as piracy, salvage and collision.

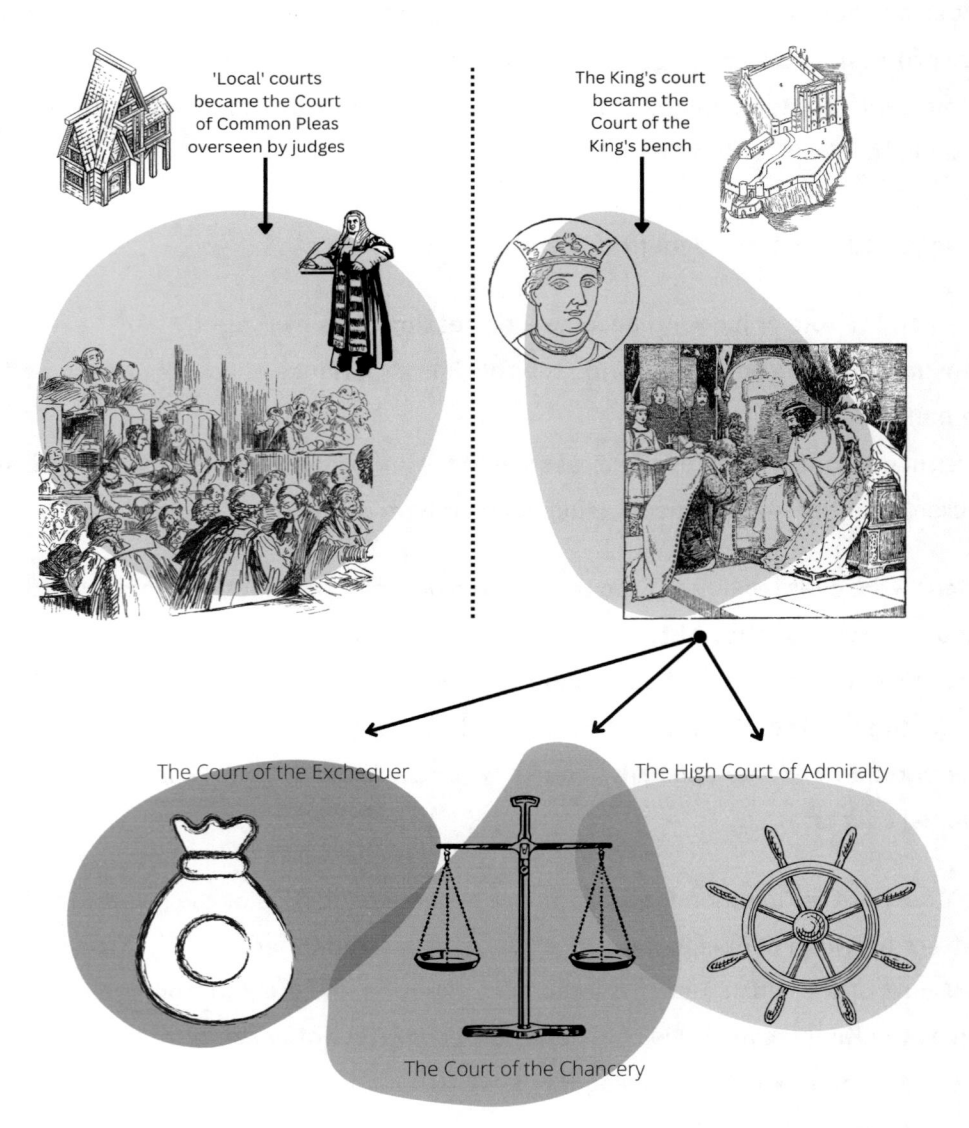

FIGURE 2.3 The fourteenth century saw the addition of the Court of the Exchequer, the Court of the Chancery and the High Court of the Admiralty to the King's Bench

Also in the fourteenth century, equity law came into being because the common law sometimes resulted in 'unfair' results when justice was weighed against conscience. Equity law enabled 'common sense' to be applied to rigid common law judgments. Equity would later be combined with common law in the nineteenth century.

Throughout the fourteenth century, judges were paid a salary by the King. The King had responsibility for making the laws and paying the judges, while the judges had the responsibility of interpreting and applying the King's law to cases that they oversaw. The situation was again not without conflict of interest because:

- if the King was unhappy with the judge's application of the law, he could dismiss the judge

- if the accused was unhappy with the judge's application of the law, he could petition the King to overrule the decision
- political alliances between the King, the judges and the accused influenced application of the law.

These arrangements continued until 1701 when an Act of Parliament addressed the matter of salary via the Act of Settlement (1701). The judges' salary was paid from the public purse, and, for the first time, judges were independent of the influence of the monarch.

The next significant changes were in 1830 when the Law Terms Act sought to improve the effectiveness of the courts by amending the circuit court system and by unifying Wales under the same justice system as England (Yates, 1856). The Central Criminal Court was formed to address criminal law and the circuit courts became county courts in order to consider civil matters of law.

These developments result in there being three basic types of law. These are:

- Criminal law which provides the definitions of criminal offences and the rules that apply when the police investigate an offence that they allege you have committed. It is the framework by which government deters and punishes crime. The individual is either guilty or not guilty.
- Civil law is concerned with the rights and property of individual people or organisations which may not always be protected by criminal laws. Civil law considers matters such as family disputes, personal injuries, duty of care responsibilities and breach of contract. A party is either liable or not liable.
- Common law started during the reign of Henry II with laws defined by the King. Today is it a set of precedents and judgments which has been established over years of the judicial system applying principles to real cases – hence the term 'case law'.

The Judicature Acts of 1873 to 1875 reformed the legal system further by changing the names, functions and number of different courts, aiming to make access to justice easier. In summary, these changes resulted in:

- Common law and equity law merged. All courts could now administer both equity and common law – with equity law (common sense) taking precedence in any dispute between the two types of law (i.e. common sense must be more important than slavishly applying the rules if the rules seem inappropriate to the specific case).
- Creation of a court hierarchy so that there was a clear pathway through the court system.
- Establishment of the High Court and the Court of Appeal.
- Provision of a right of appeal in civil cases to the Court of Appeal.

By this point, the legal system is close to the system which is in place today. One further reform of the legal system in 2006 aimed to ensure that the judiciary is truly independent of politics.

In 2006, the Legislative and Regulatory Reform Act aimed to:

- reduce the amount of resources used in regulating the legal system
- improve the quality of the legislation by removing out-of-date and complex elements
- help the UK legislation link to European Union legislation with reduced friction.

It is important to have this background overview of the evolution of the English and Welsh legal system. Having this grounding enables the reader to acknowledge why today's system can seem complex and illogical at times. It is helpful for the clinician to experience the multi-faceted nature of the legal system (and to feel somewhat confused by it) to reinforce the need to give clear and concise information to the people with whom they work.

The criminal justice system in place today

In this section, the journey through the criminal justice system, as it occurs now, will be outlined.

A crime has been committed

The journey begins with an occurrence that could be considered a criminal offence. The matter comes to the attention of the police who investigate. The investigation will seek to acquire evidence from a range of sources, such as physical evidence, witness accounts, victim statements, etc. There are three possible outcomes:

- No evidence or suspect can be identified so the investigation 'stops' (whatever information has been found is stored and can be referred to again if further evidence comes to light). It is possible that the case might be reviewed as a 'cold case' at a point in the future. This tends to occur when significant new information is found or when a technological development enables re-examination of evidence.
- There is evidence and a perpetrator for a low-level crime. The police can conclude this matter without going to court via a range of measures such as a fixed penalty notice (a fine), a caution (an instruction on what *not* to do) or a community-based resolution, also referred to as restorative justice.

- There is evidence and a suspect for a more serious crime. The police might feel that they have evidence and a case which can be referred directly to the magistrates' court. Alternatively, the police may have evidence and a suspect and the case is referred to the Crown Prosecution Service (CPS) for a charging decision.

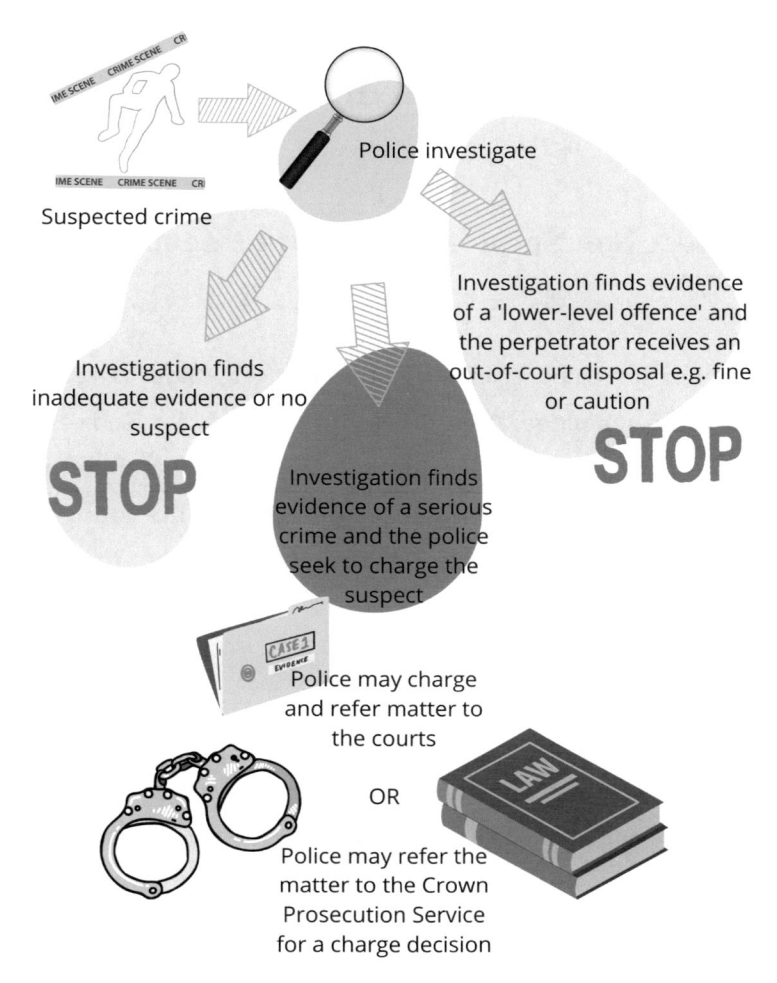

FIGURE 2.4 The process of investigation when a crime has been committed

The following text will explore the order of events following the discovery of a crime and the collection of evidence which indicates referral to court or to the CPS in the next section. The first part will consider people aged less than 18 years, and the second part will address people who are legally adults. The sequence explored is that which is in place in England and Wales.

At this stage, there are three different categories of offence:

- Summary offence: These are less serious cases such as motoring offences, taking a car without permission, criminal damage or minor assaults without serious physical injury to the victim, etc. The person charged with the crime does not need a jury trial. This type of offence is heard in the magistrates' court (no jury).

- Either-way offence: These are more serious cases such as possession of drugs, theft, burglary, fraud, serious assault causing physical harm, etc. The CPS decides if the case can be heard in the Magistrates Court or if it requires allocation to the Crown Court.
- Indictable offence – The most serious offences such as murder, rape, supplying class A drugs, manslaughter, firearms offences etc. These offences must be heard in a trial with a jury at the Crown Court.

The Crown Prosecution Service and courts – people aged under 18 years

In this section, options for disposal of a person aged less than 18 years when they are suspected of a crime are examined. Disposal is the legal term for 'end result' or resolution of the matter. Although this book focuses on adults who are in contact with the criminal justice system (CJS), many adults in prison have experienced the youth justice system, so it is important for a clinician in an adult setting to understand what that earlier experience may have entailed.

Age of criminal responsibility

The first question that will be established by the police is the age of the individual who is suspected of a crime. This is because there is an 'age of criminal responsibility' written into the law of a country. This is the age at which the government of that country has deemed that a young person has the cognitive skills to know what they were doing was against the law (or wrong).

In England and Wales, the age of criminal responsibility is ten years. In some countries, it is as low as seven years – for example, in Zimbabwe, Yemen and Thailand. In other countries, it is a figure in the teens, such as 18 years in Luxembourg, 16 years in Argentina and Mozambique, 15 years in Denmark and Burundi, and 14 years in Spain and North Korea.

Once the age of the individual is verified, the nature of the crime is considered. The seriousness of the crime is a consideration when deciding on disposal. For example, a ten-year-old suspected of shoplifting would be considered differently to a ten-year-old suspected of murder.

The options for disposal for young people who have reached the age of criminal responsibility as defined by the Ministry of Justice (2013b) are set out in Table 2.1 overleaf.

TABLE 2.1 The options for the disposal of a young person who has reached the age of criminal responsibility

Disposal option	Definition
No further action (NFA)	There is no offence or no evidence of an offence
Community Resolution	Usually, young people in trouble with the law for the first time and committing low-level crime and admitting their wrongdoing
Youth Caution	A formal caution where the young person admits their wrongdoing, the police have evidence to prove the wrongdoing, but the matter is not progressed to court/prosecuted because it is not in the public interest to do so
Youth Conditional Caution	A formal caution where the young person admits their wrongdoing, the police have evidence to prove the wrongdoing, but the matter is not progressed to court or prosecuted because the public interest is best served by managing the young person in the community with a set of conditions that they have to follow
Charged with offence	The case is progressed to court or prosecution

Youth Gravity Matrix

The disposal options are informed by a framework called the Youth Gravity Matrix (Youth Justice Board for England and Wales, 2013). This framework gives a score of 1 to 4 depending on the severity of the crime. The score can be increased by aggravating factors or deceased by mitigating factors. An example is given in Figure 2.5 below:

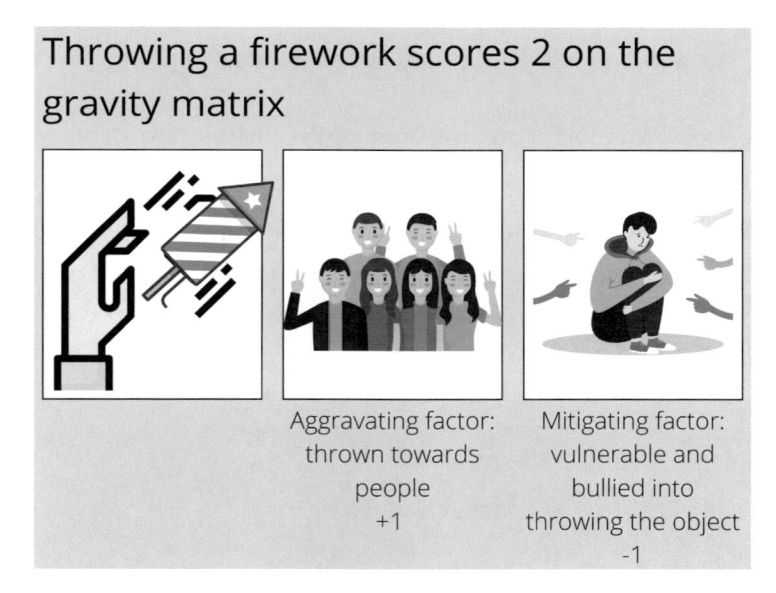

FIGURE 2.5 An example of the Youth Gravity Matrix which is employed to weigh aggravating and mitigating factors when considering the disposal of a young person

In this example, the young person scores a 2 (Youth Caution) because the crime is graded as a 2 and then the aggravating and mitigating factors cancel each other out. The options for disposal are set out in Table 2.2 overleaf (Youth Justice Board for England and Wales, 2013).

TABLE 2.2 How the Youth Gravity Matrix aggravating and mitigating factors score guides the disposal of a young person

Final score (Score from matrix for offence plus aggravating factors and minus mitigating factors)	Proposed disposal option
4	Most serious score and the young person is usually charged with a crime which is progressed to court for the court to decide on disposal
2 or 3	Consider a Youth Caution as the disposal If the Youth Caution is not adequate, consider a Youth Conditional Caution which has extra rules and supervision to help the young person avoid any more lawbreaking If the Youth Conditional Caution is not adequate, consider charging the young person with a crime which is progressed to court for the court to decide on disposal
1	Apply the minimum response – usually community resolution as the disposal

Disposal options will now be considered further.

Disposal option – Community Resolution Order

A Community Resolution Order is made when the police, the victim and the young person who has admitted the wrongdoing agree on a way to resolve the matter without the young person being convicted of a crime. It may take the form of an apology, or it may be an agreement such as cleaning up graffiti or paying compensation.

The young person who is subject to the Community Resolution Order does not have a criminal record, but the information does remain on their police information file so that it can be referred to again in the future. The information may also be disclosed if the young person or their employer applies for a Disclosure and Barring Service (DBS) check.

There are five types of community resolution:

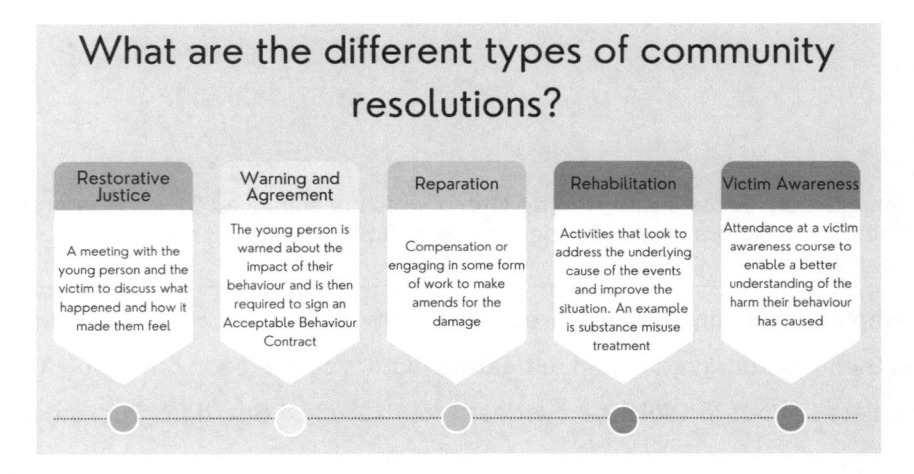

FIGURE 2.6 The five types of community resolution available when considering the disposal of a young person

Disposal option – Youth Caution

If the young person is suspected of a summary offence or an either-way offence, the police can decide to issue a Youth Caution without consulting the CPS (Ministry of Justice 2013a). If the young person is suspected of an indictable offence, then the CPS is always consulted (a Youth Caution can still be agreed as long as all the terms of the caution are in place). In the case of the most serious offences, a Youth Caution is not appropriate.

The evidence which has been collected in respect of the young person and the suspected offence is considered. In order to progress with a Youth Caution, there has to be sufficient evidence that *if* the case were taken to court, the person *may* be convicted. This is a safeguard so that the Youth Caution cannot be issued to a person when there is insufficient evidence. If there is insufficient evidence, either the matter will be discontinued at this point with no further action or the police can seek additional evidence to meet the conditions of this safeguard.

At this point in this route of disposal, the following information must be evident:

- age of criminal responsibility clearly stated
- type of offence clearly stated with the police and CPS in agreement
- sufficient evidence so that the young person would be likely to attract a conviction if the matter went to court.

In order to progress, the next step is that the young person has to 'make a clear and reliable admission to all elements of the offence' (Ministry of Justice, 2013a, p.9). This is a challenge as the young person and his or her advocates need to know the options available to them and any potential risks or benefits that exist within these options. This knowledge of options and the weighing of options must happen before the young person makes any statement of admission. If the young person does not make such an admission, a Youth Caution cannot be used as an option for disposal.

Finally, if the young person makes an admission that they committed the offence, factors such as previous offending history, impact on any victims, any public interest concerns and the young person's willingness to engage in programmes designed to minimise the likelihood of reoffending are all taken into account before the final decision to issue a Youth Caution is made. Requirements for a Youth Caution are illustrated in Figure 2.7 overleaf.

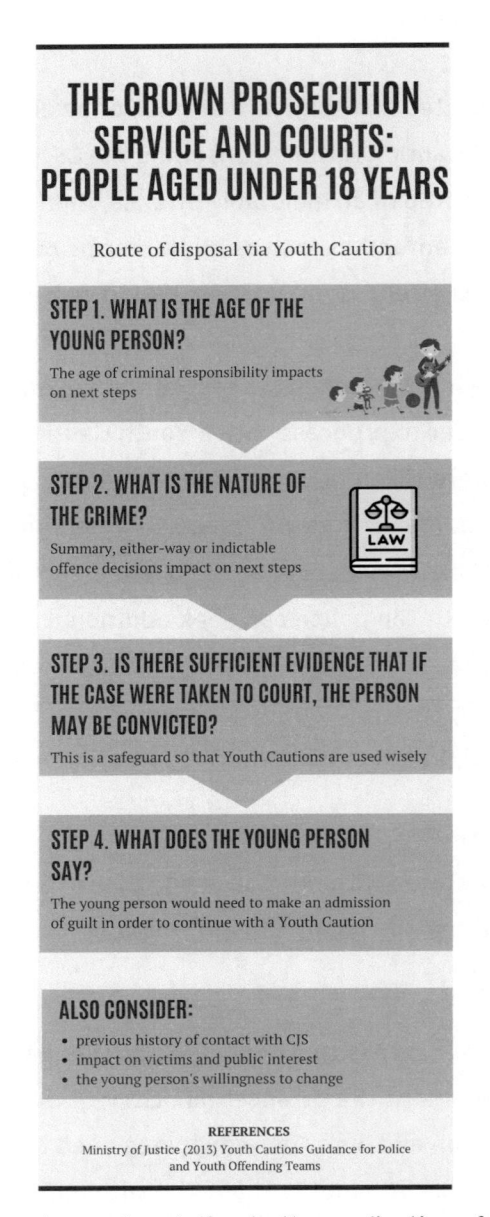

FIGURE 2.7 The stages and requirements relating to the application of a Youth Caution

The outcome of the Youth Caution disposal is:

- A record will be kept on the young person's police information file in case it is needed in the future.
- The information may be disclosed if the young person or their employer applies for a DBS check.
- If the young person finds themselves in contact with the CJS again, the information can be used in criminal proceedings.

- If the Youth Caution is associated with a sexual offence, the young person will need to follow any special instructions given to them.
- The police must notify the young person's local area youth offending team (YOT) who will offer the young person interventions to reduce the risk of them getting into trouble again. The young person does not have to engage with the YOT, but if they get into trouble again, this information will contribute to any future disposal decisions.

Disposal option – Youth Conditional Caution

A Youth Conditional Caution follows the same pattern as a Youth Caution, but with an additional element in that there are rules (or 'conditions') attached that the young person must agree to and follow. Criminal proceedings are stopped while the caution is in place, but if the person fails to comply with one or more of the conditions, the caution is deemed to have failed and the criminal proceedings can be restarted.

A Youth Conditional Caution disposal option is initiated by the police or CPS, but also involves other agencies such as the YOT. There are five basic requirements for a Youth Conditional Caution (Ministry of Justice, 2013b). These are illustrated in Figure 2.8 below:

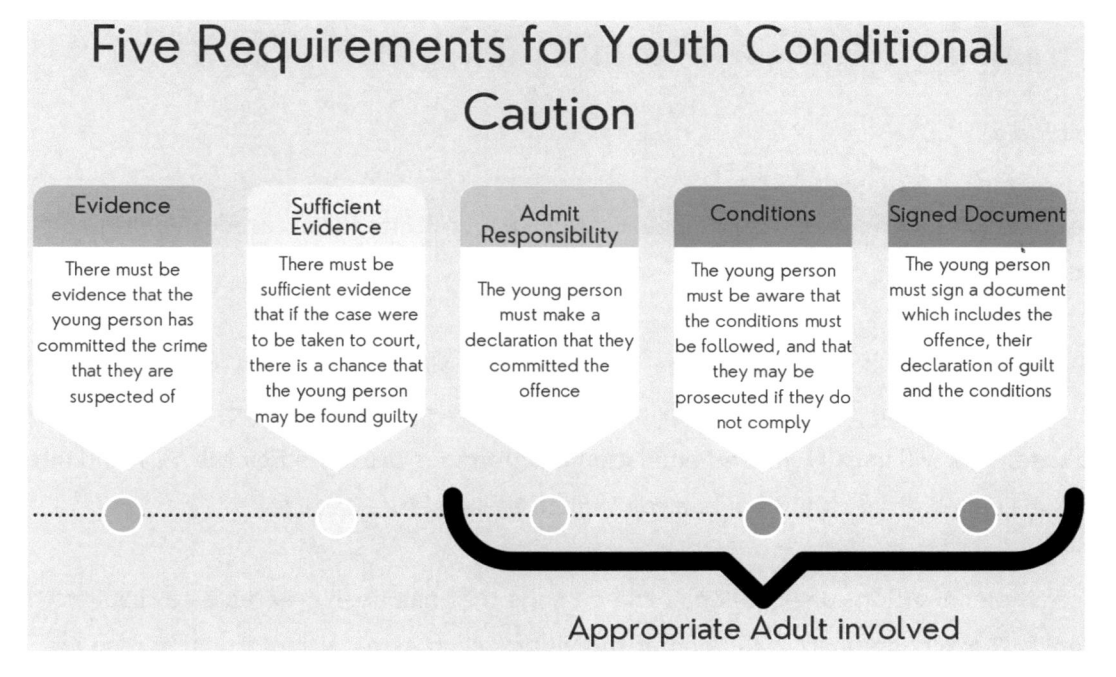

FIGURE 2.8 Five basic requirements for a Youth Conditional Caution

Expanding on the five basic requirements, a detailed outline of the requirements for a Youth Conditional Caution requires:

- Age of criminal responsibility clearly stated.
- Type of offence clearly stated with the police and CPS in agreement.
- Sufficient evidence so that the young person would be likely to attract a conviction if the matter went to court.
- A referral to the YOT for assessment of the case and recommendations with respect to the appropriateness of the Youth Conditional Caution and what the conditions should be.
- An appropriate adult (as defined by Ministry of Justice, 2013b) has been present for the process to provide advice to the young person and to ensure that the young person is treated fairly. It is important to note that an appropriate adult as defined in this document is not an intermediary. This will be discussed further in Chapter 3.
- The young person has made an admission of guilt to all elements of the offence and consents to follow the conditions of the Youth Conditional Caution.
- Factors such as previous offending history, impact on any victims, any public interest concerns and the young person's willingness to engage in programmes designed to minimise the likelihood of reoffending are also considered.
- The conditions are provided to the young person and there is a plan in place to monitor the young person's progress in completing the conditions.

Conditions

The conditions of the Youth Conditional Caution must fall into three categories – rehabilitation, reparation and punishment.

The rehabilitation conditions will be aimed at changing the young person's behaviour so that their risk of repeating a similar decision process leading to further crime will be reduced. This will usually include education programmes presented by the YOT and interventions aimed at any high-risk behaviour such as substance misuse.

Reparation conditions seek to repair the damage that has been created as a result of the offence. Reparation might be aimed at the victim, such as repairing property damage, or it may be aimed at the wider community, such as taking part in community initiatives such as litter collection. Reparation can also include work that benefits local charities or community projects.

Punishment conditions seek to penalise the young person. This includes sanctions such as monetary fines or completing unpaid work supervised by the National Offender Management Service. These conditions are usually only applied when rehabilitation or reparation are not appropriate – for example, if there are no education or interventions deemed necessary, there is no quantifiable victim or community reparation is unavailable.

The conditions must always be appropriate for the young person and victim, proportionate to the offence and achievable.

The outcome of the Youth Conditional Caution disposal is:

- A record will be kept on the young person's police information file in case it is needed in the future.
- The information may be disclosed if the young person or their employer applies for a DBS check.
- If the young person finds themselves in contact with the CJS again, the information can be used in criminal proceedings.
- If the Youth Conditional Caution is associated with a sexual offence, the young person will need to follow any special instructions given to them.
- If the young person does not complete the conditions of the caution, they may be prosecuted for the original offence.

Disposal option – charged with offence

If the young person is charge with an offence, it will progress to being heard in a court setting. The type of court setting will depend on the severity of the offence.

Moderately serious offences such as antisocial behaviour, drugs offences, knife crime, theft and burglary will be heard in the Youth Court. The most serious offences such as murder, firearms offences and rape will be heard in the Crown Court despite the young person being aged less than 18 years.

Youth Court

Youth Court is different to an adult court setting in that it is less formal, the young person is called by their first name, and the professionals working there have additional training to enable them to give the best possible care to the young person. There is an increased emphasis on the young person understanding what is happening and why.

There is additional provision from members of the local YOT, and if the young person is under 16 years old, they may be permitted to have a parent or guardian with them for emotional support. Youth Courts are also closed, so that members of the public cannot attend, and there are provisions to protect the identity of the young person such as reporting restrictions.

Youth Courts have a set of instructions which help them decide on sentencing (Sentencing Council, 2017). The instructions are underpinned by the two principles of:

- reducing reoffending (prevention)
- welfare of the young person.

Consideration of the welfare of the young person includes identifying learning disability, brain injury, mental ill-health, experience of trauma or abuse, and speech, language and communication needs (SLCN).

In a Youth Court, if the young person enters a guilty plea, the matter will progress directly to sentencing and the young person may get a reduction in their sentence for entering this plea. If the young person enters a not-guilty plea, the case will be heard and the presiding judge will make a decision on guilt. If the young person is found guilty, the matter will progress to sentencing.

Sentencing is based on consideration of:

- prevention of reoffending
- the welfare of the child or young person
- the age of the child or young person (chronologically, developmentally and emotionally)
- the seriousness of the offence including consideration of any aggravating and mitigating circumstances
- the likelihood of further offences being committed and the extent of harm likely to result from those further offences.

Table 2.3 (overleaf) gives an overview of the sentences which the Youth Court can deliver, by age (adapted from Sentencing Council, 2017).

The Magistrates Association (2022) also offer online resources, glossaries of terms and frequently asked questions information on their website.

TABLE 2.3 An overview of the sentences that the Youth Court can deliver, by age

Sentence	Age of child or young person			
	10–11	12–14	15–17	Information on when the sentence is finished (known as 'spent')
Absolute or conditional discharge or reparation order An absolute discharge means the court has decided not to impose a punishment because the experience of going to court has been punishment enough. The offender will still have a criminal record A conditional discharge means that if the offender commits another crime, they can be sentenced for the first offence and the new one	☑	☑	☑	Absolute discharge and reparation: spent on day of sentence Conditional discharge: spent on last day of the period of discharge
Financial order	☑	☑	☑	Spent 6 months after the finding of guilt
Referral order A referral order is available for young people who plead guilty to an offence The young person is referred to the YOT for a period between three and 12 months	☑	☑	☑	Spent on day of completion
Youth rehabilitation order (YRO) A youth rehabilitation order is a non-custodial community sentence with requirements that must be adhered to	☑	☑	☑	Spent 6 months after the last day the order is to have effect
YRO with intensive supervision and surveillance or fostering	☐	☑ For persistent offenders only	☑	Spent 6 months after the last day the order is to have effect
Detention and training order A detention and training order combines detention with training and is used for young people who commit a serious offence or commit a number of offences	☐	☑ For persistent offenders only	☑	6 months or under: spent 18 months after the sentence is completed (including supervision period) More than 6 months: spent 24 months after the sentence is completed (including supervision period)
An offence to which section 91(1) of the Powers of Criminal Courts Sentencing) Act 2000 applies: the court considers that it ought to be possible to impose a sentence of more than two years' detention if found guilty of the offence (also known as a 'grave crime')	☑	☑	☑	More than 6 months–30 months: spent 24 months after sentence completed (including licence period) More than 30 months–48 months: spent 42 months after sentence completed (including licence period) More than 48 months: never spent

(Continued)

TABLE 2.3 Continued

	Age of child or young person			
Sentence	*10–11*	*12–14*	*15–17*	*Information on when the sentence is finished (known as 'spent')*
Extended sentence of detention: a specified violent or sexual offence where the court is of the opinion that there is a significant risk of the young person committing further specified offences	☑	☑	☑	Never spent

Crown Court for young people

The case of a young person charged with a significant crime will be referred to the Crown Court *if* the likely outcome *if* found guilty is 'a custodial sentence substantially exceeding two years' (The Judicial College, 2022, p.45). Referral to the Crown Court will result in the young person being subject to a jury trial.

As with Youth Court, the following safeguards and supports are in place to help the young person:

- The young person's parent, a family member or a guardian can be with them.
- The young person will be referred to using their first or preferred name.
- A social worker may also be present to ensure welfare.
- Representatives from the YOT will be present.
- Reporting restrictions are in place to protect the identity of the person facing the charge.
- The judge can decide to hold the trial under 'special measures' so that the general public may not attend or may be restricted only to those who have a genuine reason to attend.
- Professional people working in the court should have skills and training specific to supporting young people in complex situations, and may change their usual professional attire for the proceedings – for example, they may remove gowns and wigs.
- An assessment of reasonable adjustments is made and implemented at a pre-trial hearing (Criminal Procedure Rule Committee, 2019).
- The young person may be offered a pre-trial visit to the courtroom.
- The court room may be arranged differently – for example, the young person may not be required to sit in the dock and may be permitted to sit with their parent.
- The use of video link as a substitute to attending in person will be considered.

- The young person may be able to have the support of a registered intermediary for some or all of the trial.

Following the Crown Court jury trial, the young person will have been found either guilty or not guilty. If they are found guilty, they are referred back to the Youth Court for sentencing as discussed previously (see Table 2.3). The only exception to this is if they are found guilty of murder, whereby the young person is sentenced by the Crown Court (Sentencing Act, 2020). In this circumstance, the young person is sentenced to Detention at His Majesty's Pleasure with a minimum term of 12 years.

This concludes an overview of the CPS and courts applied to people aged less than 18 years old. The justice system for people who are over the age of 18 – that is, people who are legally adults – will be considered next.

The Crown Prosecution Service and courts – adults

If a case pertaining to an adult suspected of a crime is referred to the CPS by the police, the CPS will review the information which has been given to them and make decisions on next steps. The CPS follow the Code for Crown Prosecutors (Crown Prosecution Service, 2017) which provides general principles that should be followed when making decisions on cases:

- Whether to charge the person suspected of a crime or not.
- What offence the person should be charged with.
- Whether there is an alternative to sending the case to court (e.g. disposal via a substitute route).
- If more evidence is needed and what type of evidence would help the prosecution in court (to make the chances of obtaining a guilty verdict stronger).
- Advise the police on strategies for the most effective investigation, use of resources and to ensure that all reasonable lines of inquiry have been explored.
- Whether prosecuting the case is 'in the public interest'. This means that the CPS have weighed up how serious the crime is, what the person did and why, what the impact has been on the victim of the crime and the community where the crime occurred, information specific to the person being charged such as their age and personal history, and lastly whether prosecution is 'proportionate' – that is, the outcome is worth applying the process.

If the CPS decides to progress a prosecution, 95% of cases will go to the magistrates' court. This is because 95% of cases are summary (less serious) offences. A panel of two or three magistrates or one district judge will hear the case. The person charged with the crime can enter a plea (guilty or not guilty), and once the case is presented to the magistrate panel or district judge, a decision will be made on their guilt. If they are found guilty, the magistrate panel or district judge can impose a prison sentence, a fine or another sanction such as a driving exclusion.

If the CPS decides to progress a prosecution for a more serious offence, it is called an either-way offence. This term comes from the fact that the case can be tried either in the magistrates' court (before a district judge or magistrate panel) or in the Crown Court (before a judge and jury). The decision on 'which way' – that is, which court – is based on a set of rules set out in the Criminal Justice Act (2003). The rules include consideration of the seriousness of the crime, the scope for the district judge or magistrate panel to be able to impose an appropriate sentence and the right of the person charged with the crime to have a trial with a jury. If the either-way offence is allocated to the magistrates' court, the process is the same as a summary offence.

For the most serious crimes such as murder or rape, the prosecution is allocated directly to the Crown Court. These offences are called indictable offences. The case will be heard by a judge and jury. These are the type of cases that attract lengthy prison sentences if the person is found guilty. The jury will decide on the verdict and the judge will apply guidelines in order to impose the most appropriate sentence or other disposal.

There are other courts for specialist functions such as County and Family Courts, Tribunal Courts, the High Court, the Court of Appeal and the Supreme Court. Detailing the functions of these courts is outside of the scope of this text, but a detailed outline is given in 'The Structure of the Courts' (Judiciary, 2021).

Disposal and sentencing

Disposal is the term used to describe how the magistrate or judge would like to resolve the case. If the person is found not guilty, disposal is release with no further action.

The magistrate or judge takes into account sentencing guidelines which are generic to all people, but they can also take into account:

- circumstances surrounding the case that might be unusual and explain elements of what happened and why
- any mitigation that the individual may offer to explain their actions
- the impact of the crime on the victim.

The goal is for the magistrate or judge to impose a sentence that offers the best chance of reducing reoffending in the future.

Disposal for people who are found guilty can be a community-based punishment such as community service, a control or restriction order or a custodial sentence. The sentence can accommodate any individual circumstances that may apply to the guilty person, such as learning disability, mental ill-health and a neurodivergent need.

Disposal and sentencing for people with individual circumstances

Options exist for disposal and sentencing for people who have individual circumstances such as learning disability, mental ill-health and a neurodivergent need.

In October 2020, new guidance was published called 'Sentencing offenders with mental disorders, developmental disorders, or neurological impairments' (Sentencing Council, 2020). This guidance requires the court to consider:

- an individualised approach to considering if the person being sentenced needs special consideration (i.e. the impact of their disability on them)
- the gender, cultural or ethnic impact of a disability and how stigma may influence how disability is supported or not at the time of the offence
- the fact that some conditions may fluctuate and may have been causing greater disability at the time of the offence
- the complex nature of hidden disability
- the possibility that the person may have a disability that has not attracted a formal diagnosis at the time of the offence; or that the disability falls into more than one diagnostic label
- that the person should not be disadvantaged if they fail to disclose their disability prior to sentencing
- the impact of chemical substances (e.g. hormones, medication, illicit drugs or alcohol) on the person and their disability
- any formal reports from suitably qualified professionals which relate to the disability.

Descriptions of illness, conditions or diagnostic labels which would be a red flag for an individualised approach to sentencing are:

- A new illness affecting a person's thinking or functioning when they have previously had a long period of stable good health. These illnesses are often linked to mental health such as schizophrenia, psychosis or depression.
- A life-long condition which has always had an influence on the person's thinking or functioning. These are often neurological conditions and usually cause thinking (cognition), feeling (emotions, affect) and actions which are outside of a neurotypical norm. Autism or learning disability would be such conditions.
- Medical conditions which have neurological and psychiatric implications on thinking and functioning such as epilepsy, head injury, stroke or dementia.
- Fluctuating conditions such as bipolar disorder or post-traumatic stress disorder which impact on thinking, motivations, impulsivity and insight.
- Difficulties with attention, concentration, impulsivity, assessment of risk and understanding causality which is often seen with people with attention deficit hyperactivity disorder (ADHD), personality disorder, conduct disorder, substance misuse disorders or brain injury. These are conditions which may have been life-long, or they may be newly acquired. They may also be co-morbid such as a person with ADHD who has sustained a head injury which changes their daily functioning associated with decision making. Issues with impulsivity and causality contribute to the person having challenges with disinhibition, which can be a factor in some offences.

In cases where such conditions should be reviewed for sentencing consideration, the court will seek information on how the condition may relate to the offence, the level of impairment that the individual experiences, medications and any triggers which preceded the offence. Speech, language and communication needs (SLCN) are often identified within this information gathering. Table 2.4 (overleaf) gives examples on how the offence, condition and sentencing may be managed (developed from source material by the Sentencing Council, 2020).

TABLE 2.4 Examples of how a criminal offence, illness, medical condition or diagnostic label and disposal may interact within the court decision making when applied to unwell adults

Conviction	Condition	Sentence
Convicted of an offence punishable with imprisonment	Mental ill-health such as depression which requires treatment but is not severe such that detention under a hospital order is indicated	A community treatment order or suspended sentence order The person can reside at their usual address but they must also have treatment by a registered medical practitioner or registered psychologist (or both) during a specified time frame
Convicted of an offence punishable with imprisonment	Disturbed mental or cognitive functioning such as schizophrenia or autism Evidence from two doctors (at least one of whom must be approved under section 12 of the Mental Health Act, 1983) that the person is suffering from a mental disorder of a nature or degree which makes it appropriate for them to be detained in a hospital for medical treatment, and that the appropriate medical treatment is available	A hospital order under section 37 of the Mental Health Act 1983 The person must reside within a secure hospital setting and a responsible clinician (usually a psychiatrist) will oversee their care and treatment as part of a multi-disciplinary team. The person's progress will be monitored and reviewed with consideration of next steps on a regular basis
The court has assessed that the protection of the public can only be achieved if the person is subject to special restrictions	A condition where the person may reasonably be expected to commit further serious crime such as a delusional disorder with command hallucinations	A restriction order under section 41 of the Mental Health Act 1983 As per hospital order (above)

These recent developments in considering all aspects of the factors that should contribute to sentencing are very welcome. However, the importance of disabilities and comorbidities being recognised is very apparent. Where such problems are overlooked or not recognised, a sentence may be inappropriate in that it does not address the key issues that have contributed to the crime (Hughes et al., 2017). In addition, it is immediately apparent that if an accused person has SLCN and cannot tell their story accurately and understandably, it may be very difficult for the court, the legal team and the police to be fully apprised of the issues relevant to the case. The negative impact of SLCN on the criminal justice journey is therefore apparent even before a sentence is received.

An overview

This chapter has covered the development of the criminal justice system from its earliest beginnings to the present day. We have also explored how the systems in place today are applied to young people and to adults when they are suspected of a crime and what outcomes may occur and why. Figure 2.9 (below) gives a summary visual representation of the CJS pathway. A copy is located at Appendix 1.

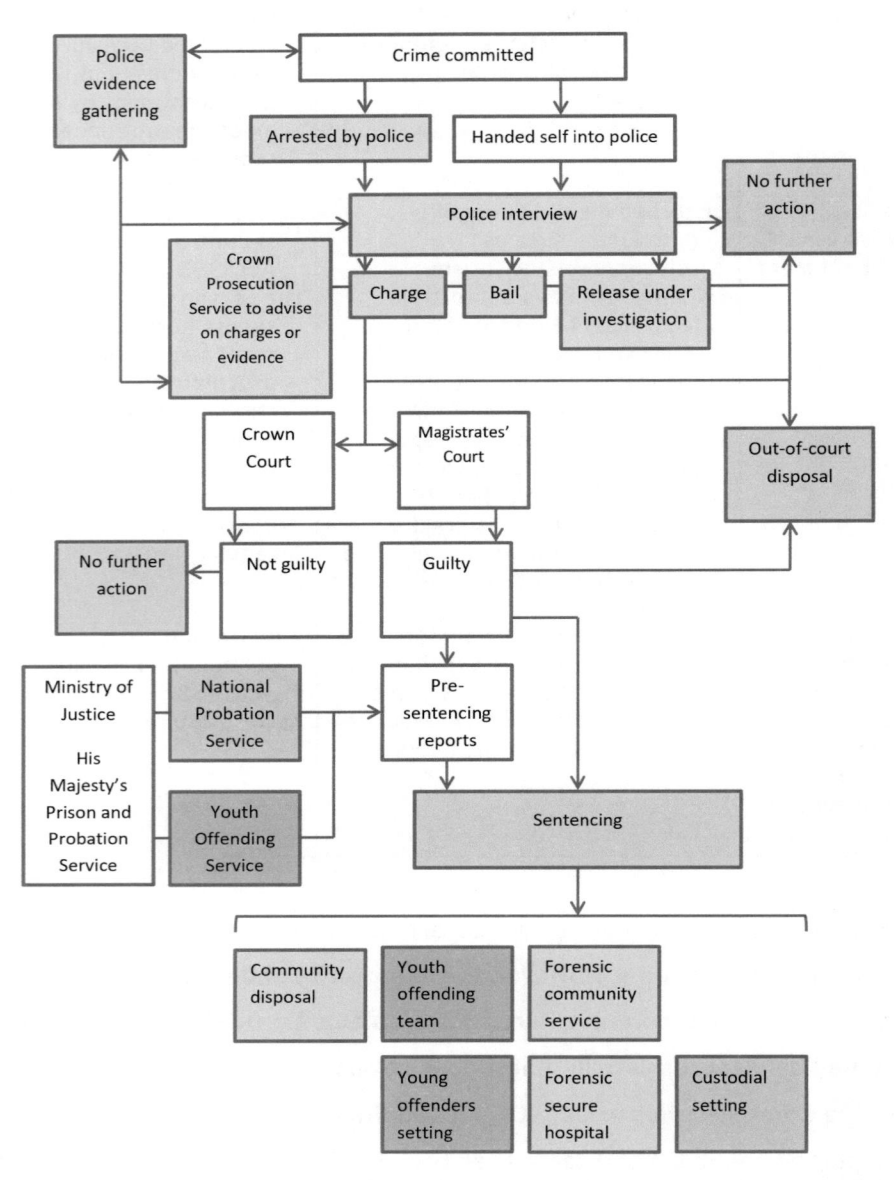

FIGURE 2.9 A visual representation of the CJS pathway from a crime being committed to disposal as applied to young people and adults

Different people involved with the criminal justice system

There is an array of people who work within the CJS or who work in organisations which participate in the CJS. Some of the roles carry ceremonial titles and robes, which adds to the sense of 'difference' that may be experienced by a person going to court. Some of the roles are part of the running of the court, and may not be introduced to a novice court attender because there is an assumption that their introduction is not required.

It is useful for the defendant (accused person) to make a pre-trial visit to the court so that the setting has been experienced before the trial date, but also to find out which professionals may be present so that any roles or responsibilities can be clarified. Figure 2.10 (below) illustrates the roles that a person may encounter in court. The figure may be a useful starting point for a conversation with a person who might require extra support.

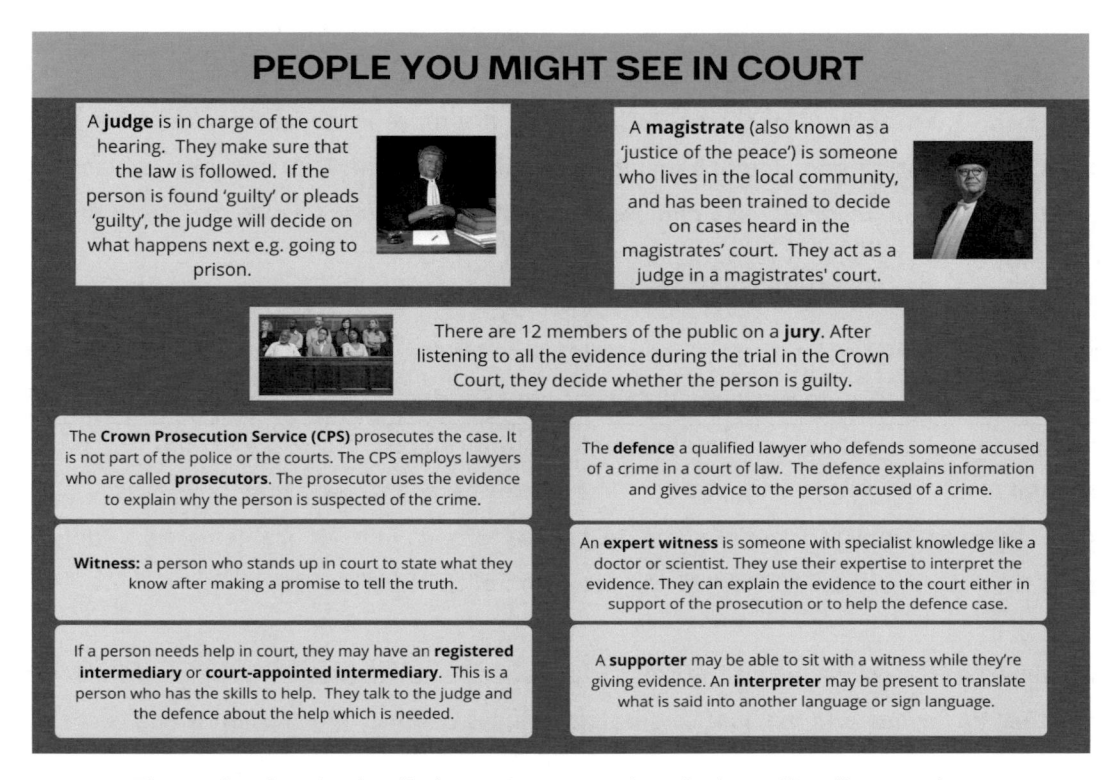

FIGURE 2.10 The professional roles that may be encountered when attending court

A more comprehensive resource for the people that are seen in court, which can be used as a communication ramp or learning tool to help a defendant or witness prepare for court appearances, is located at Appendix 2.

The role of the speech and language therapist in criminal justice services

Speech, language and communication needs play an important role in the life course of any individual (Cronin et al., 2020). Having competent communication skills gives you an advantage at every life stage (Deming, 2017; Conti-Ramsden et al., 2018). Having some communication struggles but good support also gives you opportunities to meet your potential (Buckner, Mezzacappa and Beardslee, 2003; Rowe, 2018).

But having a communication need which is undiagnosed and unsupported places a person at a disadvantage (McCool and Stevens, 2011). The communication barriers filter into learning, managing emotions, friendships and participating in communities. As the person moves through their life course, they impact on employment, earning potential, socio-economic outcomes and health experience (Beard, 2018).

People who struggle with hidden communication difficulties in education are more likely to struggle with learning, emotions and regulation of the challenges being presented to them (Law, Charlton and Asmussen, 2017). They are more likely be expelled from mainstream school and attend a pupil behavioural unit (Martindale, 2020). They are also more likely to become involved in risky choices during their teen years which can bring them to the attention of the local police (Cronin and Addo, 2021).

People who have struggled through education with hidden communication difficulties may have limited literacy, numeracy and qualifications (Søndenaa, Wangsholm and Roos, 2016). They will find it harder to gain employment, fill in forms, access services and reach their potential (Andrews and Botting, 2020). These are the people who may have less support around them and may start to become desperate to resolve their problems via a range of means that could also bring them to the attention of the local police.

The following is an overview of the work that speech and language therapists (SLTs) *may* undertake in various criminal justice services. This is generic information which is correct at the time of writing, but is also subject to change as time passes. Individual services or teams may have alternative local activities that SLTs undertake as part of their daily tasks.

In addition, SLTs may be core members of a justice service team – for example, employed full- or part-time within a prison or community setting – but in many settings, there is a formal or informal contracting arrangement to access the services of an SLT when required. In these circumstances, the SLT works in a consultative role and advises the professional who is making a referral. Access to other members of the team, residential or education staff would then need to be negotiated, along with any agreed follow-up. Issues relating to SLTs embedded in the team and SLTs as consultants are discussed further in Chapter 5.

The following section is designed to give the reader an overview of the SLT role and to help differentiate the role in different services. It is important to remember that not all of these services will have access to SLT.

SLT in youth offending teams

When a person aged between 10 years and 18 years comes to the attention of the police, a referral is made to the local YOT. The circumstances could be that the young person is at risk of offending, has committed an offence and had an out-of-court disposal, or has committed and offence and has been instructed by a court to engage with the YOT (HM Inspectorate of Probation, 2017).

An SLT in a YOT will often take a role that offers direct assessment, reporting and treatment to the young person; and indirect support, training and problem solving within the wider multi-disciplinary team (MDT). Evidence for what an SLT can add to the YOT can be found in Gregory and Bryan, 2011 and Bryan and Gregory, 2013.

Direct work would focus on exploring the strengths and weaknesses in the young person's communication profile via formal assessment, informal assessment, observation, social engagement and tasks or games. It would include the young person's self-report, as well as the reports of people in their lives such as family, teachers, friends and other professionals. The aim would be twofold: to provide a report which explains the communication issues for use by colleagues in the criminal justice system, and to help the young person understand what they are good at and how this can be used to tackle areas of challenge.

Assessment and reporting may be followed by goal setting and therapy interventions such as:

- strategies for self-autonomy so that the young person can be confident to state when they are having a problem
- work on self-esteem to have a secondary gain within the domain of communication
- sessions to teach the young person how to sequence events and understand theory of mind so that they can explain themselves more clearly
- intervention for problem solving
- emotion recognition and regulation including emotions vocabulary support
- dysfluency.

While this is not an exhaustive list, interventions often take the form of skill building rather than impairment-based treatment, which the young person may reject due to the parallel of the content with failed experiences in formal education.

Indirect work could include:

- training colleagues, families and community stakeholders in what communication is, what skills are needed and why not everyone has those skills
- training colleagues in how to notice communication difficulties and how to support and adapt their own communication style to support the young person
- support with the creation of accessible materials and interventions aiming to reduce the language burden, particularly in verbally mediated interventions such as anger management
- contributing to plans which include helping a young person with communication needs when they are in crisis
- contributing to pre-sentencing reports and progress reports.

SLT with young people in custodial settings

There are three types of custodial setting for young people:

- Young offender institutions (YOIs) are a type of secure setting which offers accommodation, education and training to young people aged 15–21 years who have been sentenced to a custodial stay by the courts. People aged 15–17 are usually housed separately from people aged 18–21 years. There are five YOIs in England and Wales. They are operated either by HM Prison and Probation Service or by private companies.
- Secure training centres (STCs) are a residential setting for young people aged 12–17 years who have been sentenced to a custodial stay by the courts. There are three secure training centres in England, each offering young people 30 hours per week of education and training. These settings are usually arranged into smaller units or 'houses' with fewer than ten young people residing in a house with key staff supporting them.
- Secure children's homes (SCHs) are the final type of residential setting for young people who have been sentenced to a custodial stay. They offer care and education to children aged 10–17 years of age. There are 14 secure children's homes in England and Wales. As of March 2021, there were 142 children accommodated in these settings, with 62% being male and 38% being female.

An SLT in a secure custodial setting will offer many of the same direct and indirect inputs as an SLT working in a YOT, but will have additional consideration of what it means for the young people to be geographically further away from their families and communities. This necessitates increased awareness of psychological models (such as attachment theory) and trauma-informed care as part of the SLT delivery (Adshead and Aiyegbusi, 2014). Examples include:

- SLT input into the communication environment to increase the sense of psychological 'safety' for the young person. This may include helping to set routines or goals and make choices about the day, creating visual prompts to help the young person with the choices, helping the young person to use tools such as mind maps to support their emotional safety. It may also include working with clinical psychology colleagues to make resources and safety plans for self-harm or risk situations.
- Working outside of the clinic room to spend time alongside the young person to build skills, support self-esteem, enable attachments and model pro-social ways of resolving issues (Children's Social Care Innovation Programme, 2016).
- Support education staff to recognise SLCN and to reduce the impact of these language difficulties on access to the curriculum and the classroom activities. The SLT may give assessment, advice, impairment-based interventions and input to education plans.
- Working as a key worker or care coordinator for a named young person where the SLT may progress care plans, write risk assessments and develop positive behaviour support strategies with the young person.

SLT in criminal justice liaison and diversion services

Criminal justice liaison and diversion services (CJLDS) aim to identify vulnerable people when they first come into contact with the CJS and offer additional support to them and the professionals around them. This service offers assessment and advice for people of any age who may be suspects, defendants or offenders. Practitioners within CJLDS may work in various locations including police stations, courts and mental health settings.

The practitioners in the team identify people coming into contact with the CJS who have mental health needs, learning disability, substance misuse difficulties, cognitive decline or other vulnerabilities. The service will support people through the early stages of the criminal system pathway, make onward referrals for appropriate health or social care input, or enable the person to be diverted away from the CJS into a more appropriate setting. An example would be to divert a person with severe and enduring mental illness to a psychiatric hospital setting.

An SLT in a CJLDS could work directly and indirectly with the people who come into the service.

Direct work would include:

- Rapid responses to requests for communication assessment often enacted in settings such as the police custody suite. The assessment might be enacted with minimal case history and be time-pressured due to the nature of the work.
- The assessment can be with a person of any age and with any underlying SLCN, so the SLT needs to have a breadth of knowledge of different conditions including developmental, neurological, psychiatric and psychological.
- The SLT has to be flexible in their assessment approaches in order to establish communication and identify the needs of the individual.

Indirect work includes:

- training colleagues and stakeholders in communication needs and how to identify these needs
- creation of screening tools to support colleagues in the identification of SLCN
- teaching skills in modifying communication to meet the needs of the individual in contexts such as police interview
- providing concise handover of information to colleagues often in a time-pressured environment
- reporting on the needs of the individual.

The work of the CJLDS SLT is different from some of the other SLT roles because of the varied nature of the work and the fast pace of the environment. It would be unusual for the SLT role to extend to identification of treatment goals and providing SLCN intervention.

SLT in forensic community teams

A forensic community team will offer care and treatment to people who, due to mental ill-health, learning disability, autism or personality disorder, have either committed a crime or pose a potential risk to themselves or others. The focus is to support the person to live in the least-restrictive environment (i.e. their community) while offering support and interventions to reduce risk. The team members provide a range of specialist knowledge in order to supervise the individual in making progress against their recovery goals.

Within a forensic community team, the SLT may offer direct interventions such as:

- assessment of the person's SLCN and reporting of the strengths and barriers

- the co-production of a communication passport and other bespoke communication tools to support the individual in reaching their communication potential
- working with the person to maximise social opportunities and build social networks
- developing accessible patient-centred resources for managing risks and safety
- supporting the autonomy and participation of the individual in meetings such as the bi-annual Care Programme Approach (CPA) review.

The key ethos of the work undertaken by the forensic community team is co-production with the person receiving the support. This means that any intervention undertaken is completed jointly with the individual and their key worker as equal partners. The SLT skills within the team are vital in helping the person who has SLCN to participate in joint working and enabling co-production.

Indirect tasks may include:

- training within the team, the community and with families or friends around the person
- preparing reports, care plans, accessible information and resources for use by the team in co-production interventions.

In agreement with the team, the SLT may offer assessment and intervention in a range of locations including the person's home, community settings such as work places and leisure or recreation settings. Some forensic community teams work across a seven-day week and a non-traditional working day.

SLT in forensic or secure hospitals

Forensic or secure hospitals are either settings for people who have been found guilty of a crime, but have been identified as needing care in a secure hospital, or are settings for people who present a significant risk to themselves or others and need care in a secure environment to support them to progress.

There are three levels of secure hospital – low, medium and high.

Low-secure services are for people who pose a significant danger to themselves and others. They may be people who have progressed from high- or medium-secure, are learning to manage their risks and who have moved to a less restrictive environment; or they may be people who have come to a low-secure setting because they cannot be cared for in an inpatient psychiatric hospital for whatever reason. Low-secure settings can offer care and treatment to people with learning disability, autism, mental health needs or psychological needs.

Medium-secure units are for people who are thought to present a serious danger to the public and have often been referred to the setting by the courts or other secure estate settings (e.g. prison). The aim is to provide care, treatment and rehabilitation in a secure setting which keeps the individuals and the public safe.

High-secure services are for those people who present a grave and immediate danger to themselves and others. There are three high-secure hospitals in England and Wales with capacity for about 750 patients.

Secure hospitals offer care for the person via a multi-disciplinary team which often (but not always) includes an SLT. The care is both pharmacological (medication for conditions which are adding to the distress of the person) and psychological (interventions aimed at helping the person to understand their thinking patterns and why they might make certain decisions, and helping them to risk-assess decisions). The whole setting will aim to be trauma-informed and therapeutic via offering choices, routine, consistent care, predictable next steps and environments that are easy to understand (Quality Network for Forensic Mental Health Services, 2019).

Within the forensic or secure hospital, the SLT may be part of the team so will work closely with other professionals to support in understanding the patient's needs and making decisions about the risks involved. However, in some settings, the SLT will have a regular or by-arrangement consultancy role.

Direct SLT work in a secure hospital may include:

- assessment of SLCN
- interventions such as helping the person participate in their own care as an equal partner
- direct work which fits with the overall plan for the person's progress and needs adaptation to be communication appropriate – for example, each person will need a safety plan which they have been involved in creating, but they may need the SLT to undertake this work because of the communication adaptations that are needed in the moment.

Indirect work includes training, accessible materials, reporting, etc., as well as creating communication-friendly environments, supporting the team with materials for specific groups, such as fire setting or violence reduction, and input into the MDT decision making (such as psychological formulation).

People tend to stay in secure hospitals for a number of years, so the SLT in this setting might be involved in a person's journey for a long time (SLT care may be slow-paced compared to SLTs in CJLDS). Some secure hospitals offer care to a small number of individuals, so the SLT may have a small caseload of people that they see often and know well.

There is a need in forensic or secure hospitals to remember that dysphagia is a risk factor for the people residing there (Dziewas et al., 2007). Medications for psychiatric conditions can cause dysphagia which may be unnoticed until there is an episode of choking (Kulkarni, Kamath and Stewart, 2017). The SLT in this setting will need to have an interest in SLCN and dysphagia.

SLT in adult prisons

Adult prisons house people aged as young as 18 years and upwards to people at the end of life. They may be people awaiting trial (housed in prison on remand) or they may be convicted of a crime and serving a custodial sentence.

Due to the challenges of data collection on the SLCNs of people in prison, it is hard to give exact figures on the incidence and prevalence of SLCN. It is suspected that between 60% and 80% of people in adult prison could have SLCN (McNamara, 2012; Royal College of Speech and Language Therapists, 2017).

Two types of prison SLT working

SLTs in adult prisons could work in small units called therapeutic communities, or they could offer a more general service to the whole prison site. The nature of the service is likely to vary significantly from prison to prison based on operational drivers in each establishment, as well as historical staffing patterns.

Therapeutic communities (TCs) are psychologically informed smaller units within a larger prison. They usually offer specific treatment to around 50–100 people. The remit may be to offer treatment via diagnostic label (e.g. to people with learning disability) or via clinical need such as substance misuse (College of Policing, 2019). The aim of a TC is to enable behavioural change for the person accessing treatment there.

An SLT may offer sessional input into a TC for assessment of SLCN, advice, reporting and MDT support and training. This is usually a part-time role. At the time of writing, there is more sessional SLT in TCs than general SLT services in a prison setting. An example is HMP Dovegate, which (at the time of writing) offers SLT sessions into a TC which has therapeutic aims of supporting people in prison who have a diagnosis of learning disability (Capone, 2017). The SLT role in this TC considers the SLCN of the individual and provides supports in the environment to increase participation. Supports include visual timetables, communication passports, pictorial minutes of meetings and other communication-friendly environment ramps (Bradshaw, 2000).

General SLT services in a prison setting are less common and can vary between geographical locations. The activity of an SLT in a general prison service might include:

- inviting referrals for communication assessment and advice
- goal setting for SLCN intervention
- SLCN intervention which is usually focused on building skills, addressing self-esteem, problem solving, stop-and-think skills
- specific work on communication breakdowns which lead to violence (violence reduction work)
- specific work on communication breakdowns which lead to self-harm or refusal of food
- input into support plans to address communication breakdowns
- working with partner agencies such as forensic psychology services, probation, prison colleagues and education providers.

This is in addition to training others, reporting and creating accessible materials. Because of the age range of people in prison, there tends to be work with younger people on psychological interventions moving to work with people as they age that is aimed at managing deterioration such as dementia. A general prison SLT will expect to see patients with wide-ranging aetiologies, complex presentations and comorbidities located in physical, emotional, psychological and mental well-being.

Conclusion

The chapter considered how the criminal justice system evolved and developed, the processes of justice including different professional roles and settings, and where SLT can contribute.

Insight is gained into why the system in place today in England and Wales is complex, with terminology that may feel alien and processes that sometimes seem to defy logic.

It is hoped that the reader has gained knowledge and understanding for themselves, and now understands why the criminal justice system is hard to comprehend for people with additional needs such as SLCN. If, at any point in this chapter, the reader has felt overwhelmed by information and new material, this can only serve as a red flag for how it must feel for a person who would benefit from support during a criminal justice journey.

It is also hoped that the chapter has outlined the contributions that an SLT can bring to criminal justice settings.

References

Act of Settlement (1701). Available at www.parliament.uk/about/living-heritage/evolutionofparliament/parliamentaryauthority/revolution/collections1/parliamentary-collections/act-of-settlement/#:~:text=The%20Act%20of%20Settlement%20was,Act%20was%20extended%20to%20Scotland. [accessed 1st March 2023]

Adshead, G. and Aiyegbusi, A. (2014) Four pillars of security: Attachment theory and practice in forensic mental health care. In A.N. Danquah and K. Berry (eds) Attachment Theory in Adult Mental Health: A Guide to Clinical Practice (pp.199–212). Routledge.

Andrews, L. and Botting, N. (2020) The speech, language and communication needs of rough sleepers in London. *International Journal of Language and Communication Disorders*, 55(6), 917–935.

Beard, A. (2018) Speech, language and communication: A public health issue across the lifecourse. *Paediatrics and Child Health*, 28(3), 126–131.

Bradshaw, J. (2000) A total communication approach towards meeting the communication needs of people with learning disabilities. *Tizard Learning Disability Review*, 5(1), 27–30. https://doi.org/10.1108/13595474200000005

Bryan, K. and Gregory, J. (2013) Perceptions of staff on embedding speech and language therapy within a youth offending team. *Child Language, Teaching and Therapy*, 29, 359–371.

Buckner, J.C., Mezzacappa, E. and Beardslee, W.R. (2003) Characteristics of resilient youths living in poverty: The role of self-regulatory processes. *Development and Psychopathology*, 15(1), 139–162.

Capone, G. (2017) Staff and service users' evaluations of therapeutic principles at a High Secure Learning Disability Therapeutic Community. Doctoral dissertation, University of Lincoln.

Children's Social Care Innovation Programme (2016) No Wrong Door: Ensuring young people access the right services at the right time and in the right place to meet their needs. Available at www.rcslt.org/wp-content/uploads/2021/08/no-wrong-door-storyboard-1.pdf [accessed 1st March 2023]

College of Policing (2019) Therapeutic communities. Available at www.college.police.uk/research/crime-reduction-toolkit/therapeutic-communities [accessed 1st March 2023]

Conti-Ramsden, G., Durkin, K., Toseeb, U., Botting, N. and Pickles, A. (2018) Education and employment outcomes of young adults with a history of developmental language disorder. *International Journal of Language and Communication Disorders*, 53(2), 237–255.

Criminal Procedure Rule Committee (2019) Plea and trial preparation hearing information form. Available at www.gov.uk/government/publications/plea-and-trial-preparation-hearings-ptph-for-1-to-5-defendants [accessed 2nd January 2022]

Cronin, P. and Addo, R. (2021) Interactions with youth justice and associated costs for young people with speech, language and communication needs. *International Journal of Language and Communication Disorders*, 56(4), 797–811.

Cronin, P., Reeve, R., McCabe, P., Viney, R. and Goodall, S. (2020) Academic achievement and productivity losses associated with speech, language and communication needs. *International Journal of Language and Communication Disorders*, 55(5), 734–750.

Crown Prosecution Service (2017) The Code for Crown Prosecutors 2018. Available at www.cps.gov.uk/publication/code-crown-prosecutors-2018-downloadable-version-and-translations [accessed 1st March 2023]

Davies, M., Croall, H. and Tyrer, J. (2009) *Criminal Justice* (4th edn). Harlow: Pearson Education.

Deming, D.J. (2017) The value of soft skills in the labor market. *NBER Reporter*, 4, 7–11.

Dziewas, R., Warnecke, T., Schnabel, M., Ritter, M., Nabavi, D.G., Schilling, M., Ringelstein, E.B. and Reker, T. (2007) Neuroleptic-induced dysphagia: Case report and literature review. *Dysphagia*, 22(1), 63–67.

Gregory J. and Bryan K. (2011) Speech and language therapy intervention with a group of persistent and prolific young offenders in a non-custodial setting with previously un-diagnosed speech, language and communication difficulties. *International Journal of Language and Communication Disorders*, 46, 202–215.

HM Inspectorate of Probation (2017) The Work of Youth Offending Teams to Protect the Public. An inspection by HM Inspectorate of Probation. Available at www.justiceinspectorates.gov.uk /hmiprobation/wp-content/uploads/sites/5/2017/10/The-Work-of-Youth-Offending-Teams-to -Protect-the-Public_reportfinal.pdf [accessed 1st March 2023]

Hughes, N., Chitabesan, P., Bryan, K., Borschmann, R., Swain, N., Lennox, C. and Shaw, J. (2017) Language impairment and comorbid vulnerabilities among young people in custody. *Journal of Child Psychology and Psychiatry*, 58, 1106–1113.

Judiciary (2021) The Structure of the Courts. Available at www.judiciary.uk/wp-content/uploads /2021/07/courts-structure-0715.pdf [accessed 1st March 2023]

Kelly, D. (2020) *Slapper and Kelly's English Legal System*. Routledge.

Kulkarni, D.P., Kamath, V.D. and Stewart, J.T. (2017) Swallowing disorders in schizophrenia. *Dysphagia*, 32(4), 467–471.

Law, J., Charlton, J. and Asmussen, K. (2017) Child language as a wellbeing indicator. Early Intervention Foundation. Available at www.eif.org.uk/report/language-as-a-child-wellbeing -indicator [accessed 1st March 2023]

McNamara, N. (2012) Speech and language therapy within a forensic support service. *Journal of Learning Disabilities and Offending Behaviour*, 3(2), 111–117. https://doi.org/10.1108 /20420921211280097

Magistrates Association (2022) FAQs and resources. Available at www.magistrates-association.org .uk/FAQs-and-Resources [accessed 1st March 2023]

Martindale, D. (2020) A world of violence, intimidation and crime. *SecEd*, 2020(3), 14–16.

McCool, S. and Stevens, I. (2011) Identifying speech, language and communication needs among children and young people in residential care. *International Journal of Language and Communication Disorders*, 46(6), 665–674.

Ministry of Justice (2013a) Youth Cautions: Guidance for Police and Youth Offending Teams. Aavailable at https://assets.publishing.service.gov.uk/government/uploads/system/uploads/ attachment_data/file/354050/yjb-youth-cautions-police-YOTs.pdf [accessed 1st March 2023]

Ministry of Justice (2013b) Code of Practice for Youth Conditional Cautions: Crime & Disorder Act 1998 (as amended by the Criminal Justice & Immigration Act 2008 and the Legal Aid, Sentencing and Punishment of Offenders Act 2012). Available at https://consult.justice.gov.uk/digital -communications/code-youth-conditional-cautions/results/code-practice-youth-conditional -cautions.pdf [accessed 1st March 2023]

Quality Network for Forensic Mental Health Services (2019) Standards for Forensic Mental Health Services: Low and Medium Secure Care – Third Edition. Available at www.rcpsych.ac.uk/docs /default-source/improving-care/ccqi/quality-networks/secure-forensic/forensic-standards -qnfmhs/standards-for-forensic-mental-health-services-fourth-edition.pdf?sfvrsn=2d2daabf_6 [accessed 1st March 2023]

Royal College of Speech and Language Therapists (2017) The provision of health and social care in the adult prison estate: Written evidence submitted by the Royal College of Speech and Language Therapists. Available at https://business.senedd.wales/documents/s90475/HSP17%20-%20Royal %20College%20of%20Speech%20and%20Language%20Therapists.pdf [accessed 1st March 2023]

Rowe, M.L. (2018) Understanding socioeconomic differences in parents' speech to children. *Child Development Perspectives*, 12(2), 122–127.

Sentencing Council (2017) Sentencing Children and Young People: Overarching Principles and Offence Specific Guidelines for Sexual Offences and Robbery – Definitive Guideline. Available at www.sentencingcouncil.org.uk/wp-content/uploads/Sentencing-Children-and-Young-People -definitive-guideline-Web.pdf [accessed 1st March 2023]

Sentencing Council (2020) Sentencing offenders with mental disorders, developmental disorders, or neurological impairments. Available at www.sentencingcouncil.org.uk/overarching-guides/ magistrates-court/item/sentencing-offenders-with-mental-disorders-developmental-disorders -or-neurological-impairments/#Annex%20A%20%E2%80%93%20main%20classes%20of %20mental%20disorders%20and%20presenting%20features [accessed 2nd January 2022]

Søndenaa, E., Wangsholm, M. and Roos, E. (2016) Case characteristics of prisoners with communication problems. *Open Journal of Social Sciences*, 4(4), 31-37.

The Judicature Act (1873). Available at www.jstor.org/stable/pdf/1276028.pdf [accessed 18th March 2023]

The Criminal Justice Act (2003). Available at www.legislation.gov.uk/ukpga/2003/44/contents [accessed 1st March 2023]

The Judicial College (2022) Youth Defendants in the Crown Court. Available at www.judiciary.uk/guidance-and-resources/youth-defendants-in-the-crown-court [accessed 23rd March 2023]

The Mental Health Act (1983). Available at www.legislation.gov.uk/ukpga/1983/20/contents [accessed 1st March 2023]

The Legislative and Regulatory Reform Act (2006). Available at www.legislation.gov.uk/ukpga/2006/51/contents [accessed 1st March 2023]

The Sentencing Act (2020). Available at www.legislation.gov.uk/ukpga/2020/17/section/250/enacted [accessed 1st March 2023]

Yates, J.B. (1856) The Rights and Jurisdiction of the County Palatine of Chester, the Earls Palatine, the Chamberlain, and Other Officers. Charles Simms & Co.

Youth Justice Board for England and Wales (2013) Youth Out-of-Court Disposals: Guide for Police and Youth Offending Services. Available at https://assets.publishing.service.gov.uk/government/uploads/system/uploads/attachment_data/file/438139/out-court-disposal-guide.pdf [accessed 1st March 2023]

INVESTIGATIONS, INTERVIEWS AND COURT

3

DOI: 10.4324/9781003288701-4

As clinicians working with adults who are in contact with the criminal justice system (CJS), it is useful to understand how investigations, interviews and a court process function. This is because:

- We will be exposed to the stages, processes and vocabulary via our role in working with suspects, defendants, witnesses or people convicted of offences.
- We may overlap with these processes – for example, if asked to provide a report or act as an appropriate adult.
- We could be required to explain the finer details of the processes to adults with speech, language and communication needs (SLCN) that we meet within our role.

In this chapter we will cover:

- investigation of wrongdoing with emphasis on police investigations in England and Wales
- systems and processes related to interviewing suspects, victims or witnesses including consideration of people who are vulnerable
- the progression of the journey from investigation and interview to attending court
- consideration of SLCN of people when in this context including the role of the speech and language therapist (SLT) and other professionals
- tools which may be useful for the clinician working in these settings.

Investigations

Investigations are a process with the aim of discovering if a crime has been committed and if there is a credible suspect (Salet, 2017). The crime may have been an act (something a person did), an intention to act (the planning of a crime) or an omission (failing to act to prevent a crime happening) (Association of Chief Police Officers, 2005a). While, in this chapter, this statement mainly pertains to the police investigating a crime, other bodies can also enact investigations into wrongdoing, such as the Health and Safety Executive in the UK (Health and Safety Executive, 2022).

The investigation will be triggered by either:

- a report of a potential crime which triggers a reactive investigation
- the suspicion of a potential future or ongoing crime which can trigger a proactive investigation.

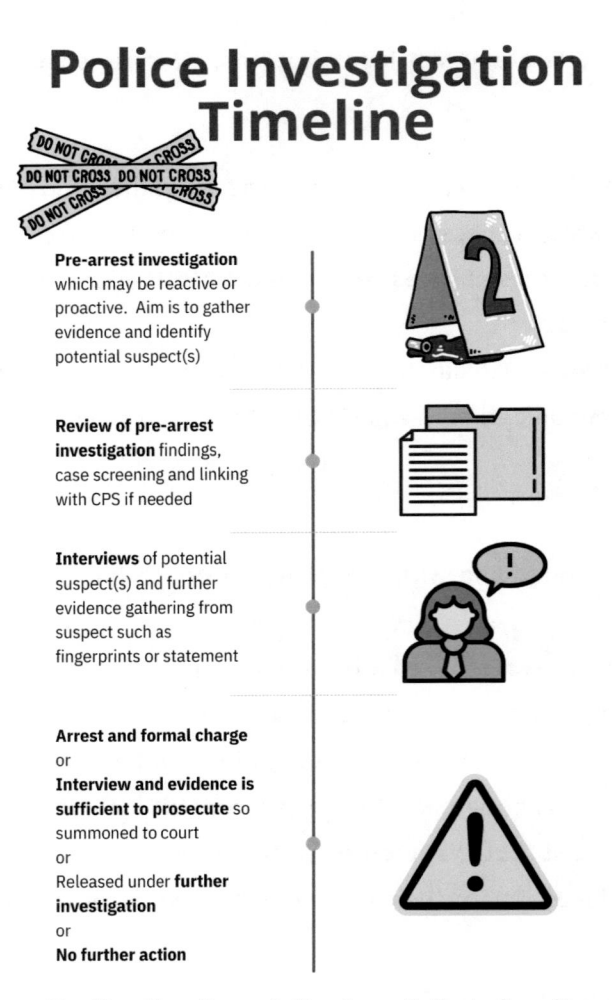

FIGURE 3.1 The police investigation timeline relating to activity before the arrest of a suspect

The reactive investigation involves an investigator responding to the report of the potential crime and attending the scene in order to discover what happened, to locate and interview witnesses, and to collect and preserve evidence (Home Office, 2020a). The information gathered is documented and escalated for 'case screening' by a senior police officer who will consider the severity of the potential crime and the possibility of solving it prior to deciding on next steps (Association of Chief Police Officers, 2005b).

The proactive investigation involves there being a suspicion of criminal activity and action by the police to confirm or deny the activity, prevent crime, gather evidence and then escalate the case for screening. This type of investigation tends to use police investigation strategies such as surveillance, monitoring electronic equipment or examining financial matters, use of information from police sources or 'undercover' policing (covert operations) and other forms of intelligence gathering (John and Maguire, 2007).

Who's who in the police custody setting?

There is an array of professionals working in the police custody setting. This chapter will refer to key roles associated with investigations, interviews and court.

FIGURE 3.2 The roles of key police custody officers

Being a suspect

In most circumstances, the individual will not know that they are a suspect until they are informed of this by the investigating team. With the police, being a suspect is indicated by either invitation to attend an interview under caution or via arrest (Home Office, 2020a).

Being invited to attend an interview under caution is also called a 'caution plus 3' interview, 'voluntary attendance' or a 'voluntary police interview' (College of Policing, 2022a). The terms can be used interchangeably and this can be unhelpful for people who are naïve about the experience of being a suspect. The important points to note are:

- Being asked to attend for an interview under caution, 'caution plus 3' interview, voluntary attendance or 'voluntary police interview' indicates that the person is under suspicion of committing a crime.
- When asked to attend for an interview under caution, the person is read the same caution as when a formal arrest is made.
- The person who is attending for an interview under caution is not under arrest and they are free to leave the police station if they wish to. While this acknowledges that the individual retains their right to liberty, leaving the police station could have adverse outcomes for the individual.
- The person who is attending for an interview under caution is entitled to free legal advice and legal representation.
- The person who is attending for an interview under caution is entitled to access Liaison and Diversion Services (NHS England & Improvement, 2019).

We can appreciate that the vocabulary is complex and that full understanding of a person's situation requires sophisticated understanding of language. This is in addition to the language demands of a verbal interview. The vulnerability of a person with speech, language and communication needs is immediately apparent.

The purpose of the interview under caution is that the police are offering the suspect the opportunity to respond to an allegation of a crime. The response could have the outcome of concluding the matter, but if this not possible, the interview under caution also gives the suspect an opportunity to offer a defence explanation. The police investigation team are obligated to take the defence explanation seriously and explore all lines of inquiry (Home Office, 2020a).

The potential outcomes of the interview under caution for the suspect are:

- No further action. The suspect is able to offer an explanation which concludes the matter and they are no longer suspected.
- Being released under investigation. The police have asked their questions and gathered information from the suspect. The police are now exploring further lines of inquiry. The person remains a suspect and has no specific rules which they must follow in relation to the suspected crime.
- Being arrested and formally charged with the crime. The interview may have given the police investigating team the information which was required in order to progress the case to a formal charge. This is covered fully in later sections of this chapter.

If a vulnerable person is being invited to attend for an interview under caution, they have the legal right to be supported by an appropriate adult (Mind, 2013). The appropriate adult is independent of the police and can be a family member, friend or healthcare professional. The appropriate adult cannot be the solicitor. The role of the appropriate adult is one of safeguarding the welfare of the suspect – ensuring that they are treated fairly and given help to participate if needed (National Appropriate Adult Network, 2018).

Being arrested

If the police suspect a person of a crime and they have sufficient evidence, the investigating team will link with the Crown Prosecution Service (CPS) in order to reach a decision on whether to charge the person and what the charge will be (Crown Prosecution Service, 2017). At this stage, the individual can be arrested (Home Office, 2020a). The arrest means that the person no longer has their right to liberty and they cannot choose to leave the situation (College of Policing, 2022a).

The important points to note are:

- If the police plan to arrest a person, they must identify themselves as police officers. The arresting officers must tell the person why they are being arrested (e.g. what crime they are suspected of committing).
- Being arrested indicates that the person is suspected of committing a crime.
- The person is not free to leave the situation.
- The police must 'caution' the individual. This is a verbal reminder to the person that they do not have to give information (The wording of the caution is: *You do not have to say anything, but it may harm your defence if you do not mention, when questioned, something which you later rely on in court. Anything you do say may be given in evidence*).
- The police are permitted to use 'reasonable' force when arresting a person. This can mean touching or holding a person, or using handcuffs (National Institute for Health and Care Excellence, 2021).

At this time, the person is accommodated at the police station and they are subject to a reception process where their personal information is entered into the computer system. This is referred to as the 'booking in' process.

The 'booking in' is overseen by the custody officer and a robust sequence is followed to ensure the safety of all people involved.

Under arrest

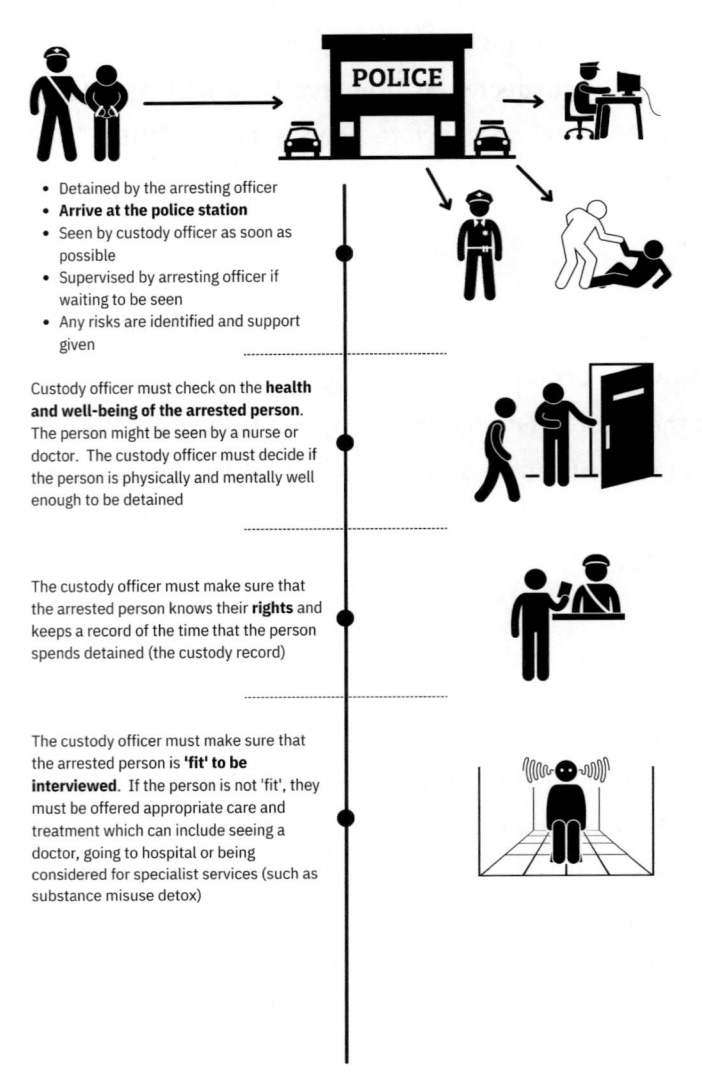

- Detained by the arresting officer
- **Arrive at the police station**
- Seen by custody officer as soon as possible
- Supervised by arresting officer if waiting to be seen
- Any risks are identified and support given

Custody officer must check on the **health and well-being of the arrested person**. The person might be seen by a nurse or doctor. The custody officer must decide if the person is physically and mentally well enough to be detained

The custody officer must make sure that the arrested person knows their **rights** and keeps a record of the time that the person spends detained (the custody record)

The custody officer must make sure that the arrested person is **'fit' to be interviewed**. If the person is not 'fit', they must be offered appropriate care and treatment which can include seeing a doctor, going to hospital or being considered for specialist services (such as substance misuse detox)

FIGURE 3.3 The process that is followed when a suspect is arrested

The custody officer has an important role at this stage as they become responsible for the person under arrest – ensuring that they are mentally and physically well, enacting a risk assessment to identify if there are any risks associated with the person, articulating the legal rights to the person and recording the information (College of Policing, 2022a). Ultimately, the custody officer will make a decision on whether the suspect is in an appropriate condition to be detained in the police station. To inform this decision, the custody officer may seek medical opinion either within the custody setting (e.g. from a custodial healthcare professional), from specialist assessment (e.g. via the suspect attending the local emergency department to be assessed by a doctor) or from a specialist team such as liaison and diversion services or substance misuse services (The Faculty of Forensic & Legal Medicine, 2022).

Once the person under arrest is 'booked into' the police custody setting, their photograph, fingerprints and DNA are taken. Other evidence such as clothing may also be taken at this point. A custody record is opened which captures detail on why the person has been arrested, medical needs including any provision put in place to care for those needs, which custody cell the person is located in and basic provisions such as food and drink (College of Policing, 2022a).

During the 'booking in' process, the custody officer should make an assessment of the vulnerabilities of the individual (College of Policing, 2022a). This may include asking the person about any specific needs that they may have, observing their presentation and making a judgement, or noting information which is already recorded on the police computer system (The Faculty of Forensic & Legal Medicine, 2022). The aim is to decide what support the person requires as part of their detention and interview (Mind, 2013). The assessment is enacted via the following questions (Association of Chief Police Officers, 2012):

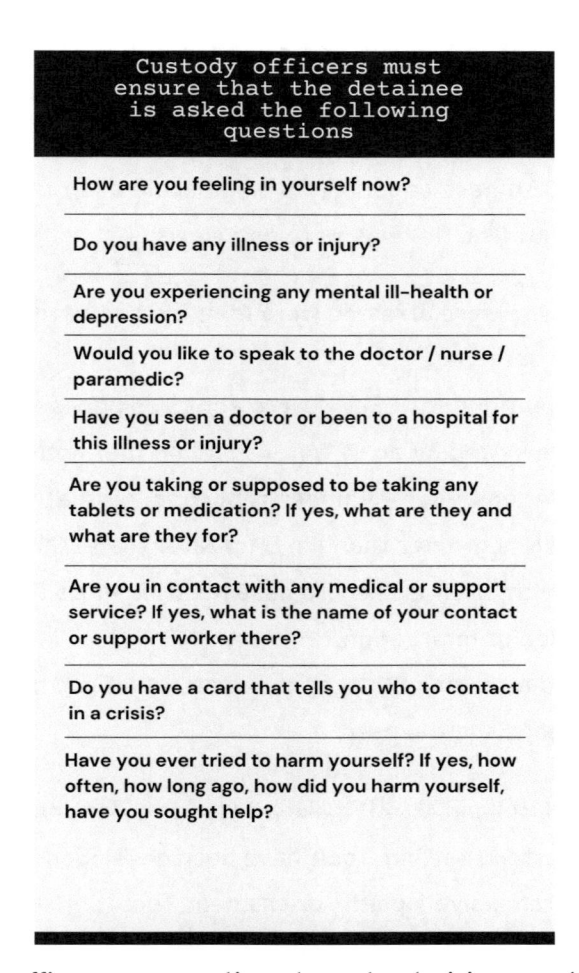

FIGURE 3.4 The custody officer uses questions to make decisions on the vulnerability of the arrested person and what support they may require

Finally, the arrested person will be reminded of their continuing rights (College of Policing, 2022a; Home Office, 2020a). These rights, which may be exercised at any stage during the time in police custody and are provided verbally and in writing (including accessible versions), are:

- the right to have someone informed of the arrest
- the right to consult privately with a solicitor and have access to free independent legal advice
- the right to consult the Police and Criminal Evidence (PACE) codes of practice (Home Office, 2020a)
- the right to interpretation and translation if needed
- the right to be informed about the alleged offence and why they have been arrested and detained.

Again, the language requirements to understand the person's situation and their rights are considerable (Rost and McGregor, 2021). There is no standardised and nationally applied requirement to screen arrested people for SLCN so that adjustments can be made to the communication environment. In England, there are pockets of good practice whereby local liaison and diversion teams have developed SLCN screens and training packages which enable non-SLTs to identify SLCN (Hutchinson, Peacock and Holland, 2021). Hutchinson, Peacock and Holland (2021) have conducted a small-scale audit of a local SLCN screen in one police force in England. The findings were as follows:

- 1 in 5 (20%) people who were arrested were identified as having SLCN when assessed by a trained non-SLT screener.
- 75% of the people identified with SLCN were adults as opposed to young people.
- When the data was reviewed by an SLT, it was found that non-SLT screeners are cautious in their observations, thereby under-reporting, so that the number of arrested people who have SLCN is greater than 1 in 5 (greater than 20%).
- An arrested person with SLCN is likely to have needs in more than one domain of comprehension, expression or interaction.
- Of the 20% identified as having SLCN on the screen, half had never attracted an SLCN identification or diagnosis in the past.

Hutchinson, Peacock and Holland (2021) make a case for wider application of screening for SLCN within the police custody setting. Tools have been developed for use with people aged 10–18 such as the Comprehensive Health Assessment Tool (Chitsabesan et al., 2014) and the Asset Plus (Youth Justice Board for England and Wales, 2016) which include recognition of SLCN. While these tools are aimed at a young offender population, they could be reasonably employed with adults in a custodial setting in the absence of other alternatives. The aim of both of these tools is to collate information about the individual to inform planning, and while this is welcome, there are criticisms that such frameworks can be inaccurate in identifying SLCN (Winstanley, 2018), can be time-consuming to complete (Young et al., 2018) and rely on individual self-report when in custody (Winstanley, Webb and Conti-Ramsden, 2021). While the authors take a 'something is better than nothing' standpoint in the application of screening for SLCN, a more robust requirement for screening, training and SLT assessment would be the ideal outcome.

Prior to police interview

Before any interview can take place, the custody officer makes an assessment of whether the person is fit to be interviewed (The Faculty of Forensic & Legal Medicine, 2022). This is in recognition of the fact that the person may be fit to detain, but may not be fit to interview. It also recognises that a person may change while at the police station, so dynamic assessment is required.

If there are concerns about the person's health and well-being, they are seen by a healthcare professional and this can be part of a process of assessment and review to ensure the care of the person over the time spent in police custody (College of Policing, 2022a). The healthcare professional can seek information from agencies involved in the care of the individual outside of the custodial setting – for example, a GP, a community psychiatric nurse or a social worker (Home Office, 2020b). The assessment and review cycle can be developed into a set of safeguards or a care plan (The Faculty of Forensic & Legal Medicine, 2022).

Information relating to the judgement of fitness to be interviewed and any assessments or plans are entered into the custody record (College of Policing, 2022a).

There is an intention to identify people who are mentally unwell or vulnerable at this stage of the care in custody (National Institute for Health and Care Excellence, 2021). Vulnerability, as defined in this situation, includes having learning disability, having a substance misuse concern that impacts on cognition or having a diagnosis that impacts on neurological function such as dementia. If a person is identified as mentally unwell or vulnerable, best practice states that the person should be referred to liaison and diversion services who are best placed to meet the needs of the individual via health and social care routes, and also to support the exchange of information between the criminal justice system and health providers (NHS England Liaison and Diversion Programme, 2014). The exchange of information is crucially important at this stage as this information supports decisions on the disposal of the person (College of Policing, 2022a) and influences charging decisions (Home Office, 1990).

The aim of the police interview is to obtain a full and accurate account of the events (Ministry of Justice, 2011). This is achieved by following principles set out by the College of Policing (2022a) as follows:

- Obtain accurate and reliable information.
- Act fairly in a non-prejudicial way, believe information offered and treat people with perceived or actual vulnerabilities with extra care or safeguards.
- The interview is part of the investigation and should test evidence or reveal new lines of inquiry.
- Ask questions without being unfair or oppressive. This can include being persistent with questions or topics, and continuing to ask questions even if the suspect is exercising their right to silence.
- Recognise the positive impact of an early admission by the suspect and the value that this can bring to the investigation.

Prior to the police interview, the investigating team are obligated to share some information with the suspect's legal advisor in what is called a 'pre-interview briefing'. The function of this is so that the legal advisor has adequate information about the crime, evidence and suspect to be able to give appropriate legal advice (Home Office, 2020a). The police are not obliged to disclose all of the information at this stage. The investigating team will have developed a strategy relating to how much material is sufficient to satisfy the legal framework while also giving optimal outcomes during the interview (thus serving the best interests of the public). Such strategies are usually considered on a case-by-case basis (College of Policing, 2022a). Following the pre-interview briefing, the suspect is offered a private consultation with their legal advisor in order to plan for the upcoming interview. This will include legal advice, potential preparation of a prepared statement and the consideration of what the suspect will say or do in the interview.

The police investigation team will have enacted an amount of planning before the interview to ensure that the aim and principles are followed as applied to the specifics of the case. This planning should include consideration of whether any special measures such as use of a registered intermediary (RI) are required. Following the planning, the interview will broadly follow the following stages (see Figure 3.5 overleaf):

FIGURE 3.5 The police interview follows five defined states

Making decisions about the suspect's vulnerability

By this stage, the person has become a suspect, has been arrested, has received legal advice and has been formally interviewed by the investigating team. Along the way, various police officers have had to make decisions about the individual and their well-being. These decisions are complex because situations that involve the CJS and the police engender heightened emotions, power dynamics, cultural influences and cognitive skills.

In order to help the police officers, a National Decision Model was developed as a framework for policing decisions. The framework places a code of ethics at the centre of all decisions (College of Policing, 2022a).

While this is welcomed, there is awareness that often the police do not operate in isolation of other services including fire and rescue, ambulance services and NHS provisions. To overcome conflicting objectives when entering into multi-agency working, a Joint Decision Model was developed (Joint Emergency Services Interoperability Principles, 2022). The Joint Decision Model is shown in Table 3.1 overleaf.

TABLE 3.1 The Joint Decision Model supports multi-agency working when considering the next steps for a suspect who is under arrest

Situation	Plan	Action
What is happening? What are the impacts? What are the risks? What might happen and what is being done about it?	What do you want/need to achieve? What are the aims and objectives of the response? What overarching values and priorities will inform and guide this?	What do you need to do to resolve the situation and achieve your desired outcomes?

If this model is applied to decisions relating to the interviewing of a vulnerable suspect in police custody, the following information and decisions might be applied, as shown in Table 3.2 below.

TABLE 3.2 A worked example of the Joint Decision Model applied to a vulnerable suspect who may have speech, language and communication needs

Situation	Plan	Action
What is happening? Police interview of a person who seems vulnerable. The person does not seem to understand everything which is being said to them so that their replies are slightly inappropriate. **What are the impacts?** If the person does not understand, then we might not acquire accurate information from them in interview. They are not saying when they don't understand. **What are the risks?** The person might give false information in the interview which will impact on the investigation. **What might happen and what is being done about it?** The person might incriminate themselves or be at risk of misleading the police.	**What do you want/need to achieve?** Obtain accurate and reliable information from a vulnerable person who seems to have some issues understanding. We need to know more about the person's skills, and help them to give accurate information. **What are the aims and objectives of the response?** • Find out more about the person's skills • Know how to help • Record the information in the custody record • Put the help in place **What overarching values and priorities will inform and guide this?** Legislation and safeguards relating to interviewing vulnerable people.	**What do you need to do to resolve the situation and achieve your desired outcomes?** • Link with liaison and diversion team to find out more about the persons medical history • Obtain speech and language therapy assessment/report • Consider use of an appropriate adult • Consider use of a registered intermediary • Develop information into a set of strategies to help the person understand • Use the strategies in the interview • Inform the person's legal representative of the needs of the person • Allow extra time for the interview

The Vulnerability Assessment Framework (Wright, McGlen and Dykes, 2012) is employed by some police forces to supplement the National Decision Model. This framework asks the police officer to use a basic A, B, C, D and E pneumonic to structure observations of vulnerability in the individual. The pneumonic cues the office to think about:

- Appearance and atmosphere: what you see first, including physical problems such as bleeding, well-being problems such as rocking or shivering, mental health problems such as responding to unseen stimuli.
- Behaviour: what the individual is doing, and if this is appropriate behaviour given the situation, what emotions are being displayed.
- Communication: what the individual is saying and how they say it, how they respond to what is said to them, what their body language says.
- Danger: whether the individual is in danger and whether their actions put other people in danger.
- Environment: where they are situated, whether anyone else is there and what impact the wider circumstances may have on the individual's health and safety.

We have explored the procedure for making decisions about the person in custody and their fitness to engage in the process, which can be summarised thus:

Fitness to detain / interview

FIGURE 3.6 The decision-making process relating to whether a suspect is appropriate to detain and interview

The person who is detained in custody should be cared for using a risk management strategy to ensure that not only are vulnerabilities identified and supported, but there is ongoing review by the custody officer which incorporates consideration of risk factors at specific time points (Home Office, 2020a). Recognised time points where the individual may be at increased risk of poor well-being are:

- within the first hour of being in custody
- after formal interviews
- following any further arrest
- following being charged with a crime
- following a phone call or visit with family, relatives or key people
- following being told that any bail application is declined
- when released from custody under investigation
- in the time period between release on bail and attending court.

These are the time points when the resilience of an individual can be affected and there is increased risk of distress, self-harm or other forms of poor decision making secondary to reduced well-being (Home Office, 2020a). Custody officers enact a risk assessment which includes a healthcare professional prior to release from custody in acknowledgement of how distressing the experience may be for the individual. This is described as 'being fit to be released'.

While any person can have impacted resilience and well-being at times of stress, the following is a list of recognised factors that are likely to affect the person's coping and should be seen as 'red flags' (Home Office, 2020b):

- suffering with a recognised mental illness such as depression, psychosis, schizophrenia
- use of substances which can be hazardous to health including illegal drugs, performance-enhancing drugs, misuse of prescribed medication, use of alcohol
- isolation from support networks or feeling rejected by community, culture or family
- previous personal history of self-harm or attempts to end own life
- family history of mental illness or ending own life
- chronic pain or illness
- significant change in recent personal history such as bereavement, homelessness, loss of protective factors
- adverse childhood experiences
- a person facing charges of a violent or sexual nature, especially involving a child or family member.

This process of ongoing review enables any changes in the person's presentation to be identified and supported. Support would include medical review by a nurse or doctor, increased pastoral support from police officers or giving the person increased supervision (such as having a police officer remain with the individual if the risks of harm to self are high) (Association of Chief Police Officers, 2005a). Similarly, the police may realise once interviewing starts that the person has hidden communication difficulties and reconsider whether a registered intermediary and other special measures need to be used.

Police interview of a vulnerable suspect

The police officer enacting the interview is termed the interviewing officer. In this role, the officer takes over responsibility for the welfare of the suspect from the custody officer for the period of the interview. The interviewing officer must be satisfied that the person is fit to be interviewed and must be fully informed of the needs of the individual (Home Office, 2020b).

The interview of a vulnerable suspect cannot be conducted unless an appropriate adult is present (Home Office, 2020a). The role of the appropriate adult was established in 1984 with the aim of reducing the risk of miscarriages of justice whereby vulnerable people had been convicted on the basis of evidence obtained in interview (Fisher, 1977). The intention is that the appropriate adult safeguards the interests, rights, entitlements and welfare of vulnerable people who are suspected of a criminal offence. This is achieved by ensuring that they are treated in a fair and just manner, and are able to participate effectively (National Appropriate Adult Network, 2018).

In the case of a vulnerable adult suspect, an appropriate adult is asked to participate as more than an observer. They are required to advise the person and help communication flow (Home Office, 2020b). The appropriate adult can be a family member, friend, health or social care worker, or a third party who has signed up to this role via a local organisation (National Appropriate Adult Network, 2018).

It is the responsibility of the interviewing officer to ensure that the human rights of the suspect are respected at all times (Human Rights Act, 1998). The Human Rights Act (1998) outlines 16 rights that apply to people living in the UK and which must be followed by authorities or bodies that exercise a public function (Social Care Institute for Excellence, 2020). In the case of police interviews, articles 3, 5 and 14 are the most relevant - protecting the suspect from degrading treatment, ensuring that the individual knows why they are arrested or charged, and prohibition of discrimination.

Figure 3.7 (below) summaries the responsibilities of the interviewing officer during the interview:

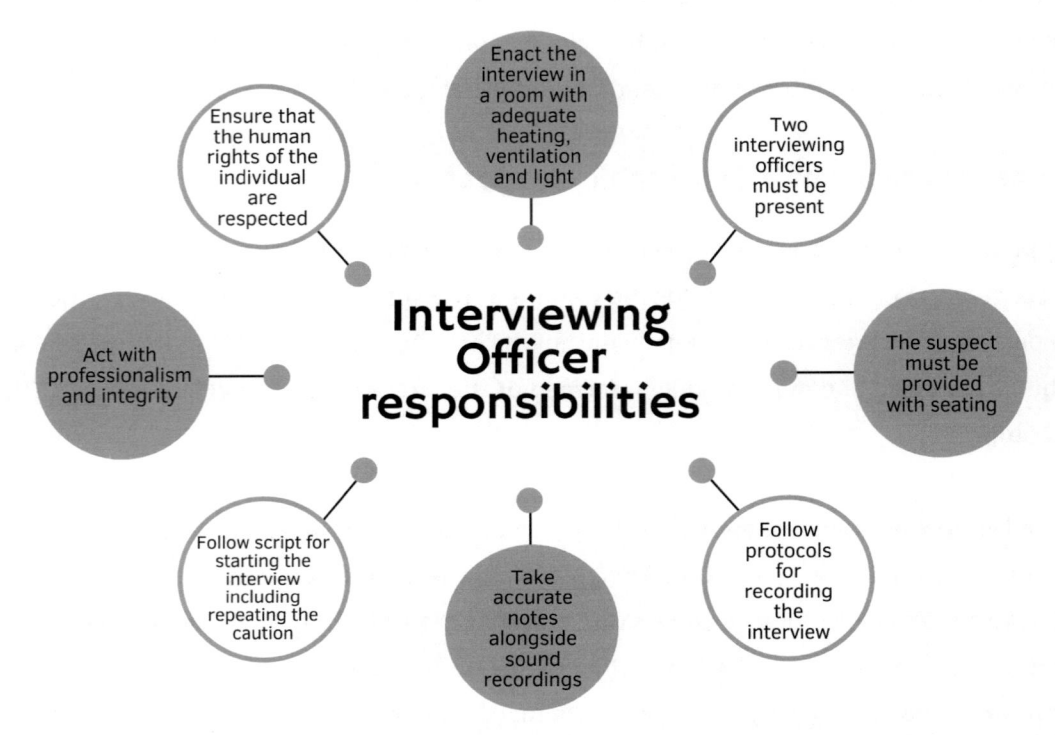

FIGURE 3.7 The responsibilities of the police officer when they are conducting the interview with the suspect

The police interview in England and Wales will follow the PEACE framework (College of Policing, 2022b); this is acknowledged as offering safeguards for vulnerable people in the domains of confessions, standards of interview technique, fairness and transparency during all stages of the interview (Gudjonsson, 2010).

The acronym PEACE stands for: Preparation and Planning; Engage and Explain; Account – clarification – challenge; Closure; Evaluation. Figure 3.8 overleaf gives a visual representation of the stages of the PEACE framework is adapted from the College of Policing (2022b). The use of such a model safeguards quality standards in relation to the interview.

The PEACE framework includes skills and knowledge drawn from aspects of psychology to try to help the interviewing officer and the suspect perform to the best of their abilities (Davison, 2008). This includes consideration of effective communication skills rooted in psychological models such as:

- Using the concept of the Betari Box which theorises that each individual influences the attitudes and behaviours of others via their own attitudes and behaviours (Wall, 2019).

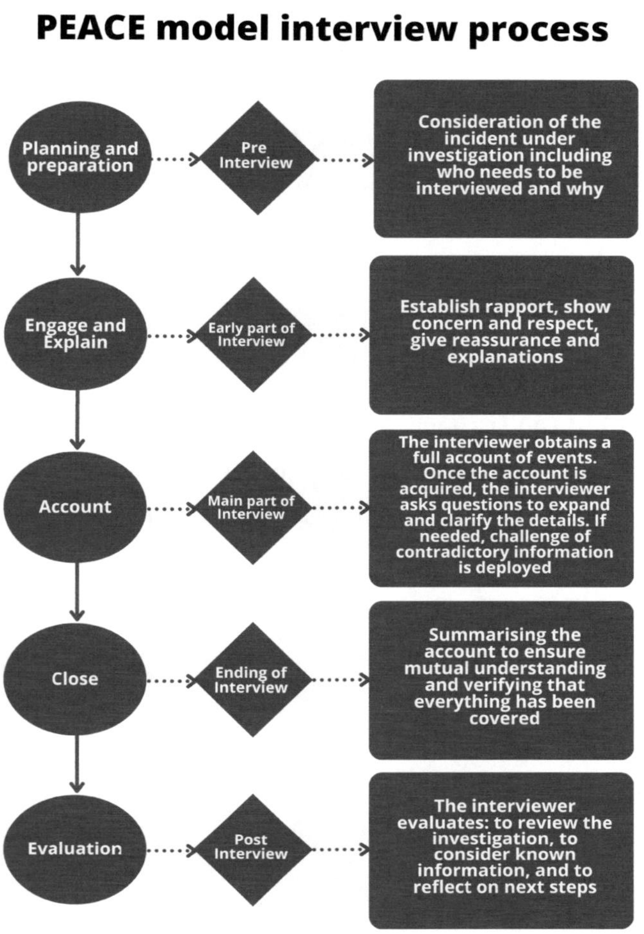

PEACE model interview process

FIGURE 3.8 The PEACE model which offers distinct stages to the police interview

- Transactional analysis which proffers that within each person there are three different ego states, and that the ego state being employed within any communication episode must be complementary to that of the conversation partner in order to have effective information exchange (Hargie, 2018).
- Employing questions which are appropriate to obtaining an account, seeking clarification and enacting challenge (Davison, 2008).
- Using conversation management strategies that enable the interview to move from open questions, to closed questions and then to asking the suspect about specific details (Shepherd, 2007).

During the application of the PEACE framework, the suspect is given numerous breaks which offer benefits to both parties: the interviewing officer can review material and consult on next steps in the interview plan, and the suspect can have time to collect their thoughts and take legal advice as needed.

While the police custody setting may have access to an SLCN screen, or very occasionally an SLT, and reasonable adjustments for communication needs may be in place, there is no obligation placed on the interviewing officer that they employ specific advice relating to communication (question type, processing time, vocabulary choices, etc.) during the interview (Asquith and Bartkowiak-Théron, 2021).

After police interview

Once the interview is concluded, the suspect waits in custody for a decision from the investigating team and CPS. If the suspect is not charged with a crime, they must be released within 24 hours. If the police need more time to gather evidence, they must obtain permission from a senior police officer or magistrates' court to keep the suspect in custody for longer (with a maximum time in custody of four days). If the suspect is vulnerable, the police should not seek to detain the person for more than 24 hours (Rethink Mental Illness, 2020).

There are limited options in regard to the next steps, and the suspect will always be informed of the decision:

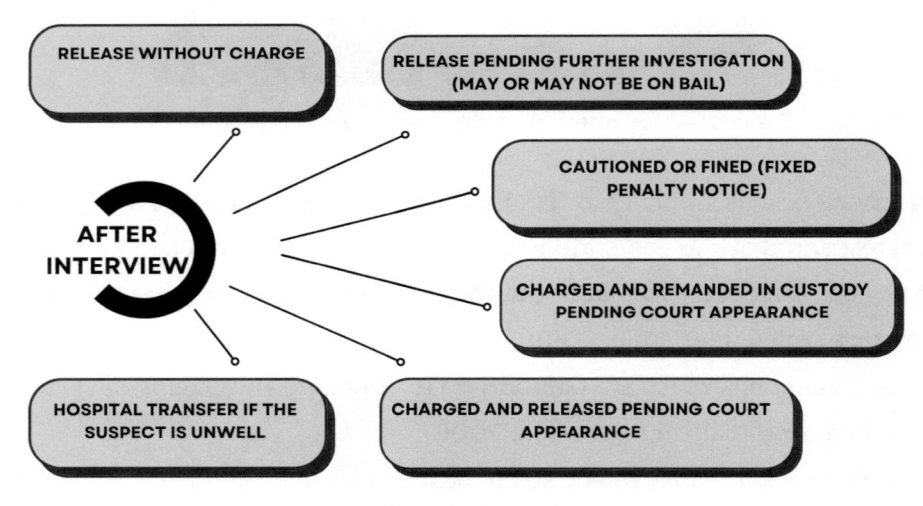

FIGURE 3.9 What happens to the suspect after the interview

Liaison and diversion services

Liaison and diversion services were identified by Lord Bradley in 2009 as key to supporting the needs of vulnerable people in contact with the CJS (Bradley, 2009). The aim of liaison and diversion services is (NHS England & Improvement, 2019):

- to train police officers to recognise signs of potential vulnerability and make an onward referral to the liaison and diversion service
- for the liaison and diversion service to screen the individual to enable appropriate assessments to be requested from appropriate professionals
- for the liaison and diversion service to have appropriate professionals within the team to be able to respond quickly to the request for assessment
- for appropriate professionals to enact assessment, specifically identify support needs and link up with services that the individual may already be under the care of
- to create routes of information sharing so that needs can be met and stakeholders can make informed decisions relating to the most appropriate care of the individual
- to report on assessment findings.

An example SLCN screening tool, liaison and diversion SLCN assessment and SLCN vocabulary measure can be found at Appendix 3 and 4. The report provided by the liaison and diversion service uses a nationally suggested template (NHS England & Improvement, 2019). An example liaison and diversion service court report using the suggested template for a fictional person (Table 3.3 overleaf).

TABLE 3.3 The standard template for a liaison and diversion court report completed to offer an example of content

Liaison and Diversion Court Report			
Name:	Brian Smith	**Date of Birth:**	14/09/2001

Brief history and current presentation of mental health, learning disabilities, substance misuse/alcohol issues and any other vulnerabilities

Are there current or relevant previous concerns regarding vulnerability? If yes, detail the history of compliance with services, any perceived links between presentation and offending, and explain how the current concerns are being managed.

Mr Smith was referred to the liaison and diversion team by New Town police following interview under caution at the police station on 27th May 2021. He was seen by the liaison and diversion service registered nurse (learning disability) and speech and language therapist in a joint visit to his accommodation address on 30th May 2021 with his social worker present.

Mr Smith was interviewed by the police in a matter relating to misuse of the internet.

Mr Smith has a diagnosis of learning disability (intellectual disability) and depression. He has a history of self-harm by cutting, substance misuse (smoking cannabis) and occasional excess of alcohol.

When he was 17 years old, he was admitted to an inpatient setting under section 3 of the Mental Health Act following a short-lived period of drug-induced psychosis which responded well to treatment.

He currently lives in a flat, maintaining his own tenancy with the support of local services. He does not have paid employment.

Mr Smith's vulnerability is located in his learning disability, his depression, his substance misuse and his history of psychosis.

Risk of suicide and self-harm

Are there current or relevant previous concerns of suicide and/or self-harming? If yes, how are the current concerns being managed?

Mr Smith has no past history or current thoughts of suicidal ideation.

Mr Smith has a history of self-harm by cutting which extends to using objects to create damage to his arms and legs. In his home setting, this is managed via a care plan that prompts Mr Smith to phone his support worker if he is considering self-harm.

In custody, Mr Smith would benefit from regular welfare checks which include a conversation about his well-being to help him maintain emotion regulation. Mr Smith is open about his self-harm urges, and agrees that police officers can ask him about this.

Risk of harm to others

Indicate both the level of risk of violence and/or psychological harm and how this would impact on possible court remand and sentencing decisions.

Mr Smith is low risk of harm to others via violence. He has no history of verbal or physical aggression.

Mr Smith is medium risk of psychological harm to others in association with the suspected offence. This risk can be mitigated via supervised use of the internet, parental controls on his electronic devices and password changes to his email account.

Accommodation and support

Identify any specific needs, available referral pathways and how they can be supported to engage with services to meet those needs including alternative accommodation where appropriate.

Mr Smith benefits from professional support to help him maintain his own accommodation. This has been stable and there are no social risk factors in his immediate geographic area. The professional support is not at risk of being reduced or removed.

Mr Smith would benefit from referral to local community services for people with learning disability and CJS needs in order to access specific support around his use of information technology. Initial information sharing with this service suggests that this support would be available to Mr Smith.

(Continued)

TABLE 3.3 Continued

Understanding of criminal justice system and ability to engage with court process
Are there concerns regarding their level of understanding of the criminal justice system and ability to engage in the court process? If yes, what reasonable adjustments are recommended to facilitate effective engagement?
Mr Smith has learning disability and depression which impacts on his ability to understand the CJS and engage with court processes in the following ways: • Mr Smith needs verbal information given to him in short sentences using everyday vocabulary • Any verbal information should be paced to allow Mr Smith to have thinking time • Verbal information should be complemented by accessible written information which includes words and images • Those speaking with Mr Smith should avoid changing topic frequently and should use verbal signposts such as 'we've finished talking about the computer – now let's talk about the phone' • Specific CJS vocabulary should be avoided or minimised • Those speaking to Mr Smith should check his understanding with open questions such as 'tell me what we have agreed' • Mr Smith should have the help of an appropriate adult in interviews • It would help Mr Smith to explain a sequence of events if visual materials are used that he can touch or move • Mr Smith should be given frequent breaks to support his emotional well-being • Mr Smith will be better at talking about concrete events where people were in the location together and it is easier for him to mentally picture the situation. He may find explaining events that happened in virtual settings (such as the internet) harder to account for because of the cognitive communication skills required for this level of explanation

Information to support remand and sentencing decisions	
Indicate how you have arrived at any recommendations, history of compliance and an assessment of current likelihood of compliance with services, and care plan (reflecting community and custody settings as appropriate).	
If remanded in custody, the author of this report will follow information-sharing protocols with the remand establishment. If returned to his own accommodation, Mr Smith will continue to access his current support systems and will be referred to local community services for people with learning disability and CJS needs. His current support systems will review his care and consider if support needs have increased.	
Report writer	Registered nurse (learning disability) Speech and language therapist
Contact number	
Date	30th May 2021
This information is only valid for use within the criminal justice system on the day that it is submitted to the court.	

The liaison and diversion service make referrals to other services for specialist assessment or treatment. However, we have no influence over specialist services accepting a person for assessment or treatment. Nor do we have any influence over the defendant attending appointments made on their behalf.

In order to support a clinician in understanding more about the report section entitled 'Understanding of criminal justice system and ability to engage with court process', Table 3.4 overleaf is offered to help cross-reference some common diagnostic labels with typical SLCN challenges associated with that label in an average person.

TABLE 3.4 Commonly encountered diagnostic labels and typical SLCN associated with that diagnostic label in an average person plus how these needs might present in formal interview

Diagnostic label	Potential impact on SLCN as a result	Potential impact on SLCN in police interview
	Adapted from Farrugia and Gabbert (2020); Herrington and Roberts (2012); Bartels (2011); Crane et al. (2016); North, Russell and Gudjonsson (2008); Bryan (2013)	
Depression	• Issues differentiating between specific memories and repeated memories • Low self-esteem and negative thoughts which can manifest as negative references to self • Decreased motivation to engage • Improved engagement and participation on structured tasks • Decreased engagement and participation on unstructured tasks with frequent topic shifts • Issues suggesting ways to resolve problems • Struggles when asked to describe situations or events • Struggles to describe own emotional experiences • Increased risk of acquiescence or submission	• Impact on giving an accurate narrative in relation to events so that it is harder to gather evidence or defence statement • Decreased willingness to invest energy in explaining events or situations leading to decreased verbal output and fewer turns taken in conversation, which may be perceived as poor cooperation • Increased risk of the interviewing officer understanding the communication style as one of a guilty suspect due to avoiding social contact or eye contact • Reduced facial expressions which might be perceived as a lack of empathy • Reduced use of intonation in narrative which could cause an investigating officer to question the underlying motives of the suspect • Likely to produce shorter utterances with less detail or range of vocabulary
Anxiety Post-traumatic stress disorder (PTSD) Paranoia	• Increased fear and panic and potential to be emotionally guarded • Increased risk of becoming overwhelmed and dissociating from situation • Inability to focus on questions or give joint attention leading to misreading of social interactions, misreading of gestures or facial expressions • Issues differentiating between specific memories and repeated memories/flashbacks • Increased restlessness • Easily triggered to experience interactions negatively • Tends to avoid social situations so may become socially isolated and have reduced social confidence which can also lead to poor self-esteem • Poor theory of mind • Issues with social interactions/ pragmatics and may find it hard to work well in a group or team • Difficulties reasoning and inferencing	• Reduced expressive output leading to shorter utterances, shorter interactions and longer periods of silence between utterances, which could influence the perceptions of the interviewing officer • Impact on giving an accurate narrative and on self-awareness of whether the narrative is accurate which could be understood as changing a statement in the face of new information • An assertive/aggressive presentation style so may be viewed as argumentative or guilty • Limited access to emotions vocabulary impacting on narrative skills so may present as emotionally cold to the situation

(Continued)

TABLE 3.4 Continued

Schizophrenia	• Issues with episodic memory such that a memory which is being asked about might not be accessible • Issues processing information with working memory deficits when acutely unwell or un-medicated • Issues ordering information • Altered thoughts or perceptions • Can misrepresent as emotionally unaffected and have issues accessing vocabulary for emotions • Can find attention and listening impacted by hallucinations • Can find it hard to create a clear and easy-to-comprehend sentence/utterance due to problems with syntax and semantic processing (accessing nouns and verbs) • Manner and tone of expressive language can be impacted by internal symptoms of illness • Impacted social skills/pragmatics/conversational cues and difficulties with non-literal language • Skills relating to theory of mind are impacted • Difficulties understanding facial expressions/gestures of others • Difficulties interpreting prosody • Difficulties reasoning and inferencing	• Problems with recall of specific events in accurate order which may arouse suspicion of guilt • Difficulty concentrating and following instructions which could be seen as poor cooperation or being avoidant • Problems attending to and decoding questions in various forms so that responses are not always on topic and present as evasive • Perseveration and echolalia in expressive output which can be perceived as poor cooperation in a police interview • May produce strings of empty speech which may be interpreted as falsehoods or guilt
Psychosis	• Impacted concentration and listening skills • Reduced understanding of verbal instructions or information due to inattention • Reduced following of instructions or information due to processing via the lens of own perception which is impacted by psychosis • May be highly distractible • Likely dominant interaction style • Impacted theory-of-mind skills • Difficulties with pragmatics and inferencing	• Difficulty concentrating and following instructions which could be seen as poor cooperation or being avoidant • Problems attending to and decoding questions in various forms so that responses are not always on topic and present as evasive • Increased risk of the interviewing officer understanding the communication style as one of a guilty suspect due to distractibility and dominance • Issues with theory of mind and inferencing could impact on the content of narrative which is entered into evidence

(Continued)

TABLE 3.4 Continued

Mood disorder	• Selective attendance to emotional cues • Negative interpretations of ambiguous questions/information • Negative bias when processing information	• Impact on giving an accurate narrative in relation to events so that it is harder to gather evidence or defence statement • Selective attendance to emotional cues impacting on narrative skills so may present as emotionally cold to the situation • Problems decoding ambiguous questions so that responses are not always on topic and present as evasive • Negative bias which influences expressive output in terms of content and tone, so that the person may be perceived as defensive or guilty
Poor emotional well-being Issues relating to psychological resilience/vulnerability Lived experience of adverse childhood experiences Long-term impacts of substance misuse	• Heightened levels of suggestibility, compliance and potential to acquiescence • Not coping with stress which decreases cognitive skills further • Low levels of self-efficacy • Can be influenced by the body language or facial gestures of others in the room • Risks of creating an answer rather than offering a 'don't know' response • Difficulties making informed decisions • Problems understanding questions and the implications of the answers • Can misread the interviewer as disapproving or angry • More processing time is needed to decode questions and access memory • Belief that own guilt or innocence is obvious to interviewer	• Risk of false admissions of information leading the interviewing officer to suspect underlying guilt • Tendency to change narrative over time to 'please' the interviewer • Impact on giving an accurate narrative and on self-awareness of whether the narrative is accurate which could be understood as changing a statement in the face of new information • Problems attending to and decoding questions in various forms so that responses are not always on topic and present as evasive
Learning disability Borderline IQ	• Issues decoding open questions • Difficulties adapting to new environments appropriately • Difficulties generalising from one environment to another • Slower processing speed for verbal information • Problems switching attention between verbal and visual information • Decreased working memory for verbal choices • Heightened levels of suggestibility, compliance and acquiescence • May present with emotions that mismatch questions or circumstances	• Quality and accuracy of information is degraded, which may suggest guilt to an interviewing officer • The person will likely select the last item offered in a verbal multiple choice question so may implicate themselves in a crime • Problems attending to and decoding questions in various forms so that responses are not always on topic and present as evasive • Tendency to provide a preferred response to the interviewer rather than the factual information • Mismatch of emotions to questions may present as suspicious to interviewing officer

(Continued)

TABLE 3.4 Continued

Personality traits/ personality disorder	• Heightened levels of suggestibility, compliance, and acquiescence • Non-standard interpersonal/ interaction style • Difficulties expressing needs and opinions which leads to frustration • Sometimes immature phonology • High likelihood of co-existing anxiety • Problems with empathy and emotions vocabulary • Issues with theory of mind • May miss the emotional subtext of messages • May present as wanting to 'control' interactions so take more conversational turns and fast pace of speech • May struggle with at 'personal space' and overuse gesture, make longer and more intense eye contact	• Risk of false admissions of information leading the interviewing officer to suspect underlying guilt • Increased risk of the interviewing officer understanding the communication style as one of a guilty suspect due to interaction style • A frustrated presentation style so may be viewed as argumentative or guilty • Impact on giving an accurate narrative in relation to events so that it is harder to gather evidence or defence statement • Limited access to emotions vocabulary impacting on narrative skills so may present as emotionally cold to the situation
Autism traits	• Difficulties with cause and affect/ consequential knowledge • Barriers to identifying the intentions of the interviewer due to problems with understanding social cues • Sensitively to feelings of being treated with respect, dignity, fairness • Risks of sensory overload and lack of control to reduce sensory stimulation • May miss the emotional subtext of messages • High likelihood of co-existing anxiety • May have difficulties reasoning and inferencing • Issues with theory of mind • Heightened levels of suggestibility, compliance and acquiescence in order to avoid conflict	• Impact on giving an accurate narrative in relation to events so that it is harder to gather evidence or defence statement • Potential for strong feelings of disrespect when the interviewing officer checks information, which could impact on interaction style and cooperation • Reduced expressive output leading to shorter utterances, shorter interactions and longer periods of silence between utterances, which could influence the perceptions of the interviewing officer • Changes to body language and physical gestures so that the investigating officer might perceive the individual as a physical risk • May present with emotional responses that are incongruent with the question and seem suspicious • Risk of false admissions of information leading the interviewing officer to suspect underlying guilt

Going to court

Following police investigation, a suspect may be charged with a crime. If this happens, the matter will be referred to court and the suspect becomes a defendant. What happens next depends on the severity of the alleged crime and any concerns relating to the defendant or witnesses or evidence. The following process map gives a flavour of the variables which affect next steps:

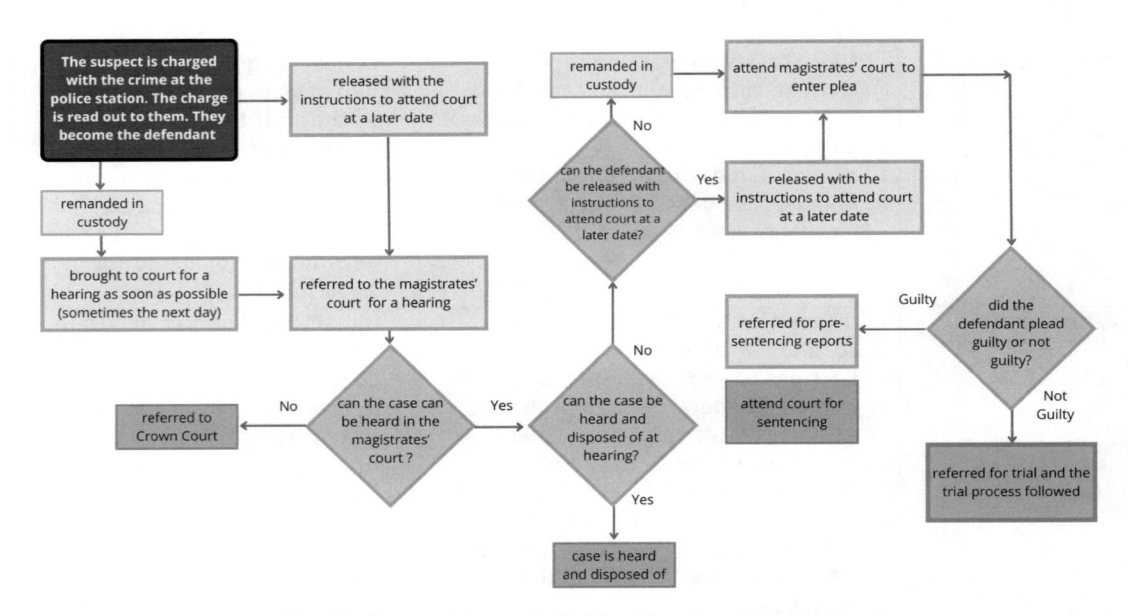

FIGURE 3.10 The process that follows once an individual is charged with a crime

Other variables which impact on individual cases:

- Timescale: the length of time between being charged and going to court will vary depending on the severity of the crime, the complexity of the case and legal arguments.
- Mental ill-health: if the person is mentally unwell at the time of being charged, they can be remanded in custody and presented at court for a hearing. The judge can direct that the defendant is transferred to an inpatient mental health setting (hospital) for a period of assessment and treatment. This can be a period of time between 28 days and 12 weeks (Mental Health Act, 2007).

Fitness to plead

One of the first stages in a criminal case is when the defendant attends court for an arraignment. An arraignment is a type of court hearing whereby the defendant is named by the court clerk and the charges are read out. The charges are called the indictment. It is important that consideration of vulnerability has been applied prior to the arraignment hearing, and this is to ensure that the defendant is 'fit to plead'. Fitness to plead is determined by five criteria (The Criminal Procedure Rules, 2020) given in Figure 3.11 below:

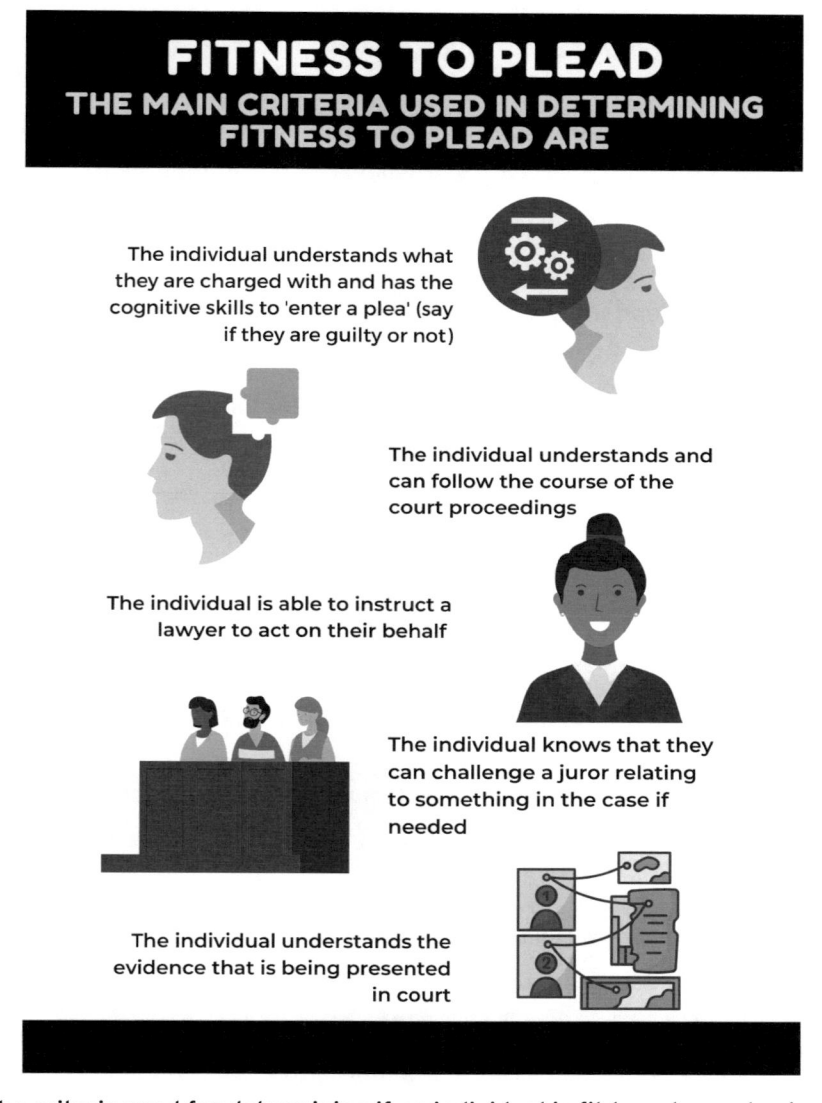

FITNESS TO PLEAD
THE MAIN CRITERIA USED IN DETERMINING FITNESS TO PLEAD ARE

The individual understands what they are charged with and has the cognitive skills to 'enter a plea' (say if they are guilty or not)

The individual understands and can follow the course of the court proceedings

The individual is able to instruct a lawyer to act on their behalf

The individual knows that they can challenge a juror relating to something in the case if needed

The individual understands the evidence that is being presented in court

FIGURE 3.11 The criteria used for determining if an individual is fit to enter a plea in court

The proceedings may stall at this point because the court needs to be certain that the person is fit to plead, so they may request a specialist opinion such as a psychiatric report. The court may decide that the person could be fit to plead if they had additional support to understand information and express themselves. The additional support comes in the form of special measures which may include the use of a registered intermediary.

Intermediaries for defendants

Although the law allowing registered intermediaries (RIs) to be used with defendants in criminal courts has been passed, it has not yet been implemented. In some cases, the judge will determine that without communication support the defendant will not be able to give evidence. In that case, an instruction to the matching service for RIs for victims and witnesses is given. Very recently, a new scheme called court-appointed intermediaries (CAIs) has been implemented to manage use of intermediaries for courts other than the criminal courts (e.g. family courts). This is a welcome development given that victims and witnesses in these courts had no access to RIs previously.

The RI will assess the defendant and write a report making clear what is required to facilitate communication during the trial. The RI will only be present for the period that the defendant's evidence is being given. Backen (2017) has outlined the approach taken during trials involving a defendant.

Court process

Once the court is satisfied that the defendant is fit to plead and has support if needed, the court process will progress via the defendant entering a plea (a statement of guilt) to the charges that were detailed in the indictment. See Figure 3.12 overleaf.

A guilty plea will result in the matter being referred for pre-sentence reports, followed by a sentencing hearing.

A not-guilty plea will result in a trial being initiated. A trial follows the process of all parties preparing for court, the case being opened and presented by the prosecution, the defence case being presented followed by any response from the prosecution, and then a summary. Following the summary, a decision will be reached either by the judge or the jury on the guilt of the defendant. If the person is found guilty, they will be referred for pre-sentence reports, followed by a sentencing hearing. If they are found not guilty, they will be released from custody (or the charges on the indictment).

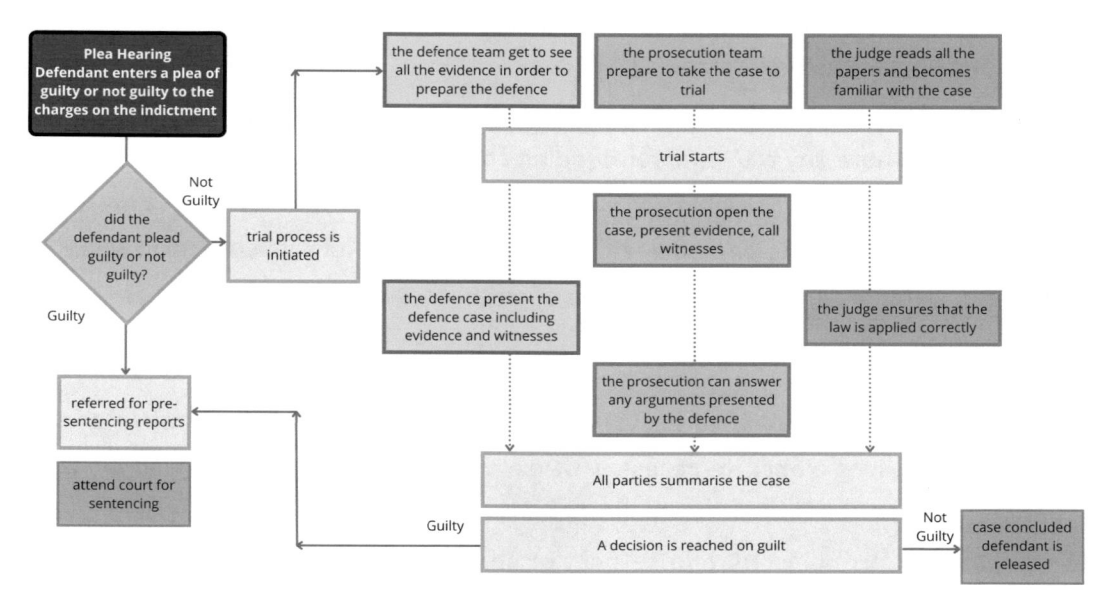

FIGURE 3.12 The process that follows the entering of a plea in court

Pre-sentence reports

Once the defendant has been convicted either by entering a guilty plea or by the court process, the judge can ask for pre-sentencing reports which are compiled by the National Probation Service. The aim of the reports is to ensure that the judge can understand the person who has been convicted, their circumstances and needs relating to the offence, and how they have been in prison if they were remanded in custody. There will be detail on the crime, and any risks that the person poses to the general public. The report concludes with a recommendation in relation to sentencing.

When considering vulnerable people, the pre-sentence report should include information on:

- How the person's vulnerability interacted with culpability – for example, were they responsible for their conduct at the time of the criminal act, and did they understand cause and effect?
- Does the person's vulnerability result in them being at increased risk to the general public? For example, does the vulnerability suggest that they may commit further crimes? Are they a risk to themselves or others? Can the risks be managed so that they are reduced?
- What are the implications of the person's vulnerability when considered against different sentencing options? For example, could the person remember and follow the

instructions in a community order? Would incarcerating the person be an unfair disposal because of their vulnerability?

- How does the person's vulnerability interact with any goals of rehabilitation? For example, are there any reducing reoffending courses which would benefit the person? Where are the courses available and can the person engage with the course given their vulnerability? Would the person need additional supervision and what form would this take (e.g. working with NHS services, ensuring that medication regimes were followed, support from adult social care)?

These factors can be exemplified if applied to a case study. Imagine a gentleman aged 76 years old who lives alone. He accesses GP services if he initiates them and his family live in another town, so do not see him often. The gentleman has had increased contact with the police in his home town in respect of shouting at the general public, removing items from people's gardens and shoplifting. The gentleman enters a plea of guilty and pre-sentence reports disclose a diagnosis of early dementia. Dementia has impacted on the gentleman's understanding of cause and effect so his culpability is reduced. The gentleman's vulnerability indicates that he is likely to repeat the same actions so he may be a risk to himself and the public. The gentleman would not be able to follow conditions in a community order and he would not benefit from incarceration in prison. He would also not benefit from rehabilitation or crime reduction courses because he lacks culpability. It is likely that in this scenario a guardianship order would be recommended alongside assessment from healthcare providers and adult social care. An SLT working in a community forensic team may be involved in this case to help the gentleman understand what has happened and why, help him make decisions about his care and provide functional memory aids to help him orient himself to situations.

Sentencing

The judge will sentence the person once guilt is established either by the defendant entering a guilty plea or by the court convicting the defendant. Options for sentencing for adults in England and Wales include the following (Sentencing Act, 2020):

- Fine: the court sets a monetary fine based on the severity of the crime and the financial resources of the convicted person. The matter is concluded with the payment of the fine.
- Discharge: a release from court with no further action needed. The convicted person will have the conviction on their criminal record. An absolute discharge is when the

court has decided that the matter is closed. A conditional discharge is when the court has decided that no further action is needed at this time, but if the individual is convicted of another crime in the future, then this conviction can be taken into account. This means that a person can be sentenced for the conditionally discharged conviction and the new conviction.

- Community sentence: this type of sentence aims to punish the convicted person, prescribe a programme which will address the underlying courses of why the crime was committed and provide restorative justice to the victim or community. A community sentence usually has an amount of time spent completing unpaid work, the requirement to access rehabilitative courses or treatment for substance misuse and directions on lifestyle (where to live, curfew, restrictions on whom the convicted person can associate with). The community sentence is tailored to the circumstances of the community, the convicted person and the crime.

- Suspended sentence: this type of sentence is the court giving the convicted person a chance to lead a lawful lifestyle for a defined period instead of going to prison. It is categorised as a custodial sentence. During the defined period, the person will follow a set of directions which resemble a community sentence. Failure to comply with the directions results in imprisonment for the remainder of the sentence. If the convicted person breaks the law during the suspended sentence period, they will be required to serve the custodial sentence in prison (plus face charges for the new offence).

- Determinate custodial sentence: the court directs that the convicted person should serve time in prison for the protection of the public. The amount of time that should be served in prison is prescribed by the Sentencing Act (2020) and is dependent on past criminal convictions and the severity of the crime associated with the new conviction. Most custodial sentences are determinate. This means that there is a set amount of time to be served in custody and the prospect to be released before the whole sentence has been served. Generally, the convicted person will serve at least half of the sentence in custody. The release includes licence conditions which must be followed. Some people are suitable for release with a home detention curfew device (commonly known as a 'tag'). This is used to ensure that they stay at home (e.g. during night-time hours when they had previously committed burglary offences). The police are automatically alerted if the 'tag' is detected other than where it should be.

- Extended custodial sentence: this is a type of sentence that the court decides on if the convicted person is judged to be violent or involved with terrorism. The convicted person would need to have a previous criminal record and there would need to be risks to the safety of the general public. The extended sentence means that the person is not automatically eligible for release on licence during their custodial stay. The convicted person serving an extended sentence is expected to serve two-thirds of their sentence and then apply for a parole hearing. The parole hearing will consider whether risks have reduced and direct whether release on licence is appropriate. If the convicted person is not released on licence following a parole hearing, they will serve their entire sentence in prison and be released on completion of the sentence.

- Life sentence (including discretionary life sentence): this is a sentence which is assigned to the convicted person for the rest of their life. There is a prescribed amount of time that the convicted person is expected to remain in prison – this is called a tariff. Once the tariff period has been served, the convicted person can apply for a parole hearing. The parole hearing will decide if the person's risks have reduced and if they are appropriate to be released on licence. If released on licence, there is a set of conditions that must be followed for the rest of their life. If the conditions are breached, the individual is recalled to prison regardless of the amount of time they have been living in the community.

- Whole-life order: this is a type of life sentence where the convicted person is sentenced to life in prison without the option of release on licence. This type of sentence is reserved for the most serious cases of murder and has been used around 100 times since its creation in 1983. Since 2003 (when there was a review of this type of sentence), there have been 63 whole-life orders given by the courts (Criminal Justice Act, 2003; Sentencing Council, 2022).

- Hospital order: this type of sentence is considered when the convicted person has a vulnerability such as mental illness, developmental disorders such as learning disability or neurological impairments such as risky behaviours following head injury. The convicted person is sentenced to reside in hospital for assessment and treatment. The person remains in hospital until the treatment is completed.

- Guardianship order: the convicted person is placed under the guardianship of local social services or an approved person.

- Ancillary order: an ancillary order is additional to the sentence and has the aim of preventing future offending. It is a rule or set of rules which are specific to the conviction and can include, for example, being disqualified from driving, being excluded from certain geographic locations, being disqualified from attending events such as football matches, a restraining order which prevents contact with another person, the requirement to follow instructions associated with the Sex Offender Register.

Where a sentence includes conditions, it is essential that the person fully understands these. The conditions are set out within a very complex legal document. SLTs will often work with the person to produce a simple, pictorial version to ensure that the person really understands what they must comply with. In addition to the sentence, the convicted person is also expected to pay a surcharge. This is a fee charged to the convicted person (in addition to any fine) that is used to fund victim services through the Victim and Witness General Fund. The surcharge can be as low as £22 for people who are discharged, and as high as £190 for other sentence types.

An example of sentencing (based on UK court reports)

A middle-aged man was driving on unfamiliar roads in a rental campervan with his family on holiday. He had no past convictions and had good moral standing in his community. While driving the campervan, he sought to enact a three-point turn in a passing place on a rural road. During this manoeuvre, he was in collision with a motorbike. The man and his family immediately called for emergency help, assisted the casualty and attended the police station for questioning. The motorcycle user died of his injuries and the man was charged with death by dangerous driving. In summing up, the judge explained that this was a first offence, that the suspect had assisted police and entered a guilty plea, that he had displayed remorse and had provided character references. The pre-sentencing report found that the man had a clean driving licence, was not under the influence of drugs or alcohol, was well rested and driving in safe conditions. The unfamiliar roads and vehicle were noted as factors. The man was assessed as a minimum risk of reoffending. The judge handed down a two-year suspended sentence with 300 hours of unpaid community work to be completed in two years (with an interim report on progress after one year) plus an ancillary order of being disqualified from driving for three years.

To conclude this section, a short glossary of terms is provided at Appendix 5 to help clinicians and vulnerable people with specific specialist vocabulary.

Victims and witnesses

So far this chapter has addressed suspects, defendants and convicted people when they are in contact with the CJS. But it is important to note the needs of victims and witnesses, and what support they can access in their contact with CJS.

A note about terminology – often people who have experienced crime refer to themselves as a 'survivor' of the experience. Alongside this, the police may call the person who has experienced crime the 'complainant'. In this chapter, we will use the term 'victim' as this is the vocabulary used by the Crown Prosecution Service and Ministry of Justice whose source materials we will reference. The use of the word 'victim' is not intended to be stig-matising or minimising to the people who have experienced acts of crime.

The Ministry of Justice (2020a) define a victim as a person who has endured physical, mental or emotional harm, or economic loss, as a direct result of a criminal act. This can be as the person who experienced the criminal act first-hand, or as a witness to the criminal act. If the victim has died as a result of the criminal act, a close relative or spokesperson for the victim can assume the legal rights of the victim. Likewise, if the victim is aged under 18 years or has a vulnerability such as mental or neurological illness, a spokesperson can assume their legal rights.

Being identified as a victim of crime is important as the person who is the victim has 12 legal rights which are applicable to their case (as shown in Figure 3.13 overleaf).

Figure 3.13 is created from information provided by the Ministry of Justice (2020a). It is important to note that not all rights apply to all cases. Rights 1, 4 and 12 apply to all victims:

> The right to be able to understand and be understood: all victims have the right to be given information in a way that is easy to understand and to be provided with help to be understood, including, where necessary, access to interpretation and translation services

> The right to be referred to services that support victims and the support be tailored to meet individual needs: all victims have the right to be referred to services that support victims, which includes the right to contact them directly, and to have specific needs assessed so services and support can be tailored to meet individual needs. If eligible, the victim has the right to be offered a referral to specialist support services and to be told about additional support available at court – for example, special measures includ-ing registered intermediaries

> To make a complaint about victim rights not being met: if a person who is the victim of crime believes that they have not received their rights, they have the right to make a complaint. If they remain unhappy after following the complaints protocol, they can contact the Parliamentary and Health Service Ombudsman.

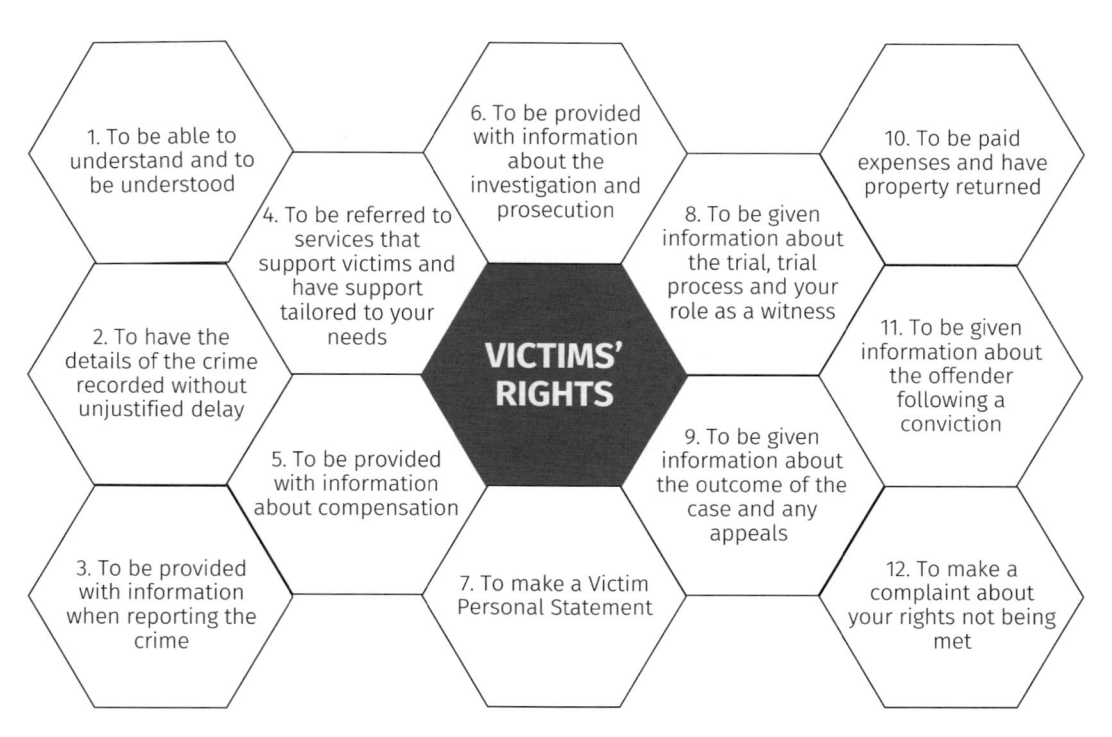

FIGURE 3.13 The 12 legal rights of a person who is the victim of a crime

The Ministry of Justice (2020a) give additional weight to the needs of vulnerable victims by offering 'enhanced rights'. In order to be considered vulnerable, the victim should have a mental illness, an identified need in respect of intelligence, cognition or social functioning such as learning disability, or a physical health need. The victim may also be termed vulnerable if they are intimidated by the process such that they feel intense anxiety which would impact on their ability to give evidence in court. Enhanced rights means being offered the same 12 victim rights as any other victim, but having shorter waiting times or being referred to certain providers who specialise in meeting the individual's needs.

Special measures for vulnerable victims and witnesses

Any person who is identified as a vulnerable victim or witness can access special measures (Crown Prosecution Service, 2018; Crown Prosecution Service, 2021). Special measures are adaptations to the court or trial process to allow the individual to have every opportunity to give evidence to a high standard. The aim is to reduce the emotional burden associated with giving evidence. Typical special measures include:

- a visit to the court room prior to the trial in preparation
- help travelling to and from the court

- accommodation near the court if the vulnerable victim or witness requires this to support their attendance
- financial help with expenses such as childcare costs
- agreement from the vulnerable victim or witness in relation to certain personal information being disclosed in court, such as gender identity or sexual orientation
- ground rules in relation to the length of time the person will be giving evidence or the nature of any cross-examination
- using screens around the witness box so that the vulnerable victim or witness does not need to see the other people in the court
- using videolink technology so that the vulnerable victim or witness can give evidence from a different location
- giving evidence in closed court so that no press or members of the public are present
- giving evidence via pre-recorded video in advance of the trial
- reducing the formality of the process by having formal dress adapted (e.g. removal of wigs and gowns)
- having access to or the use of communication aids, or the support of a registered intermediary.

Registered intermediaries for vulnerable victims and witnesses in the Criminal Court Jurisdiction

Registered Intermediaries (RIs) are matched to the communication or disorder information that police or court officers submit to the national matching service for England and Wales. The RI is matched against their skills and experience. The RI meets with the victim or witness and conducts an assessment of their speech, language and communication abilities. The RI also assesses whether the person understands the difference between truth and lies.

The RI writes an evidence-based report specifically highlighting the support that the person will need and the strategies that should be included for the police interview. If the case goes to court, the RI writes a further report specifically addressing the communication needs for the court setting. This may refer to particular aspects of grammar that should be avoided, preferred vocabulary such as referring to body parts, the need for questions to be reworded by the RI. Where the individual is physically disabled, the RI may set out how a signing system will be used. The RI does not interview the person; rather, their job is to enable the police officer or the lawyer to conduct the interview or cross-examination.

The RI should be involved in planning the police interview, and before a court case involving special measures, the judge will normally hold a Ground Rules Hearing meeting including the RI so that the required communication measures can be agreed. The RI will also agree with the judge how he or she will intervene should the lawyer inadvertently not comply with the agreed measures or if the RI becomes aware that the person is not understanding or needs a break.

An important distinction in the role of the RI is that they are not a supporter of the individual. The RI role is to facilitate communication so that the person can give their evidence to the best of their ability. The person should be supported by others such as an appropriate adult or a Witness Service Officer (Ministry of Justice, 2020b).

Conclusion

This chapter has considered the journey from criminal investigation of wrongdoing, to police interview practices and through the court process to sentencing largely from the standpoint of a vulnerable person. The chapter has also discussed the SLCN of people when in this context, including the provision of resources that may be useful. While the CJS does not separate needs associated with speech, language and communication in its systems and processes, SLCN are included under the umbrella terms 'vulnerable' and 'vulnerability'.

Summary

- Investigations can be proactive or reactive.
- An individual will not know that they are a suspect until they are invited to attend a police interview or are arrested.
- The police will look for signs of vulnerability in the suspect, victim or witness from the first contact and as an ongoing process.
- A vulnerable suspect has the right to be interviewed with the support of an appropriate adult.
- A vulnerable victim or witness has the right to a registered intermediary in the criminal court and a court-appointed intermediary in other courts.
- A vulnerable defendant only has the right to the support of an intermediary in court if the judge determines this.
- Liaison and diversion services are also available to support vulnerable suspects and defendants.

- Pre-sentence reports will include information about vulnerability.
- The sentence and disposal will take into account any vulnerabilities.

References

Association of Chief Police Officers (2005a) *Core Investigative Doctrine* available at www .whatdotheyknow.com/request/387377/response/939365/attach/html/2/ACPO%202005 %20Practice%20Advice%20on%20Core%20Investigative%20Doctrine%20002.pdf.html [accessed 3rd March 2023]

Association of Chief Police Officers (2005b) *Core Investigative Doctrine*, Section 4. Available at www.whatdotheyknow.com/request/387377/response/939365/attach/html/2/ACPO%202005 %20Practice%20Advice%20on%20Core%20Investigative%20Doctrine%20002.pdf.html [accessed 3 March 2023]

Association of Chief Police Officers (2012) *Guidance on the Safer Detention and Handling of Persons in Police Custody: Second Edition*. Available at https://assets.publishing.service.gov.uk /government/uploads/system/uploads/attachment_data/file/117555/safer-detention-guidance -2012.pdf [accessed 3 March 2023]

Asquith, N.L. and Bartkowiak-Théron, I. (2021) Interviewing Vulnerable People. In *Policing Practices and Vulnerable People* (pp.107–127). Cham: Palgrave Macmillan.

Backen, P. (2017) *They Just Don't Get It: Communication and the Work of an Intermediary in the Vulnerable People in the Justice System*. Independently published.

Bartels, L. (2011) Police interviews with vulnerable adult suspects. Available online at www .researchgate.net/profile/Lorana-Bartels/publication/256041391_Police_Interviews_with _Vulnerable_Adult_Suspects/links/5642f6f508aec448fa62bc65/Police-Interviews-with -Vulnerable-Adult-Suspects.pdf [accessed 3rd March 2023]

Bradley, K. (2009) The Bradley Report: Lord Bradley's review of people with mental health problems or learning disabilities in the criminal justice system. Available online at https://webarchive .nationalarchives.gov.uk/ukgwa/20130107105354/http://www.dh.gov.uk/prod_consum_dh/ groups/dh_digitalassets/documents/digitalasset/dh_098698.pdf [accessed 3rd March 2023]

Bryan, K. (2013) Psychiatric Disorders and Communication. In L. Cummings (ed.) *Handbook of Communication Disorders* (pp.300–318). Cambridge: Cambridge University Press.

Chitsabesan, P., Lennox, C., Theodosiou, L., Law, H., Bailey, S. and Shaw, J., (2014) The development of the comprehensive health assessment tool for young offenders within the secure estate. *The Journal of Forensic Psychiatry & Psychology*, 25(1), 1–25.

College of Policing (2022a) Authorised Professional Practice. Available at www.app.college.police .uk/app-content [accessed 3rd March 2023]

College of Policing (2022b) Investigative Interviewing. Available at www.app.college.police.uk/app -content/investigations/investigative-interviewing [accessed 3rd March 2022]

Crane, L., Maras, K.L., Hawken, T., Mulcahy, S. and Memon, A. (2016) Experiences of autism spectrum disorder and policing in England and Wales: Surveying police and the autism community. *Journal of Autism and Developmental Disorders*, 46(6), 2028–2041.

Crown Prosecution Service (2017) *The Code for Crown Prosecutors 2018*. Available at www.cps .gov.uk/publication/code-crown-prosecutors-2018-downloadable-version-and-translations [accessed 3rd March 2023]

Crown Prosecution Service (2018) Speaking to Witnesses at Court. Available at www.cps.gov.uk/legal -guidance/speaking-witnesses-court [accessed 3rd March 2023]

Crown Prosecution Service (2021) Special Measures. Available at www.cps.gov.uk/legal-guidance/ special-measures [accessed 3rd March 2023]

Davison, J. (2008) *The Science of Interviewing: P.E.A.C.E. A different approach to investigative interviewing*. Available at www.fis-international.com/assets/Uploads/resources/PEACE-A -Different-Approach.pdf [accessed 3rd March 2023]

Farrugia, L. and Gabbert, F (2020) Vulnerable suspects in police interviews: Exploring current practice in England and Wales. *Journal of Investigative Psychology and Offender Profiling*, 17(1), 17–30.

Gudjonsson, G.H. (2010) Psychological vulnerabilities during police interviews. Why are they important? *Legal and Criminological Psychology*, 15(2), 161–175.

Hargie, O. (2018) Skill in Theory: Communication as Skilled Performance. *The Handbook of Communication Skills* (4th edn) (pp.9–40). Routledge.

Fisher, H. (1977) Report of an Inquiry by the Hon. Sir Henry Fisher into the circumstances leading to the trial of three persons on charges arising out of the death of Maxwell Confait and the fire at 27 Doggett Road, London, SE6. Available at https://assets.publishing.service.gov.uk/government/uploads/system/uploads/attachment_data/file/228759/0090.pdf [accessed 3rd March 2023]

Herrington, V. and Roberts, K. (2012) Addressing psychological vulnerability in the police suspect interview. *Policing: A Journal of Policy and Practice*, 6(2), 177–186.

Health and Safety Executive (2022) When and how we investigate. Available at www.hse.gov.uk/enforce/when-how-investigate.htm [accessed 3rd March 2023]

Home Office (1990) Home Office Circular No 66/90 Provision for Mentally Disordered Offenders. Available at www.cps.gov.uk/sites/default/files/documents/legal_guidance/Home%2520Office%2520Circular%252066%252090.pdf [accessed 3rd March 2023]

Home Office (2020a) Police and Criminal Evidence Act 1984 (PACE) codes of practice. Available at www.gov.uk/guidance/police-and-criminal-evidence-act-1984-pace-codes-of-practice#pace-codes-of-practice [accessed 3rd March 2023]

Home Office (2020b) *Interviewing Suspects Version 7.0*. Available at https://assets.publishing.service.gov.uk/government/uploads/system/uploads/attachment_data/file/864940/interviewing-suspects-v7.0.pdf [accessed 3rd March 2023]

Human Rights Act (1998) available at www.legislation.gov.uk/ukpga/1998/42/contents [accessed 3rd March 2023]

Hutchinson, P., Peacock, D. and Holland, C. (2021) Speech, Language and Communication Needs (SLCN) in Police Custody Settings: The importance of screening and intervention. Unpublished public lecture, University of Sunderland.

John, T. and Maguire, M (2007) Criminal Intelligence and the National Intelligence Model. In T. Newburn, T. Williamson and A. Wright (eds) *Handbook of Criminal Investigation* (1st edn) (pp.225–251). Willan. https://doi.org/10.4324/9780203118177

Joint Emergency Services Interoperability Principles (2022) The Joint Decision Model (JDM). Available at www.jesip.org.uk/joint-decision-model [accessed 3rd March 2023]

Mind (2013) *At Risk Yet Dismissed: The Criminial Victimisation of People with Mental Health Problems*. available at www.mind.org.uk/media-a/4121/at-risk-yet-dismissed-report.pdf [accessed 3rd March 2023]

Ministry of Justice (2011) *Achieving Best Evidence in Criminal Proceedings Guidance on interviewing victims and witnesses, and guidance on using special measures*. Available at www.cps.gov.uk/sites/default/files/documents/legal_guidance/best_evidence_in_criminal_proceedings.pdf [accessed 3rd March 2023]

Ministry of Justice (2020a) Code of Practice for Victims of Crime in England and Wales. Available online at https://assets.publishing.service.gov.uk/government/uploads/system/uploads/attachment_data/file/936239/victims-code-2020.pdf [accessed 3rd March 2023]

Ministry of Justice (2020b) The Witness Intermediary Scheme Annual Report 2019/20. Available online at https://assets.publishing.service.gov.uk/government/uploads/system/uploads/attachment_data/file/919858/witness-intermediary-scheme-annual-report-2019-2020.pdf [accessed 3rd March 2023]

National Appropriate Adult Network (2018) About appropriate adults. Available at www.appropriateadult.org.uk/information/what-is-an-appropriate-adult [accessed 3rd March 2023]

National Institute for Health and Care Excellence (2021) Violence and aggression: Short-term management in mental health, health and community settings. NICE Guideline 10. Available at www.nice.org.uk/guidance/ng10/resources/violence-and-aggression-shortterm-management-in-mental-health-health-and-community-settings-1837264712389 [accessed 25th January 2022]

NHS England & Improvement (2019) Liaison and Diversion Standard Service Specification, Version Number 10. Available online at www.england.nhs.uk/wp-content/uploads/2019/12/national-liaison-and-diversion-service-specification-2019.pdf [accessed 3rd March 2023]

NHS England Liaison and Diversion Programme (2014) *Liaison and Diversion Operating Model*. Available at www.england.nhs.uk/wp-content/uploads/2014/04/ld-op-mod-1314.pdf [accessed 3rd March 2023]

North, A.S., Russell, A.J. and Gudjonsson, G.H. (2008) High functioning autism spectrum disorders: An investigation of psychological vulnerabilities during interrogative interview. *The Journal of Forensic Psychiatry & Psychology*, 19(3), 323–334.

Rethink Mental Illness (2020) Police stations: What happens if I'm arrested. Available online at www.rethink.org/advice-and-information/rights-restrictions/police-courts-and-prison/police -stations-what-happens-if-im-arrested [accessed 23rd March 2023]

Rost, G.C. and McGregor, K.K. (2012) Miranda rights comprehension in young adults with specific language impairment. *American Journal of Speech-Language Pathology*, 21(2), 101–108. https:// doi.org/10.1044/1058-0360(2011/10-0094)

Salet, R. (2017) Framing in criminal investigation: How police officers (re)construct a crime. *The Police Journal*, 90(2), 128–142. doi:10.1177/0032258X16672470

The Mental Health Act (2007) available online at www.legislation.gov.uk/ukpga/2007/12/contents [accessed 3rd March 2023]

The Criminal Justice Act (2003) available online at www.legislation.gov.uk/ukpga/2003/44/contents [accessed 3rd March 2023]

The Criminal Procedure Rules (2020) available online at www.legislation.gov.uk/uksi/2020/759/ contents [accessed 3rd March 2023]

The Sentencing Act (2020). Available online at www.legislation.gov.uk/ukpga/2020/17/contents/ enacted [accessed 3rd March 2023]

The Faculty of Forensic & Legal Medicine (2022) Healthcare of detainees in police stations. Available at https://fflm.ac.uk/resources/publications/healthcare-of-detainees-in-police-stations [accessed 3rd January 2023]

Sentencing Council (2022) Life sentences. Available online at www.sentencingcouncil.org.uk/ sentencing-and-the-council/types-of-sentence/life-sentences [accessed 3rd March 2023]

Social Care Institute for Excellence (2020) The Human Rights Act (HRA). Available at www.scie.org .uk/key-social-care-legislation/human-rights-act?gclid=CjOKCQiAybaRBhDtARIsAIEG3kmP6q2 V91dyXn8sJ_YOb2N4UL5WEdKkcF42420gHl1A31TDzcCFRBMaAt1uEALw_wcB[accessed3rdMarch 2023]

Shepherd, E. (2007) *Investigative Interviewing: The Conversation Management Approach*. New York: Oxford University Press.

Wall, I.R (2019) Policing atmospheres: Crowds, protest and 'Atmotechnics'. *Theory, Culture & Society*, 36(4), 143–162

Winstanley, M. (2018) Young offenders and restorative justice: Language abilities, rates of recidivism and severity of crime. Unpublished, University of Manchester.

Winstanley, M., Webb, R.T. and Conti-Ramsden, G. (2021) Developmental language disorders and risk of recidivism among young offenders. *Journal of Child Psychology and Psychiatry*, 62(4), 396–403.

Wright, K., McGlen, I. and Dykes, S. (2012) Mental health emergencies: Using a structured assessment framework. *Emergency Nurse*, 19(10), 28–35.

Young, S., Gudjonsson, G., Chitsabesan, P., Colley, B., Farrag, E., Forrester, A., Hollingdale, J., Kim, K., Lewis, A., Maginn, S., Mason, P., Ryan, S., Smith, J., Woodhouse, E., & Asherson, P. (2018). Identification and treatment of offenders with attention-deficit/hyperactivity disorder in the prison population: A practical approach based upon expert consensus. *BMC Psychiatry*, 18(1), 281. https://doi.org/10.1186/s12888-018-1858-9

Youth Justice Board for England and Wales (2016) Asset Plus Guidance: Assessment and Planning Interventions Framework. Available at https://webarchive.nationalarchives.gov.uk/ukgwa /20221215003856/https://www.iicsa.org.uk/key-documents/7585/view/HMP000340.pdf [accessed 3rd March 2023]

DETENTION AND PROGRESS THROUGH
THE CRIMINAL JUSTICE SYSTEM

DOI: 10.4324/9781003288701-5

In this chapter, we will explore further what happens to a person following conviction and sentencing in court.

The chapter offers the reader the 'gold standard' care that a person should be in receipt of post-conviction and sentencing, but also acknowledges that sometimes, for various reasons, this level of input is not always available or provided. The reader should keep this in mind during this chapter.

Topics covered will include:

- an overview of the National Probation Service, inpatient secure hospital services and prison settings from first contact to resolution of the sentence
- the impact of speech, language and communication needs (SLCN) when entering the care of such services
- practical resources for professionals to use with individuals to support SLCN.

The sentence that a judge imposes on a convicted person is an important part of the criminal justice system (CJS) because it is a demonstration to victims, the public and people who break the law that justice is seen to be done (see Chapters 1 and 2 for discussion relating to this assertion). The principles of sentencing are:

- punishment of crime,
- reduction of future crime,
- reparation to the victim,
- rehabilitation of the convicted person, and,
- public protection.

(Ministry of Justice, 2020a)

The sentence may have been informed by a pre-sentence report from the National Probation Service, although, at the time of writing, only approximately 50% of sentences are subject to pre-sentence reporting (HM Prison and Probation Services, 2021).

As discussed in Chapter 3, when a person is convicted, there are a limited number of options available to the judge in respect of sentencing. These are outlined below with an indication of the frequency that each disposal option is used (HM Courts & Tribunals Service, 2022):

- fixed penalty notice (FPN) which is a monetary fine and the outcome in around 75% of court cases
- community disposal (such as community orders, suspended sentences, etc.) which is the result in around 10% of court cases

- custodial sentence which is the consequence in around 8–9% of court cases
- court order to an appropriate service, such as a secure hospital, which is the conclusion in around 5% of court cases.

A monetary fine is by far the most common outcome of a court case.

The National Probation Service (NPS)

The role of the National Probation Service can apply to an individual case from the court appearance – via pre-sentence assessment and reporting – to sentence management during the serving of the sentence, to resettlement input towards the end of the sentence (Viglione, Burton, and Basham, 2019). It is possible for a convicted person to have a long-standing relationship with the probation member of staff over a period of years (which may include more than ONE conviction and sentence) (Appleton, 2019).

The aims of the National Probation Service are to support the CJS in the application of effective justice, to offer public protection and to rehabilitate people who have attracted a conviction (Barton, 2019). This remit results in a complex role that has different objectives at different points in the person's journey through their sentence (Davis, Houston, and Rudes, 2021):

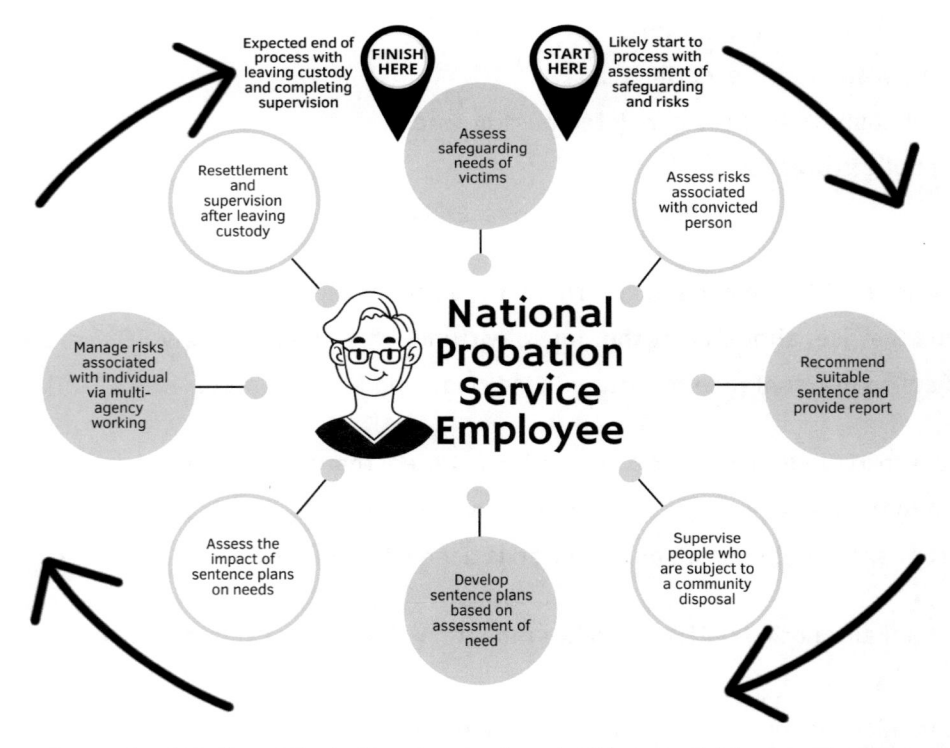

FIGURE 4.1 The cycle of National Probation Service input with an individual as they move through the process of justice, protection and rehabilitation

It is useful to consider the role in segments that reflect different stages or sentence types. At each stage, the professional has a responsibility to the individual who has committed the crime, the victim of the crime and the public (Pycroft and Gough, 2019).

At the stage of court, the National Probation Service employee undertakes the following tasks (Robinson, 2018):

- Explores the vulnerability, safeguarding necessities and wishes of the victim in order to ensure that the victim is safe, and so that any requests can be included in the pre-sentence report.
- Completes a risk assessment of the person who has committed a crime which includes understanding risk, but also deficits and proportionate responses.
- Consideration of sentencing guidance and which evidence-based interventions are available to address the needs of the convicted person (and where they can access these interventions).
- A recommendation of a suitable sentence which can be realistically delivered so that justice is served and the convicted person has the best chance of rehabilitation.

If the sentence is a community disposal, the National Probation Service role is undertaken by a community offender manager (COM). The COM undertakes the following tasks (Yukhnenko, Blackwood and Fazel, 2020):

- Develops a sentence plan which addresses the risks that were identified in the pre-sentence report. If there was no pre-sentence report, the COM conducts the risk assessment and then develops the sentence plan.
- If the sentence plan identifies interventions that the person must complete, the COM will make referrals to multi-agency partners who provide the intervention. An example is if the convicted person requires a domestic violence reduction programme, they will be referred to an accredited provider. The sentence plan aim is to address education, training, employment and dependency (such as drug or alcohol) requirements.
- Risk management – the COM will complete assessments that explore the potential for the person to reoffend and development opportunities to address any issues such as emotion management, criminal attitudes, thinking skills and choices that may lead to reoffending.
- Supervision of the individual to ensure that they are engaging with the sentence plan, the risk management work and following any licence conditions. The supervision usually takes the form of meetings at various community locations (e.g. at work, at the probation offices or in the home). As supervision progresses over a period of time, the frequency and duration of the meetings reduce. In some cases, the supervision moves

from face-to-face meetings to phone calls. There are expectations relating to probity and engagement in the supervision relationship.

- Finally, the COM will ensure that the sentence plan and the risk management work has had an impact. At this stage, there might be resettlement requirements such as help with employment or debt, assistance to support ongoing recovery from substance misuse or prerequisites around accommodation. The goal of resettlement is to reduce the risk of reoffending by supporting with social factors that can lead to crime.

If the convicted person attracts a custodial sentence, the National Probation Service work is completed by a prison offender manager (POM). The POM is usually located within the prison setting to enable relationship building via close proximity. The POM undertakes the following tasks (Fox et al., 2018):

- Development of the sentence plan which includes consideration of accredited intervention programmes. If the convicted person is located in a prison that does not offer a required intervention, the POM may need to arrange for the individual to transfer to another prison in order to access the required intervention. This task in itself can be complex and time-consuming as the POM must match the individual to the intervention, find a providing prison and then apply for a space in that setting. There may be a psychological cost for the individual in respect of losing location close to family and tolerance of being moved.
- The elements of the sentence plan which consider education, training, employment and dependency may be easier to accommodate within the prison setting as college courses and work opportunities are factored into the prison day.
- The risk management work is also different in the prison setting as multi-agency colleagues from the prison service or health and social care may be involved. The monitoring of risk is changed as the day-to-day activities of a person in prison are captured on their electronic record, so is easier to consider and review.
- Supervision of a person in prison can be supported by engagement of multi-agency colleagues and reviewed by committee.
- Towards the end of the prison stay, the POM will consider resettlement options. Resettlement requirements will often include accommodation, employment, financial arrangements and onward referrals to community providers.
- Some people are released from prison with licence conditions. These are a set of rules which must be followed. If they are not followed, the person can be returned to prison. A person released from prison with licence conditions will have their care transferred to a COM, who becomes involved in the case in the months before release to ensure that there is a supported transition from one professional to another. It is the COM who writes the licence conditions.

In the case of a person being sentenced to a secure hospital, the National Probation Service allows the care and treatment of the person to be driven by health and social care input. The responsibility for the individual is located with a senior doctor at the setting (known as the responsible clinician). The offender manager (OM) becomes part of a multi-agency review team rather than having a key relationship with the individual (Chester, 2018).

Ethos of National Probation Service model of care

HM Prison and Probation Services (2021) in England and Wales employ an evidence-based approach to sentence management and offender rehabilitation:

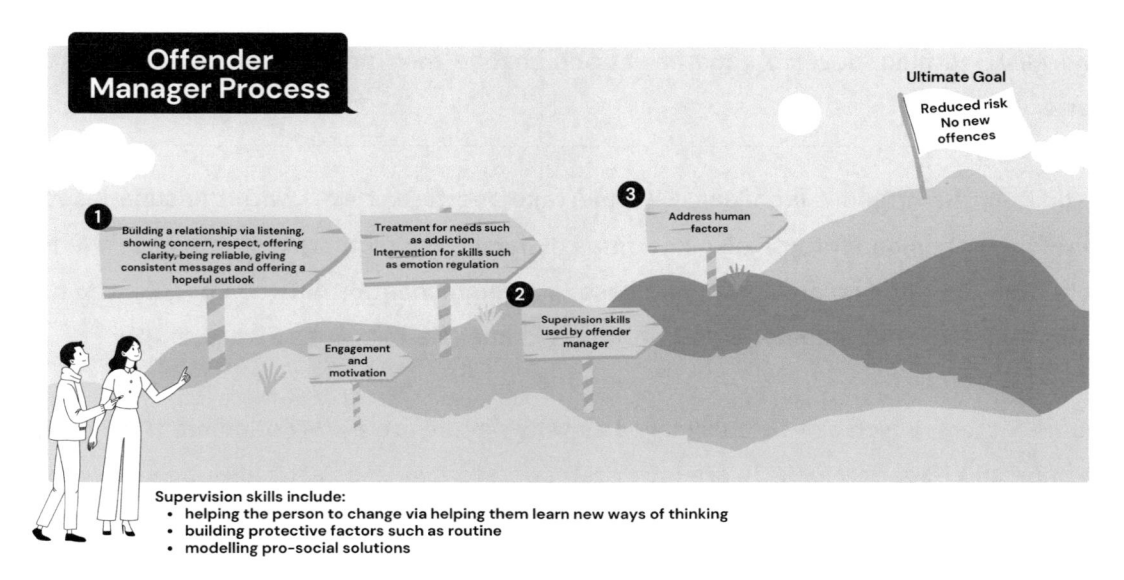

FIGURE 4.2 The process followed by offender managers when working with sentenced individuals

The initial focus of the OM and supervisee relationship is focused on building a foundation for the supportive but complex relationship that is required (Shapland et al., 2012). This is dependent on the skills of the OM to foster a good working alliance. Skills required include (Maguire et al., 2010):

- listening and being interested
- showing concern for the individual and their situation
- respect for the individual and their lived experience

- clarity of roles and clarity of information provided
- reliability in the alliance in terms of timekeeping, completing actions and honesty
- consistency of information and interaction style
- hopefulness in respect of the person having an optimistic future.

The aim of employing these skills is to create engagement and motivation within the working relationship. It is hoped that mutual respect is fostered.

The OM will develop this further by supporting the supervisee to access opportunities which will help them as part of their sentence plan or licence conditions. Opportunities of this nature may include access to substance misuse treatment or access to a course that addresses a need, such as a course aimed at reducing violence as a means to resolve conflict. Alongside accessing such treatment or courses, the OM uses supervision skills to help the supervisee generalise learning, develop good habits and change their previous patterns of thinking (Duwe, 2017).

In addition, the offender manager will undertake one-to-one work with the supervisee to identify any 'human factors' (also known as dynamic risk factors) that influence the person's risks of offending or reoffending based on commonalities between people who have committed crimes as a homogenous group over time (Heffernan and Ward, 2019).

Human factors, which can be considered as 'why people are at risk of committing crimes' (Herman and Pogarsky, 2020), are internal moderators such as attitudes, beliefs and values; external moderators such as peer networks or positive relationships; lifestyle choices such as substance misuse; related to opportunity such as employment or accommodation; part of lived history such as socio-economic background; or a health experience such as brain injury.

It is possible to appreciate why a person who has a positive attitude to law breaking, and who is mixing with peer networks who also break the law, and who has few opportunities in respect of employment, might commit crime in order to obtain money. Figure 4.3 (overleaf) gives a range of human factors that are a risk for potential criminality (see Chapter 1 on why people commit crimes).

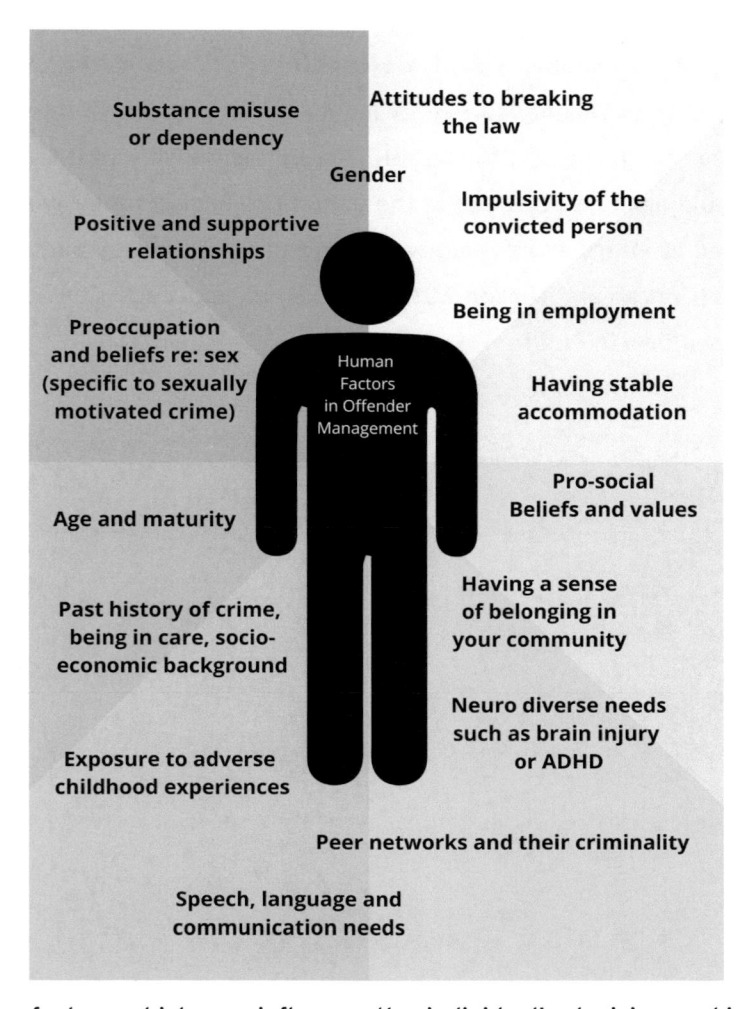

FIGURE 4.3 Human factors which can influence the individual's decision making in relation to future crime

The probation officer's knowledge of the human factors can be based on records and reports, assessment of risk and self-report from the individual. While awareness of human factors is useful for the probation officer because these are dynamic risk factors, this model is impacted by the following flaws:

- It is dependent on the individual being able to give a consistent coherent narrative, which is often difficult for people with SLCN, lived experience of trauma or significant substance misuse histories (Taylor et al., 2014).
- It is derived from social norms or cultural values that are socially constructed and may not apply to all people and all situations (Heffernan and Ward, 2019).
- It is subjective, based on the probation officer's views in the moment, the individual's self-report and the quality of any behavioural records which are available (Cording, Beggs Christofferson, and Grace, 2016).

In order to elicit an improved self-report, especially in people with SLCN, using a multimodal approach which includes visual representations is beneficial (Melvin, Langdon, and Murphy, 2020). While Talking Mats is a validated semi-structured interview tool which would lend itself to this purpose (Stans et al., 2019), it is unlikely that National Probation Service teams would have had training in the use of use such a tool. Given that probation officers are trained in interview techniques, hybrid card-sorting resources might be reasonably employed (Conrad and Tucker, 2019). An example of a card-sort activity for human factor reporting is shown in Figure 4.4:

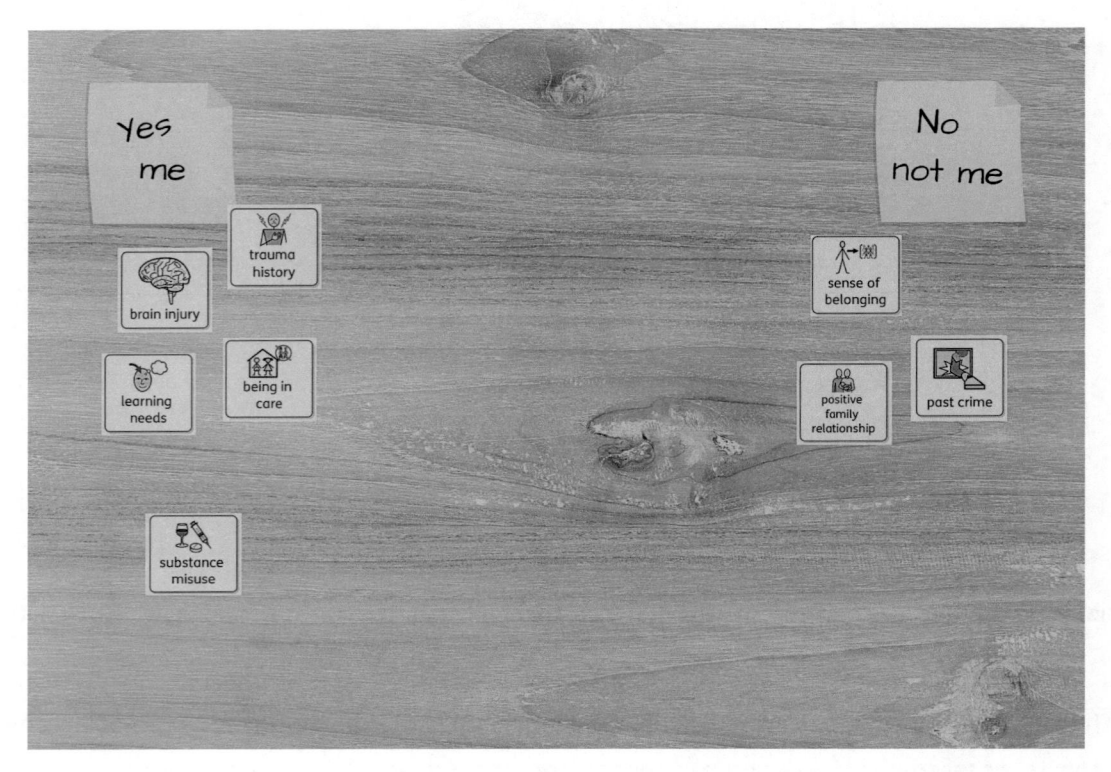

FIGURE 4.4 Hybrid card-sorting resources support an individual with speech, language and communication needs to express their past experiences

A copy of a card-sort resource for exploring this topic is located at Appendix 6.

Once human factors are identified, HM Prison and Probation Services (2021) recommend face-to-face sessions to:

- co-produce a plan for building new skills either by training or employment, or via using probation officer supervision for reflection
- maintain and improve family ties, which may be via supported contact
- reflect on identity with the aim of building pro-social identity

- discussion of motivations to help the person remain focused on goals and to break plans into achievable stages.

The OM will use skills in motivational interviewing (Witbrodtet al., 2019) and cognitive behaviour therapy (Raynor, 2019) to help the individual have autonomy, build on their strengths to address areas of need and acquire skills in emotion regulation.

The OM will also seek to identify protective factors (HM Prison and Probation Services, 2021) which can be used to counter the risk factors (Serin, Chadwick and Lloyd, 2016). Protective factors are one of three things (Dickens and O'Shea, 2018):

1. the opposite to a risk factor (e.g. having somewhere to live and a job which keeps you in a good sleep-to-wake routine)
2. personal characteristics or skills which reduce risk or mitigate risks when they are encountered (e.g. a person who is using their internal resilience to attend a substance misuse group and who has said 'no' to drugs when offered)
3. activity which promotes pro-social identity such as volunteering in a community garden project.

The protective factors may be captured in diagram form which has been completed as a joint piece of work with the OM and the individual. An example is given in Figure 4.5 below:

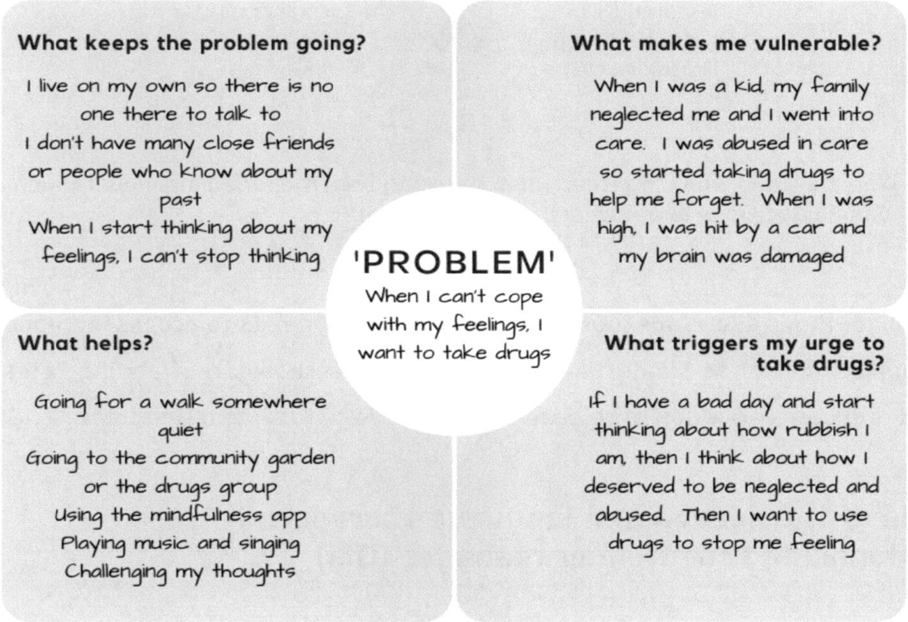

What keeps the problem going?

I live on my own so there is no one there to talk to
I don't have many close friends or people who know about my past
When I start thinking about my feelings, I can't stop thinking

What makes me vulnerable?

When I was a kid, my family neglected me and I went into care. I was abused in care so started taking drugs to help me forget. When I was high, I was hit by a car and my brain was damaged

'PROBLEM'
When I can't cope with my feelings, I want to take drugs

What helps?

Going for a walk somewhere quiet
Going to the community garden or the drugs group
Using the mindfulness app
Playing music and singing
Challenging my thoughts

What triggers my urge to take drugs?

If I have a bad day and start thinking about how rubbish I am, then I think about how I deserved to be neglected and abused. Then I want to use drugs to stop me feeling

FIGURE 4.5 An example completed assessment of protective factors for a person with speech, language and communication needs who is at risk of using substances to self-medicate when they experience intense emotions

A blank copy of this protective factors' formulation form is located at Appendix 7.

To conclude this section, it must be noted that the National Probation Service must also employ rigour in the effective deployment of resources. This requires the NPS to use tools to consider risk (e.g. risk assessment), need (e.g. needs assessment associated with human factors) and responsivity (supervision skills) to provide the best possible outcomes in respect of victim justice, recidivism and public safety. See Figure 4.6 below:

Who to target:
Target resources
at higher-risk people who might
commit the most serious crimes
(e.g. more serious high-risk crime =
more supervision)

How to target:
Adapt the work to the
needs of the
individual (e.g.
accessible
information, regular
sessions that match
the attention span of
the individual, using
visual to help support
memory, etc.)

What to target:
Focus on the need
that is most likely to
lead to re-offending
(e.g. if the person
commits crimes to
finance a substance
misuse habit, address
the substance misuse
to reduce re-
offending)

FIGURE 4.6 Who, how and what to target when reducing the risks of an individual which supports making decisions about where to expend resources

Using such methods allows for those with higher risks or needs to access increased supervision support. Evidence suggests that this model decreases reoffending rates (Drake, 2011) and reduces revocation of release on licence (Paparozzi and Gendreau, 2005).

The role of the speech and language therapist (SLT) alongside the offender manager (OM)

Offender managers will work with people in contact with the CJS who have SLCN. While OMs are highly skilled in their role, the information provided around SLCN is minimal (HM

Prison and Probation Services, 2021). This creates the context whereby professionals working in CJS may be unaware of SLCN and are at risk of making subjective opinions of a person because of lack of awareness (Brooker, Collinson and Sirdifield, 2022). SLCN can lead to shorter utterances, communicating via body language and reduced eye contact, which can result in the OM perceiving the individual as uncooperative (Houston and Butler, 2019). Houston and Butler also comment on the 'tendency to assume that individuals understood' (Houston and Butler, 2019, p.33) which hints at the under-recognition of SLCN in this field.

The reader will have also noted that much of the OM's work with the individual is verbally mediated, which creates opportunities for joint working between OMs and SLTs. However, in settings where there is no access to SLT, there is no support for OMs to manage SLCN or to make the verbally mediated processes more accessible for people with SLCN.

Special interest should be drawn to the work that OMs undertake as part of the supervision of an individual. This work addresses matters such as consequences of actions, the perspectives of third parties, discussion of emotions and skills in relationships, employment and leisure. All of these domains have the potential to be impacted by SLCN.

Top tips for colleagues, such as OMs working in verbally mediated systems with people with SLCN:

1. Use accessible vocabulary with no complex words or specialist terminology. As a general guide, try to pitch vocabulary at the level of a person starting secondary school as many of the people working with OMs stopped school around this time. (Where an SLT assessment has been made, ensure that you routinely remind yourself of the vocabulary and language recommendations).
2. Any specialist terms which must be used, such as approved premises, should be explained and understanding checked as per 6 below. Always think 'Would my next-door neighbour understand this term?' as a safeguard to using specialist vocabulary.
3. Slow down the pace of information. Try to plan information into bite-sized chunks. Give thinking time as information is offered. A strategy might be to pause after three minutes and say, 'I'm going to pause there to make sure that I've remembered everything' and then pause for at least 30 seconds.
4. Group by topic. Group information by topic (e.g. where to live) and remain with that topic for this conversation. Save other topics for other conversations so that the information

does not blend together. Use an informal agenda to help such as a piece of paper with one topic from the OM and one topic from the person with SLCN (any additional topics can be noted for a future conversation agenda).

5. Use visuals for every conversation. This could be calendars, bullet points, photographs of places, clocks, visual timetables or written key words, maps, etc.

6. Check understanding via asking an open question such as 'What have we agreed?' or 'Remind me of the plan'. Do not ask 'Have you understood?' as the person will often reply 'yes' even if they are not certain. It always helps to give a written breakdown of any plan in bullet point form.

7. Write down names, places, dates and times for the person so that reliance on auditory memory is reduced.

8. Any verbal strategies such as points 3 and 6 above should always be framed as the OM needing thinking time or to check the plan so that the individual does not feel patronised.

A visual aid of these top tips to share with colleagues is included at Appendix 8.

After court for people with an impairment or disability

The Sentencing Council (2020) offers a framework which should be applied when disposing of people with an impairment or disability after court. The framework offers three categories of disability which should be considered:

• being mentally unwell as defined in psychiatric terms – a condition that causes problems with everyday functioning which starts after a sustained period of normal function

• having a neurological impairment which may be defined using a medical or psychological model – a condition that impacts on daily functioning and is acquired after a sustained period of normal function

• a developmental disability which can be considered as medical or psychological – a condition that has been present since birth and which causes an individual to be below average function when compared with age-matched peers.

The framework informs a process whereby the court takes into account the person's impairment or disability, details about the crime and a judgement on culpability. This enables a person to be disposed of in the most appropriate setting for the individual. In this context, 'disposed of' is the CJS term for 'placed' or 'admitted to' in the context of a secure hospital. Figure 4.7 overleaf shows the information that the court will consider to decide

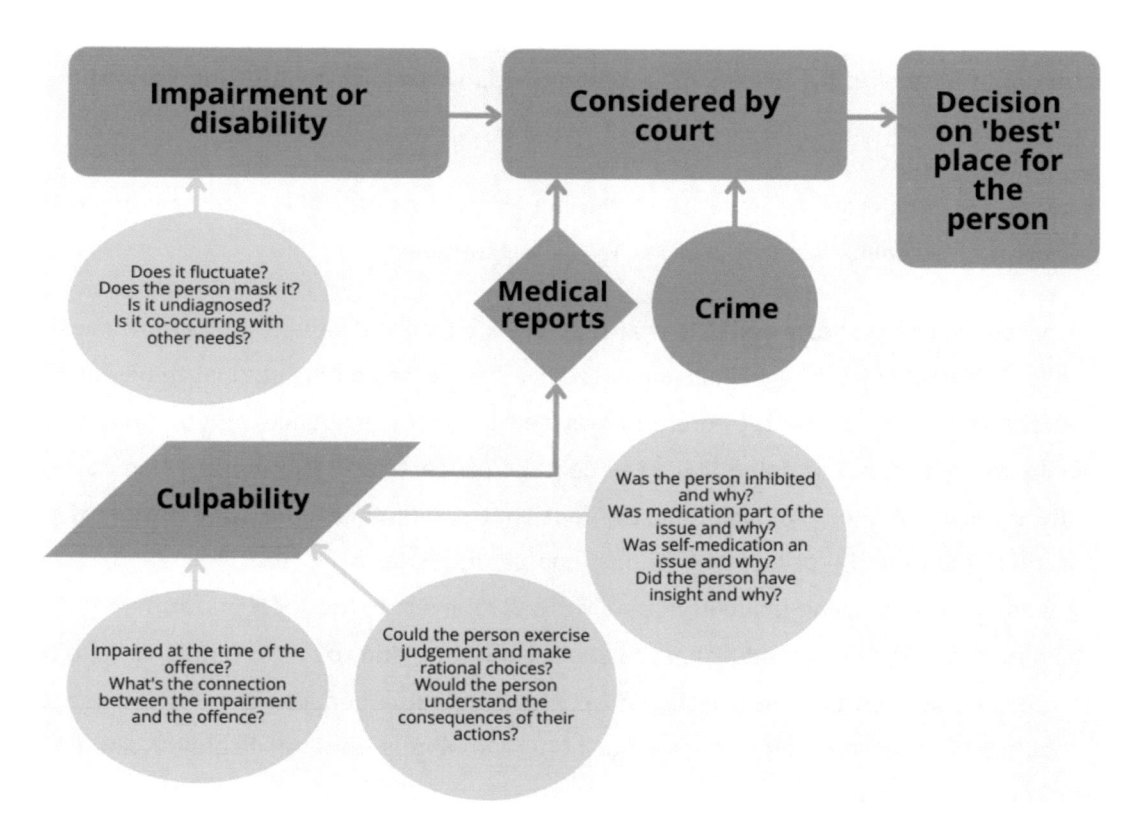

FIGURE 4.7 The process for consideration of culpability when considering a person with impairment or disability

upon culpability. Should the court be missing crucial information, the judgment may be delayed or made in good faith based on partial information.

It is incumbent on the court to decide if the impairment or disability impacted on the culpability of the individual at the time of the offence. In law, culpability means whether the person has any responsibility for the act – whether the person can be legally blamed. Terms often associated with legal culpability are purposely, knowingly, recklessly and negligently. Examples to illustrate these terms are:

- Person A is culpable in relation to stealing, because they purposely waited until the item was unsecured and unsupervised to remove it.
- Person B is culpable in relation to a driving offence because they knowingly drove when under the influence of alcohol with an awareness that this was against the law.
- Person C is culpable for people being injured at work because they recklessly stacked heavy items on a shelf which was not strong enough to hold the load and had signed the heavy item risk assessment.

- Person D is culpable for a road traffic accident because they were negligent in their role of maintaining the brakes on a heavy goods vehicle which subsequently collided with a car.

The court will decide on the severity of the impairment or disability, and how much the impairment or disability was a factor in the crime. Examples:

- A person with psychosis believes that they are a police officer searching for a missing child. They believe that the child is located in a house, being held against their will. The person with psychosis enters the property searching for 'evidence' and to 'rescue' the child. In the process of doing this, they damage property and frighten the homeowner. The severity of the psychosis and the fact that it influenced the commission of the crime resulted in the person not being culpable in this case.
- A woman with learning disability has a work placement in her local supermarket. She has been taking snack foods from the shop without paying to eat at home. To take the food, she hides it in her bag. In this case, she is culpable because she knows that she should pay for items before removing them from shops and her disability was not a factor in the crime.
- A man with a head injury is impulsive and prone to feeling threatened because of his reduced understanding of body language, facial expression and tone of voice. At a football match, he becomes violent and assaults a member of the public after that person shouted at him for knocking into him. The man is partially culpable because, while his head injury reduces his culpability and is a factor in the crime, he was knowingly not taking his anti-anxiety medication which would have reduced his risks. Figure 4.8 overleaf illustrates the types of issues that will influence court decisions. Where SLCN has not been identified, the court will be unaware of this factor.

As a result of weighing the impairment or disability, culpability and circumstances of the crime, the court may direct one of the following outcomes:

- Mental health treatment requirements as part of a community order or suspended sentence so that the person can access care and treatment without being detained under the Mental Health Act 1983. The care and treatment are usually via a community-based medical or psychological practitioner. A person receiving this disposal after court would usually access community-based SLT if needed. The SLT service may not know the circumstances of the individual as such information would not be disclosed by the court. The referral criteria for a community-based SLT service vary across geographic reasons, so whether the referral would be accepted would be based

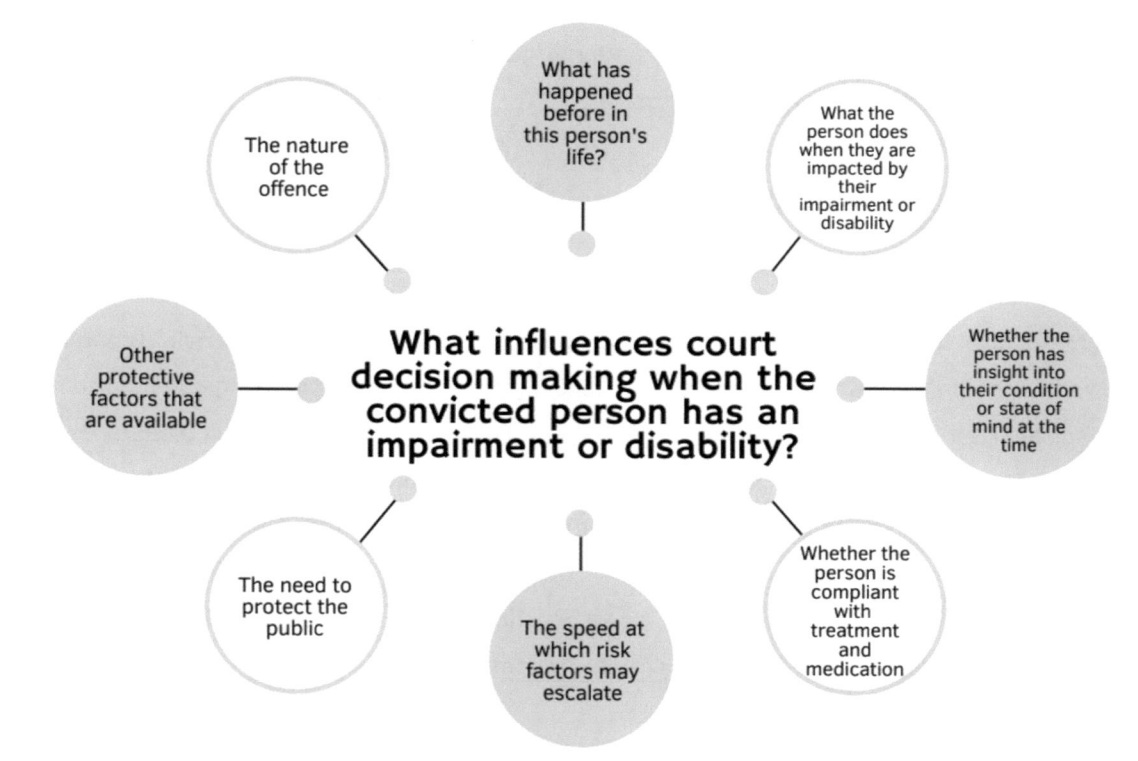

FIGURE 4.8 Factors that influence court decision making when the convicted person has an impairment or disability

on this. The commissioning of SLT within mental health services also varies across England and Wales, so it should not be assumed that an SLT will form part of the multi-disciplinary team.

- Care in a mental health inpatient hospital under the Mental Health Act 1983 via a hospital order, where the care is provided by a multi-disciplinary team who are overseen by a psychiatrist. A person receiving this disposal after court would ideally access mental health inpatient hospital-based SLT if needed. The SLT would be part of the team and would have full access to information about the person's history. However, in many settings, SLT is not routinely available.

- Supervision and treatment under a guardianship order whereby geographically local social services or a relative approved by the local authority support the person to live at a prescribed address and attend treatment, occupation, education or training. A person receiving this disposal after court would ideally access community-based SLT if needed. The SLT service may know the circumstances of the individual in this case due to the involvement of social services, but transfer of detailed information does not always occur.

The Sentencing Council (2020) are at pains to point out that such disposals after court focus on care and treatment so that risks are mitigated while the individual is supported to have positive health and well-being outcomes.

Mental health inpatient hospital settings

A person convicted of an offence can be considered for care and treatment in a mental health hospital if they have an impairment or disability which impacted on their culpability at the time of the crime. If a person meets these circumstances and is being considered for a hospital order after court, specific criteria need to be met. The person will transfer from legislation that is designed to meet the needs of law breaking to legislation that protects vulnerable people – specifically the Mental Health Act (1983 amended 2007).

The Mental Health Act (2007) allows for a person who is convicted of an offence to go to hospital instead of prison in the following circumstances:

- Two suitably qualified doctors agree and have provided evidence to the court that the person would be more appropriately placed in a hospital setting.
- There is a hospital which can offer fitting care and treatment.
- The court agrees that hospital is a preferred disposal.
- It can be arranged for the person to move to a hospital setting within 28 days of sentencing.

The Mental Health Act (2007) offers a definition of 'mental disorder'. While this terminology may seem at odds with more current vocabulary, it is nonetheless used by the courts when considering people with an impairment or disability. The definition is:

> mental disorders include mental illnesses such as schizophrenia, bipolar disorder, anxiety or depression, as well as personality disorders, eating disorders, autistic spectrum disorders and learning disabilities associated with abnormally aggressive or seriously irresponsible conduct on the part of the person concerned.
>
> *(Mental Health Act, 2007, section 1, point 17 and 20)*

Care and treatment are defined in the act as:

> 'medical treatment' includes nursing, psychological intervention and specialist mental health habilitation, rehabilitation and care.
>
> *(Mental Health Act, 2007, section 7, point 38)*

The courts can ask clinical commissioning groups (in England) or health boards (in Wales) to provide information about mental health inpatient settings which may be appropriate for the care and treatment of the individual. This includes for assessment and what arrangements can be made to admit a person to a hospital location (Department of Health, 2015).

Assessment for mental health inpatient hospital usually takes the form of a request for assessment either from the court, a legal representative or a specialist doctor (such as a consultant psychiatrist). The request should be accompanied by reports explaining the person's mental disorder, their past history, their conviction and any requests for treatment. This information informs the pre-assessment considerations. The mental health inpatient hospital setting will decide which professional(s) should conduct a face-to-face assessment and will arrange for these representatives to meet the individual. To some extent, assessment may be limited by service availability – for example, if there is no in-house SLT service, assessment is unlikely to include SLCN. Should the initial assessment indicate SLCN, the team may then decide to commission an external SLT to report, but availability of a suitable SLT and funding issues can lead to lengthy delays. Following a face-to-face assessment, information will be discussed by the hospital admissions group where a decision on whether the setting can meet the care needs of the individual will be made.

If the individual is accepted for admission, the mental health inpatient hospital will begin the pre-admission processes which include:

- informing the referrer and the individual of their acceptance for treatment
- provision of written information to the individual in the form of an information leaflet about the hospital, what to expect and photographs (hospitals who cater for people with learning disability will provide this leaflet in accessible forms)
- pre-admission nursing assessments so that the needs of the person are met immediately on arrival – this can be physical or medical, as well as assessing well-being needs
- the development of a bespoke care plan which offers the least-restrictive options for the person coming to hospital from the earliest opportunity
- identifying early treatment targets which are individualised, gender sensitive, recovery orientated, and address needs related to mental and physical health and management of risk.

During pre-admission processes, the professionals involved will arrange for formal transfer of care which will include documentation from the Ministry of Justice to enable the person to move from one setting to another. They will arrange for appropriate transport which is least restrictive and promotes the dignity of the individual, and inform family members of developments.

Levels of security

Mental health inpatient hospital settings offer three levels of security. These are:

- Low-secure services provide care and treatment to those adults who present a significant risk of harm to others and whose escape from hospital must be impeded.
- Medium-secure services provide care and treatment to those adults who present a serious risk of harm to others and whose escape from hospital must be prevented.
- High-secure services provide care and treatment to those adults who present a grave risk of harm to others and who cannot be managed in lower levels of security and who must not be able to escape from hospital.

The appropriate level of security will be identified during the referral and assessment phase.

Medium- and low-secure hospitals

Medium- and low-secure hospitals (also known as forensic hospitals) provide accommodation, care and treatment to people who:

- pose a serious risk of harm to others and whose escape from hospital should be prevented (medium-secure level)
- or pose a significant risk of harm to others and whose escape from hospital should be impeded (low-secure level).

The majority of people admitted to secure care go to medium- and low-secure settings with only a small number held in high-secure conditions (Duke et al., 2018). Following admission to a medium- or low-secure hospital, there is a settling-in period. The person is orientated to the hospital setting (which is often called a ward or unit), the routine of the day or week, the professionals who work there and their care coordinator. Good practice is that the hospital has a 'buddy system' whereby the new person is matched to a peer to help them settle in and a welcome pack in a format which meets the needs of the person, such as accessible materials (Georgiou, Oultram and Haque, 2019).

Often wards provide specific services such as care and treatment for people with mental illness, people with learning disability or people with autism. Wards can also specialise in the treatment (psychological services) which they offer such as violent offender programmes, sex offender programmes or fire-setting treatment. The ward is staffed by a multi-disciplinary team under the supervision of a consultant psychiatrist who specialises in a clinical area which is congruent with the patient group. The consultant psychiatrist has the role of 'responsible clinician' (RC).

There is an expectation that certain events will happen in the early days of being transferred to secure hospital (Georgiou et al., 2019):

- Information is given about rights, consent, advocacy services and how to complain.
- Information is given to the person and their family about the care, treatment pathway and contact or visiting arrangements.
- The person will see a doctor for a physical health review within 72 hours of arrival and any concerns will be developed into a physical health care plan. This is because people who are residing in secure services have increased physical health risks such as diabetes, dyslipidaemia, hypertension, epilepsy, asthma or obesity. The care plan will include items such as health education, exercise, oral health or information on nutrition. It will include any specialist screens that are recommended for people in certain high-risk groups, such as blood tests, and any specialist appointments with external services such as respiratory clinics.

The ethos of the care and treatment is one of recovery and risk reduction. Written plans are co-produced with the individual and their family or friends (where appropriate) including the following areas, illustrated in Figure 4.9 below:

RECOVERY AND RISK REDUCTION

FIGURE 4.9 The ethos of the care and treatment within a secure hospital is one of recovery and risk reduction using six domains to influence change

The written plans are reviewed monthly and updated if required. They are often adapted into a visual progress tool which is more engaging for the individual. An example is given in Figure 4.10 below:

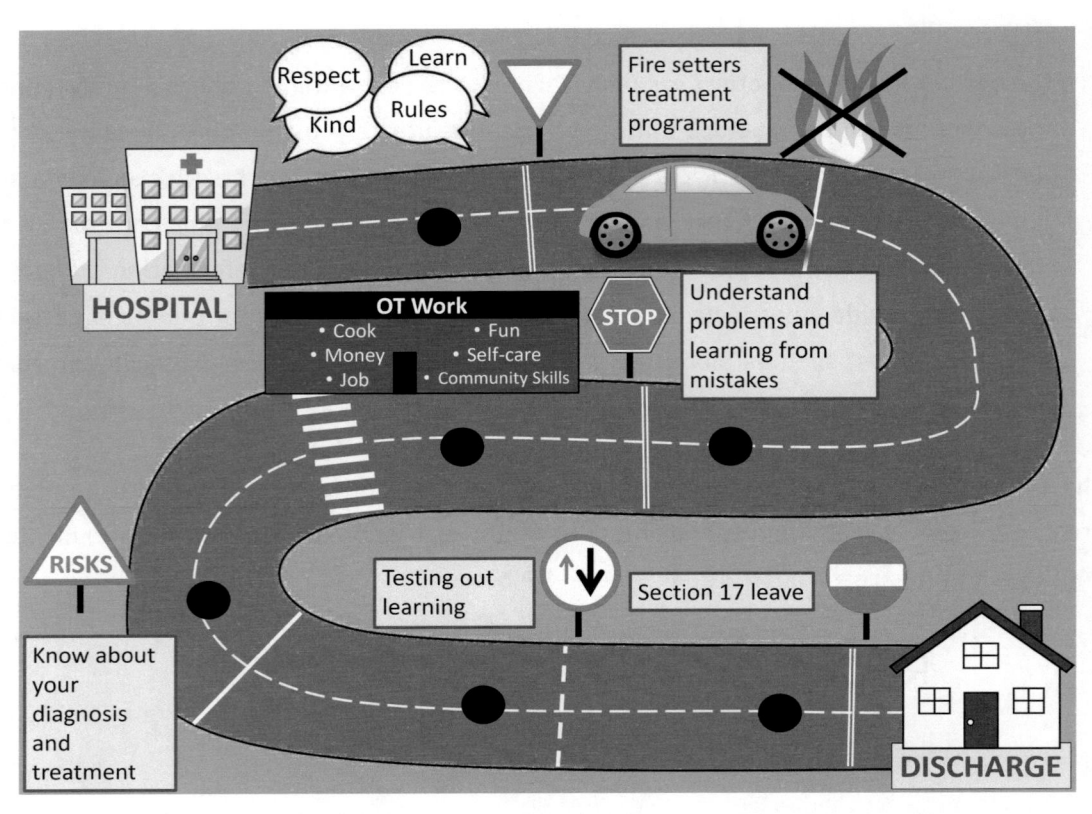

FIGURE 4.10 Care and treatment plans are often offered in motivating and accessible forms

There is a blank version of this visual progress tool at Appendix 9 including a choice of 'cars' which can be laminated and attached with Velcro to move along the road as the person progresses in their treatment.

Alongside visual tools for progress, skill building such as managing own time, recognition of emotions or seeking help when needed can also be represented with visual aids to help the person to understand. Figures 4.11–4.13 (on pages 141 and 142) illustrate individual examples.

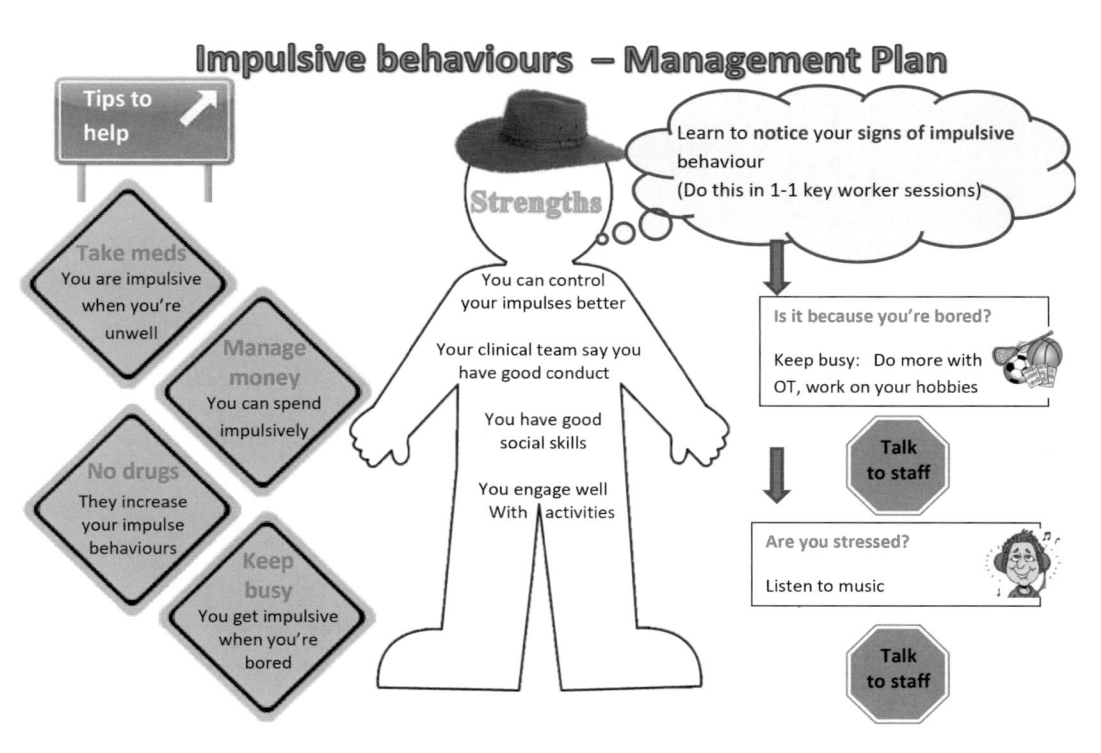

Substance Use – Management Plan

Strengths

Not taken drugs in a long time
Motivated to receive treatment

Work with key worker in 1-1 sessions

Recognise relapse warning signs

Utilise the help from a substance use worker

Attend a substance misuse group

Learn to cope with urges and cravings

Try new hobbies and activities

Engage with OT

Reduce boredom

You said you want to move to a drug-free area

Find hobbies and activities you like

Build relationships that will help

Spend time with non-drug users

Keep building relationships with non-users

Now in hospital → — → — In the Community

FIGURE 4.11 An example skill-building plan to help an individual in secure hospital progress to living in their community with the skills/knowledge to avoid taking substances

Impulsive behaviours – Management Plan

Tips to help

Strengths

Learn to **notice** your **signs** of impulsive behaviour
(Do this in 1-1 key worker sessions)

Take meds
You are impulsive when you're unwell

Manage money
You can spend impulsively

No drugs
They increase your impulse behaviours

Keep busy
You get impulsive when you're bored

You can control your impulses better

Your clinical team say you have good conduct

You have good social skills

You engage well With activities

Is it because you're bored?

Keep busy: Do more with OT, work on your hobbies

Talk to staff

Are you stressed?

Listen to music

Talk to staff

FIGURE 4.12 An example skill-building plan to help an individual in secure hospital who has impulsive behaviours which add to their risks

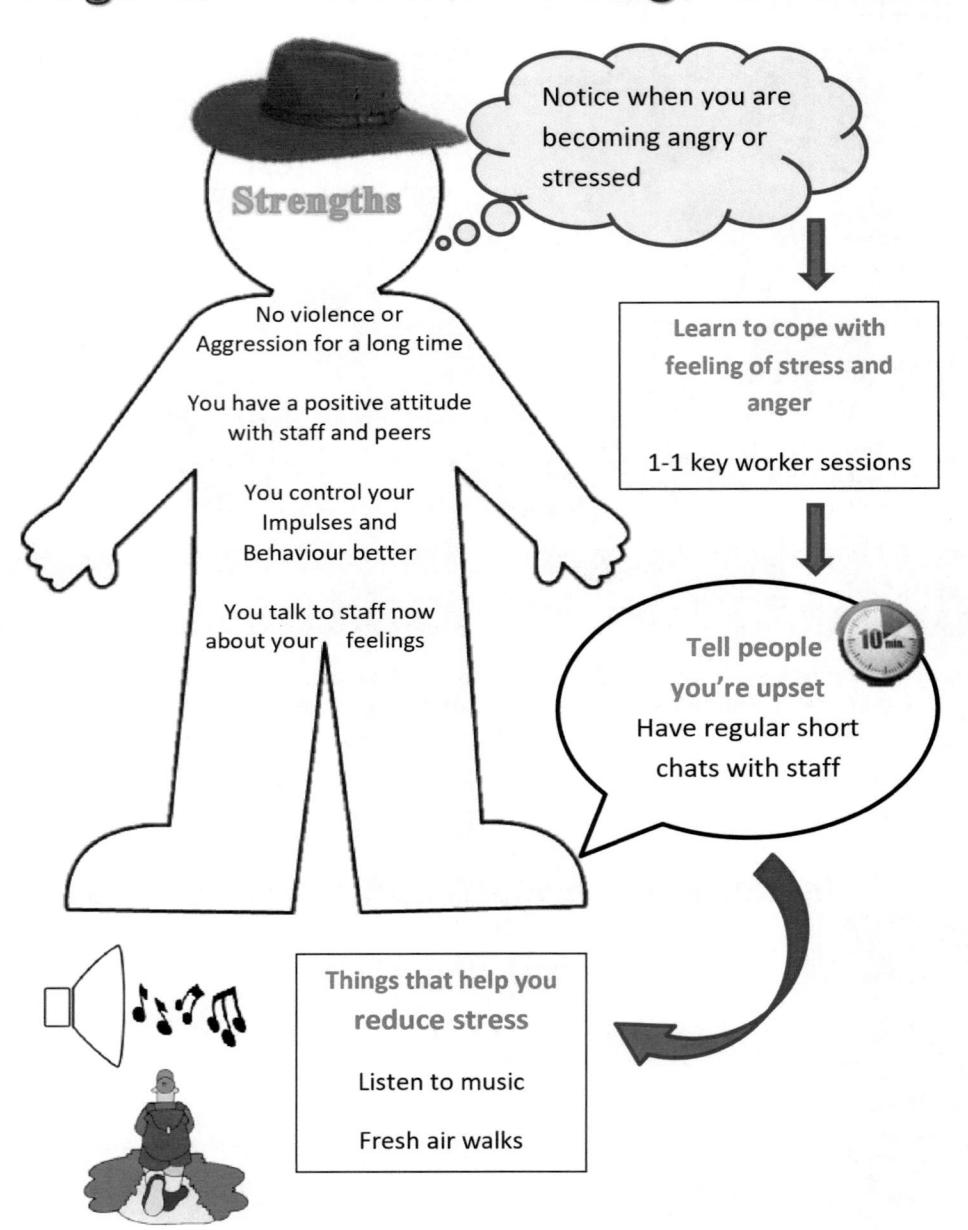

FIGURE 4.13 An example skill-building plan to help an individual in secure hospital who has a past history of anger and violence

Care programme approach

Progression through treatment in secure hospitals in England is supported and measured via the Care Programme Approach (CPA). This is a framework that focuses on the strengths, goals and support needs of the individual and promotes joined-up working across different agencies – especially as the person moves from treatment to discharge planning (Department of Health, 2008).

Under the CPA model, the individual has a named care coordinator who is responsible for developing care plans, ensuring that goals are met and working face to face with the patient (Simpson, Miller, and Bowers, 2003). The person who is newly admitted to secure hospital should have their first formal CPA review meeting after the initial three months. This should be followed by regular reviews every 6–12 months depending on the goals set. The person should be active in planning their review meeting – who should attend, setting a date and sending invitations, chairing the meeting themselves if they wish and having stakeholder input into decisions (Rethink Mental Illness, 2020).

While each setting will have slightly different ways of managing a CPA review meeting, every opportunity should be taken to make it accessible and motivating for the individual.

Case example

Mr S resides at a low-secure setting in England. He is detained there under section 37/41 of the Mental Health Act 2007 because he had a mental disorder (autism) which results in seriously irresponsible conduct and risks to the general public. He has been at the hospital for two years and is managed under the CPA model. Because he has autism, many of his needs are related to social communication. For this reason, his care coordinator is a speech and language therapist. He has a review meeting every six months. He chairs the meeting with the help of a mental health advocate, and his care coordinator makes a visual record of things that people say or do on large sheets of paper attached to the wall. In this way, he has a total communication scaffold which he can refer to in the meeting if he needs extra support. The care coordinator writes key words, draws emotion faces, adds thinking bubbles with thoughts and notes any questions which Mr S asks. This process helps Mr S manage his social communication needs and the strategies support his theory-of-mind skills. After the meeting, the care coordinator takes photographs of the large sheets of paper and makes them into a visual record for Mr S to keep.

Care and treatment

The care and treatment offered in low- and medium-secure settings will comprise of three strands:

- Pharmacological and psychiatric which will include the diagnosis of conditions that would benefit from medication, the provision of medication and its review/management as per prescribing guidelines. This is usually led by the RC with the support of the multi-disciplinary team (MDT).

- Psychological treatment or interventions which are usually led by a clinical psychologist. These are generally group or individual sessional treatments aimed at making the person more aware of themselves, their risks and their experiences.
- Care associated with skill building which is usually led by occupational therapists (OTs) and nurses with the input of the MDT. This usually involves skills that would be used every day such as budgeting, personal hygiene, activities of daily living (ADL). Some medium- and low-secure settings have invested in SLT as part of their MDT, which adds skill building in relation to SLCN to the portfolio of care, but this is not a consistent model across all medium- and low-secure services.

The pathway of care and treatment begins with the initial settling-in phase (as discussed) and progresses to individualised care plans which offer rehabilitation in a sequence that allows for increased levels of challenge as the person progresses through their care. An example of a staggered approach to care and treatment that increases the level of challenge is given in Figure 4.14 below:

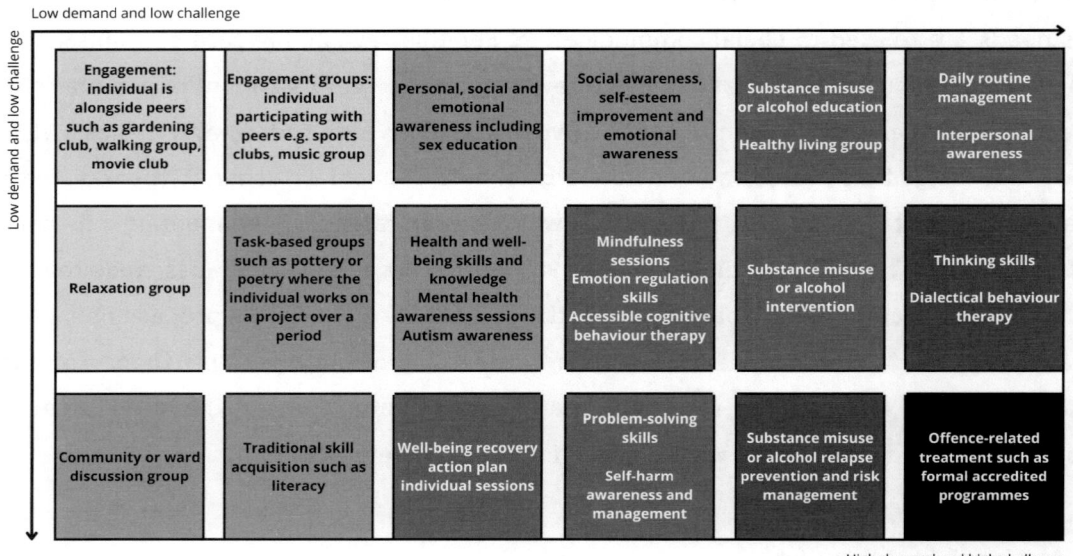

FIGURE 4.14 A staggered approach to care and treatment which enables the individual in a secure hospital to move from low-demand activities to more difficult risk-reduction treatment

In this figure, the demands and challenges placed on the individual are low in the top-left area (light grey shading) and increase to higher demand and challenge as the person progresses towards the bottom-right area (dark grey shading). The spread of demand from top left to bottom right acknowledges the work which the individual will be doing with a range of professionals and often in parallel. Group intervention as well as one-to-one intervention occurs across the pathway, depending on the needs of the person. Often generic information such as healthy living skills is offered in a group setting, whereas sensitive and personal information is discussed in private, such as the well-being and recovery action plan completed traditionally with the care coordinator.

Section 17 planned leave

As well as care and treatment within the hospital ward, the team around the patient will consider whether community access would be useful for the individual to help develop skills. When the person is sectioned under the Mental Health Act 2007, community access is called Section 17 planned leave (Mental Health Act, 2007).

Section 17 planned leave must be part of the care and treatment for the individual, and the therapeutic aim must be outlined by the MDT and approved by the consultant psychiatrist who is the RC.

Case example

Miss J has been in hospital for 18 months and is mentally stable. As part of her rehabilitation and reducing her risks, she is working on her skills with money and cooking with the ward occupational therapist. These goals were set at her CPA review meeting. The MDT agrees with the goals, and the OT has made a plan for Miss J to save up some money, research some recipes online, go to the local supermarket to buy ingredients and then return to the ward to make a meal in the therapy room kitchen. Miss J's risks have been reviewed by the RC who agrees that this proposal is appropriate. The RC signs the Section 17 planned leave paperwork so that Miss J can leave the hospital to go to the supermarket on a certain date, for two hours under the supervision of a named registered nurse (RN).

Section 17 planned leave usually takes the form of a hierarchy of progression, from leave in the hospital grounds to accessing places locally, and then travelling further afield. The supervision usually starts high, and then is reduced as the person reduces their risks in treatment. The eventual goal is unescorted Section 17 planned leave to an agreed location.

It is useful to have a visual aid to help the person consider the stages of Section 17 planned leave and what is required of them to help them progress. The ladder diagram shown in Figure 4.15 (overleaf) is valuable in this respect.

My Section 17 Leave Stage Ladder

Shadowed community leave ☐

Unescorted grounds leave ☐

Shadowed grounds leave ☐

Escorted 1:1 community leave ☑ Next step to finish safety plan

Escorted 2:1 community leave ☐

Escorted 1:1 grounds leave ☐

Escorted 2:1 grounds leave ☐

FIGURE 4.15 A Mental Health Act Section 17 leave plan helps the individual in a secure hospital to progress through the stages of high supervision to low supervision with clear next steps to support progress

A proforma of this visual aid is located at Appendix 10 for use in clinical practice.

Formulation

Formulation is a term used by psychologists and teams within secure care settings. A formulation is a process whereby the individual and members of their care team bring together everything that they know about the person and try to construct the knowledge into a format that helps the individual understand themselves and their difficulties (Lewis-Morton et al., 2015). There is evidence to suggest that this type of self-examination is helpful to the individual as they have raised awareness of their strengths and barriers, and helpful to the care team as they can target person-specific needs (Casares and Johnstone, 2015).

There are many different formats and models for psychological formulation. Most include the following (Selzer and Ellen, 2014):

- predisposing factors – the things that have happened in the past which make a person vulnerable to the issue
- precipitating factors – the things that triggered the most recent occurrence of this issue
- perpetuating factors – the things that are happening currently to keep the issue alive
- protective factors – the things that can make the issue better
- the issue is sometimes called the 'problem' – for example, 'What happened in the past to make you vulnerable to this problem?'
- biological causes such as poor physical health, brain injury, pain or substance misuse

- psychological causes such as self-esteem, thinking skills, personality traits or resilience to stress
- social factors such as economic resources, connectedness in the community and the quality of important relationships.

Formulation using these domains can be used for physical health needs such as diabetes, psychological intervention needs such as offender rehabilitation, or resettlement needs such as helping the person to be safe after discharge from hospital. Formulation can be in diagram form, written statement form or visual form. See examples in Figures 4.16 (below) and 4.17 (overleaf).

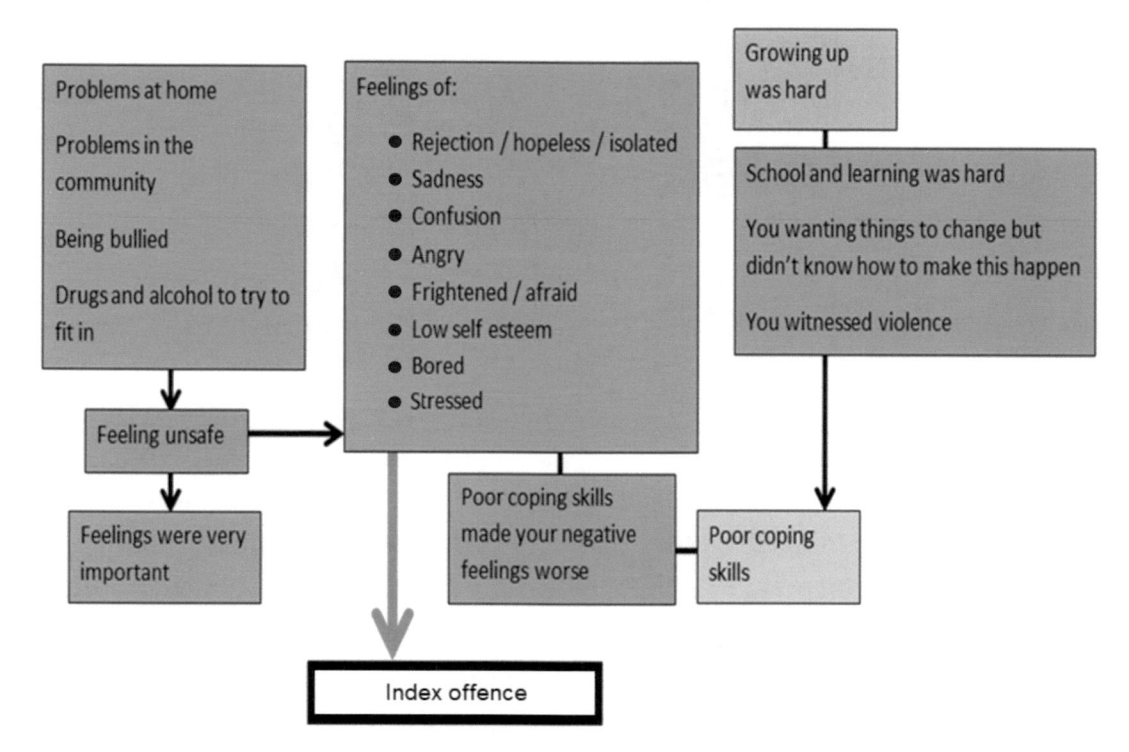

FIGURE 4.16 An example of a formulation of an individual in a secure hospital using a box and arrows chart

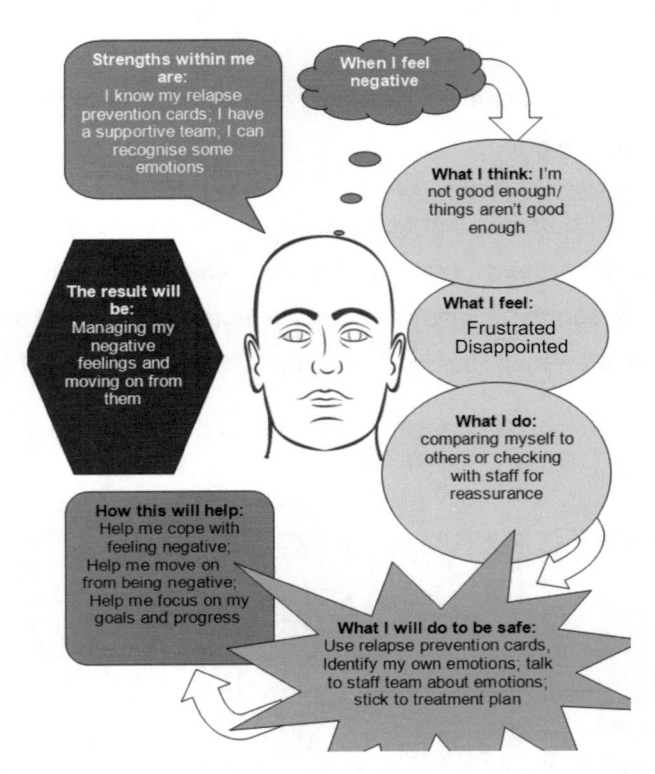

FIGURE 4.17 An example of a formulation of an individual in a secure hospital using a visual aid

Case example

Mr M is a gentleman with learning disability. He grew up with limited stability and as a result can feel insecure with low self-esteem. His learning from being a young person was that to 'be good' he should supress negative emotions. In the past, he has damaged property when he felt a negative intense and unwanted emotion. When this happened, he was given support and 'extra care' by people around him, which he found pleasing. He is residing in a secure hospital following a conviction for arson when his property damage escalated to fire setting. Formulation work included him and resulted in the production of a formulation figure which informs how Mr M and his team understand him (see Figure 4.18 overleaf).

Mr M has SLCN. Part of his formulation is that the people who support him should use consistent strategies to help him when he is distressed. Table 4.1 table is a more complex document which incorporates SLCN (predisposing factors) on page 150, what Mr M will do and what the team around him will see (precipitating and perpetuating factors) and strategies that will help (protective factors) which are sorted into red, amber and green depending on Mr M's level of distress. This document is for use by staff and not Mr M.

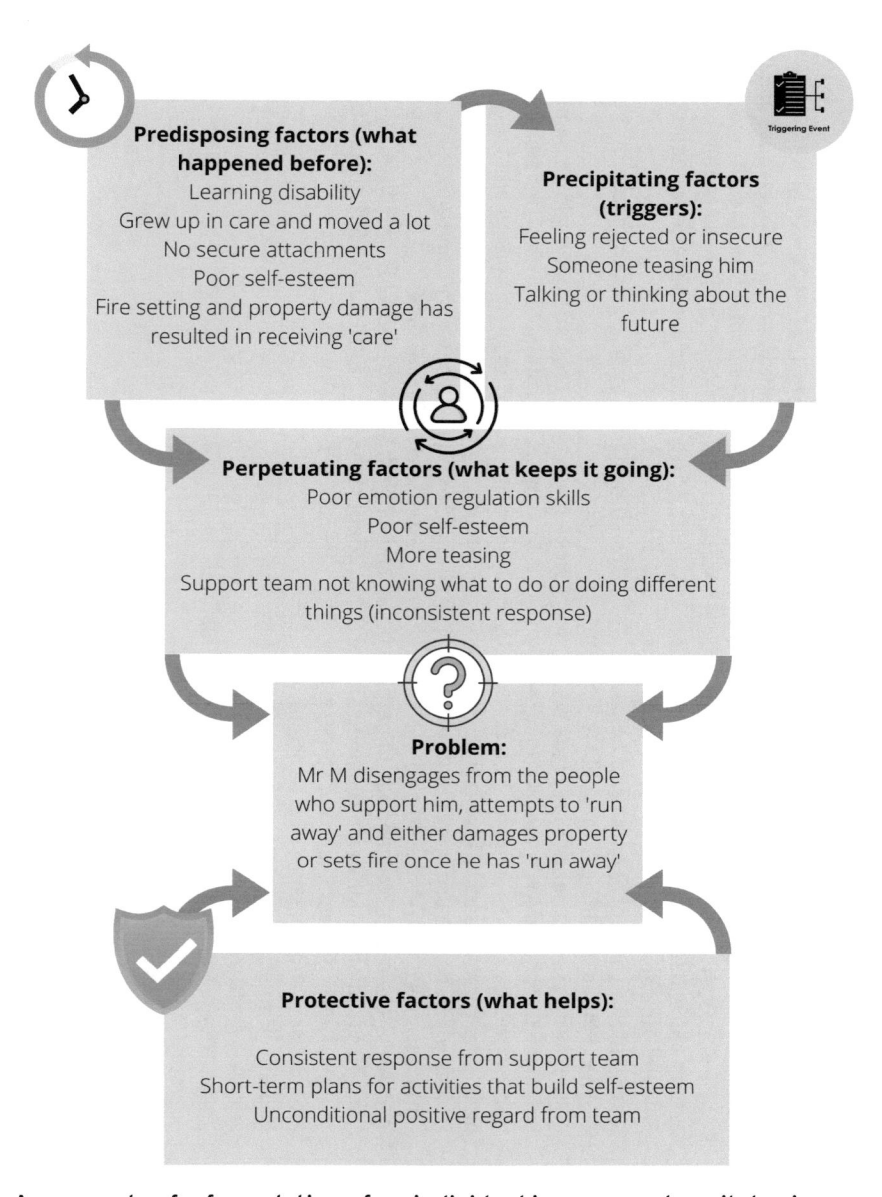

FIGURE 4.18 An example of a formulation of an individual in a secure hospital using a more formal format

Formulation can be a long and complex process which involves exploring a person's past experiences and current challenges. It can be adapted to include the individual – for example, using a communication framework such as Talking Mats (Boardman, Crichton and Butterworth, 2016) – but significant language barriers and risks of re-traumatising a person who may have had past trauma remain (Johnstone, 2013). It is recommended by Johnstone (2013) to consider ways to involve the individual, but also ways to feedback to the person the results of a team formulation. Johnstone (2013) advocates for a carefully written letter that summarises the key information to be shared with the individual. This approach supports SLCN as it is multimodal and can include accessible principles in the letter writing.

TABLE 4.1 An example of a formulation of an individual in a secure hospital which has been developed into a support plan for SLCN to be utilised by nursing staff

Predisposing factors – communication needs	Precipitating and perpetuating factors in communication	Protective factors – how staff can support at different stages
Attention and listening: Good attention to the conversation partner when motivated or discussing a preferred topic. Less good attention and avoidance seen when discussing a dispreferred topic. Can attend to task for up to 45 minutes when motivated. **Receptive language:** Understands simple sentences. Is better when information is given in 'bite-size' pieces. Has a processing delay for verbal information so needs 'thinking time'. Has an adequate knowledge of vocabulary for everyday conversations but does not possess an age-appropriate vocabulary. The conversation partner will need to check understanding of verbal messages and explain some elements. **Expressive language:** Can provide verbal information in sentences. Can state own needs. Has significant disordered speech sounds and so requires careful listening from the conversation partner. Will repeat information if he thinks that he has not been understood. Will recast information into an alternative form if he thinks that he has not been understood.	Mr M enjoys social interaction with trusted people. He finds it hard to initiate social interaction and will use well-scripted jokes to engage the conversation partner before drawing them towards the topic of his choice. Mr M is not assertive when social interaction is cut short and will feel dissatisfied if an interaction did not include his preferred topic. When this happens, he can feel rejected and be upset. Mr M has limited vocabulary to label his emotions and limited assertiveness to express his emotional state, so when feeling rejected, he may withdraw to his room and isolate himself. The intervention to limit this is his 'I need to talk' cards which he can use to guarantee a quality interaction with trusted staff. Mr M does have receptive language impairment and needs information given to him in simple forms, slowly and with easy vocabulary. It is the conversation partner's responsibility to do this. If the conversation partner does not do this, Mr M will not disclose if he has not understood. He will guess at the meaning. This can result in communication breakdown and misunderstandings. If misunderstandings occur, Mr M can feel rejected and be upset (as above). Mr M has disordered speech sounds that cannot be improved. Mr M has good awareness of his speech sound problems. Mr M will employ his disordered speech sounds in order to elicit attention or support (special care) in some social situations (e.g. from members of the public).	**Green (most calm):** Encourage use of 'I need to talk' cards. Ask open questions that enable Mr M to have an equal turn in an exchange (an open question is one that requires a longer answer). Model social interactions that do not follow a script so that Mr M can experience non-scripted situations. Give information in bite-size chunks with time to think. Write down key words and draw stick-men pictures to support attention, listening, understanding, learning, social problem solving and theory of mind. Label positive and negative emotions as experienced in real time. You can ask Mr M to wait until you have an opportunity to talk/listen 1:1 but ensure that this 1:1 is offered.

(Continued)

TABLE 4.1 Continued

Predisposing factors – communication needs	Precipitating and perpetuating factors in communication	Protective factors – how staff can support at different stages
Receptive language: Understands simple sentences. Is better when information is given in 'bite-size' pieces. Has a processing delay for verbal information so needs 'thinking time'. Has an adequate knowledge of vocabulary for everyday conversations but does not possess an age-appropriate vocabulary. The conversation partner will need to check understanding of verbal messages and explain some elements. **Expressive language:** Can provide verbal information in sentences. Can state own needs. Has significant disordered speech sounds and so requires careful listening from the conversation partner. Will repeat information if he thinks that he has not been understood. Will recast information into an alternative form if he thinks that he has not been understood.	Mr M will use scripts/jokes to start a conversation. He will also return to scripts or jokes when he wants to redirect the topic aware from emotions or difficult topics. He prefers it when the conversation partner follows his lead with scripts and jokes. If the conversation partner is not redirected by Mr M's device, he can either withdraw (end the interaction to avoid) or be confrontational (shout or swear in order to end the interaction). This has been seen when supporting Mr M with dispreferred tasks such as budgeting and room cleaning. Mr M is keen to please the conversation partner and be seen as 'good'. This impacts on his social assertiveness and his ability to express opinions that he thinks will not be well received.	**Amber (mild agitation):** Staff to initiate 1:1 support and give frequent short chats for support. Staff to respond to Mr M requests for 1:1 time in a responsive/rapid time frame (as much as practicable). Ask closed questions (questions that require a yes/no answer) so that Mr M can give his view but with lower demands on him. Ask questions that offer a forced alternative choice to lower demands (e.g. 'Do you mean _____ or _____?') Allow more time for communication. Give more thinking time. The more agitated he is, the less you should say to avoid language increasing agitation. Acknowledge and label his feelings for him (e.g. 'I can see that you are frustrated') Try to notice and praise Mr M to increase self-esteem and promote positive communication. Once Mr M returns to 'green'/calm, move to 'green' communication strategies.

(Continued)

TABLE 4.1 Continued

Predisposing factors – communication needs	Precipitating and perpetuating factors in communication	Protective factors – how staff can support at different stages
Pragmatic skill level: Has highly developed awareness of the conversation partners' facial expression and uses this to check their understanding of his expressive language. Can follow standard pragmatics (e.g. take turns, be relevant, give appropriate quantities, present information in an appropriate manner and adapt for different social situations). Finds opening conversations hard and uses jokes to do this. Tends to follow the same script rather than generate novel content for basic social discourse.		**Red (agitated):** Allow Mr M to withdraw from a situation and give him 'communicative space' (aim = allow flight from a situation that stresses Mr M). Offer Mr M 1:1 talking time once he returns to interactive levels (aim = demonstrating acceptance of Mr M's emotions and showing him that he does not need to be 'perfect'). Use empathetic listening to allow Mr M to talk with no attempt to problem-solve (aim = allowing Mr M to express his views and feelings without challenge). Offer Mr M 1:1 talking time for up to 10 minutes every hour to explore how he is feeling (aim = support of emotions in order to promote him returning to amber or green). Staff interaction: Pause between each sentence to allow Mr M the conversational turn if he would like it Do not interrupt Mr M Follow Mr M's topics Once Mr M returns to 'amber'/mild agitation, move to 'amber' communication strategies.
Reading and writing: Not formally assessed but can read some easy-read materials. Requires help with spelling.		
Other: Poor vocabulary for labelling emotions and will tend to talk about positive emotions only. Will avoid discussing 'hard' topics via redirection of the conversation partner.		

High-secure hospital

The Secretary of State for Health (England and Wales) has a duty, under Part One, Section 4 of the National Health Service Act 2006, to provide hospital accommodation and services for persons who are liable to be detained under the Mental Health Act 1983, and who, in the opinion of the Secretary of State, require treatment under conditions of high security on account of their dangerous, violent or criminal propensities.

The UK has four high-secure services. In England, three hospitals provide the following high-secure services, with around 700 beds available:

- services for people who are deaf (Rampton Hospital)
- male mental illness (Broadmoor, Rampton and Ashworth Hospitals)
- personality disorder services (Broadmoor, Rampton and Ashworth Hospitals)
- learning disability services for men (Rampton Hospital only)
- women's service (Rampton Hospital).

The State Hospital Carstairs provides care for Scotland with 140 beds.

High-secure services provide care and treatment to those adults who present a grave risk of harm to others and who cannot be managed in lower levels of security and who must not be able to escape from hospital. High-secure services provide a model of integrated services incorporating all elements of the service pathway and aim to deliver effective, timely, therapeutic recovery-focused services for patients with a mental disorder assessed as presenting a serious risk of harm to others.

The core objectives of high-secure care are to:

- assess and assertively treat mental disorder
- provide a safe and therapeutic environment
- protect others by reducing the likelihood of current and future interpersonal violence
- maintain dignity through individualised compassionate care
- improve health and well-being (including physical, mental and spiritual).

The principles of care are:

- patient-centred physical and mental health care pathways
- integrated security

- focus on recovery
- robust evidence-based interventions/treatment
- efficient pathway management
- therapeutic environments
- structured rehabilitation activities
- effective multi-disciplinary team working
- carer involvement *(NHS England, 2021)*.

The main difference between high-secure care and other forms of secure care is the level of security.

Patients entering high-secure hospitals have very high levels of security need (Williams et al., 2020). Clearly, security protocols impact on the hospital staff also. All hospital staff members are searched via airline-style screening on entry – items such as mobile phones (and many other items) cannot be taken into the hospital.

There are strict security protocols for all staff to abide by while undertaking their role. For example, an SLT would need to:

- book appointments in advance
- check in with staff colleagues on the ward or unit to see if the appointment can go ahead
- take advice on the day as part of a dynamic risk assessment of the patient to determine whether enhanced security is advised. For example, ward-based staff might advise than an SLT session can go ahead but with a member of ward-based staff observing outside the room or present in the room. Ward-based staff directly observing can be a source of anxiety for professionals as well as for patients. Patients are possibly more used to this, and it is important to prioritise these safety measures. Another way to consider this is to see such requirements as training opportunities. A member of the nursing staff directly observing in the room may be there for security reasons but will often ask afterwards about what you were doing and why, thereby creating an opportunity to discuss hidden SLCN.

Confidentiality is also subject to a security constraint. Any information relevant to the care of the patient or to the security of the establishment must be disclosed. Any issues about this should always be discussed with the lead clinician or a manager. While patient consent would always be sought, information must be disclosed. If a patient refused an assessment, this would be reported in the notes. Where an SLT is required to provide a written report, this would be done even if the patient objected (such objection is rare in our experience).

Security also leads to restrictions on materials used. Computers can only be accessed in very controlled settings within high-secure establishments. Items such as paperclips, biro caps, pens, etc. can be fashioned into weaponry. It is advisable to remove such items and to organise any materials into a closed folder or pouch to ensure that all material is removed; leaving advice sheets or exercises with patients may not be permissible and requires discussion with the patient's team.

Mandatory induction is provided to all staff working in high-secure settings, giving an opportunity to think through issues. Where an SLT (or other professional) is conducting commissioned work, the commissioning agent should explain any security protocols and the process for entering and moving around the hospital. Where an SLT is not part of staff and is visiting, they will be accompanied at all times. An inevitable consequence of the security is that it can be slower than usual to accomplish tasks, but it is important not to lose sight of the priority that security has.

The principles of a care programme and a care pathway outlined for low- and medium-secure care, also apply to high-secure environments. The remainder of this section will highlight communication issues and the role of SLT in high-secure care.

Patients are admitted to an assessment ward initially and will typically stay there for at least three months to undergo very detailed assessment. In some cases, the patient may have unclear or multiple diagnoses. The team will gradually work out what the diagnosis is. In some cases, medication can be withdrawn under a carefully agreed protocol to try to establish the essence of the patient's difficulties. Assessment is provided by psychiatrists, forensic psychologists, forensic social workers and occupational therapists. SLT input varies from Rampton having a well-established SLT service to the other establishments having provision varying from a small team to sessional input to periods with no service.

When a patient is ready for assessment will be determined by the clinical team. Ideally, they will be initially stabilised (in terms of any pressing physical health needs and their medication), but in some circumstances SLT input will be requested as part of this process.

Case example

A 28-year-old male with acute psychosis exacerbated by ceasing to take medication was admitted as an emergency from police cells. The patient was also profoundly deaf and unable to communicate. Initial SLT assessment showed that the patient could not use sign language, but did have basic lip-reading abilities. He was frightened and bored and desperately wanted to go outside to kick a ball around. The SLT worked with the psychiatrist to obtain basic information to determine immediate care needs and to establish the most effective way to communicate with him on the ward.

Speech and language assessment is routinely used in some high-secure settings. The purpose of the assessment may vary, but in all cases a profile of communication abilities can be provided, specific diagnoses can be highlighted (e.g. a stammer or a motor speech problem), any limitations on the person's ability to communicate can be highlighted, and any communication implications for other aspects of the patient's care can be stated. For example, a person may have insufficient language skills to manage verbally mediated interventions such as psychotherapy; other patients may lack language skills to cope with group work, or may need the group facilitator to reduce the verbal loading.

There is no standardised assessment of speech and language for adults with severe mental health difficulties, so some years ago SLTs at Broadmoor hospital developed a minimum data set to guide assessment with consensus input from the specialist interest group of SLTs. The Broadmoor Assessment (Bryan 2000) is given in Appendix 11.

While this might seem a very formal approach to assessment, patients who are suspicious, paranoid or highly distractable may find a formal situation with relatively simple-to-understand instructions and repetitive activities such as naming pictures much less threatening.

In many cases, more functional assessment, discussion of topics, etc. will not follow for many months until a relationship of trust has been negotiated.

Case example

A 20-year-old man was referred to SLT after being in the hospital for some time. He rarely spoke, was making little progress and did not leave his ward, which was one of the most restrictive wards. The patient initially would not come into a room with the SLT but would non-verbally interact for a few seconds in the corridor and did not object to the SLT returning. Over the next nine months, the patient gradually sat in a room with the door open and with his chair close to the door with no barrier to his exit. Gradually, he would join in with silent tasks such as card sorting designed to de-sensitise him to one-to-one non-verbal interaction, and when that was established, verbal interaction was gradually introduced.

Eventually, over many sessions, the formal assessment was completed. The assessment showed that he had more language than usually apparent with a developmental level equivalent to ten years. Some insight into his thinking could be carefully explored, and this subsequently contributed to achieving a more informed risk assessment which 'reduced' his risk level (within the high-secure setting).

With the agreement of the team, a functional language programme commenced but was unsuccessful because the ward team were unable to continue this between short SLT sessions. Subsequently, a ward change (less restrictive) enabled an off-ward programme to commence with staff supported by SLT to reduce communication loading and to manage basic structured communication and checking back for meaning. The key worker was also supported to manage very structured conversation during physical activity (e.g. table tennis or washing-up).

Over the next year, the patient's activity programme ramped up, therapeutic engagement with his psychiatrist commenced, and the team agreed that SLT input should be suspended as the sessions were getting in the way of his off-ward activities. It was, however, agreed that he should be referred back to SLT for further input before any verbally mediated interventions commenced. This case does highlight that for many people in high-secure settings, their progress though the care pathways is slow, which reduces the pressure to complete the task and allows the SLT to watch and wait or gradually build up interaction.

Suitability for verbally mediated interventions is a further area where SLT advice may be helpful. Group interventions such as anger management require a high level of verbal ability as well as knowledge and experience of how to behave in a group situation. Group-based intervention has been shown to be effective in enabling patients to progress through high-secure care pathways (Sturgeon, Tyler and Gannon 2018). However, dropping out of a group or being asked to leave due to being unable to tolerate group dynamics will hinder the patient's progress. Where the patient has insufficient language skills to manage group work, this should be discussed with the clinical team. In many cases, if the group material can be adapted to be more accessible, the patient will have a better chance of coping. A protocol to guide staff can be personalised to an individual patient and is included in the

Broadmoor Assessment in Appendix 11. For individual interventions, music or arts therapy might be a less verbally demanding alternatives to, for example, psychotherapy.

Murphy has written extensively about managing and treating patients with autism in high-secure care (Murphy 2020; Murphy and Mullens 2017; Murphy and Broyd 2019; Murphy and Allely 2019). Autism is an example of a disorder that is developmental in origin, but which persists into adulthood. An example of SLT input is given below in relation to a patient with autism and personality disorder.

Case example

The Broadmoor Assessment showed that Jason presents with low normal language abilities with some restrictions on his ability to convey information via language. His comprehension is rather literal with difficulties in shifting topic. His style of interaction can be loud, with fast bursts of speech and frequent use of derogatory comments and expletives which listeners may interpret as indicating aggression. Jason tends to focus on topics that interest him and has limited awareness of listener perspectives. Jason has difficulties with written language, which are suggestive of long-term developmental difficulties.

Jason was able to engage in interpersonal communication, although this usually arose where the listener responded to his complaints or comments. Jason did ask for clarification when he did not understand, and he engaged well in discussion of interpretation of word meanings. Sometimes he stated a brief point, but occasionally he tended to dominate the conversation and to revert to personal topics. Jason tended to assume that the listener knew more about him than was the case, and had limited awareness of the listener's perspective. Jason has a number of idiosyncratic views about language that relate to his literal interpretations; for example, he was greatly irritated by the use of social stereotypes such as 'good morning' which he perceives to be stating the obvious and possibly inaccurate. Jason had limited facial expression and little eye contact.

On the Social Avoidance and Distress Scale (Watson and Friend, 1969), Jason scored 25/28, indicating a high level of social distress and a high degree of avoidance. His profile on the Communication Checklist – Adult (CC-A) (Whitehouse and Bishop, 2009) showed:

Parameter	Scaled score
Language structure	6
Pragmatic difficulties	2
Social engagement	1

This profile is strongly suggestive of autistic spectrum disorder (or autism, as is more popularly used by individuals to define themselves at the time of writing). The profile shows language ability within the low normal range, but considerable difficulties with pragmatic aspects of language and social engagement.

Initial recommendations to the clinical team were that:

- Jason has some restrictions on his verbal language abilities and that he is unlikely to understand written information (particularly if it is of no interest to him).
- Jason is experiencing a high degree of distress when involved in interpersonal communication.
- Jason has a speech style that is often associated with aggression. Staff should ensure that they do not react to this.
- Jason should have a limited number of sessions of SLT to explore whether his awareness of communication issues can be improved. He may also benefit from learning some alternative strategies to deal with some of his reactions. For example, it may be possible to negotiate an alternative to verbal abuse in relation to other people. It should also be possible to agree a set of guidance for communicating with Jason.
- Jason would benefit from opportunities to use his language skills positively within his interests. For example, a physics discussion group or facilitated session with another patient who shares the same interest or involvement in small group activities where word definitions are discussed.

The team agreed to a short series of SLT sessions, and during that time it became apparent that ward-based staff were struggling with interpersonal communication. The SLT subsequently refined the advice for professionals and provided a training session for all staff in contact with the patient, aimed at raising awareness of his communication difficulties and providing consistent strategies for managing his issues. This is a lengthy case example, but it brings into sharp focus the impact of SLCN on progress through the care pathway. Difficulty with day-to-day communication affects care, and makes risk assessment very difficult, given that risk assessment is a verbally mediated process, so that patients can end up housed in more restrictive parts of high-secure establishments.

Case example

Some patients present with SLCN that pre-date the development of their mental health condition. An example would be a patient with a stammer. Intervention would be the same as for any other setting but adapted to the setting. Explaining his stammer to staff is helpful. Below is an example, for a 35-year-old patient with schizophrenia.

The stammer is severe and the patient associates the stammer as arising due to sexual abuse experienced as a child. The key features of his stammer are:

- blocking at laryngeal level with no sound produced
- disrupted shallow breathing
- repetition of sounds in the beginning, middle and end of words
- word repetitions
- phrase repetitions
- sound prolongations
- tension in the face, jaw and neck regions
- facial tic
- poor posture for speaking.

One-to-one therapy focused on relaxation, breathing and posture. Eventually, a simple 'easy stammer' structured approach (Irwin 1972) was used which involves stretching the first word and stopping and re-starting a word with a stretch if a stammer occurs. The only adaptation to the technique is not touching the patient (e.g. during breathing exercises), as this is not permitted for security reasons. The patient gradually learned the technique but remained selective in its use, partly due to lack of motivation, partly because achieving more communication led to more demands to communicate, which he could not always cope with. Professionals working with him needed support to ensure that language demands did not overwhelm him. The patient did manage some therapeutic engagement with his team and also managed to re-establish contact with a family member.

Within this book, there is discussion of ageing within the prison population. The same issues become evident in high-secure care. Some patients remain in high-secure services for many years; others enter at an older age. It is common to see patients with conditions such as stroke and Parkinson's disease. It should be noted that a significant number of patients in mental health settings have physical health problems (Voller et al., 2016). In addition, patients may develop communication difficulties as a side effect of mediation. Some antipsychotic medications can lead to dry mouth, and clozapine is an example of a medication that commonly causes hyper-salivation which impacts on speaking and quality of life (Maher et al 2016).

Drug-induced dysarthria can also occur in people who have taken significant amounts of antipsychotic medication. The Frenchay Dysarthria Assessment (Enderby and Palmer, 2008) can be modified to ensure that the SLT does not touch the patient. Intervention can address both speech and swallowing issues. Therapy would be individualised, with common modifications being to proceed slowly using a very structured approach. Ensuring that staff understand the difficulties and take a systematic approach to managing them is also crucial. Such patients need reinforcement 'little and often', so incorporating a speech practice routine into routine interactions with a key worker or regular sessions with an occupational therapist can help to keep the patient focused and to support memory for the techniques if the patient has other cognitive problems. Typically, well-established, regular support will be effective, but the patient may deteriorate, for example, if the key worker leaves or if the patient changes ward. In this circumstance, a short period of SLT input is required to re-establish the most effective communication possible.

The above discussion indicates that a person in a secure hospital with SLCN is likely to have barriers to accessing the stepped psychological interventions offered to address the reason for being in hospital. The individual will also have challenges with learning new skills and embedding the skills into their daily lives. There is a need for specialist SLT assessment and input so that such care and treatment can be made accessible and effective when patients have SLCN (Gregory and Bryan, 2015; Cronin and Addo, 2021). However, despite improvements in SLT availability, there are still many secure settings without an SLT service.

Most patients leaving high-secure provision will move to a medium-secure setting or may be returned to prison if they have a custodial sentence to complete.

Leaving hospital

As the person progresses through their hospital stay, they will move from treatment to recovery and towards discharge from hospital. If the person started their care in medium-secure hospital, a move to a low-secure setting will usually occur (Clark et al., 2017; Sustere and Tarpey, 2019). If the person has a criminal conviction and a sentenced period to serve, they may transfer to prison to complete the remainder of their sentence. Discharge from any secure hospital setting can be complex and time-consuming and should be structured via careful discharge planning (Gowda et al., 2019). Areas that need to be addressed include: involvement of the individual and their family or friends; ensuring that all required services are involved and working together; managing the transition from one setting to another with care for the emotional well-being of the people involved; the involvement of an independent mental health advocate (IMHA) (National Institute for Health and Care Excellence, 2016).

If a person moves from low-secure services to the community, there is a requirement to consider ongoing support during the transition after the person has left hospital (National Institute for Health and Care Excellence, 2016). Risks associated with leaving a secure hospital setting include homelessness, self-harm, suicide and reoffending, so discharge plans should be comprehensive in order to address these needs (National Institute for Health and Care Excellence, 2016; Fazel et al., 2016a).

Some geographic locations in the UK have specialist community forensic teams (SCFTs) who are commissioned to provide least-restrictive care to people as they transition from a secure hospital setting to living in their community (Mental Health Taskforce, 2016).

If the person moved from prison to a secure hospital, their progression route may include returning to prison and being released from that location at the end of their custodial sentence. This will be managed via the offender manager pathway (HM Prison and Probation Services, 2021). The important factor in the transition from secure hospital to prison is ensuring that all assessment and treatment data is transferred with the individual so that all parties are aware of the progress made (National Institute for Health and Care Excellence, 2016).

Five good communication standards

In recognition of the prevalence of SLCN in specialist hospitals that cater for people with learning disabilities or autism, the Royal College of Speech and Language Therapists published the 'Five good communication standards: Reasonable adjustments to communication that individuals with learning disability and/or autism should expect in specialist hospital and residential settings' in 2013. The document (which is available online) details the five standards that should be met to reduce the risk of communication breakdown (Royal College of Speech and Language Therapists, 2013):

1. There is a detailed description of how best to communicate with the individual person.
2. Services (such as secure hospital settings) demonstrate how they support the individual person with communication needs to be involved with decisions about their care and their services.
3. Staff value and use competently the best approaches to communication with each individual person that they support.

4. Services create opportunities, relationships and environments that make individual people want to communicate.
5. The individual person is supported to understand and express their needs in relation to their health and well-being.

While this document details the communication standards for secure hospital settings, it is expected that a version for all criminal justice settings will be available in the near future.

The prison estate

Following the legal processes in court, an individual can be sentenced to custody – which results in a transfer from court to prison. This section will outline details of the prison estate and indicate what is prescribed to happen in the early days of custody.

His Majesty's Prison and Probation Service (HMPPS) manages the 117 prisons in England and Wales. The Scottish Prison Service and Northern Ireland Prison Service manage the prisons in their respective countries. Prisons in England and Wales can be operated by either the public sector or under contract to the private sector via competitive tender (Beard, 2021).

Prisons are subject to inspection by His Majesty's Inspectorate of Prisons (HMIP) who judge the standard of the detention within a prison under the four domains of safety, respect, purposeful activity and rehabilitation and release planning (HM Inspectorate of Prisons, 2021a). This is to ensure that the prison setting meets the minimum standards of International Human Rights (Office of the High Commissioner for Human Rights, 2022). Despite this inspection regime, it is reported that UK prisons are largely old buildings with poor facilities, of poor design for present-day regimes, are overcrowded and in need of maintenance to the fabric of the building (Beard, 2021). For this reason, transfer from court to prison can be a stressful experience as the newly convicted person may not know which prison they will be accommodated in and what to expect when they arrive.

While the prison estate is a collection of prisons, each one varies in a range of ways, by:

- security category
- the nature of people who are accommodated there (e.g. gender, type of conviction)
- the establishment function of the prison (i.e. the types of prisoners that can be held there)
- the design of the buildings and site

- the local governance of the prison senior leadership team
- any investment into the prison and what the expenditure is used for.

Each of these variables will be explored in more depth in order to set the scene for early days in custody.

Prison security category falls into four levels (Ministry of Justice, 2020b):

- Category A establishments cater for people who would pose the most threat to the public, the police or national security should they escape. They are people who pose a high risk of violence. Security conditions in category A prisons are designed to make escape impossible.
- Category B prisons offer accommodation to people who do not pose a threat such that they need to be held in the highest security conditions but do need to be housed in a setting where the potential for escape should be made very difficult. They are people who pose a risk of violence.
- Category C prison settings house people who require more supervision and monitoring than would be offered in an open prison but are considered to be people who are unlikely to make a determined attempt to escape. They are people who pose some risks of violence in some circumstances.
- Category D prisons are 'open conditions'. These prisons house people who are low risk for escape or violence. They may have been tested at higher levels of security and been found to be trustworthy. Open conditions allow for people to leave the prison site unaccompanied for agreed work or leisure activities.

Prison as a concept has three overarching goals – to protect the public, to provide a deterrent against crime, and to rehabilitate people who have been convicted of crimes so that future offending is decreased (Gauke, 2018). In order to achieve this, each prison has one or more establishment function – an operation that the prison offers to the wider custodial estate. This is so that a prison can offer certain services or interventions to a high standard, rather than trying to meet the needs of a diverse population. This model requires the convicted person to be residing at the establishment that can offer appropriate services as defined in their sentence plan (HM Prison and Probation Services, 2021). The result is that a sentenced person can move prisons numerous times during their sentence.

Prison establishment functions (National Offender Management Service, 2017):

- Remand prisons offer accommodation to people who are charged with a crime and are awaiting the conclusion of their legal process. These are people who were not granted bail when charged with a crime due to risks associated with them, so were 'remanded in custody'. Because people who are in custody on remand are not convicted, remand prisons may offer more privileges than a prison offering accommodation to sentenced people.

- A local prison, also known as 'nearest reception prison', is the prison closest in geographic distance to the court which sentenced the person. This is the prison that most people will be taken to on the day of sentencing prior to being moved (depending on specifics such as where the person is from, length of sentence, severity of crime, links with organised crime, etc.). This is also the prison that a person may be transferred to in the last weeks of their sentence for release if it is local to where they live.

- Dispersal prisons house people who are higher risk (category A or B prisoners) and who are serving longer sentences such as life sentences. The name 'dispersal' comes from the function of the prison – that the prison staff can move, or disperse, a person at short notice in order to disrupt any criminal activities.

- Training prisons offer accommodation for category C prisoners with increased emphasis on skills for employment. All of the UK training prisons are adult male prisons.

- Resettlement: resettlement is the term used for the support that a person in prison has prior to release to help them have the best possible outcomes. Most category C and D prisons offer a resettlement function.

- Closed prisons are all category A, B and C prisons where security is such that the convicted person should not be able to escape.

- Open prisons are category D prisons where there are lower levels of security, more privileges, fewer prison officers and a more individualised daily routine.

- Specialist units within a larger prison. Some prisons offer specialist care and treatment within smaller 'units' inside the grounds of a larger prison. Such units are aimed to meet the needs of specific convicted people such as those who have attracted certain diagnostic labels or those who need trauma-informed care in order to progress in their sentence. Units such as this are referred to as therapeutic communities (TC) or psychologically informed planned environments (PIPE).

- Separate units within a larger prison. Some prisons offer separate units in order to accommodate people in prison who require separation from the general prison population. This can be accommodation for people who have been convicted of certain crimes (e.g. crimes of a sexual nature), people who are vulnerable in prison (e.g. because they disclosed information about a peer) or people who have declared that they need to be separate for their own protection (e.g. because of past employment such as being a police officer).

- Offer specialist rehabilitation. Some prisons offer specialist rehabilitation for certain convictions such as Violent Offender Treatment Programmes (VOTP) and Sex Offender

Treatment Programmes (SOTP). A smaller number of prisons offer adapted VOTP (AVOTP) and adapted SOTP (ASOTP) for people with lower IQ, literacy issues or learning needs.

- Young offender institutions (YOIs) offer a custodial setting for boys aged 15–17 and young adult men aged 18–21 or for women aged 15–21.

Some prisons offer a combination of functions – for example, a prison can be a category C training and resettlement prison which has a remand function to serve the local courts and offers a number of separate bed spaces for people who are vulnerable or isolating for their own protection.

Prisons of different ages have different designs. Of the 117 prisons in use today, the oldest were purpose-built in Victorian times and tend to be within towns – often close to amenities as towns have developed over time. These purpose-built Victorian prisons have mostly become local prisons. They usually offer space for large numbers of people within large house blocks over numerous floors. There is often limited outdoor space (Beard, 2021).

The next phase of prison development was the mid-twentieth century in the era after the Second World War. Prisons established at this time were the redevelopment of sites that had been built for other purposes such as military bases or airfields. These prisons tend to be larger sites, with more green space and located further away from population centres. The buildings themselves tend to be over one or two floors. These prisons have mostly become category D establishments (Karthaus, Block, and Hu, 2019).

The most recent phase of prison building has been in the last 30 years, where prison design has aimed to offer purpose-built buildings which are more suited to rehabilitation – offering space for sports, education and employment skills training. The more recently constructed prisons offer better security features such as improved line of sight, and some offer improved conditions for prisoners such as in-cell showers and telephones (Beard, 2021).

The prison experience can be very much influenced by the prison that a person is housed in, as well as their personal resilience. 'Individuals do not arrive in prison as blank slates but import pre-existing coping styles, values, experiences and characteristics into prison with them, shaping how they respond to prison' (Muirhead, Butler and Davidson, 2021, p.3). Muirhead and colleagues (2021) investigated how individuals respond to sharing a cell and found that if the person in prison has skills in developing positive relationships with peers, they reported improved well-being while sharing a cell. Denkers and McGinty (2022) found that a person's ability to acquire skills, to self-regulate their emotions, and to understand situations from different perspectives all influenced substance misuse and self-harm in a UK prison. Social skills and problem-solving abilities increased the individual's potential to tolerate the prison setting (Kızılkaya, Ünsal and Karaca, 2022). The prison's size in terms of population numbers, overcrowding, facilities, staffing levels, proximity to family support networks and incidence of violence also play a role in the individual's ability to cope in prison (Western, 2021). Prisons vary in terms of provision of interventions that can help a person to cope, and limited access to such interventions can increase the potential for poor experiences when combined with the personal history of the individual (Zhong et al., 2021).

Each prison has some local decision making which is the responsibility of the prison senior leadership team. This enables the governing team to make decisions relating to budgets, expenditure, staff recruitment, service contracts and local priorities within the setting (House of Commons Justice Committee, 2019). This has also resulted in some variation between prisons based on the decisions made, such as investment in technology or sports facilities.

In addition, it is universally recognised that the prison estate in the UK is in poor condition (National Audit Office, 2020). The majority of the buildings are old, of a poor design and overcrowded (Beard, 2021). There are significant building maintenance issues with four out of ten prisons in need of repair in order to remain operational (National Audit Office, 2020). Prison cells that were designed to house one or two people are offering housing for more than that number, resulting in overcrowding, and facilities such as bathrooms are in a poor state of repair (Ismail, 2020). Add to this the reducing staffing levels, the potential for violence, the increase in self-harm within the prison estate and the increasingly complex health needs of prisoners, which give a very daunting overall picture of the prison setting (Perrett et al., 2020). The aim for the future is to provide clean, ventilated single-accommodation cells with private bathroom facilities that offer the individual a single bed, storage for possessions, a chair and table (Beard, 2021).

Arrival in prison

Whether a person is arriving in prison on remand, or whether they are arriving from court having been sentenced, the process remains very similar. This section will refer to the person coming into the prison as the 'arriving person' so as not to differentiate between a remanded person and a sentenced person.

An arriving person is escorted to the prison in secure transport which is often a bus with blacked-out windows and small compartments inside to contain the passengers. The arriving person is usually taken to the nearest reception prison.

Following entry of the bus to the prison setting via numerous gates and doors, the secure transport staff team will provide paperwork to the prison reception staff prior to moving the arriving people one by one to a holding cell. The holding cell resembles a waiting room and will contain all the arriving people who are received at the prison in that time period.

On a one-by-one basis, arriving people are asked to participate in their reception process. This includes (National Offender Management Service, 2020a):

- A check of all legal paperwork to ensure that the detention in prison is lawful.
- A check of the Person Escort Record (PER) paperwork to ensure that any immediate medical needs or vulnerabilities are identified as soon as possible.
- Identity is checked to ensure that they are the person who has been remanded or sentenced. A photograph and fingerprints are taken, and a prison identity card with a unique prison number is provided. The identity card is required on a daily basis in the prison setting, so should be kept securely by the individual.
- An electronic account is created for the arriving person on the prison digital system. This account is where the arriving person will accrue moneys, complete personal shopping and operate everyday activities such as ordering prescriptions. The account is also required for using the telephone to contact friends and family. Because it can take up to 48 hours for telephone access to be applied to the account, a newly arriving person is usually offered a phone call to a friend or family member to let loved ones know that all is well after the journey.
- The arriving person will be searched to ensure that they do not have contraband on their person. This may be a 'pat down search', passing through a metal detector, sitting on a metal-detecting chair or being passed through a body scanner. The advent of body scanners has reduced the need for intrusive searches where the arriving person is required to undress.
- All the property that the arriving person has with them is handed in to be searched. Any contraband items such as mobile phones, cash or cigarettes will be removed and stored. Any inappropriate items such as sunglasses or slogan tee shirts will also be stored. These items are returned to the arriving person when they are released from prison.
- The arriving person is permitted a limited amount of property within the prison due to storage limitations, so they will be invited to select which items they would like to retain for daily use (e.g. clothes, personal hygiene products, books, photographs).
- The arriving person will have a face-to-face interview with a member of the prison reception staff to ensure that they know their legal rights, to have an assessment of their well-being, to check for any risks of self-harm or suicide and to consider if there are any risks of violence to other people (staff or peers). If required, the arriving

person can be supported via a care plan (known as an Assessment, Care in Custody and Teamwork (ACCT) document). The arriving person will also have their suitability to share a cell assessed at this point (known as Cell Sharing Risk Assessment (CSRA)).

- Lastly, the arriving person will have a face-to-face interview with a medical doctor or a registered nurse. This is to complete a health and well-being assessment aimed at identifying any physical or emotional health needs. It covers previous medical history, social history and medication. It is the earliest opportunity for the arriving person to discuss any medical needs and be referred to any specialist professionals such as opticians, therapists or substance misuse services. Well-being needs such as thoughts to self-harm are discussed, and the healthcare professional can implement the ACCT document care plan.

- If this is the arriving person's first time in prison, if they are identified as vulnerable, if they are a young offender, if they have been given a life sentence or if they have been charged with or convicted of homicide of a family member, special attention is paid to their well-being. This is because these factors increase the potential for the arriving person to have suicidal ideation.

The reception process can take some time, but the intention is that the arriving person is supported through these tasks as quickly as possible. The arriving person is offered food, drink and the use of toilet facilities during their time in the reception department.

Once the reception process is complete, the arriving person is offered access to shower facilities and located in a cell. They are provided with bedding, towels, clothes if needed and a first-night pack which contains basic toiletries, hot drink ingredients and sweets. They may be sharing the cell with a new person. The cell should contain (in addition to furniture) a television, a kettle, a telephone and basic plastic cutlery. If the arriving person is being supported on an ACCT document care plan, they will be checked by a prison officer at regular intervals.

Prison induction

Arrival at prison is often overwhelming, especially if this is the first time in prison (Cadet, 2019), and 58% of arriving people report that coming to prison provokes anxiety and stress (Jacobson, Edgar and Loucks, 2007). It is acknowledged that the arriving person will have struggled to take in information during the reception process due to intense emotions, unfamiliarity with the terminology and the unaccustomedness of the environment (National Offender Management Service, 2020a). To address this, each prison offers an induction which provides information about the prison day, the services on offer, employment and education.

Prison induction is formed of two parts. The first part is 'induction to custody' in general – this is generic to all prisons and covers the legal matters, offender management and the rights of people in prison. The second part is specific to the prison where the arriving person is located and is called 'local induction'. This part of the induction will be more person-centred, such as exploring the individual's learning needs, and will allow for the arriving person to start gaining an understanding of the routines which they are part of (National Offender Management Service, 2020a).

In recent times, the induction process has included asking arriving people about their needs in terms of learning, communication or neurodiversity via a rapid screening tool (Criminal Justice Joint Inspection, 2021). Depending on the setting, this may be verbally mediated or a computer-based self-assessment which is designed for the purpose. In some prisons, the screening is conducted by professionals from the in-house education provision, while in others it may be an unqualified person who has had some training to complete the task. It is well documented that the value of any screening is impacted by the training and support level that trainers have (Bryan et al., 2015). This screening process, while crude, should identify pre-existing conditions such as neurodivergent needs, and can inform referrals to specialists to support the individual.

The Ministry of Justice defines neurodivergent needs as:

> learning difficulties and disabilities (LDDs) which generally include: learning disability, dyslexia, dyscalculia, and developmental coordination disorder (DCD, also known as dyspraxia); other common conditions, such as attention deficit hyperactivity disorder (ADHD, including ADD), autism spectrum conditions (ASC), developmental language disorder (DLD, including speech and language difficulties), tic disorders (including Tourette's syndrome and chronic tic disorder); and cognitive impairments due to acquired brain injury (ABI).
>
> *(Criminal Justice Joint Inspection, 2021, p.12)*

This information is sought as part of the prison local induction because of the high prevalence of learning, communication or neurodivergent needs in the prison population. The data has been summarised as (Barton and Hobson, 2017; Criminal Justice Joint Inspection, 2021):

- 20% of the adult prison population are reported as requiring help with reading, writing or numeracy, while 80% of the adult prison population reported problems reading and comprehending standard written information.

- 20-30% of adults in prison are reported to have a learning difficulty which interferes with their ability to fully understand criminal justice processes.
- In custody, the rates of learning difficulty are reported as 36% for men and 39% for women (the incidence of learning difficulty in the general population is around 10%).
- People with learning difficulties in prison are more than three times as likely to have clinically significant depression or anxiety compared with peers who have no learning difficulty.
- Prevalence in the adult prison population of dyslexia is thought to be over 50% (10% in general population).
- Rates of ADHD are around 30% of adults in prison (the incidence of ADHD in the general population is around 4%).
- Within prisons, the prevalence of autistic 'traits' or 'indicators' are captured as 16-19% compared with 1-2% in the general population.
- It is estimated that around 50% of the adult prison population have sustained an ABI compared to around 12% of the general population.
- It is estimated that as many as 80% of adult prisoners have speech, language or communication needs.

Because screening for neurodivergent needs is a relatively new practice within prison induction, the data is variable. While some prisons report neurodivergent needs on screening in as few as 12% of arriving adults to prison, other prison sites report incidence as high as 85%. This could be attributed to factors such as screener skills, screener support, application to the screening process by the arriving person at a time of stress, or demographic variations in regions associated with socio-economic needs. Neurodiversity is thought to be between 15% and 20% in the general population, and tacit knowledge from those working in adult prisons suggests that incidence would be much higher in the prison setting. The function of screening for neurodivergent needs is to indicate a potential need, thus enabling onward specialist referral and reasonable adjustments as the person enters the prison establishment (Criminal Justice Joint Inspection, 2021).

Prison induction should also include information in various forms to support the understanding of the arriving person: written information, verbal presentations, one-to-one sessions, accessible information and information in alternative forms should all be available. While this is the ideal position, we acknowledge that there is variability in the availability of accessible information between prisons.

The local induction will include information on facilities at the prison such as the education provision, sports and gym, chaplaincy and faith, health and well-being, training and employment opportunities, and access to key professionals such as offender managers.

Prisons operate on the basis of incentives, so that if a person follows the rules and contributes to the good order of the establishment, they can rise from basic level, to standard level and to enhanced level. Each level offers increased privileges such as employment opportunities a person can benefit from, access to gym sessions and increased family visits. The incentive scheme, as well as the discipline process, is explained during local induction. There is also scope for a person to have extra support in place which allows them to progress in the incentive levels via an MDT approach which is called Challenge, Support and Intervention Plan (CSIP) which was introduced to the prison setting in February 2019 (Pickering, Blagden and Slade, 2022).

Lastly, the internal economy is outlined for the arriving person. Within prison, when the arriving person is actively engaged in employment or education, they attract a small financial remuneration. This is paid electronically into their account and can be used for telephone credit, to purchase items from the internal prison 'online' shop or saved.

Jacobson et al. (2007) said of prison induction that the most important factors in helping the arriving person to settle into the prison setting were:

- relationships with other prisoners and reassurance that peers would be friendly
- prison officer attitudes, including being approachable, taking time to explain and treating prisoners with respect
- first-night environment being clean and having been able to let family know of safe arrival
- healthcare information as many arriving people had concerns relating to medical conditions or medications
- prison information relating to facilities, visits, telephones and property so that the early days in prison can be as comfortable as possible.

Progress in prison

The secure hospital stay described earlier in this chapter detailed a significant amount of team-led person-centred care and support for the individual. Conversely, the prison environment is less person-centred as it caters for larger numbers and expects individuals to be more autonomous in their progression. After the arriving person has completed their induction process, they will move to a location in the prison where they will reside for a longer period.

The key figures for supporting progression in the prison sentence are:

- The individual's personal officer (also known as key worker). This is a prison officer who is assigned to the individual following induction. Their role is to have one-to-one conversations with the individual and to engage, motivate and support. The time allocated is 45 minutes per week (Prison and Probation Ombudsman, 2020).
- The individual's offender manager – as discussed earlier in this chapter (HM Prison and Probation Services, 2021).
- The prison officers who work at the individual's residing location (often called wing or community) who will have day-to-day interactions with the individual (HM Prison and Probation Services, 2022).
- Any prison staff member who might have regular interactions with the individual such as their teacher in college, their religious leader, their workplace supervisor.
- Any member of the health and well-being team who is offering regular interactions such as a substance misuse worker or a registered mental health nurse.
- Any member of the interventions team who is providing a risk-reduction intervention as detailed on the individual's sentence plan such as a VOTP (HM Prison and Probation Services, 2021).
- Any peer support that the individual might be accessing such as the listener scheme (HM Inspectorate of Prisons, 2016).

All prisons use a computer-based system called National Offender Management Information System (NOMIS) where information about the individual and their activities is recorded. This becomes the record of progression for the individual and is used as evidence in progression reviews. The information recorded on this system is not failsafe, in that information can be missing, inaccurately recorded or influenced by unconscious bias (Rogers and Thomas, 2022).

Progression reviews occur every 6–12 months with the offender manager depending on the type and length of sentence that the individual is serving (National Offender Management Service, 2020b). The aim of the review is to consider the security category of the individual, which includes reviewing the risk of the threat that the individual poses, and whether they are a candidate for a lower level of security. The review will also ensure that progress is being made against the sentence plan (HM Prison and Probation Services, 2021). Any information which is documented on NOMIS is discussed so that the individual is getting specific feedback on strengths and areas that would benefit from reflection. The offender manager will also seek updates from other key figures for progression so that they have an overview of the individual's activities since the last review.

Parole hearings

Another form of progression review is a parole hearing (The Parole Board Rules, 2019). Whether the parole process applies to an individual is dependent on the type of sentence that the person is serving (the sentence must be over four years in length and the person must be close to, or over, the minimum time that the judge stated must be served) (Rodin, 2019). The parole hearing is conducted by a panel made up from parole board members. The panel will usually include a judge, a specialist panel member (e.g. a criminologist) and a lay panel member (Hood, Shute, and Wilcox, 2000).

The parole panel review the case in order to decide if the individual continues to present a risk to the general public (Rodin, 2019). This review will decide if the person remains at the same level of security, whether the person can be moved to a prison with a lower level of security, or whether the person can be released to the community with a set of rules to follow (licence conditions) (The Parole Board Rules, 2019).

In order to request a parole hearing, the individual must complete an application form. If the individual meets the criteria for a parole hearing, the application is accepted. The key figures for progression for the individual will gather information and written reports which explore the person's progression. This will usually include a risk assessment completed by a forensic psychologist, which is based on time spent with the individual (Fazel and Wolf, 2018). Key figures for progression, such as the offender manager and the forensic psychologist, will generally conclude their report with a recommendation relating to the individual's progression, such as release, move to a lesser level of security or completion of more risk-reduction intervention (Hood et al., 2000).

The reports and assessments are assembled to form a 'dossier'. The dossier is provided to the individual for them to read and comment on prior to their parole hearing. If the individual disagrees with anything in the dossier, they can make their own comments, which are called 'representations' (Hood et al., 2000). In some cases, the dossier can be hundreds of pages long, which presents a clear and obvious challenge to the incarcerated person in terms of literacy and SLCN (Kelly, McIvor and Richard, 2020).

The parole panel that has been allocated the case will read the dossier and representations. The parole panel might be satisfied that a decision on progression can be made by reading the papers alone (Rodin, 2019) or the panel might decide that a face-to-face hearing is required. If a face-to-face hearing is decided on, the panel, the key progression figures and the individual will be included. The face-to-face hearing may be in person or via video link technology (Suhartono and Sarayar, 2021). If the individual has financial resources or is entitled to legal aid, the individual can have a legal representative to support them. If the individual does not have access to this support, they can represent themselves in the face-to-face hearing (The Parole Board Rules, 2019).

The parole panel will focus their decision making on whether the individual has reduced their risks via successfully completing risk-reduction interventions, the recommendations from the key progression figures, whether there is a robust plan to support the person if they are progressed and whether the person has presented with good order and discipline within the prison setting in recent months or years (Padfield, 2016).

While this outline of the parole process gives a flavour of what happens, it is important to note that it can be a long and drawn-out process (Padfield, 2018), that individuals subject to the process find it stressful and that often the person finds it hard to understand what is happening and why (Kelly et al., 2020).

Release from prison

Release from prison is based on the length of the person's custodial sentence and the choices that the person has made while in prison. The three most common release situations are (Beard, 2020):

- Released from prison automatically at the halfway point of the full sentence term and serving the remainder of the sentence on licence in the community (supervised by a community offender manager (COM)).
- Released at the two-thirds point of the sentence by the parole board because the individual no longer represents a risk to the general public and serving the remainder of the sentence on licence in the community (supervised by a COM).
- Release at the end of the minimum term of a life sentence if the parole board assesses the individual as no longer presenting as a risk to the general public and serving the remainder of the sentence on licence in the community (supervised by a COM).

The rationale for releasing a person before the full term of the sentence is that this eases overcrowding in prisons, gives the individual incentive to follow good order and discipline while in prison and supports rehabilitation by creating the conditions for a period of supervision by an offender manager (Beard, 2020).

Prior to release, there is an expectation that key professionals within the prison and the community plan the release with the individual (HM Inspectorate of Prisons, 2021b). This should include:

- Allowing the person in prison to be released from a prison which is local to where they plan to live (known as local release and arranged by the Offender Manager Unit).
- Work is completed to support the individual to have a successful release. This should include housing, employment, family relationships, access to benefits, ensuring that identification and bank accounts are in place and onward referrals to services such as substance misuse services or adult social care (this work is completed by the individual and a range of professionals).
- Any risks or support needs are discussed at a multi-disciplinary meeting which can include colleagues from the police, child protection services, social workers and voluntary agencies.
- That licence conditions are formalised and that the individual is provided with a copy and given explanations to ensure understanding (completed by the individual and the offender manager).

Many prisons have a 'resettlement' team who are specialists in supporting the practical arrangements surrounding release such as housing. A voluntary organisation called Prison Advice and Care Trust (PACT) also offer support to people in prison and their families, including at the point of release. The prison healthcare provision and substance misuse service will be involved in release planning and ensuring that onward referrals and medication are provided.

While release planning is desirable and gives the optimum preparation for release, sadly not all individuals are offered robust and long-standing arrangements. Many are released to temporary housing, unemployment and gaps in their medical care (Meyler, 2021).

Release from prison can be a very difficult time for individuals – there is fear of failure, pressure to rebuild financially and socially, concerns around lifestyle choices and very real risks to the well-being of the released person (Chang et al., 2015). Two of the predictors of good outcomes following release from prison are the individual having positive mental health and the person not being a user of illicit substances (Hopkin et al., 2018).

Employment is the other predictor of outcome, in that if the individual can find and retain paid employment, their potential for positive outcomes increases (Ramakers, 2022).

Improving the prison environment

Within the prison environment, there are adjustments that could be made to improve the communication environment and lessen the impacts of SLCN. Where there is an SLT service embedded in the establishment, there is leadership and expertise to help shape such adjustments and integrate them into the establishment, ideally alongside training and support for other staff. Where there is not an SLT service, that may be harder to achieve; however, an indicative list of suggestions is given below to guide consideration of improving the communication environment within a prison for the benefit of everyone:

- Prisons tend to be noisy and crowded, with bright lights and lots of distractions. To support the sensory needs of neurodivergent people and the attention needs of the individual, planning interactions in quiet spaces at less busy times is helpful. Treatment spaces should be adjusted to have noise-absorbing furnishings and natural daylight where possible.
- Adding signage, clocks, calendars and visual planners support orientation to person, place and time. HMP Berwyn offers visual planners and pictorial menus via in-cell computers so that the individual can self-cue in ways that do not highlight the individual as vulnerable.
- All written materials should be offered in accessible form as standard as this meets the needs of the whole population without the requirement to store or provide different materials to different people (while also minimising the risk of highlighting the individual as vulnerable).
- Training for all staff in being communication aware and how to adapt communication styles. While this is possible in-house for some settings, there is training available free of charge via the Royal College of Speech and Language Therapists website (Royal College of Speech and Language Therapists, 2022).
- Provision of everyday items that support neurodivergent people to participate in communication such as eye masks, tinted glasses, earplugs, headphones and ear defenders (to reduce sensory overload and aid attention toward communication); sensory soothing objects such as 'fidget objects' and sensory diet items such as dry crunchy foods provided alongside meals also aid attention toward communication.
- Provision of information via video formats which can be viewed 'on demand' via the use of technology. HMP Berwyn has a health and well-being TV channel which provides

local information to viewers, thus supporting access to information in accessible forms, the processing needs of individuals and the need for repetition.

- Step-by-step guides with words, photographs and symbols for people who might be approaching a new situation for the first time (e.g. first time in prison, first parole hearing).
- Allowing more time for interactions with people who are suspected to have SLCN to allow for information to be given at a slower pace and to check understanding. Use of total communication strategies during the interaction to increase the chances of success (a resource for total communication strategies is located at Appendix 12).
- Using visual scales to check how people are feeling or what their opinion is. Visual scales can be used at the beginning, in the middle or at the end of the conversation. They allow either party to give feedback on their views without it feeling personal, and with emotions contained. They also support the labelling of emotions for those who find it hard to expression emotions (alexithymia) (a visual scale resource is located at Appendix 13).
- To address challenges with pragmatics and social skills, it is helpful to co-produce a set of ground rules for an interaction. This can be agreed on at the first meeting and carried over to subsequent meetings, or renegotiated as needed (an example and a resource for ground rule setting is located at Appendix 14).
- Using post-it notes or other pieces of paper when meeting with a person to set an agenda. Each person in the meeting can offer one or two agenda items, and as each is discussed, they can be turned over or put in the bin. This will help both parties feel thar their preferred topic was included in the conversation.

While these adjustments support SLCN and can be employed by any professional within the prison setting, if concerns persist about an individual's ability to communicate, a referral to SLT should always be sought.

Conclusion

In this chapter, there has been explanation of the National Probation Service, inpatient secure hospital services and prison setting from the first point of contact to the resolution of the court-imposed sentence. It is hoped that the chapter has allowed the reader to gain some awareness of the differences in these court disposals, and who the key figures are within the rehabilitation of the individual.

Of note is the incidence of SLCN in the sentenced population, especially in those who are subject to a hospital order or a custodial sentence in prison. When the aetiology of SLCN is broken down, as it is in this chapter, the reader will be left with no doubt that the SLCN of this population are exceptionally high and overtly complex with additional diagnostic overshadowing and poor health outcomes also apparent.

There is tacit knowledge from those working in the CJS that many people within the CJS will not be aware of their SLCN and are unlikely to have been under the care of an SLT (Bryan et al., 2015). There is a call for more SLT resource within prison settings, but until that is achieved, the responsibility sits with all professionals involved in the CJS to be mindful of the communication needs of those in contact with services, and to make their own informal assessment and adjustments. It should, however, be noted that many of the prison officers and other professional staff working in prisons will have had little if any training around SLCN. Signs of communication problems, which may be helpful for the wider staff to be aware of, include:

- the person having problems giving attention and being unable to listen for more than a few minutes at a time
- the person asking questions that have already been answered
- the person being unable to explain what has happened when asked (e.g. what happened in court today)
- the person explaining what has happened differently each time because they have not understood
- the person seeming to be 'behind' the topic because they are still processing something that was talked about five minutes ago
- the person using strings of 'empty speech' (e.g. saying a lot of words but without much information being conveyed)
- the person being over reliant on social phrases to 'bulk out' their speech (e.g. 'you get me', 'and another thing', etc.)
- the person using words in ways that are slightly 'wrong' because the word is new to them and they are learning its use
- unusual interaction styles and intense emotions which 'spill out' in interactions
- the conversation being heavily weighted towards the staff member because where responses are minimal or not forthcoming, there is a natural tendency to fill the gap
- the person agreeing with that which is put to them, even when it is clear that contradictory information has been offered.

This chapter has also offered ideas for adjustments and practical resources for the professional within CJS to try with individuals. While some professionals might feel that their communication style is accessible, this book challenges them to try new ideas in order to enhance accessibility, and to support the invisible disability that is SLCN.

References

Appleton, C.E. (2019) *Finding common ground: Relationship building and communication between PO and client within a community supervision setting* (Doctoral dissertation, Portland State University).

Barton, A. and Hobson, A. (2017) Learning to fail? Prisoners with special educational needs. *Prison Service Journal*, (232), 4-10.

Barton, J. (2019) 'Strengthening probation, building confidence': The task of re-designing probation. *Probation Journal*, 66(1), 131-137.

Beard, J (2020) Release from prison in England and Wales. Briefing Paper No. 5199. Available at https://researchbriefings.files.parliament.uk/documents/SN05199/SN05199.pdf [accessed 6th March 2023]

Beard, J (2021) The prison estate. Research Briefing No. 5646. Available at https://researchbriefings.files.parliament.uk/documents/SN05646/SN05646.pdf [accessed 6th March 2023]

Boardman, L., Crichton, C. and Butterworth, S. (2016) When you can't talk about it: Using Talking Mats to enable an offender with communication difficulties to express his thoughts and beliefs. *Probation Journal*, 63(1), 72-79.

Brooker, C., Collinson, B. and Sirdifield, C. (2022) Improving healthcare in adult probation services: Learning from Youth Offending Teams. *Probation Journal*. https://doi.org/10.1177/02645505211070088

Bryan, K. (2000) Broadmoor Assessment. Unpublished.

Bryan, K., Garvani, G., Gregory, J. and Kilner, K. (2015) Language difficulties and criminal justice: The need for earlier identification. *International Journal of Language and Communication Disorders*, 50(6), 763-775.

Cadet, N. (2019) 'They haven't done the course in becoming a prisoner yet': Exploring the induction experiences of neo-phyte older prisoners. *Prison Service Journal*. www.crimeandjustice.org.uk/sites/crimeandjustice.org.uk/files/PSJ%20245%20September%202019%20Journal.pdf [accessed 6th March 2023]

Casares, P. and Johnstone, L. (2015) Integration of formulation in adult multidisciplinary services across a large NHS Foundation Trust-Phases 1 and 2: Training and integration. *Clinical Psychology Forum*, 275, 20-27.

Chang, Z., Lichtenstein, P., Larsson, H. and Fazel, S. (2015) Substance use disorders, psychiatric disorders, and mortality after release from prison: A nationwide longitudinal cohort study. *The Lancet Psychiatry*, 2(5), 422-430.

Chester, V. (2018) People with intellectual and developmental disorders in the United Kingdom criminal justice system. *East Asian Archives of Psychiatry*, 28(4), 150-158.

Clark, L.L., Shurmer, D.L., Kowara, D. and Nnatu, I. (2017) Reducing restrictive practice: Developing and implementing behavioural support plans. *British Journal of Mental Health Nursing*, 6(1), 23-28.

Conrad, L.Y. and Tucker, V.M. (2019) Making it tangible: Hybrid card sorting within qualitative interviews. *Journal of Documentation*, 2, 397-416.

Cording J.R., Beggs Christofferson S.M.and Grace R.C (2016) Challenges for the theory and application of dynamic risk factors. *Psychology, Crime & Law*, 22(1-2), 84-103.

Criminal Justice Joint Inspection (2021) neurodiversity in the criminal justice system A review of evidence. Available at www.justiceinspectorates.gov.uk/cjji/wp-content/uploads/sites/2/2021/07/Neurodiversity-evidence-review-web-2021.pdf [accessed 6th March 2023]

Cronin, P. and Addo, R. (2021) Interactions with youth justice and associated costs for young people with speech, language and communication needs. *International Journal of Language & Communication Disorders*, 56(4), 797-811.

Davis, L., Houston, P.J. and Rudes, D.S. (2021) Probation Officers, Discretion, and Participatory Management. In *Oxford Research Encyclopedia of Criminology and Criminal Justice*. Oxford University Press.

Denkers, C.J. and McGinty, A. (2022) Innate health: A novel examination of what explains well-being, prosocial behavior, and aggression among men living in a UK prison. *Preprints* 2022, 2022060023. doi:10.20944/preprints202206.0023.v1

Department of Health (2008) Re-focussing the Care Programme Approach: Policy and positive practice guidance. London: Department of Health.

Department of Health (2015) Reference Guide to the Mental Health Act 1983. Available at https://assets.publishing.service.gov.uk/government/uploads/system/uploads/attachment_data/file/417412/Reference_Guide.pdf [accessed 6th March 2023]

Dickens, G.L. and O'Shea, L.E. (2018) Protective factors in risk assessment schemes for adolescents in mental health and criminal justice populations: A systematic review and meta-analysis of their predictive efficacy. *Adolescent Research Review*, 3(1), 95–112.

Drake, E.K. (2011) 'What works' in community supervision: Interim report. Olympia: Washington State Institute for Public Policy. http://dx.doi.org/10.13140/RG.2.1.3781.0404

Duke, I.H., Furtado, V., Guo, B. and Völlm, B.A. (2018) Long-stay in forensic-psychiatric care in the UK. *Social Psychiatry and Psychiatric Epidemiology*, 53(3), 313–321.

Duwe, G. (2017) The use and impact of correctional programming for inmates on pre-and post-release outcomes. US Department of Justice, Office of Justice Programs, National Institute of Justice. Available at www.ojp.gov/pdffiles1/nij/250476.pdf [accessed 6th March 2023]

Enderby, P. and Palmer, R. (2008) *Frenchay Dysarthria Assessment 2nd Edition* (FDA-2). London: Pearson.

Fazel, S., Fimińska, Z., Cocks, C. and Coid, J. (2016a) Patient outcomes following discharge from secure psychiatric hospitals: Systematic review and meta-analysis. *The British Journal of Psychiatry*, 208(1), 17–25.

Fazel, S. and Wolf, A. (2018). Selecting a risk assessment tool to use in practice: A 10-point guide. *Evidence-Based Mental Health*, 21(2), 41–43.

Fox, C., Harrison, J., Marsh, C. and Smith, A. (2018) Piloting different approaches to personalised offender management in the English criminal justice system. *International Review of Sociology*, 28(1), 35–61.

Gauke, D (2018) Prisons reform speech: The Justice Secretary delivers his first major speech on prison reform at the Royal Society of Arts in London. Available at www.gov.uk/government/speeches/prisons-reform-speech#:~:text=First%2C%20protection%20of%20the%20public,it%20is%20an%20important%20one [accessed 6th March 2023]

Georgiou, M., Oultram, M. and Haque, Q. (2019) *Standards for Forensic Mental Health Services: Low and Medium Secure Care – Third Edition*: Quality Network for Forensic Mental Health Services. Available at www.rcpsych.ac.uk/docs/default-source/improving-care/ccqi/quality-networks/secure-forensic/forensic-standards-qnfmhs/standards-for-forensic-mental-health-services-fourth-edition.pdf?sfvrsn=2d2daabf_6 [accessed 6th March 2023]

Gowda, M., Gajera, G., Srinivasa, P. and Ameen, S. (2019) Discharge planning and Mental Healthcare Act 2017. *Indian Journal of Psychiatry*, 61(Suppl. 4), S706–S709. https://doi.org/10.4103/psychiatry.IndianJPsychiatry_72_19

Gregory, J. and Bryan, K. (2015) Speech and language therapy intervention with a group of persistent and prolific young offenders in a non-custodial setting with previously undiagnosed speech, language and communication difficulties. *International Journal of Language & Communication Disorders*, 50, 1–14.

Heffernan, R. and Ward, T. (2019) Dynamic risk factors, protective factors and value-laden practices. *Psychiatry, Psychology and Law*, 26(2), 312–328.

HM Courts & Tribunals Service (2022) Statistical data set HMCTS Management Information – January 2022. Available at www.gov.uk/government/statistical-data-sets/hmcts-management-information-january-2022 [accessed 6th March 2023]

HM Inspectorate of Prisons (2016) Life in prison: Peer support. Available at www.justiceinspectorates.gov.uk/hmiprisons/wp-content/uploads/sites/4/2016/01/Peer-support-findings-paper-final-draft-1.pdf [accessed 6th March 2023]

HM Inspectorate of Prisons (2021a) Our Expectations. Available at www.justiceinspectorates.gov.uk/hmiprisons/our-expectations [accessed 6th March 2023]

HM Inspectorate of Prisons (2021b) Release planning. Available at www.justiceinspectorates.gov.uk/hmiprisons/our-expectations/prison-expectations/rehabilitation-and-release-planning/release-planning [accessed 6th March 2023]

HM Prison and Probation Services (2021) The Target Operating Model for probation services in England and Wales: Probation Reform Programme. Available at https://assets.publishing.service.gov.uk/government/uploads/system/uploads/attachment_data/file/1061048/MOJ7350_HMPPS_Probation_Reform_Programme_TOM_Accessible_English.pdf [accessed 6th March 2023]

HM Prison and Probation Services (2022) Life as a prison officer. Available at https://prisonandprobationjobs.gov.uk/prison-officer/life-as-a-prison-officer [accessed 6th March 2023]

Herman, S. and Pogarsky, G. (2020) Morality, deterrability, and offender decision making. *Justice Quarterly*, 39(1), 1–25.

Hood, R., Shute, S. and Wilcox, A. (2000) *The Parole System at Work: A Study of Risk Based Decision-Making*. Research, Development and Statistics Directorate. London: Home Office.

Hopkin, G., Evans-Lacko, S., Forrester, A., Shaw, J. and Thornicroft, G. (2018) Interventions at the transition from prison to the community for prisoners with mental illness: A systematic review. *Administration and Policy in Mental Health and Mental Health Services Research*, 45(4), 623–634.

House of Commons Justice Committee (2019) Prison Governance. Available at https://publications.parliament.uk/pa/cm201919/cmselect/cmjust/191/191.pdf [accessed 6th March 2023]

Houston, S. and Butler, M. (2019) More than just a number: Meeting the needs of those with mental illness, learning difficulties and speech and language difficulties in the criminal justice system. *Irish Probation Journal*, 16(1), 22–41.

Irwin, A. (1972) The treatment and results of 'easy-stammering'. *International Journal of Disorders of Language and Communication*, 7, 151–156.

Ismail, N. (2020) Rolling back the prison estate: The pervasive impact of macroeconomic austerity on prisoner health in England. *Journal of Public Health*, 42(3), 625–632.

Jacobson, J., Edgar, K. and Loucks, N. (2007) There When You Need Them Most: PACT's First Night in Custody Services. Birbeck Institutional Research Online. Available at www.prisonreformtrust.org.uk/uploads/documents/Pact%20-%20final%20with%20cover.pdf [accessed 6th March 2023]

Johnstone, L. (2013) Using Formulation in Teams. In L. Johnstone and R. Dallos (eds) *Formulation in Psychology and Psychotherapy* (pp.236–262). Hove: Routledge.

Karthaus, R., Block, L. and Hu, A. (2019) Redesigning prison: The architecture and ethics of rehabilitation. *The Journal of Architecture*, 24(2), 193–222.

Kelly, L., McIvor, G. and Richard, K. (2020) Prisoners' understanding and experiences of parole. *Criminal Behaviour and Mental Health*, 30(6), 321–330.

Kızılkaya, M., Ünsal, G. and Karaca, S. (2022) The effect of psychoeducation on the social skills and problem-solving skills of female prisoners. *Journal of Psychiatric Nursing/Psikiyatri Hemsireleri Dernegi*, 13(1), 1–8.

Lewis-Morton, R., James, L., Brown, K. and Hider, A. (2015) Team formulation in a secure setting: Challenges, rewards and service user involvement – A joint collaboration between nursing and psychology. *Clinical Psychology*, 1(275), 65–68.

Maguire, M., Grubin, D., Lösel, F. and Raynor, P. (2010) 'What works' and the correctional services accreditation panel: Taking stock from an inside perspective. *Criminology & Criminal Justice*, 10(1), 37–58.

Maher, S., Cunningham, A., O'Callaghan, N., Byrne, F., Mc Donald, C, McInerney, S. and Hallahan, B. (2016) Clozapine-induced hypersalivation: An estimate of prevalence, severity and impact on quality of life. *Therapeutic Advances in Psychopharmacology*, 6, 178–184.

Melvin, C.L., Langdon, P.E. and Murphy, G.H. (2020) 'I feel that if I didn't come to it anymore, maybe I would go back to my old ways and I don't want that to happen': Adapted sex offender treatment programmes: Views of service users with autism spectrum disorders. *Journal of Applied Research in Intellectual Disabilities*, 33(4), 739–756.

Mental Health Act (1983). Available online at www.legislation.gov.uk/ukpga/1983/20/contents [accessed 6th March 2023]

Mental Health Act (2007). Available online at www.legislation.gov.uk/ukpga/2007/12/contents [accessed 6th March 2023]

Mental Health Taskforce (2016) The Five Year Forward View for Mental Health. Available at www.england.nhs.uk/wp-content/uploads/2016/02/Mental-Health-Taskforce-FYFV-final.pdf[accessed 6th March 2023]

Meyler, A. (2021) Building bridges to successful reintegration. *Irish Probation Journal*, 18, 197–212.

Ministry of Justice (2020a) A Smarter Approach to Sentencing. Available at https://assets.publishing.service.gov.uk/government/uploads/system/uploads/attachment_data/file/918187/a-smarter-approach-to-sentencing.pdf [accessed 6th March 2023]

Ministry of Justice (2020b) Security Categorisation Policy Framework. Available at https://assets.publishing.service.gov.uk/government/uploads/system/uploads/attachment_data/file/1011502/security-categorisation-pf.pdf [accessed 18th March 2023]

Muirhead, A., Butler, M. and Davidson, G. (2021) Behind closed doors: An exploration of cell-sharing and its relationship with wellbeing. *European Journal of Criminology*, 20(1), 335–355.

Murphy, D. (2020) Autism: Implications for high secure psychiatric care and move towards best practice. *Research in Developmental Disabilities*, 100, 1–9.

Murphy, D. and Allely, C. (2019) Autism spectrum disorders in high secure psychiatric care: A review of the literature, future research and clinical directions. *Advances in Autism*, 6, 17–34.

Murphy, D. and Broyd, J. (2019) Evaluation of autism awareness training provided to staff in a high secure psychiatric care hospital. *Advances in Autism*, 6, 35–47.

Murphy, D. and Mullens, H. (2017) Examining the experiences and quality of life of patients with an autism spectrum disorder detained in high secure psychiatric care. *Advances in Autism*, 3, 3-14.

National Audit Office (2020) Improving the prison estate. Available at www.nao.org.uk/wp-content/uploads/2020/02/Improving-the-prison-estate.pdf [accessed 6th March 2023]

National Health Service Act (2006). London: Stationary Office.

National Institute for Health and Care Excellence (2016) Transition between inpatient mental health settings and community or care home settings. Available at www.nice.org.uk/guidance/ng53/evidence/full-guideline-pdf-2606951917 [accessed 6th March 2023]

National Offender Management Service (2017) The Prison Estate in England and Wales, including public and contracted prisons, NOMS Immigration Removal Centres operated on behalf of the Home Office and Secure Training Centre. Available at https://assets.publishing.service.gov.uk/government/uploads/system/uploads/attachment_data/file/582255/Breakdown_List_of_the_Prison_Estate_and_CPAs.pdf [accessed 6th March 2023]

National Offender Management Service (2020a) Early Days in Custody – Reception in, First Night in Custody, and Induction to Custody. Available at www.justice.gov.uk/downloads/offenders/psipso/psi-2015/psi-07-2015-pi-06-2015-early-days-custody.pdf [accessed 6th March 2023]

National Offender Management Service (2020b) Categorisation and Recategorisation of Adult Male Prisoners. Available at www.justice.gov.uk/downloads/offenders/psipso/psi-2011/psi-40-2011-categorisation-adult-males.doc [accessed 6th March 2023]

NHS England. (2021) High Secure Mental Health Services: Schedule 2: The Services. Available at www.england.nhs.uk/wp-content/uploads/2021/02/service-specification-high-secure-mental-health-services-adult.pdf [accessed 6th March 2023]

Office of the High Commissioner for Human Rights (2022) International Bill of Human Rights. Available at www.ohchr.org/en/what-are-human-rights/international-bill-human-rights [accessed 6th March 2023]

Padfield, N. (2016) Parole Board Oral Hearings 2016 – Exploring the Barriers to Release: Avoiding or Managing Risks? Report of a Pilot Study. University of Cambridge Faculty of Law Research Paper No. 62/2017. Available at http://dx.doi.org/10.2139/ssrn.3081035.

Padfield, N. (2018) Parole: Reflections and possibilities A discussion paper. Howard League for Penal Reform. Available at https://howardleague.org/wp-content/uploads/2018/05/Parole-reflections-and-possibilites.pdf [accessed 6th March 2023]

Paparozzi, M.A. and Gendreau, P. (2005). An intensive supervision program that worked: Service delivery, professional orientation, and organizational supportiveness. *The Prison Journal*, 85(4), 445-466.

The Parole Board Rules (2019) UK Statutory Instrument No. 1038. Available at www.legislation.gov.uk/uksi/2019/1038/made [accessed 6th March 2023]

Perrett, S., Plugge, E., Conaglen, P., O'Moore, E. and Sturup-Toft, S. (2020) The Five Nations model for prison health surveillance: Lessons from practice across the UK and Republic of Ireland. Journal of Public Health, 42(4), e561-e572.

Pickering, A., Blagden, N. and Slade, K. (2022) 'You can have a bit of my pain, see how it feels' – Understanding male prisoners who engage in dual harm behaviours. *Psychology, Crime & Law*, 1-24.

Prison and Probation Ombudsman (2020) The Key Worker Scheme. Available at www.ppo.gov.uk/blog/the-key-worker-scheme [accessed 6th March 2023]

Pycroft, A. and Gough, D. eds. (2019) *Multi-Agency Working in Criminal Justice 2ème: Theory, Policy and Practice*. Policy Press.

Ramakers, A. (2022) Secrecy as best policy? Stigma management and employment outcomes after release from prison. *The British Journal of Criminology*, 62(2), 501-518.

Raynor, P. (2019) Supervision skills for probation practitioners. *HM Inspectorate of Probation Academic Insights*, 5.

Rethink Mental Illness (2020) Care Programme Approach (CPA). Available at www.rethink.org/advice-and-information/living-with-mental-illness/treatment-and-support/care-programme-approach-cpa/?gclid=CjOKCQjw1tGUBhDXARIsAIJxO1mWRvN4Mo2jQAFXVDPWL1ouuYX7Pw-_dMZgVhVKEYeg_DO1tZVjAdOaAtZAEALw_wcB [accessed 6 March 2023]

Robinson, G. (2018) Transforming probation services in magistrates' courts. *Probation Journal*, 65(3), 316-334.

Rodin, B (2019) The Parole System of England and Wales. Available at https://researchbriefings.files.parliament.uk/documents/CBP-8656/CBP-8656.pdf [accessed 6th March 2023]

Rogers, J. and Thomas, I. (2022) Twenty suicides of care experienced people in custody: A scoping review of the Ombudsman's fatal incident reports for care experienced people who died in custodial settings between 2004 and 2020. *Prison Service Journal*, 258, 25-31.

Royal College of Speech and Language Therapists (2013) *Five Good Communication Standards.* London: RCSLT

Royal College of Speech and Language Therapists (2022) The Box: Understanding and supporting people with speech, language and communication needs in the justice system. Available at www .rcsltcpd.org.uk/courses/the-box-learning-journey [accessed 6th March 2023]

Selzer, R. and Ellen, S. (2014) Formulation for beginners. *Australasian Psychiatry*, 22(4), 397–401.

The Sentencing Council (2020) Sentencing offenders with mental disorders, developmental disorders, or neurological impairments. Available online at www.sentencingcouncil.org.uk /overarching-guides/magistrates-court/item/sentencing-offenders-with-mental-disorders -developmental-disorders-or-neurological-impairments [accessed 6th March 2023]

Serin, R.C., Chadwick, N. and Lloyd, C.D. (2016) Dynamic risk and protective factors. *Psychology, Crime & Law, 22*(1–2), 151–170.

Shapland, J., Bottoms, A., Farrall, S, McNeill, F., Priede, C. and Robinson, G. (2012) The quality of probation supervision – A literature review. University of Sheffield, Centre for Criminological Research.

Simpson, A., Miller, C. and Bowers, L. (2003) Case management models and the care programme approach: How to make the CPA effective and credible. *Journal of Psychiatric and Mental Health Nursing*, 10(4), 472–483.

Stans, S.E.A., Dalemans, R.J.P., de Witte, L.P. and Beurskens, A.J.H.M. (2019) Using Talking Mats to support conversations with communication vulnerable people: A scoping review. *Technology and Disability, 30*(4), 153–176.

Sturgeon, M., Tyler, N. and Gannon, T.A. (2018) A systematic review of groupwork interventions in UK high secure hospitals. *Aggression and Violent Behavior*, 38, 53–75.

Suhartono, A. and Sarayar, D.R.O. (2021) Optimization of technology use in the new normal parole program: A Comparative Study of Indonesia, the United States and the United Kingdom. Proceedings of the 2nd International Conference on Law and Human Rights. Available at www .atlantis-press.com/proceedings/iclhr-21/125963845 [accessed 6th March 2023].

Sustere, E. and Tarpey, E. (2019) Least restrictive practice: Its role in patient independence and recovery. *The Journal of Forensic Psychiatry & Psychology*, 30(4), 614–629.

Taylor, R., Evans, J., Stuart-Hamilton, I., Roderique-Davies, G., Pierpoint, H. and Bartlett, H. (2014) A Review of the Speech, Language and Communication Needs of Young People from Wales in the Youth Justice System. http://dx.doi.org/10.13140/RG.2.2.28807.19362

Viglione, J., Burton, C. and Basham, S.L. (2019) The balancing act of probation supervision: The roles and philosophies of probation officers in the evidence-based practice era. In P. Ugwudike, H. Graham, F. McNeill, P. Raynor, F.S. Taxman and C. Trotter (eds) *The Routledge Companion to Rehabilitative Work in Criminal Justice* (pp.967–981). Abingdon: Routledge.

Voller, F., Silvestri, C., Martino, G., Fanti, E., Bazzerla, G., Ferrari, F., Grignani, M., Libranchi., S., Pagano, A.M., Scarpa, F., Stasi, C. and Di Fiandra, T. (2016) Health conditions of inmates in Italy. *BMC Public Health*, 16, 1162. https://doi.org/10.1186/s12889-016-3830-2

Watson, D. and Friend, R. (1969) Measurement of social-evaluative anxiety. *Journal of Consulting and Clinical Psychology*, 33(4), 448.

Western, B. (2021) Inside the box: Safety, health, and isolation in prison. *Journal of Economic Perspectives*, 35(4), 97–122.

Whitehouse, A.J.O. and Bishop, D.V.M. (2009) *Communication Checklist – Adult*. London: Pearson

Williams, H.K., Senanayke, M., Ross, C.C., Bates, R., and Davoren, M. (2020) Security needs among patients referred for high secure care in Broadmoor Hospital England. *BjPsych Open*, 6, 1–5.

Witbrodt, J., Polcin, D., Korcha, R. and Li, L. (2019) Beneficial effects of motivational interviewing case management: A latent class analysis of recovery capital among sober living residents with criminal justice involvement. *Drug and Alcohol Dependence, 200*, 124–132.

Yukhnenko, D., Blackwood, N. and Fazel, S. (2020) Risk factors for recidivism in individuals receiving community sentences: A systematic review and meta-analysis. *CNS Spectrums, 25*(2), 252–263.

Zhong, S., Senior, M., Yu, R., Perry, A., Hawton, K., Shaw, J. and Fazel, S. (2021) Risk factors for suicide in prisons: A systematic review and meta-analysis. *The Lancet Public Health*, 6(3), e164–e174.

5

ASSESSMENT OF COMMUNICATION

DOI: 10.4324/9781003288701-6

Assessment of communication is the first stage in the assessment and intervention continuum. The reasons for assessment of speech, language and communication needs (SLCN) will vary, based on the individual, their circumstances and what is desired to be known. Assessment may establish an initial language profile and may inform intervention. Later, further aspects of language processing may need to be investigated, or reassessment may be used to evidence progress in achieving key outcomes.

This chapter aims to offer ideas and information that would be useful for professionals from a range of backgrounds when considering the SLCN of people within the criminal justice system (CJS). The guidance and information can and should be applied across different settings and situations as the person moves through the CJS. This is because communication, and the demands placed on the individual, will change at different time points.

Some of the information in this chapter will be useful for anyone with an interest in SLCN in CJS, some information will appeal to those working directly with people and some is specifically aimed at speech and language therapists (SLTs).

The following topics will be discussed:

- a three-tiered approach to supporting people with SLCN
- guidance for non-SLT professionals working within the universal approach
- a framework for assessment for SLTs within the targeted approach
- a framework for multi-disciplinary (MDT) assessment within the specialist approach
- trauma-informed practice and communication outline for SLTs
- suggested resources that are identified as appropriate for a professional to use, or which would be expected to be used by a registered SLT.

A word about terminology

In this chapter, the following terms are used with the following intended meaning:

- Professional — An appropriately qualified person of a related professional discipline working in the setting.
- Speech and language therapist (SLT) — A registered speech and language therapist.
- Patients, clients or service users — A person engaging in a service in order to support their progression or address their risks.
- Person or individual — A person who is located on a CJS pathway.

It is important to note that there is an active conversation within health, social care, research and education settings relating to 'person-first language' (PFL) and 'identity-first language' (IFL) (Botha, Hanlon and Williams, 2023).

PFL became popular in the 1970s when there was a drive to put the person before their diagnostic label. Phrases such as 'person with aphasia' or 'person with a stammer' were used.

IFL would use phrases such as 'autistic person', 'diabetic person' or 'ADHDer' to describe people. This phraseology has come from a drive to 'reclaim' diagnostic labels as part of a pro-social model of identity. Those who use IFL feel that it is a form of empowerment.

Some people have a preference for IFL, while others prefer PFL (Buijsman, Begeer and Scheeren, 2022). In this book, we will take the sage advice of Buijsman, Begeer and Scheeren who write that those writing materials for the general population should 'use a mix of person-first language and identity-first language to cover the full range of preferences' (Buijsman et al., 2022, p.1).

The challenge when writing this particular book has been PFL v IFL in health, social care and research alongside the PFL v IFL in the CJS. The CJS favours PFL so that 'people who are in prison' is favoured over the IFL of 'prisoner'. While we will write with a mix of PFL and IFL generally, when we are referring to people who are being defined by their status within the CJS, we will use PFL.

Variations in service models

The SLT within the CJS will encounter a range of differences within service delivery models and types of clinical setting (Turner, 2019). The authors would like to note the following variations in service delivery which will impact on the way that SLT assessment and intervention is provided (see the Introduction of this book for further information on models of SLT delivery).

The SLT may or may not be located in the clinical setting as part of the MDT.

The SLT may be located in an alternative team, or be an independent practitioner, and be requested to attend a CJS setting to provide assessment, advice or intervention. When this is the case, the reason for referral is usually explicitly stated by the referring clinician. Once the reason for referral is satisfied and information is provided to the referring clinician, any further input would need to be discussed and negotiated on a case-by-case basis.

If the SLT is located within the team, referrals may be less defined and the SLT may have a broader scope to explore different aspects of SLCN as directed by the presentation of the person in the setting. The SLT may or may not attend MDT meetings depending on the service design.

Following referral, the timescale for meeting the reason for referral may vary based on the setting and the reason for referral. Within a prison setting, a referral for communication assessment of a person on remand may demand a more rapid response than a referral within a high-secure hospital where there may be less time pressure to satisfy the reason for referral. Examples include:

- A person in prison on remand may need a rapid assessment and report in order to gain reasonable adjustments during the court processes.
- A person who is having a very difficult time associated with SLCN, which is resulting in potential impacts on their health and well-being, would require a more rapid response in order to reduce risks of harm to self and others.
- An older person in prison or a person in a high-secure hospital whose presentation has changed significantly would need more urgent assessment.
- A person who is not expected to move from their current setting for a number of months or years may receive a less rapid response.
- A person who is close to release from prison or discharge from hospital, and who requires a communication plan for transition, would require a timely response in order to support their progression.

The SLT autonomy to respond to referrals and offer intervention is likely to be on a continuum. While some SLTs are highly autonomous, such as a lone SLT working in a police custody suite, others may be less so and may be offering care within a framework where SLT interventions are described by a service-level agreement.

SLT activities may be based on the setting, with some secure hospitals having a team of SLTs embedded in the wider MDT. Some settings will have a culture that is influenced by the medical model, while others will operate within a biopsychosocial model of care.

There is an assumption that an SLT in CJS is highly specialist, and while they can be, they can also be 'expert generalists'. However, there will be times when the SLT may make observations that inform referrals to more specialist teams such as video fluoroscopy or voice specialists.

Information sharing will also be different in different settings. Within the prison setting, sharing medical information with medical colleagues is acceptable but the SLT would not share medical information outside the medical team (such as with the offender manager or the forensic psychologist) without clearly stated written consent. Within a secure hospital, information sharing is defined by the Mental Health Act (Department of Health, 2015) and patient consent is not required in the same way.

Finally, a variation in service model can be in the frequency and duration of any offered SLT intervention. Some settings may offer a specific intervention for a set period (e.g. eight weeks of dysfluency intervention) while other settings may offer a process of review and further goal setting so that SLT input can continue over many months or years as long as new meaningful SLT goals are set.

SLCN within the CJS adult population

SLCN in the adult population who are in contact with CJS are thought to be at the following levels:

- Approximately 50% of adults in prison have problems with language (the words that are known and how they are used to express ideas or experiences) (Morken, Jones, and Helland, 2021).
- Approximately 40% of people in prison aged over 55 have cognitive impairment (Combalbert et al., 2016) which can impact on SLCN.
- Approximately 50% of adults attending court from prison have mental illness which can impact on SLCN (Brown et al., 2022).
- Around 20% of people attending court have learning disability (Marshall-Tate et al., 2020).
- Almost 80% of people referred to a forensic support service for people with learning disabilities had communication impairment affecting their understanding of information (McNamara, 2012).

For this reason, we can assume that most professionals working within the CJS will meet people with SLCN on a regular basis. Many of these service users will:

- Be unaware of their own SLCN because they have never accessed SLT.
- Be skilled at 'masking' their SLCN. This is a mechanism that they will have developed unconsciously in order to disguise vulnerability. An example would be that they have developed topics which they feel confident with and will drive interactions to these topics in order to equal the proficiency of the conversation partner.
- Have unconscious ways to terminate interactions that feel overwhelming such as aggression or disengagement.

- Function well with superficial and social chat.
- Disobey social conventions around pragmatics, such as taking longer conversational turns so that they can limit an interaction to topics where they are skilled.
- Use lots of 'empty phrases' within their interaction as 'fillers' such as 'you get me', 'well, it's one of those things', 'you know what I'm saying'. This gives an impression of a lot of talk but very little information conveyed.

SLCN are not confined to the ability to understand information and express a response. When in contact with professionals within the CJS, the person will be experiencing intense and unwanted emotions which will be impacting on their ability to communicate (Fowler, Phillips, and Westaby, 2017). This is often triggered or amplified by the power imbalance within the relationship where the individual feels 'controlled' by the professional (Brown and Völlm, 2016). Figure 5.1 (below) demonstrates the component parts of a communication exchange:

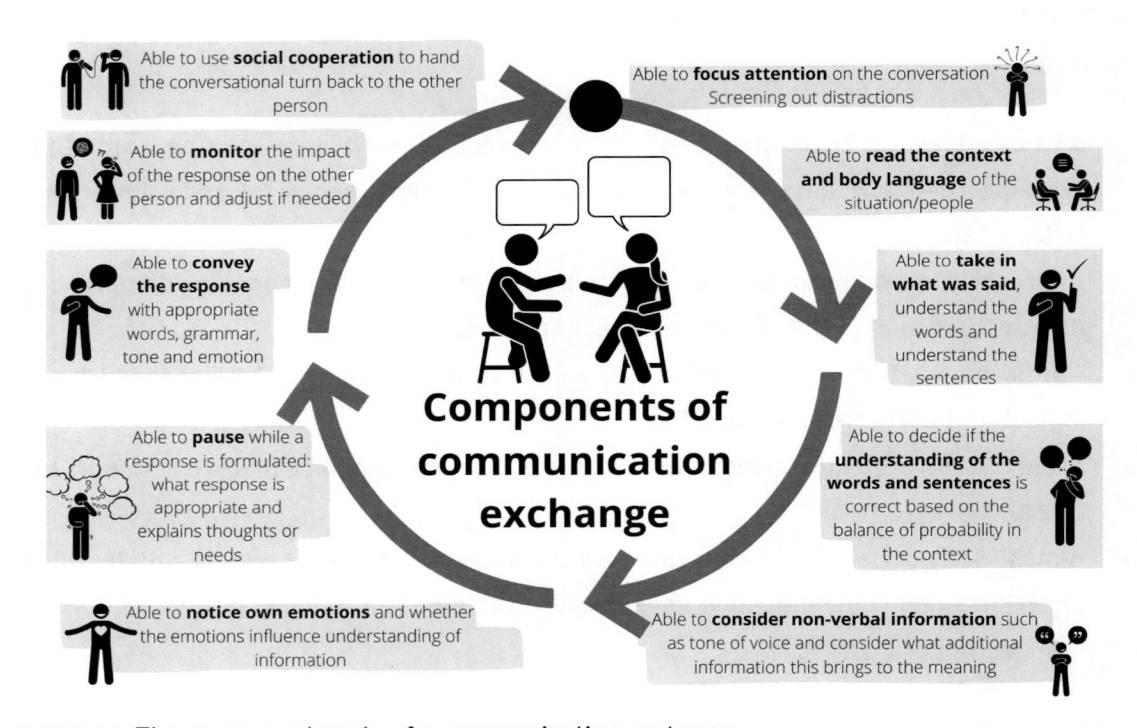

FIGURE 5.1 The component parts of a communication exchange

Emotions will also impact on the individual's decision-making processes (Modecki, Zimmer-Gembeck, and Guerra, 2017). The person may have poor skills in tolerating emotions, so the flight-and-fight response will be activated, and they will feel 'in danger', which will also influence the communication style (Zsolnai, 2015). As a result, the individual may be hard to engage, and any formal activities might be rejected. The person may also be worried about trusting a new professional, which could result in disengagement or masking of difficulties.

Here are some examples of individuals' experiences in relation to communication needs and the CJS journey.

Case example

Mr A had fallen from a height when he was a teen and sustained a significant head injury. He knew that he was 'brain injured' but did not know what this meant in real terms. Now aged 22, he had trained to be a plasterer and had a girlfriend, and life was going well for him. Subsequent to a violent argument, he was arrested for assaulting his girlfriend. Following the criminal justice pathway, he was ultimately sentenced to a custodial stay for the assault. On asking, he said the following, which has been paraphrased for this example:

> I just went along with whatever I was asked because I thought that it would be over quicker... I didn't understand most of what was said and I just wanted to go home, so I agreed to anything.

Case example

Mr B had grown up in a violent household, had a stammer and had learned to express himself in actions rather than words – 'in the playground, other kids would tease me and I'd make my point with my fists'. As an adult, he was charged with a violent crime. He said the following, which has been paraphrased for this example:

> They asked me in the police station but I just couldn't speak. I was tense and they thought that I was going to kick off, so they cut it short. There was no time. And then in court I didn't say a word, because, can you imagine stammering in front of all those people...it would have been awful. So I just shut down.

Case example

Mr C is a man in his 40s. He has learning disability but he was not formally diagnosed before being incarcerated. He had grown up in the parental home in a small village where everyone knew him and so a formal diagnosis was never needed. After his parents had both died, he was alone. He ran out of money and to resolve this he attempted to enter a house to steal items of value. During the CJS pathway, he struggled to understand what was happening and why. He was grateful to be fed but he was scared. He said the following, which has been paraphrased for this example:

They said all these words. I didn't know what they were on about. I just pretended I did. I was polite to them and I thought that they would be polite to me, but then they sent me here [prison].

A three-tiered approach to supporting individuals

With this in mind, it is useful to apply a workforce pyramid model to consider the SLCN of people in the CJS and their access to specialist services (Soloff, 2011). This approach is used to manage or justify the level of specialist input needed. A workforce pyramid suggests a tiered approach to supporting people via three levels:

- A universal approach which can benefit all and which any professional would be able to implement with indirect support or training by an SLT.
- A targeted approach which will be used for the support of people with moderate needs and which involves direct and indirect application of targeted resource such as an SLT or therapy assistant. Equally, in some settings, a language plan could be implemented by an education worker or an occupational therapy (OT) assistant with the support of an SLT.
- A specialist approach which would target specialist resources at the most complex people who may have the most intensive needs, and would benefit from a multi-disciplinary understanding of the individual which includes a specialist SLT.

The pyramid is illustrated below in Figure 5.2:

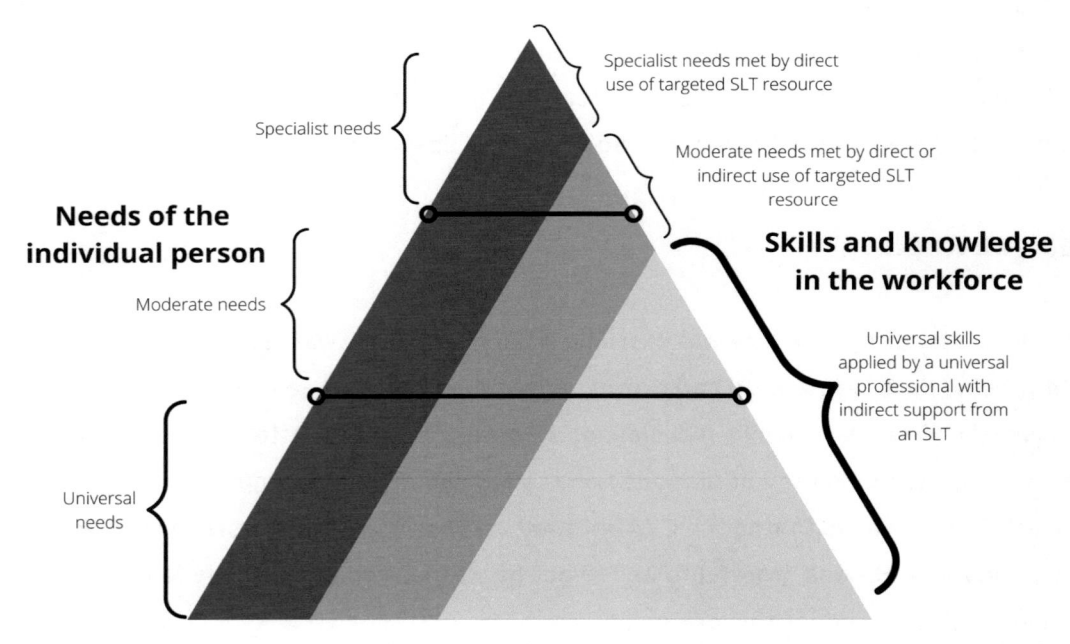

FIGURE 5.2 A tiered approach to supporting people via three levels – universal, targeted and specialist

The universal approach

The universal approach involves all professionals working within the CJS having the knowledge and skills to identify people who may have SLCN via noticing 'red flags' (indicators of potential SLCN). The knowledge and skills are developed via continued professional development, which would ideally include training from a SLT in identification of need, and modification of their own communication style.

The universal approach also involves modifications to the general environment, which benefits all people, such as written materials that are designed to be accessible for all, signage supporting wayfinding, the use of picture menus and orientation tools such as calendars and clocks.

Within the universal approach, professionals from a range of backgrounds would be able to use basic tools which would help the identification of communication risks in the environment and associated with an individual. The following tools are provided in the appendices for use by non-SLT professionals:

- A tool which allows the non-SLT to explore the communication environment which is located at Appendix 15. Each page on the Communication Environment Tool indicates whether the communication environment can be improved based on the number of 'grey' squares that are 'ticked'. Improving the communication environment is considered in Chapter 6.
- A screen that allows a non-SLT to predict whether a person has SLCN which is located at Appendix 16. Each page on the screen indicates whether the non-SLT should suspect SLCN based on how many 'grey' squares are 'ticked'.
- A tool that supports the gathering of communication information by a non-SLT professional which can be completed as part of the referral to SLT and which is located at Appendix 17. The completion of this tool aids the SLT in prioritising the referral and understanding the issues that the person is facing. As part of the universal approach, the professional would know how to access support from an SLT and how to refer an individual for additional assessment. The professional would also be able to articulate some of the findings from the tools to other agencies either in writing or verbally – for example, if the individual is leaving a setting to move to another.

Universal approach to interaction

When a professional within CJS is meeting a person, the most helpful things to talk about first in order to gather red flags for SLCN are:

- any diagnosis or past events such as head injury, dementia, learning disability, ADHD, etc.
- an idea of what happened to the individual in school, college, work
- what life is like for them (e.g. who is at home, what is home like, were they a looked-after child, are they in a relationship now?).

It is recommended that this takes the form of a conversation rather than a formal interview structured by a template. The suggestion is that the professional does not follow a scripted template with the aim of recording the person's replies, but that the professional engages the person in a way that feels more conversational. This allows for noting the individual's replies, but also the times when they needed a question explaining, needed more thinking time or were unable to explain their thoughts in a way that felt easy to follow. The aim is to capture more than replies on a template. The aim is to note potential communication needs which would trigger making a referral for SLCN assessment.

A helpful strategy is that the conversation is undertaken using a blank piece of paper which both the professional and the individual can see. The professional jots down key words or phrases in the form of direct quotes as a memory aid for writing the details down in full afterwards. The individual feels listened to because they can see that their own words are being captured, and trust is commenced because the paper can be seen by both parties.

Red flags for SLCN

A summary of the red flags that the professional may note during conversation is summarised in Figure 5.3 below:

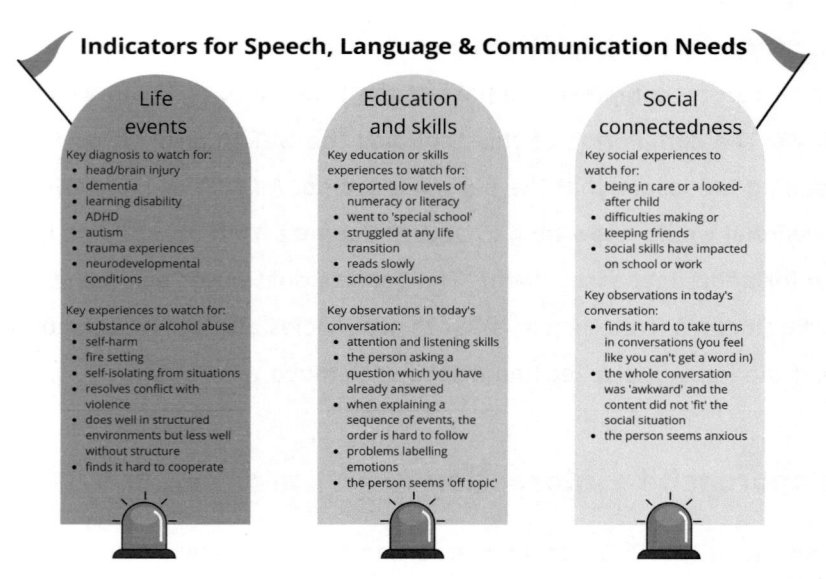

FIGURE 5.3 The red flags that the professional may note during conversation which may be an indication of SLCN

For the professional within the CJS, once red flags are noted, it is useful to utilise the demands and capacities model (Starkweather and Gottwald, 1990).

The demands and capacities model was first developed to understand ways to help children who stammer achieve fluent speech. The concept was that the child (or individual) has a set amount of 'capacity' within a conversation, and that if the demands of the conversation are too high, there will be an imbalance and a communication problem will result. Figure 5.4 (below) gives a worked example for an ADHDer in respect of the demands of the conversation and their capacity:

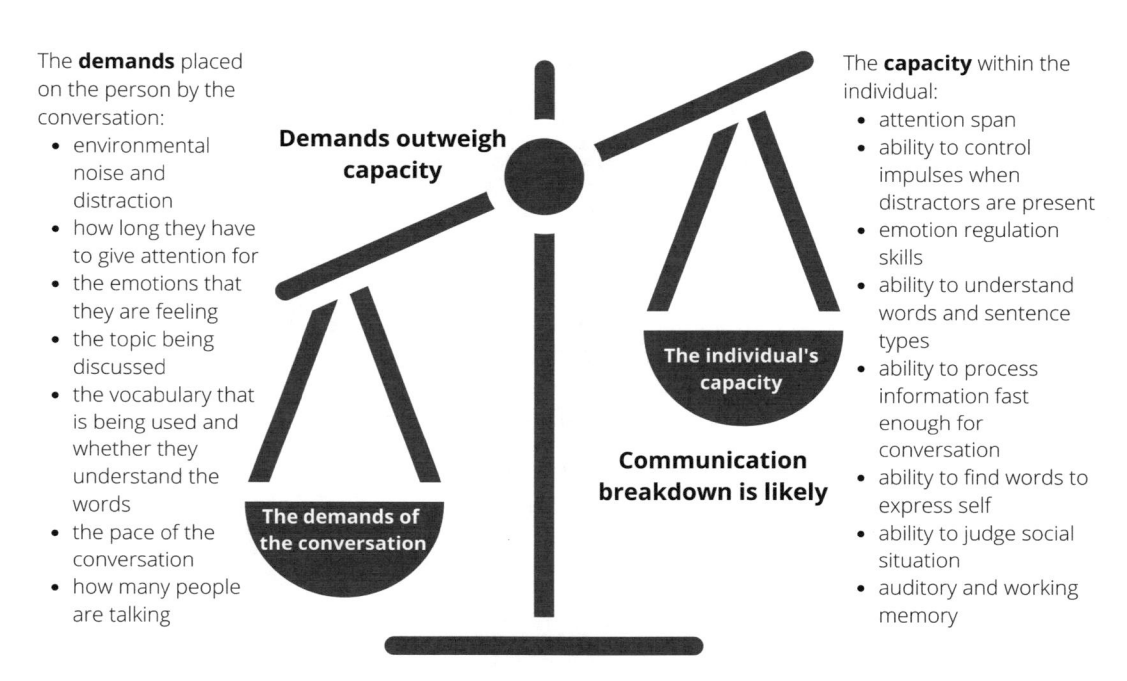

FIGURE 5.4 The demands of a conversation and the capacity of an ADHDer

In this example, the conversation is placing too many demands on the individual and a communication breakdown occurs. Demands can be managed by the professional (i.e. the other speaker), and reducing demands will reduce the potential for communication breakdown (See Figure 5.5 overleaf).

How to reduce demands placed on the person by the conversation:

- **Plan the time of day** to have the conversation. When is the person at their best?
- **Plan the content** of the conversation. Consider how many topics to cover in one conversation.
- **Plan the words** used. Keep vocabulary simple and use the same terms consistently to help the person process information.
- **Let the person know**. Help the person prepare for the demands by letting them know when, where, what and who.
- **Go slowly**. Make sure that there is enough time for the conversation and pause to allow thinking time.
- **Create calmness** if possible. Provide a glass of water, offer to make notes for the person so that they feel more relaxed, remove distractions, offer fidget objects if you know that this helps.
- **Use visual aids** if possible, draw stick-men pictures, write down key words, use photos, maps or pictures. Use self-rating scales (see appendices for resources).
- **Offer the person ways to control the conversation**. Provide a way that the person can take a break or leave the room such as a visual stop card or button (see appendices for resources).
- **Set ground rules** (see appendices for resources).
- **Use help in meetings** resources (see appendices for resources).

FIGURE 5.5 Ideas to support the reduction of demands placed on the conversation partner who has presented with red flags for speech, language or communication needs

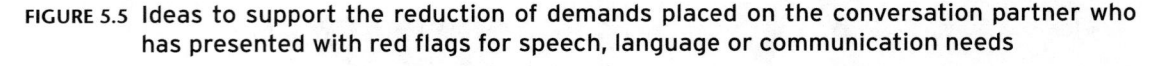

Alongside this, increasing capacity of the individual may also help. Capacity tends to be harder to measure and can be difficult for the individual to quantify (Starkweather and Gottwald, 2000). Ideas for increasing capacity are shown in Figure 5.6 below:

How to increase capacity within the individual:

- **Manage fatigue:** plan the conversation for when the person is well rested. Offer sleep hygiene advice or suggest consulting a GP if fatigue is an ongoing problem.
- **Healthy routines:** help the person get into a daily routine which includes food, rest, social engagement and meaningful occupation. This will support the best possible well-being of the individual and increase their capacity.
- **Therapeutic alliance:** build a relationship with the person before having a high-demand conversation so that they feel some level of alliance and safety.
- **No surprises:** let the person know information in advance so that they have time to prepare.
- **Advocacy:** allow the person to bring a 'supporter' to the conversation if possible.
- **Variability:** be aware that the person may have different capacity on different days based on what else has happened recently.
- Recovery time: be aware that if the person has reduced capacity at the moment, this may not recover quickly and the conversation may have to be planned for another time. Professionals cannot predict the recovery time of individuals as each person is unique.

FIGURE 5.6 Ideas to support the capacity of a conversation partner who has presented with red flags for speech, language or communication needs

The overarching goal of using the demands and capacities model is to match the demand and capacity to achieve an equal 'balance' which will minimise the possibility of a communication breakdown. Total communication was discussed in Chapter 4 and would also apply in this situation to help balance demand and capacity. See Appendix 12 for total communication strategies.

Help in Meetings Tools

Help in Meetings Tools are part of the universal approach and are based on resources that were presented at a National Autistic Society (2019) conference. They have been adapted for use with people who have SLCN and are in contact with CJS.

The aims of these resources are to:

- offer a small, portable and printable tool which can be used in meetings in a variety of locations
- cue professionals that individuals with SLCN need support to prepare for a meeting
- offer practical tools to help the individual with SLCN have some autonomy in a context that may be very hard for them
- act as a visual reminder for all people attending a meeting that reasonable adjustments are in place (it's very easy for able people to forget an adjustment when they are 'in the moment').

The tool comprises of a leaflet and some cards. The cards can be inserted into a clear plastic clip badge or just used on the table top. The resources are located at Appendix 18 for use in practice.

To conclude the universal approach, written materials in the form of fact sheets that may be helpful to provide guidance relating to a range of conditions and the associated SLCN are provided at Appendix 19. These materials are designed to support the non-SLT professional to identify and recognise SLCN, and to make some observations using the fact sheet as a supportive framework. The materials are particularly useful if the person has a diagnosis (e.g. ADHD or learning difficulties) but their communication needs are not flagged or recognised. The fact sheets should assist the non-SLT professional to note potential communication difficulty and increase confidence when considering whether to make a referral to SLT for assessment. The non-SLT professional is invited to write notes on the reverse of the factsheet to support information gathering.

It should be noted that these guidance sheets are generic and do not replace individualised assessment of language and communication.

The targeted level

This approach in the three-tiered model includes all elements of the universal approach plus access to SLT assessment, advice and intervention. The professional working at the universal level will have noted the SLCN of the person and made a referral for targeted input. At this stage, the SLT will undertake information gathering to support understanding of the person's needs. Two tools are offered to support the information-gathering process:

- a Functional Communication Matrix which helps the SLT to consider five domains of the individual's daily functional communication (this is located at Appendix 20)
- a Communication Risk Assessment Tool which helps to identify factors, likelihood and consequence of hazards arising from SLCN (located at Appendix 21).

These tools have been developed and refined via clinical practice, but have not been subject to any testing of reliability or validity.

The Functional Communication Matrix is designed to allow the SLT to consider how well the person functions in the environment. This is because many people will perform below expected levels of communication on formal assessments, which may suggest a significant challenge in activities of daily living. However, when the person is considered from a functional standpoint, they are scaffolded (or supported) by the environment. In this situation, the SLT and the individual would need to carefully consider the goals of referral and decide whether formal assessment or SLT intervention is appropriate at that time. There is potential to damage a person's self-esteem if they are formally assessed and found to have 'impairment' when the impairment is not a factor limiting participation. There is potential for the individual to receive intervention which is an additional burden on their time. The Functional Communication Matrix can be repeated as an indicator for intervention or as an outcome measure following intervention.

The Functional Communication Matrix should be 'scored' using a holistic understanding of the person and their needs. For example, a person may score low on all domains except one, and the SLT would make a clinical decision with the service user on the impact of this one domain on the person's participation and well-being.

The Communication Risk Assessment Tool was also developed in clinical practice and has only been subjected to testing of reliability and validity 'in house' at HMP Berwyn with a small sample of SLTs.

Case example

Peter is a man who has been in prison for more than 20 years. He has an IQ of 61 so is a learning-disabled person who would be expected to score very low on formal SLT assessments. He functions very well in prison where the routine supports him to know what he is doing and why, where the professionals around him know him well and where his job role has been adapted to accommodate his needs. Peter can sustain long periods where he is in the range of 'no concern' when considered using the Functional Communication Matrix.

However, Peter becomes of concern when he has a parole board. He has experience of parole boards being negative, and entering his parole window introduces new people into his structured environment. The parole board also involves several long meetings, lots of written reports and a considerable amount of anxiety. During periods such as parole windows, Peter moves from no concerns to moderate concerns. His triggers are:

- past experience of parole boards being negative
- the introduction of new people who are part of the parole board process who may offer him complex information in a form which is hard for him to engage with
- receiving his parole dossier which is a set of papers that he cannot read or engage with
- changes to his routine where he has to attend appointments which are related to his parole board such as a review of his sentence plan.

His emotional response is:

- thinking about the past, which makes him feel shame and guilt
- thinking about the parole board, which makes him anxious
- thinking about the future, which makes him frightened.

The build-up of emotions and the additional triggers impact on Peter's daily functioning so that:

- He finds it hard to ask for help from people he knows well because his high emotional load is impacting on his cognition and self-awareness.
- There is an increase in episodes of shouting, swearing and withdrawing from protective factors such as art club.
- There are increased episodes of miscomprehension of information, which in turn increases anxiety impacting on his cognition and his communication.

- There are changes in interaction style where Peter interrupts others and introduces a topic with no preamble so that the conversation partner struggles to be on the same topic (decreased awareness of theory of mind on Peter's part due to impacted cognition).

The impact of Peter's difficulties is reflected in this entry on Peter's electronic record:

> Yesterday Peter attended the People Hub to meet with a psychologist who he has not met before. The psychologist talked to him about his offence for approximately one hour. Afterwards, Peter returned to the house block and went to his cell. He would not come out for his dinner, declined to attend the gym session and did not want to speak to his key worker. In the evening, Peter was shouting out of his window. The night staff report that he did not sleep well, and this morning he was swearing at peers who he usually gets on with. He had not attended to his personal hygiene, and when prompted to have a shower, Peter became emotionally overwhelmed and tore some notices from the notice board. He was guided back to his cell, and when staff checked on him, he was crying.

The professionals working with Peter believe that the changes in his communication style would make it hard for him to participate in the parole hearing without additional support.

While formal SLT assessment was not previously required, there is now a need for that assessment to profile Peter's needs for the parole board, and to set goals for intervention to help him to manage this situation.

Risk assessment

Risk assessment is a useful tool for identifying hazards and whether those hazards are going to impact on the safety (effectiveness) of any activity (Health and Safety Executive, 2014). The ethos of risk assessment can be applied to SLCN in that we can explore what the hazards are, and what the impacts might be.

A hazard can be anything that impacts on the communication success of an interaction. Examples include:

- communication materials such as visual aids being in the wrong language or too complex

- equipment such as the type of lighting in the room and if this causes a communication barrier (e.g. too dark to see the faces of the people talking)
- practices such as changing the topic often and quickly which disorientates the conversation partner
- strong smells triggering sensory overload which stop the conversation partner from processing auditory information
- within the custodial or hospital settings, using materials that are not permitted or which could be associated with an individual's offence or trauma - see section in this chapter which discusses forensic setting considerations.

The impacts of these hazards might be that the person cannot give information, or that incorrect information is given and that this results in a criminal charge. The ultimate impact of hazards to communication is unsafe convictions (Prison Reform Trust, 2008).

An example of a completed Communication Risk Assessment Tool for a person in police custody is shown in Table 5.1 overleaf.

The SLT has considered the needs of the individual and has captured 'impacts' or 'risk factors' which are associated with the communication needs of the person not being met. Often there are risk factors which are unknown or potentially present, so the Communication Risk Assessment Tool allows for this. The total number of risk factors is captured.

The SLT also considers the implication of communication breakdown for the individual. If the individual is known to have frequent communication breakdowns which result in violence, this is considered by estimating the likelihood of the breakdown and the consequence.

Lastly, the risk factors score is added to the 'likelihood x consequence' score to obtain a total. The total can be used to direct a response within the three-tiered model. The example is based on a person in police custody, so the response is modelled on this setting. The response can be adapted to be suitable for alternative settings and based on local resources but should continue to reflect the three-tiered approach.

TABLE 5.1 Example SLCN Risk Assessment Tool completed for a person entering police custody

CJS SLCN RISK ASSESSMENT TOOL	
Name: *RW* **NHS number:** *123 456 7890* **DOB:** *21st June 1995*	
Description of person's current situation, communication needs and applicable history:	
This gentleman has been referred to SLT by police officers at Low Town police station. He has been arrested and has a communication passport completed by SLT in the local brain injury team. Has ADHD and head injury. Gets headaches when exposed to bright lighting.	
Is this person felt to be at increased risk of poor outcomes due to communication skills and/or needs reasonable adjustments in place?	
Yes	
Potential or actual impact *(Potential risks to individuals from communication needs not being addressed)*	Y – yes P – potential ? – unknown N – no
A lack of choices and involvement in everyday decisions	*N*
Reliance on other people and loss/lack of independence	*P*
Limited engagement with others	*N*
Poor health literacy	*Y*
Increased use of behaviour which challenges to elicit communication or attention	*?*
Diminished physical and mental health	*P*
Reduced access to or involvement in other therapeutic input	*N*
Professionals consistently overestimating an individual's abilities, impacting negatively on perceptions/affecting the individual's overall care	*Y*
Isolation	*N*
Relationship breakdown	*?*
Increased vulnerability to abuse and hate crime	*?*
Low mood, anxiety and depression	*P*
Reduced employment and/or education opportunities	*Y*
Placement breakdown / frequent transfer of location	*P*
Number of risk factors currently present – score 1 for each Y or P	*7*
Current level of risk	
(This may be from one single risk factor or more or an accumulation of a number of factors) Comment: *Has 7 risk factors, can be impulsive so likelihood of something happening is present, can be violent or emotional which can impact on decisions.* *Likelihood 4 x consequence 2 = 8*	

	Likelihood 1 = least likely 5 = certain					
Consequence 1 = least impact 5 = most impact		1	2	3	4	5
	1 – small					
	2 – minor					
	3 – moderate					
	4 – major					
	5 - severe					

Total risk score: Add risk factors score to likelihood and consequence score
Risk factors 7 + LC score 8 = 15

(*Continued*)

TABLE 5.1 Continued

Current management to mitigate risk:
This man is medium risk of communication problems. He is being managed via the universal approach in the three-tiered model by colleagues from other professional backgrounds. He is referred to SLT for assessment.

Impact of current management:
Currently calm and settled following conversations with other professionals and information provided about SLT appointment.

Communication risk management/action plan:
Change lighting in the room due to headaches *Interviews for 20 minutes at a time* *Fidget objects in the interview room* *To be offered a walk between interviews* *Routinely use questions to check his understanding of information*

To be reviewed by	
Name *PC Bellows 386*	Date of review

Today's date:
Completed by: *PC Bellows 386*

Score	Priority
2-8	Low risk - Arrange support from appropriate adult or intermediary if in police custody - Follow any advice from professionals involved or communication passport - Universal approach within the three-tiered model - Use easy words, visual aids, and give regular breaks - Check understanding with open questions such as 'tell me what we've said so far'
9-18	Medium risk All of the above Targeted approach within the three-tiered model Be aware of emotions which may be triggered if the person does not understand such as frustration or anger
19 -30	High risk All of the above Consider obtaining advice from CPS or senior investigating officers prior to next steps if in police custody

The SLT will also meet with the individual in order to ask about communication skills. This will include asking about:

- attention and listening (including distractibility in the environment)
- sensory processing
- understanding information
- processing abilities with information
- expressing themselves
- use of standard pragmatics
- memory
- narrative skills
- body language and facial expression.

This is a lot of information to gather, and it would be reasonable to expect to complete this inventory over more than one meeting. Where a person is in a custodial setting, and likely to be there for some time, the SLT can take time over multiple short settings to make an initial assessment. Sometimes people in prison are willing to engage, but initially reluctant to complete any form of assessment. In such situations, slowly building up trust is necessary. The SLT can also gain valuable information by observing the person communicating in different settings and with different staff. It would be helpful to initiate fact finding from the individual via conversation in the first meeting, and offer explanation of the role of the SLT, what information is being gathered and why, and how this might help the person. Three explanatory sheets covering information which should be shared by the SLT in the early stages of working with a new person are located at Appendix 22 and may help to structure the conversation. The appointment should always conclude with explaining what will happen at the next appointment and asking the person if they would like to engage.

Table 5.2 (overleaf) offers ideas for the SLT on how to obtain useful data in time-limited settings with minimal resources. The table suggests nine domains that can be observed during informal assessment, and topics which may be explored to inform decision making. The observations can be used to inform a decision on whether to offer formal assessment, or whether to refer on to another professional such as a registered mental health nurse.

Information about communication strengths and needs can be gathered informally via means such as:

- Observation of the person in function or everyday activities.
- Asking key stakeholders for their input on strengths and needs using a checklist such as the two screens developed by Crew and Gregory (2008) which are reproduced in Appendix 23.
- Asking the person to reflect on different situations using comic-strip conversations or timelines as an aid to reflection.
- Asking the person to provide a narrative and note skills and themes while listening.
- Using a visual semi-structured interview approach such as Talking Mats (Boardman, Crichton and Butterworth, 2016).
- Undertaking a joint task together such as building a Lego model, playing a game or teaching each other a skill. This enables participants to undertake different roles and enables the SLT to see the person when they are in a leading role. The skilled clinician can note attention, comprehension, processing, expression and pragmatics during such informal activities.
- Setting the person a problem to solve such as providing a picture of a finished model and the components which are needed to make the model. This allows the clinician to note attention, problem solving, cognition, processing of information and self-advocacy.

TABLE 5.2 Ideas for the SLT to obtain useful data in time-limited settings with minimal resources presented by different domains which impact on SLCN

SLCN domain	What the SLT may observe	Tasks the SLT may try
Attention and listening (including distractibility in the environment)	Does the person give you attention? Are they distracted by something (e.g. an object in the room, sitting on a chair with wheels, something outside of the room which is on their mind)? How long can they give attention for? Does their attention come and go? If they are distracted, how quickly are they able to give attention back to the task?	Observing their skills during the initial conversation about the person's life and experiences Asking the person about their attention Asking about different activities which are arranged in a hierarchy of attention such as watching easy TV dramas, reading a magazine, watching an action movie or football match, watching a long movie like *Forrest Gump*, reading a book, watching a documentary Asking the person about how they like to communicate with others (e.g. text message, phone call, in person chat, serious longer conversations) Tell the person a short piece of narrative and ask them closed questions about the content
Sensory processing, physical presentation, emotions and unseen stimuli	Is the person staying very still or moving a lot? Are they seeking sensory contact like rubbing their hands on their jeans or rocking on the chair? Do they seem to be listening to or watching something which you cannot see? Are they unusually tearful or entertained?	Observing the way that they sit, move and reposition themselves while conversing Watching facial expressions, eye movements and head posture Paying attention to their emotions both verbally stated and observed to see if the emotion seems appropriate for the situation
Understanding information especially verbal information	The person demonstrating that they understand what is said to them	During the initial conversation, note if the person gives information which seem appropriate to the question or topic Ask the person to do something or follow an instruction very informally: 'We are in the room at end – the last door on the left?' 'Can you pass me the red pen?' More formally, ask the person if they have heard of certain words, if they can tell you what they mean, if they can tell you when the word is used (e.g. 'Tell me about the word "assault"') Try a task where you describe an object, a person or an event and the listener should tell you what you are talking about
Processing abilities with information	Does the person pause for longer than you would expect before answering? Do they start talking and then ask you what the question was? Do they start talking but the information is off topic?	Observing their skills during the initial conversation about the person's life and experiences

(Continued)

TABLE 5.2 Continued

SLCN domain	What the SLT may observe	Tasks the SLT may try
Expressing themselves	Does the person speak in utterances or sentences with appropriate grammar? Are they struggling to find the word, with lots of filled pauses or empty speech? Is the speech clear and easy to understand? Do they stammer or have slurred speech? Do they use words which feel age and context appropriate?	Observing their skills during the initial conversation about the person's life and experiences Asking about a stammer or slurred speech Extend the task on words that they have heard (used for comprehension) to using the word in a sentence (the sentence can have past, present or future tense to check grammar)
Use of standard pragmatics	Do they take turns in conversation? Are the turns equal? Do they give abrupt answers or say too much? What is the volume and tone of voice like? Is it too loud or too quiet? Does the person stay on topic? Are they offering information which is relevant to what is being discussed? Does the person dominate the conversational floor?	Observing their skills during the initial conversation about the person's life and experiences
Memory	Can the person remember recent facts such as orienting themselves to who they are, where they are and when? Can they remember a piece of information which you told them a few minutes before? Can they remember information from a long time ago such as their address as a child? How many items can the person remember and repeat in sequence?	Observing their skills during the initial conversation about the person's life and experiences Look for specific information which you can verify such as date of birth or address Give a piece of information and ask them to remember it until you ask for it again List objects, numbers or adjectives and ask the person to remember the list and repeat it in sequence. Offer a hierarchy of challenge where you offer high-frequency/high-imageable targets first, then low-frequency or low-imageable, then semantically related items. Start with three items and build up until the ceiling is reached

(Continued)

TABLE 5.2 Continued

SLCN domain	What the SLT may observe	Tasks the SLT may try
Narrative skills	Can the person sequence events and explain the sequence to you in a logical order so that you understand what happened, when, where and with whom?	Ask the person to tell you how they would make a cup of tea – explaining each stage to you as if you had never made tea Ask them to explain a more complex task such as making grilled cheese on toast Ask them to explain a complex sequence such as the football offside rule or how to play poker Tell the person a short piece of narrative and ask them to re-tell it to you with all details included Ask them to explain to you the plot of their favourite TV show, book or film
Body language and facial expression	Does the person present with body language which is appropriate to the conversation and setting? Does the person's facial expression match the topic of conversation or what they are saying? Does the facial expression change or remain the same?	Observing their skills during the initial conversation about the person's life and experiences

Resources for use in informal assessment can include:

- *Getting the Picture: Inference and Narrative Skills for Young People with Communication Difficulties* by David Nash which provides resources to explore inference, narrative and sequencing skills in young people and adults
- magazine and newspaper short articles which can be used for comprehension, expression and narrative observation
- game materials such as playing cards, dominoes, Pictionary, general knowledge quizzes or Jenga to consider engagement, turn taking, tolerance of emotions, comprehension and expression in task and pragmatics
- construction-type kits such as Lego, puzzles or K'nex to consider attention, problem solving, self-esteem, comprehension, expression and pragmatics
- pre-assembled bags of resources for 'challenges' with instruction cards (e.g. a set of ten objects which each have a tenuous link whereby the person has to explore the objects and ask questions to discover the link).

It is important to note that these are not used just as tasks to occupy the person being informally assessed but should be used as tools to facilitate a particular assessment question that the SLT is considering. As with any resource, infection control may also be important and this may require all items to be either single use or able to be cleaned for infection prevention. Exact requirements will depend upon the setting and any current level of infection control required.

Possible resources to assist the SLT in engaging the person and in obtaining particular information about them might include:

- pens and paper for 'drawing your perfect future', creating mind maps, drawing comic strips
- a bag of fidget objects or sensory objects
- conversation starter cards or cubes
- 'Would you rather' cards
- 'What's missing?' or 'What's wrong in this scenario?' resources
- puzzle or joke books
- dice games such as Yahtzee
- sand timers, cooking timers, clocks, calendars, etc. for setting agreed time limits and orientation
- post-it notes or wipe boards for noting agendas.

Case example

An SLT was invited to an MDT meeting in a medium-secure hospital at the request of a colleague who had some unspecified concerns about a service user on the ward. The meeting included the service user. The aim of attending was to inform the decision to refer the individual to SLT (i.e. the targeted level in the three-tiered model). The SLT employed observation of the nine domains discussed in table 5.2 and used this to form a hypothesis relating to the SLCN of the service user. As a result, the service user was identified as potentially having signs of ADHD, and an ADHD assessment was initiated.

The SLT may decide to use a formal assessment of SLCN. The clinical decision to undertake a formal assessment will be based on the following questions:

- What was the reason for referral?
- Do I need to conduct a formal assessment to satisfy the reason for referral?

- Would this person tolerate a formal assessment?
- Would formal assessment results add anything meaningful to the understanding of this individual?
- Do I have access to an appropriate assessment which is valid for this person?
- Is the assessment suitable for age, gender, skill level and culture?
- Will the assessment offer information that I cannot obtain in other ways?
- Do I need to compare this individual to a standardised norm or an expected level?

Many referrals will be for communication assessment in order to articulate the strengths and barriers that the person faces in their daily life, and to report on this with advice to overcome barriers. In these circumstances, formal or informal means can be utilised. It should also be noted that some people in prison may be very wary of interpersonal inter-action and may cope better with formal assessment, particularly where the test is simple in design and repetitive such as the British Picture Vocabulary Scale (Dunn and Dunn, 2009). Similarly, some people may find it easier to talk while conducting a task. For example, someone who is very uncomfortable about eye contact may communicate more easily while conducting a card-sorting task. The SLT's approach of careful observation, hypothesis testing and noting of facilitators to communication will be very important. For such a person, advice to a key worker might be to have any significant discussions while conducting a task where eye contact is naturally reduced (e.g. washing and drying dishes).

Some referrals may be to inform legal processes such as court hearings or release plans. In these circumstances, formal assessment might be required to give comparative or norm-referenced data that can help the individual to access reasonable adjustments or sup-port. Norm-referencing can invoke anxiety in professionals. Is it inappropriate to refer to an adult as having the understanding of a seven-year-old? It probably is, but this can be worded more appropriately – for example, 'the person has a language comprehension level equivalent to that of a seven-year-old, which is partially masked by his use of slang terms and expletives'. Such norm-referencing may be very helpful, for example, to a judge who needs to make crucial decisions about a person's future very rapidly. Reports which are requested in order to help people access financial support also benefit from such data being included.

Formal assessments may be applicable to the assessment of communication depending on the reason for referral, the age of the person, whether the assessment is culturally appro-priate and whether the person can tolerate assessment.

Suggested formal assessments which are worth consideration within the CJS are:

- Cognitive Linguistic Quick Test Plus (CLQT+) which considers attention, memory, executive functions, language and visuospatial skills in people aged over 18 years (Helm-Estabrooks, 2001–2017).
- Test of Everyday Attention (TEA) which considers three aspects of attention – selective attention, sustained attention and attentional switching – in people aged over 18 years (Robertson et al., 1994).
- Doors and People, which assesses long-term memory in adults (Baddeley, Emslie and Nimmo-Smith, 1994).
- Clinical Evaluation of Language Fundamentals – Fifth Edition (CELF-5 UK), which is a language assessment suitable for people up to 21 years and 11 months (Wiig, Semel and Secord, 2013).
- Test for Reception of Grammar (TROG-2), which examines understanding of grammatical contrasts and is suitable for young people and adults (Bishop, 2003).
- British Picture Vocabulary Scale: 3rd Edition (BPVS III), which is a tool to consider vocabulary development. While this assessment is norm-referenced to young people aged up to 16 years, it can be used with people over the age of 16 years (Dunn and Dunn, 2009).
- Test of Adolescent and Adult Language Fourth Edition (TOAL-4) which is a language assessment suitable for people up to 24 years and 11 months (Hammill, Brown, Larsen and Wiederholt, 2007).
- The Mount Wilga High Level Language Test (Christie, Clark and Mortensen, 1986), which is a resource originally developed for clinical use in the field of brain injury in the 1980s, and which has been refreshed in 2006 (Simpson et al., 2006). It was developed in clinical practice so is not validated or standardised against any population. Some subtests of the Broadmoor Assessment were developed from the structure of the Mount Wilga High Level Language Test. The Broadmoor Assessment is included at Appendix 11.
- The Quick Aphasia Battery (QAB), which considers aphasia in adults (Wilson et al., 2018).
- The Comprehensive Aphasia Test (CAT), which considers aphasia in adults in more detail (Swinburn, Porter and Howard, 2023).
- The Everyday Memory Survey (EMS), which is a screen for individual memory-related behaviours in daily life to determine if a person with suspected dementia would benefit from a referral to a specialist service (Hall, 2004).
- The Brief Cognitive Status Exam, which considers the cognitive functioning in people with dementia or suspected dementia (Ireland, 2012).

- Expressive Vocabulary Test Third Edition (EVT-3), which is an assessment of expressive vocabulary and word retrieval in adults (Williams, 2019).
- Communication Checklist – Adult (CC-A), which helps to identify subtle communicative difficulties which may be present in adults with neurodiverse needs (Whitehouse and Bishop, 2009).

If the reason for referral is assessment and intervention using a co-production ethos where therapy goals are mutually agreed, formal assessment may offer limited data to guide therapeutic engagement, particularly where this is designed to facilitate another intervention such as engagement in emotion regulation support or drug rehabilitation. The SLT may use a formal assessment after set periods of time to establish whether formal gains are detectable on standardised assessment. This can be particularly useful in settings where continued SLT therapeutic input needs to be demonstrated e.g. in an external consultancy situation, or in a situation where evidence of progress is required e.g. by an MDT to determine readiness to move from high-secure to medium-secure care. A test such as the CC-A (Whitehouse and Bishop, 2009) can be very helpful in such circumstances.

Case example

Jim is a young man serving a short prison sentence. Jim is from the Traveller community. There are concerns around Jim as he finds it hard to express his ideas in coherent ways, so there are frequent communication breakdowns. When the communication breakdowns occur, it impacts on Jim's well-being and sense of identity. Jim was offered SLT assessment and intervention at the targeted level but felt that this was not for him. Professionals continued to be worried about Jim and, via linking with the onsite chaplain, Jim agreed to have a conversation with the SLT.

The conversation happened at Jim's place of work in the prison, which was the horticulture centre. With prior planning, Jim was asked to build a bird table kit but was set the challenge to complete this without the instructions. The SLT role was to ask questions, encourage Jim to comment on what he was doing and why, and to ask Jim to explain his plan for the bird table. If Jim was 'stuck', the SLT could offer suggestions. The activity created a situation where the SLT could observe Jim's attention, comprehension, cognition and self-advocacy, and also ask Jim about his communication experience.

After Jim had made the bird table, the SLT discussed with Jim how the process felt and facilitated the labelling of his emotions during the task.

The SLT was able to use the information to make the following visual for Jim:

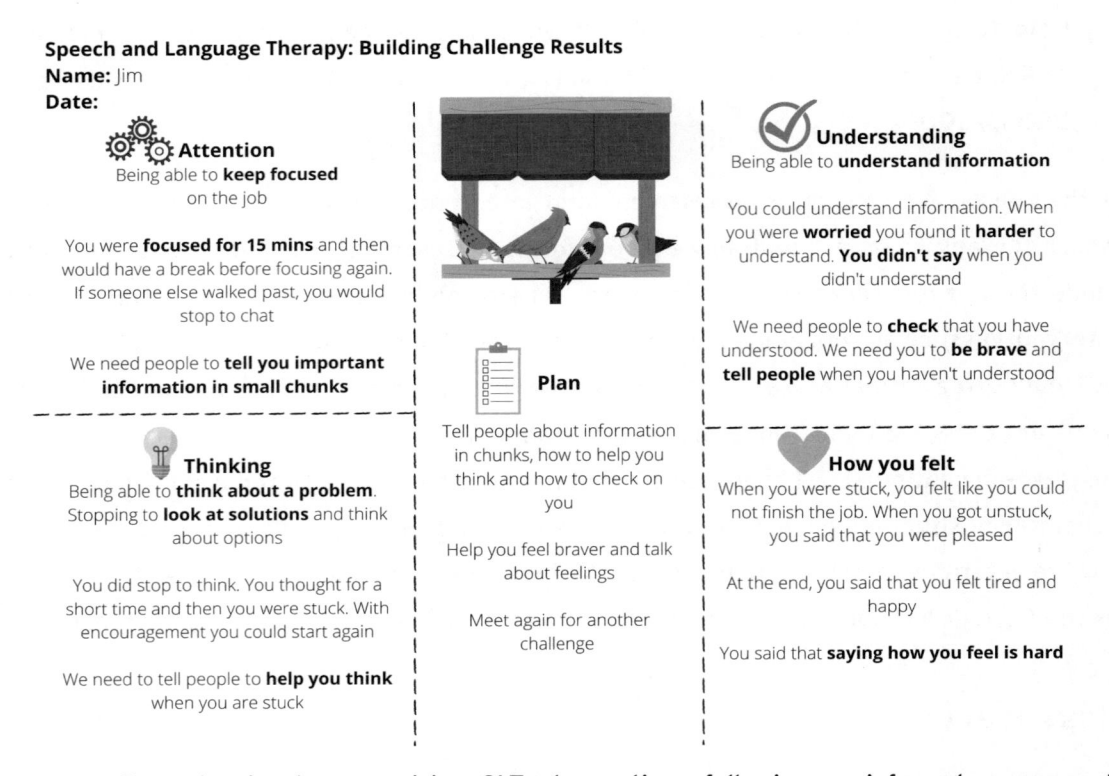

FIGURE 5.7 Example visual summarising SLT observations following an informal assessment activity

Case example

PJ is a man in his early 20s residing in a low-secure hospital setting. He has a trauma history and learning disability. His SLCN are significant such that his receptive language skills require considerable adaptation to help him understand information. His expressive skills are also reduced, and he finds it hard to talk about his experiences or emotions. Talking Mats have been the most successful communication tool to assist PJ in expressing his views (Stans et al., 2019). When PJ wanted to say more about his experiences, he asked to create his own Talking Mat symbols – setting himself a problem to solve.

PJ was given access to symbol software in his planned computer sessions, and the SLT supported him in using the software, thinking of words, spelling words and symbol choices. During the sessions, PJ drifted away from his original idea to make his own Talking Mat. This change to plan was not questioned as PJ was engaged in his task and the SLT did not want to influence his process. He created symbols sets which were sequences of symbols.

On first view, the sequences were not easy to follow, and the SLT asked PJ to help with understanding the meaning. PJ printed out the symbols and used scissors and glue to create what he called 'story strips'. Alongside the story strips, PJ could add some verbal narrative to help the listener – thus beginning to construct his own retelling of some of the events of his years at school.

He was offered a scrapbook and used this to begin to make his own life story book over a period of 18 months. His story strips formed the basis of each piece, which he would expand verbally or with photos which he would print from the internet.

PJs book was shared in key worker sessions using the principles of trauma-informed conversations (see Appendix 28).

CJS communication passport

Once information gathering and assessment is complete, the results can be collected into a single document which the person can use to help explain their SLCN to others. This would be in addition to any formal reporting to the MDT or the referring agent. It may be that the information gathered is captured in a communication passport if the individual feels that this style of document is useful for them.

The SLT should consider the following concerns:

- Who is the communication passport for and what content should be included based on this?
- What negotiations should be undertaken with an individual to help them decide if a communication passport is appropriate for them?
- When should the communication passport be offered and when might it make a person vulnerable (e.g. vulnerable to bullying from peers in a prison setting)?
- How will a person with a communication passport make the judgement on sharing the information if it might make them vulnerable?
- Would a list of 'where to use this passport' be helpful?
- Is there a training need for the individual who holds a communication passport, and how will this be supported to generalise outside of the clinic setting?
- Would having a communication passport make the individual 'different' to their peers which could impact on self-esteem?

Communication passports are a simple tool which help people to share basic information at times when they cannot do so themselves (Communication Matters, 2022). For example, hospital communication passports have long been an established good practice for people with learning disability going into hospital. If this good practice is extended to any person with SLCN in a range of situations, communication passports for people who are at risk of coming into contact with the CJS seems a potential measure to help promote awareness of the needs of the individual. However, the clinician should weigh the pros and cons of such a document and its appropriateness in some situations. The clinician should also be mindful of a top-down approach to the provision of communication passports which are given as a 'sticking plaster' but which do not offer any tangible benefits for the person or their communication context (Bradshaw and Pringle, 2019).

When thinking about a design of a communication passport for this client group, we must be respectful of age, dignity, portability, accessibility in the moment, content and any security restrictions (e.g. it may be inappropriate to show pictures of children in some settings). The examples given (see Figure 5.8 overleaf) are each a two-page document which could be printed on A5 paper and kept in a person's wallet.

A template of this resource is located at Appendix 24. In less secure settings, another idea is to complete the passport and allow the person to keep a photograph of it on their phone which they can show to a stakeholder if needed.

The Communication Risk Assessment Tool, which may have been completed during the information-gathering stage of the episode of care, might be usefully shared with stakeholders alongside the communication passport to ensure a full understanding of the person's needs.

Communication report

One of the reasons for referral to the targeted approach may be to obtain a communication report which explains the individual's SLCN.

CJS COMMUNICATION PASSPORT

NAME AND ADDRESS

*Richard Davies
32 High Street
Low Town*

DATE OF BIRTH / AGE

21st June 1995

PREFERRED NAME *Rich*

ABOUT ME

PHOTO OR WRITTEN DESCRIPTION OF ME

MEDICAL NEEDS / MEDICATIONS / SPECIAL NEEDS

*ADHD - on concerta
Head injury - can be tearful*

ALLERGIES OR OTHER IMPORTANT PHYSICAL HEALTH THINGS YOU NEED TO KNOW

Bright lights give me headaches

HOW YOU CAN HELP MY SPECIAL NEEDS

*Turn off bright lights
box of tissues
give me my medication every day*

WHO TO CONTACT FOR ME

Head Injury care worker - Emma Smith 01583 592 564

CJS COMMUNICATION PASSPORT

MY SPEECH, LANGUAGE OR COMMUNICATION NEEDS ARE

*Attention and listening are hard
Understanding new words / long words is a problem
When I talk, I might copy your long words without knowing what they mean
I also go off topic and find it hard to explain a sequence of events*

IN ORDER TO HELP ME, PLEASE DO

*Give me a fidget object to help me listen
use easy words
don't rush me*

PRACTICAL MATTERS

*I can only concentrate for 25 minutes so need breaks
I'm better if I can walk around between conversations
I'd like an intermediary please*

HEALTH OR SOCIAL CARE PROFESSIONALS WHO KNOW ME ARE

*Social worker Wendy Whitehead at local council
Telephone - 01990 475896
GP - Dr Albert at Low Town GP Surgery*

THIS COMMUNICATION PASSPORT WAS PREPARED BY

Amy Highlander - speech and language therapist at Head Injury Service telephone - 01990 536596

FIGURE 5.8 Example communication passport for use in a criminal justice setting for a person with SLCN – page 1.

Considerations relating to this reason for referral vary based on the type of CJS setting:

- In liaison and diversion teams, there is an expectation to report on the SLCN needs of the individual so that reasonable adjustments can be made to ensure that any conviction is 'safe'. The report is likely to be factual, relating to SLCN only with limited past medical history content. The aim is for this to be a report which is shared with other professionals with the consent of the individual. If consent is not obtained, other professionals will seek to obtain a copy of the report via legal disclosures.
- In community forensic teams, reports on SLCN are written as needed and shared with the clinical team. The individual would not be expected to give consent for this report to be shared with the responsible clinician (RC). It would be expected that the report had been shared with the individual by the SLT.
- Within secure hospitals, it would be expected that the SLT would write a formal report for the clinical team. The individual would not be expected to give consent for this report to be shared with the RC. While it would be desirable for the report content to be shared with the subject of the report, this is not required if the person is cared for under the Mental Health Act and a best-interests decision is made not to share the contents.
- Within the prison setting, reporting of SLCN is more complex. People in prison have the right to keep their medical information confidential and separate from their legal matters. For this reason, the SLT in a prison setting would not write a report unless the individual had provided written consent in advance. There is an expectation that the individual will have read the report prior to it being shared so that they can withdraw consent to share if they are unhappy with the contents.

A further consideration when preparing a communication report, depending on the setting, is whether the individual has been consulted on the style of report (e.g. accessible style, formal style, giving a focused specific piece of information, focusing on function over impairment). Does the referrer expect a report in a set format? There are occasions where this is not negotiable, such as parole reports.

The tone and style of a report can vary based on the reason for reporting and 'who' you are writing to. If the report is to help the individual appreciate their progress in their communication goals, it can take the form of a letter to the person. Ideas for report style:

- Accessible report which is factual and written in terms that the individual can engage with. This can include photos of completed work or Talking Mats, symbols and key words. The subject of the report would generally feel more ownership of this document.

- A professional report which is factual and written in a more formal tone, usually without pictures and symbols, although it may include graphs of assessment results. This type of report may be written for a court process or a manager's hearing.
- A completed proforma report which uses a template that has been provided by a third party such as the parole board. The rationale for the template is that such reports are standardised and it is easier for the parole board members to find information quickly.
- A client letter which can be more informal and personal, include photos and examples of work and build a sense of achievement in the reader.

Is accessible material required?

Accessible material is not solely based on the person's skills in literacy. The need for accessible material includes consideration of concentration, attention, how information is processed and stored within memory, preferred terminology, adaptations to vocabulary to support the individual and visual design which supports understanding and expression.

Think about the person and their skills first:

- How well can they understand what is said to them?
- Can they read or understand pictures?
- Can they read text or understand written information?
- Are they a confident reader or writer, or is the presentation of writing likely to cause distress?
- Can they concentrate well to take in information?
- How able are they to ask questions if they do not understand?
- What is their knowledge and previous experience of the topic?
- How are they in respect of making sense of the topic and understanding the implications and relevance to them?

Remember when a person is upset, anxious, tired or ill, their demand and capacity skills change, which could also impact on their ability to engage with written materials. Figure 5.9 overleaf is offered to help the clinician decide whether the provision of accessible information would help.

Assessible information needed?

Problems understanding of verbal information
Communicates mostly about here and now
Struggles with reading and writing
Poor concentration and easily distracted.

Yes: always

Assessible information needed?

Limited understanding of verbal information but better with familiar people, topics or contexts
Struggles with reading and writing
Concentrates for 10 to 20 minutes
Visual aids help understanding and memory

Yes: always

Assessible information needed?

Good understanding of verbal information
Good literacy skills
Good concentration in most situations
Can express themselves well

Use standard written forms

FIGURE 5.9 A summary to support decision making relating to whether accessible information should be provided to an individual

An example accessible communication report is shown in Table 5.3 overleaf.

The style and design of accessible reports can vary and there is no 'perfect' example. With this in mind, a comprehensive advice sheet on how to create an accessible document is included at Appendix 25 and summarised in Figure 5.10 on page 221.

TABLE 5.3 Example accessible SLT report

Easy-Read Speech and Language Therapy Report

Date of report:

Your details

Name:
Date of birth:
NHS number:
Address:

About you

	You went to different schools You said your reading and writing is not good
	You learned 2 languages You have had a stutter all your life
	You said that sometimes you do not understand what people say to you You said that you have a bad memory

Attention and Listening

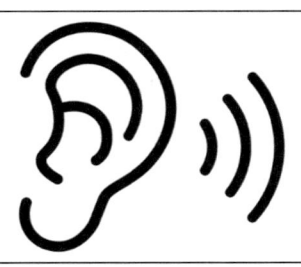	When you saw Jacqui, your **listening was very good**

Understanding

	We did a test to find out how good you are at understanding **You said you found it hard**

(Continued)

TABLE 5.3 Continued

	The test showed that you find it **hard to understand** when people talk to you People need to use SMALL sentences
	Jacqui found that your **memory is not very good**
	People need to give you **time to think**

Talking

	You can make good sentences and ask for things you need
	You do not know all the words for things This is because you have 2 languages

Reading and writing

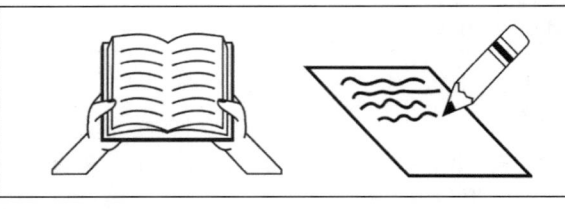	You could read some words which Jacqui wrote down **You find reading and writing hard** **You want to be better at reading and writing**

What will happen now?

- *Jacqui will work with you to write a communication passport about you and how to help*
- *Jacqui will tell your team about your communication needs*
- *We would like you to tell us if you do not understand something*
- *We will write things for you in 'easy-read' – pictures, words and symbols*
- *Jacqui and you will think about what work you might want to do and how*

Report written by:
Date:
Report finalised with client on (date):

FIGURE 5.10 A summary to support decision making relating to whether accessible information should be provided to an individual

Communication advice

The referrer will often seek advice that can be used to reduce the risk of communication breakdown and increase the person's ability to engage in rehabilitation. The main domains for communication advice are:

- attention and listening
- understanding of verbal information
- ability to process verbal information and comment on processing time
- auditory memory
- access to and use of working vocabulary
- cognition
- expression of verbal information including dysfluency or voice
- social skills including emotions impacting on interaction skills.

The communication advice is developed as a result of analysis of speech, language and communication assessment findings and observation of application of skills by the individual. The advice should be discussed and agreed with the individual so that they are comfortable with any suggested strategies. The advice should also take into account any situations which the individual will be exposed to in the coming months. Ideas for communication advice per domain are given in Table 5.4 overleaf.

TABLE 5.4 Ideas for communication support by different domains which impact on SLCN

Domain	Example of information which could be included	Example strategies to help
Attention and listening	Comment on how long a person can give attention and listening Comment on how this changes in 1:1 conversation and in groups Comment on most common barriers to attention and listening Comment on how the person refocuses once attention has lapsed Comment on when attention and listening varies and why	What helps the person to listen? How can attention and listening be supported in certain situations? Are there sensory needs located in this person's communication profile?
Understanding of verbal information	Comment on the types of words and sentences which the person can understand Comment on how total communication supports comprehension	Advice on which strategies help this person to understand such as easy words, short sentences, avoidance of inference, use of communication ramps
Ability to process verbal information and comment on processing time	Comment on accuracy of processing verbal information Comment on any points in verbal information where processing often fails, such as the end of sentences Comment on how long the person takes to process Comment on how time pressure changes the person's processing accuracy	A specific idea of amount of processing time to offer Advice on sentence types to use to support processing such as active sentences Advice on managing time pressure such as allowing time, using conversation agendas or 'parking' information for another time
Auditory memory	Comment on how many items the person can hold and process within the auditory memory	Advice on environmental supports to reduce the load placed on the auditory memory, such as clocks, calendars, written prompts, visual minute takers in group meetings, recapping at the end of the conversation
Access to and use of working vocabulary	Comment on semantic processing and lexical access including any word-finding issues or semantic errors Comment on extent of working vocabulary for comprehension and expression Comment on any environmental or personal factors which impact on this domain	Ideas which support word-finding or semantic errors that the individual has pre-approved Information on types of words known and used Information relating to whether the person masks their vocabulary needs or is overt with them Ideas to check understanding of vocabulary in sensitive ways

(Continued)

TABLE 5.4 Continued

Domain	Example of information which could be included	Example strategies to help
Cognition	Comment on the person's ability to seek help or solve problems using communication skills Comment on impulsiveness and how this interacts with communication skills Comment on the person's skill to sequence information in a way that shows consideration of the conversation partner's knowledge Comment on application of theory of mind within communication Comment on emotional liability and how this impacts on communication Comment on the person's self-awareness of their communication needs	Advice on strategies to promote thinking, self-awareness and planning of communicative content Advice on visual ramps such as comic-strip conversations Advice on non-judgemental positive regard in communication Ideas on how to give communication feedback in a way that is supportive and nurturing
Expression of verbal information including dysfluency or voice	Comment on the person's ability to express ideas, request help, explain situations and give a coherent narrative Comment on any barriers such as fluency or voice quality Comment on any specific needs such as access to emotion vocabulary (alexithymia)	Practical suggestions on how best to support the person to express information such as pre-planning, using visual aids, thinking time, choices, etc. Suggestions to support fluency based on the person's preferences Suggestions to support voice such as environmental modifications Information on the types of words, concepts or feelings that the person is able to articulate and what is reasonable to expect
Social skills including emotions impacting on interaction skills	Comment on turn-taking skills in 1:1 and in group situations; quantity of information provided in any social context; ability to maintain a topic or change topic Comment on use of potentially offensive vocabulary such as swearing or racially inappropriate words Comment on ability to understand and use non-verbal information such as facial expression to support comprehension Comment on use of any communication device which seems different to social expectations (e.g. laughing when nervous or telling jokes during important conversations) Comment on any social masking which is used by the person in order to support their participation so that the individual is not misperceived	Offer strategies which the individual agrees will support their social interactions Suggest ways to give feedback on inappropriate topics or vocabulary without stigmatising the individual Suggest whether masking or devices should be accepted or challenged, and if so, when and by whom in agreement with the person

This advice can be developed further into a communication contract which the individual uses in certain situations or with certain people. The communication contract takes the form of 'If I do this, you can do____' and 'If you do____, I can do_____'. When negotiating the communication contract, each party agrees and tries to understand the other's point of view on why the support is necessary. Once agreement is reached, a time period is assigned, and a reward is set for both parties so that co-production and joint working are embedded into the communication support. An example of a communication contract is given in Figure 5.11 below, using the example of a man in a low-secure hospital setting who swears in public and supports football:

Communication contract	
Situation: Daniel often swears in public when on section 17 leave from hospital. The swearing is often in a loud voice and can be heard by passers by	
___Daniel___ has agreed to: Be reminded about swearing before he leaves the hospital grounds. Have the same rule as football. Staff can 'book' him for swearing by showing him a yellow card. If Daniel is 'booked' twice, he is 'sent off' and will return to the hospital. Daniel will not argue with the escorting staff about being 'booked'.	Escorting staff has agreed to: Remind Daniel about swearing before he leaves the hospital grounds. Follow the football rule consistently and fairly. Apply the football rule in a way which is respectful like a referee. Remind Daniel not to argue and to support him to use 'sportsmanlike conduct'. Not 'go on about it' if Daniel gets booked of sent off.
This contract was agreed on: 14th February 2023 This contract will last until: 1st August 2023 If everyone keeps the contract: Daniel and staff will go and see Leeds Utd FC in a pre-season friendly game	

FIGURE 5.11 Example of a communication contract between a person with SLCN residing in a secure hospital and their clinical team

A blank communication contract is located at Appendix 26 for use in practice.

SLT intervention after assessment is discussed in the next chapter. This segment on assessment in the targeted approach concludes at this point, and we now move on to discuss the top tier of the three-tiered model.

The specialist level

This approach in the three-tiered model includes all elements of the universal and targeted approach plus specialist resources aimed at the most complex people who may have the most intensive needs, and who would benefit from multi-disciplinary input which includes a specialist speech and language therapist.

Complex people with intensive needs should be defined locally by each setting, but examples may include:

- people who are making choices that have serious or potentially life-changing consequences such as choosing to set fires recklessly
- people whose communicative actions place themselves and professionals at risk of harm such as deciding to take a professional hostage as a means to get your problems resolved
- people with complex trauma or mental health needs which result in them being a risk to themselves or others
- people with such an intense response to triggers that they have the potential to escalate to violence very quickly and are hard to de-escalate
- people with long-term difficulties.

The differentiation between targeted approaches and specialist approaches lies in:

- the need for highly experienced and skilled professionals to be involved in the direct care of the individual
- the need for each component of intervention to be specifically articulated, implemented and monitored
- the expected time and demands placed on the professionals involved in the case would be higher than targeted approaches
- the expected time to see a change in the individual receiving care would be over a longer duration
- the expectation of integrated strategies across the team and of individualised care.

People may move between the targeted and specialist levels of input depending on their progress and changing needs.

Assessment of SLCN within the specialist approach includes the strategies within the targeted approach but will also include information from a wider group of professional colleagues. This will be drawn together in a series of professional meetings, depending on the setting. The individual may be included in some or all of these meetings if they are able to tolerate the discussion without emotional or psychological distress (McKeown et al., 2020). A useful framework for synthesising information is the psychologically informed formulation framework which allows for the co-creation of a hypothesis that perhaps explains how the individual has arrived at their current situation (Logan, 2017). The formulation should offer the following:

- An outline of a need that the person would like support with. Support does not suggest a 'cure' but does offer skill building within the milieu where the person functions.
- Suggestions of how different elements of the person's life and experience relate to one another.
- Suggestions of how unhelpful responses may be developed in the current milieu and how they may be perpetuated.
- Indications of what might help, which can be the foundation of a plan.
- An opportunity to try something that may help and then revise what is known based on reviewing the formulation.

In Figure 5.12 overleaf, Person J has a history of reckless fire setting. He has SLCN and learning disability. The formulation shows elements of his overall picture and suggests the hypothesis that:

- J is unable to solve a problem when feeling distressed, so withdraws and sets fire.
- SLCN, attachment needs and core beliefs relate to the decision to set fire. Fire setting has become a tool whereby J can obtain quality interactions and reassurance.
- Communication tools will help J if they are used consistently each day to help him understand, express, solve problems and feel listened to.
- Being able to understand, express, solve problems and feel listened to will help attachment needs but cannot 'cure' them.
- This is likely to be an ongoing process with J as his presenting problem has been reinforced over many years and his core beliefs are going to take many years to resolve (if at all).
- Involving J in the formulation and use of communication tools is key so that he feels that the intervention is acceptable to him.

In this scenario, assessment of SLCN is on a continuum with intervention. The SLT suggests communication tools to embed in the person's day based on MDT knowledge and observation, and then tests the tools over a period to see if the presenting problem is reduced in frequency and duration. This allows for a sequence of assessment plan (information gathering, observation, J's views, etc.) (via formulation including J), After the formulation has provided a rationale for intervention, and the intervention completed with J, the formulation can be reviewed to test whether the intervention was successful in changing the presenting problem. The formulation sheet featured above is included at Appendix 27 for use in practice.

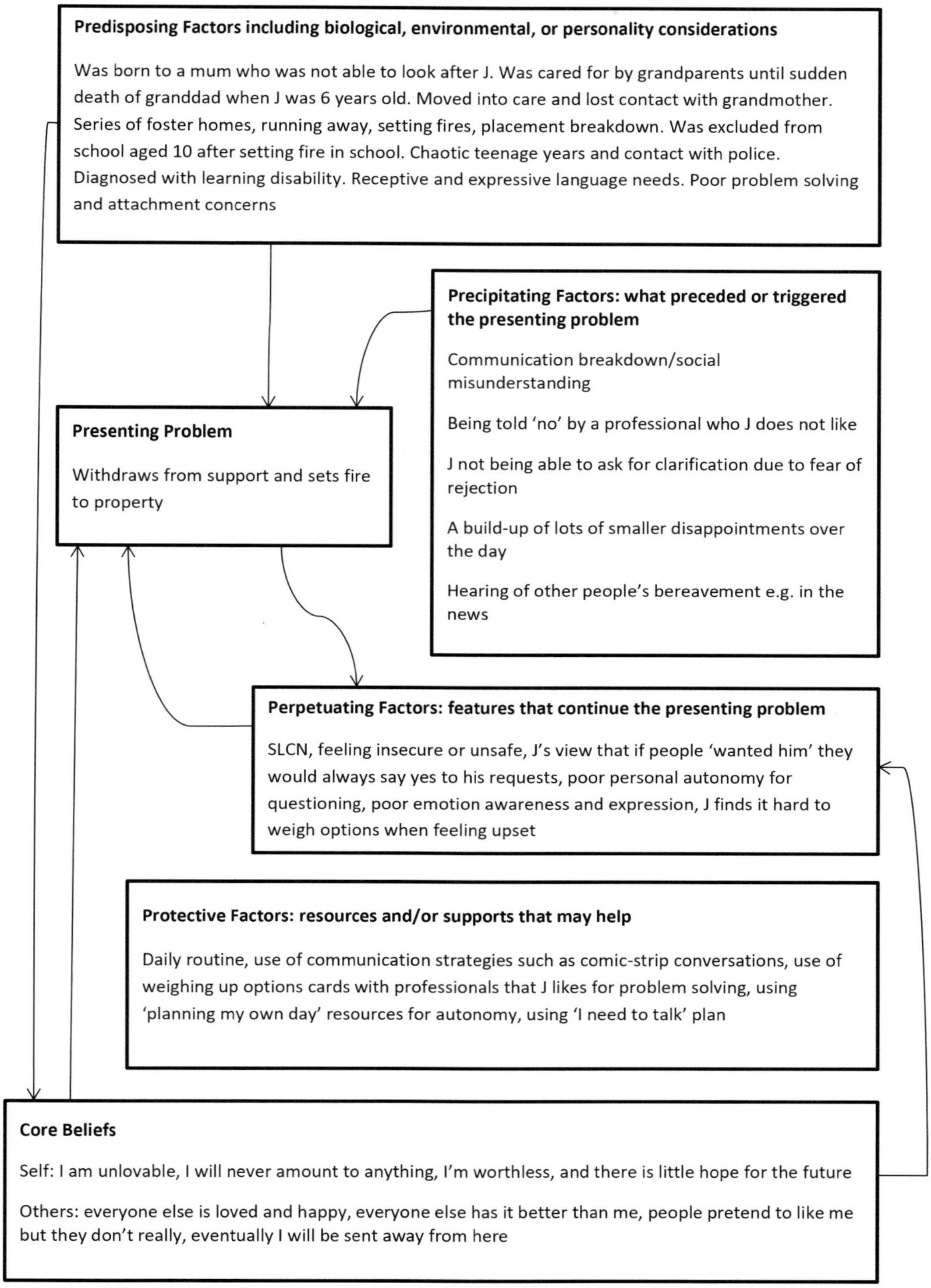

Predisposing Factors including biological, environmental, or personality considerations

Was born to a mum who was not able to look after J. Was cared for by grandparents until sudden death of granddad when J was 6 years old. Moved into care and lost contact with grandmother. Series of foster homes, running away, setting fires, placement breakdown. Was excluded from school aged 10 after setting fire in school. Chaotic teenage years and contact with police. Diagnosed with learning disability. Receptive and expressive language needs. Poor problem solving and attachment concerns

Precipitating Factors: what preceded or triggered the presenting problem

Communication breakdown/social misunderstanding

Being told 'no' by a professional who J does not like

J not being able to ask for clarification due to fear of rejection

A build-up of lots of smaller disappointments over the day

Hearing of other people's bereavement e.g. in the news

Presenting Problem

Withdraws from support and sets fire to property

Perpetuating Factors: features that continue the presenting problem

SLCN, feeling insecure or unsafe, J's view that if people 'wanted him' they would always say yes to his requests, poor personal autonomy for questioning, poor emotion awareness and expression, J finds it hard to weigh options when feeling upset

Protective Factors: resources and/or supports that may help

Daily routine, use of communication strategies such as comic-strip conversations, use of weighing up options cards with professionals that J likes for problem solving, using 'planning my own day' resources for autonomy, using 'I need to talk' plan

Core Beliefs

Self: I am unlovable, I will never amount to anything, I'm worthless, and there is little hope for the future

Others: everyone else is loved and happy, everyone else has it better than me, people pretend to like me but they don't really, eventually I will be sent away from here

FIGURE 5.12 **A completed formulation of a person with SLCN demonstrating how SLT input is integral to the individual's risk reduction**

Within a secure hospital setting or a community forensic team, the majority of people would be offered care at the specialist approach level. Within a prison setting, it is likely that every person would benefit from the universal approach, as many as 50% would benefit from a targeted approach and a lower number of perhaps 5–10% would require a specialist approach. These estimations are based on tacit knowledge of the SLT service at HMP Berwyn.

This concludes discussion of the three-tiered approach to SLT services in CJS.

Trauma-informed practice

Trigger warning: the next section of this text discusses trauma and trauma-informed approaches. It may not be suitable for all readers and caution is advised.

Trauma is important when considering services and care for people within CJS. But what is trauma? The accepted definition of trauma is:

> Individual trauma results from an event, series of events, or set of circumstances that is experienced by an individual as physically or emotionally harmful or life threatening and that has lasting adverse effects on the individual's functioning and mental, physical, social, emotional or spiritual well-being.
>
> *(Substance Abuse and Mental Health Services Administration*
> *(SAMHSA), 2014)*

Trauma negatively affects the individual's ability to (King, 2017):

- cope with the circumstances that led to their trauma
- recover from the trauma
- tolerate emotions such as fear, hopelessness, shame, guilt and a sense of violation that mirror the emotions experienced when exposed to trauma-inducing events.

An experience of trauma can be acute (time limited with high intensity), chronic (ongoing) or complex (multiple different experiences which are trauma-inducing). The effects of trauma are usually long-standing and are more impactful if experienced by a person during their developmental years (Randall and Haskell, 2013).

Trauma is especially relevant to the population discussed in this book because people who are exposed to adverse childhood experiences (ACEs) (which are trauma-inducing) are likely to also be people in contact with the CJS. This cohort has the following demographic outline (Ace Aware Wales, 2022):

- A higher rate of multiple, traumatic bereavements including of parents compared with the general population in the UK (Vaswani and Paul, 2019).
- 40% of people in prison will have lived exposure to domestic violence as a child.
- 40% of people in prison have been physically abused in childhood.
- 17% of people in prison have been sexually abused in childhood.
- 60% of young people incarcerated in young offender settings have experienced four or more ACEs.
- Being subject to childhood trauma increases the likelihood that a person will serve an increased number of prison sentences.
- Being subject to childhood trauma correlates to the length of time a person serves in their sentence (more trauma is likely to lead to longer periods of incarceration).
- People who had been exposed to greater levels of trauma during their childhood were more likely to commit multiple crimes.
- People who had been exposed to greater levels of trauma during their childhood were more likely to commit violent crimes.
- There is a correlation between the amount of violence witnessed or experienced and the potential to commit violence against others.

The evidence base argues that trauma is so fundamental to offending and recidivism risks that all services working within the CJS should be trauma-informed to reduce the potential for new trauma or re-traumatisation (Ace Aware Wales, 2022; Auty et al., 2022). Trauma-informed practice should be implemented at all levels in the three-tiered model with all individuals. The rationale for this is that lived experience of trauma is highly prevalent in this population, and some individuals will not have disclosed a trauma history despite having experienced it. A professional working in the field of CJS should not assume that there is no trauma history. The risk of triggering trauma in a person has such dramatic consequences that it should be controlled for at all times.

So what is trauma-informed practice? Paterson (2014) explains that trauma-informed practice is:

> A model [of service provision and care] that is grounded in and directed by a complete understanding of how trauma exposure affects service users' neurological, biological, psychological and social development.

To unpack this further, trauma-informed practice employs an ethos of (Vaswani and Paul, 2019):

- being sensitive to the fact that many people using the service will have experienced trauma
- being careful that any care and treatment does not harm the individual
- being aware that trauma affects the way that a person interacts and engages
- being able to adapt to the individual's needs to minimise their distress, maximise trust and work jointly to co-produce outcomes
- being able to notice any potential by the service, professionals or individuals to trigger re-traumatisation and prevent this.

Figure 5.13 (below) offers a hierarchy of needs which should be met in order to offer a clinical environment that is responsive to trauma needs. Each level builds on the last from the bottom of the hierarchy towards the top. The rate that people move from one level to another varies from person to person, informing the clinician that creating a trauma-informed therapeutic alliance may take an extended period of time.

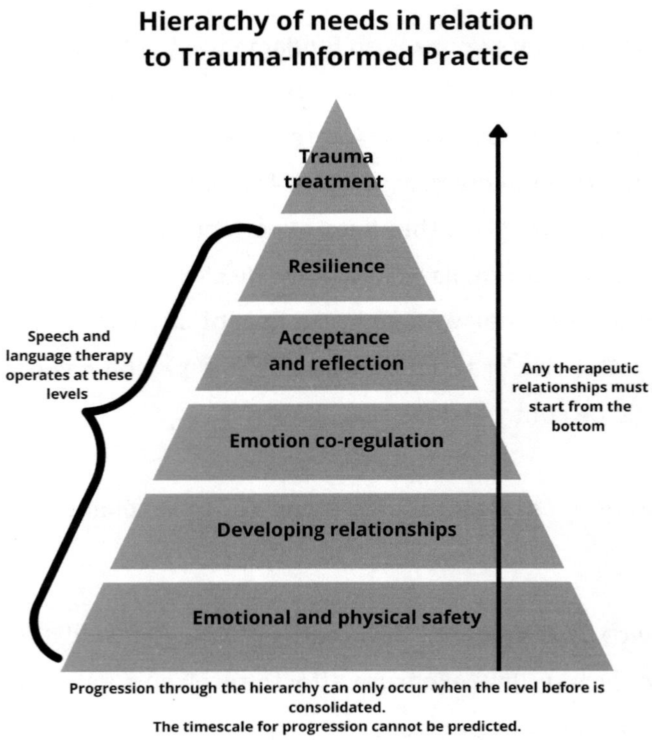

Hierarchy of needs in relation to Trauma-Informed Practice

Trauma treatment

Resilience

Acceptance and reflection

Emotion co-regulation

Developing relationships

Emotional and physical safety

Speech and language therapy operates at these levels

Any therapeutic relationships must start from the bottom

Progression through the hierarchy can only occur when the level before is consolidated.
The timescale for progression cannot be predicted.

FIGURE 5.13 A hierarchy of needs which should be met in order to offer a clinical environment which is responsive to an individual's trauma needs

All services and professionals working with CJS should be trauma-informed regardless of the care that they are offering. This is because trauma-informed practice is not aimed at directly addressing the trauma, but is aimed at providing an environment in which trauma is not exacerbated and does not become an impediment to engaging with the care on offer (Vaswani and Paul, 2019).

Case example

Dave came to prison after being remanded in custody for a suspected violent crime. Very little was known about Dave and his past history when he arrived. The act of coming into custody had trauma triggers for him, such as the large numbers of people in crowded environments, bright lights, high noise levels, confinement behind locked gates and doors, fear of the unknown, anxiety about the criminal charge and the threat of potential violence from peers. This was coupled with rapid withdrawal from substances so that Dave felt physical withdrawal symptoms that were distressing for him.

In the prison reception, Dave was argumentative with prison officers and uncooperative. He declined to follow polite requests, and his verbal interactions were perceived as aggressive by officers. Dave was supported to complete the prison reception process, and as part of this he was referred to speech and language therapy due to his interaction style. The SLT phoned Dave to ask if he would be open to meeting, including arranging when and where based on his preference.

The SLT met Dave in his place of work, in the prison, as this was where Dave felt he would like the first meeting. Dave showed the SLT what he does at work and introduced her to his work supervisor. Gradually, appointments moved to a more confidential space so that the SLT could ask Dave about his interaction style when he came to prison. Dave talked about feeling anxious and overwhelmed. The SLT did not ask Dave why this was the case and employed non-judgemental positive regard for his explanation. Dave agreed to commence joint work on understanding how his emotions impact on his interaction style. The agreement included the assurance that the SLT would not ask him questions about his emotions before he came to prison. Further details such as frequency and place of appointments, how Dave can send the SLT a message if he cannot attend, the boundaries of confidentiality and an agreement that the SLT would not touch Dave (such as a handshake) were all finalised.

Trauma-informed SLT service within CJS

While an SLT service within CJS would not be aiming to directly address trauma via treatment, the service would be expected to be trauma-informed. Figure 5.14 (below) provides an overview of how a trauma-informed SLT service may present itself (Chaudhri et al., 2019):

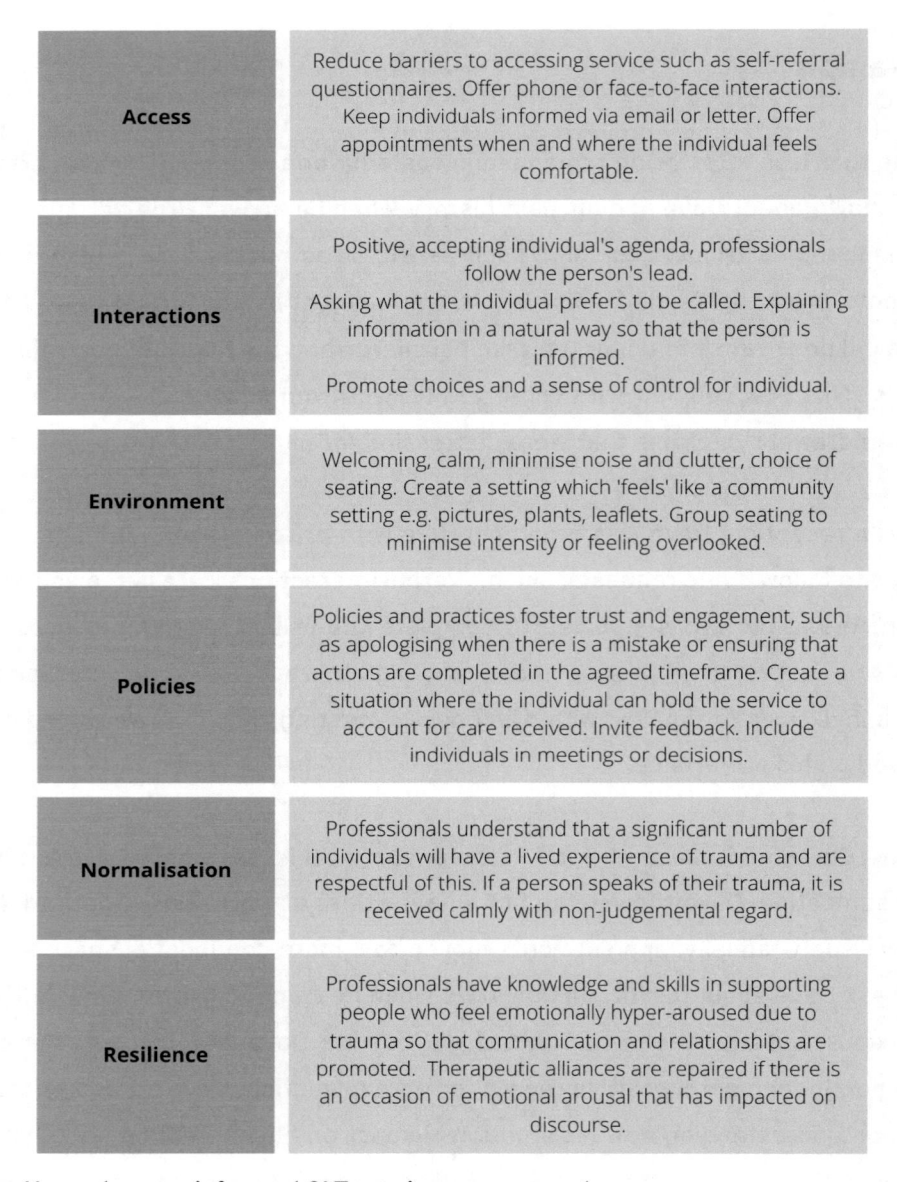

FIGURE 5.14 How a trauma-informed SLT service may present

The service is welcoming and affirming; there are reduced or zero barriers to access; there are explanations of the SLT role and service aims; any intervention is informed by co-produced treatment goals; the duration, frequency and location of care is mutually agreed; there is honesty and accountability; feedback is sought and used to drive service change; all interactions are based on positive regard and respect.

The professionals should be able to adapt communication strategies in response to the individual's current emotional and psychological needs. If a person is in a distressed state, communication should be adjusted to reduce demands (as per the demands and capacities model discussed in this chapter). Figure 5.15 (below) illustrates this point and offers communication advice to reduce or increase demands as required:

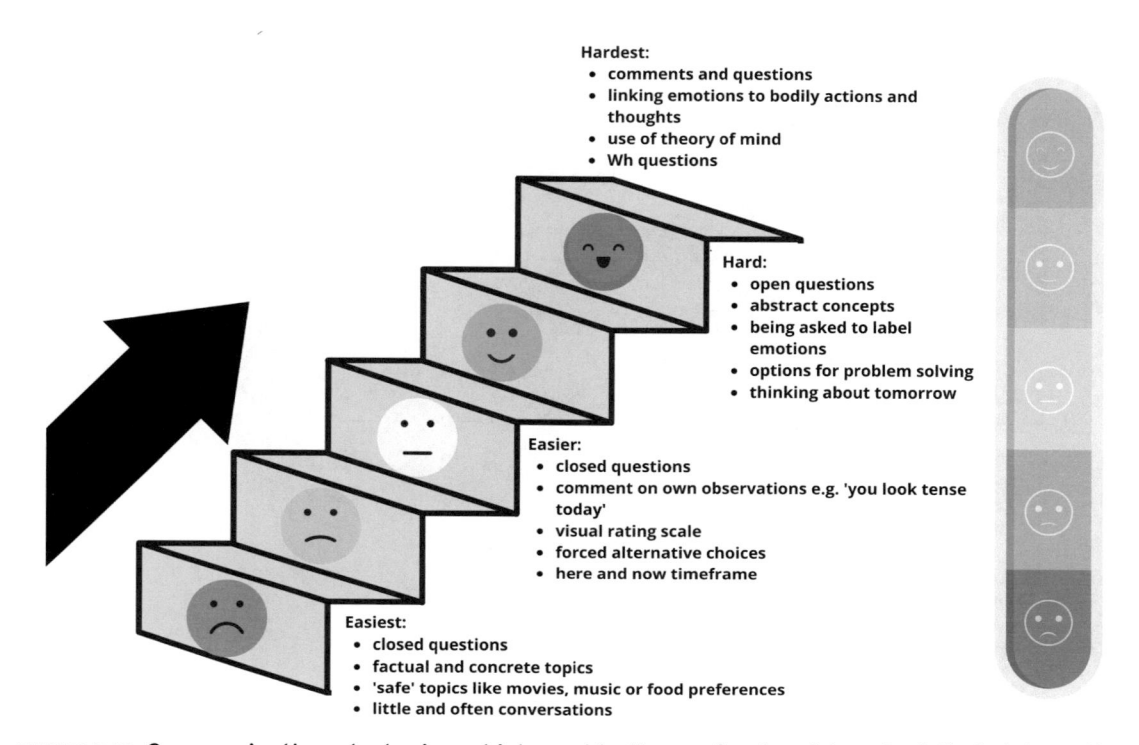

Hardest:
- comments and questions
- linking emotions to bodily actions and thoughts
- use of theory of mind
- Wh questions

Hard:
- open questions
- abstract concepts
- being asked to label emotions
- options for problem solving
- thinking about tomorrow

Easier:
- closed questions
- comment on own observations e.g. 'you look tense today'
- visual rating scale
- forced alternative choices
- here and now timeframe

Easiest:
- closed questions
- factual and concrete topics
- 'safe' topics like movies, music or food preferences
- little and often conversations

FIGURE 5.15 Communication strategies which enable the professional to adapt their interaction style in response to the individual's current emotional and psychological needs

Being exposed to ACEs not only creates emotional and psychological trauma within a person, but also leads to a greater risk of changes to the neural landscape of the brain. Sexual trauma in childhood has been linked to increased levels of anxiety in adult survivors due to neurological changes (Lovett, 2018). ACEs are associated with hampering structural connectivity in critical cortico-limbic networks that are required for cognitive reasoning and experience of emotions (Benedetti et al., 2014). ACEs also negatively influence thalamic volumes which cause people who have experienced ACEs to experience more acute episodes of post-trauma stress symptoms (Xie et al., 2022). Figure 5.16 (overleaf) illustrates neuroanatomy, trauma responses and where they are experienced within the brain, the person's psychological response and basic communication advice within one visual.

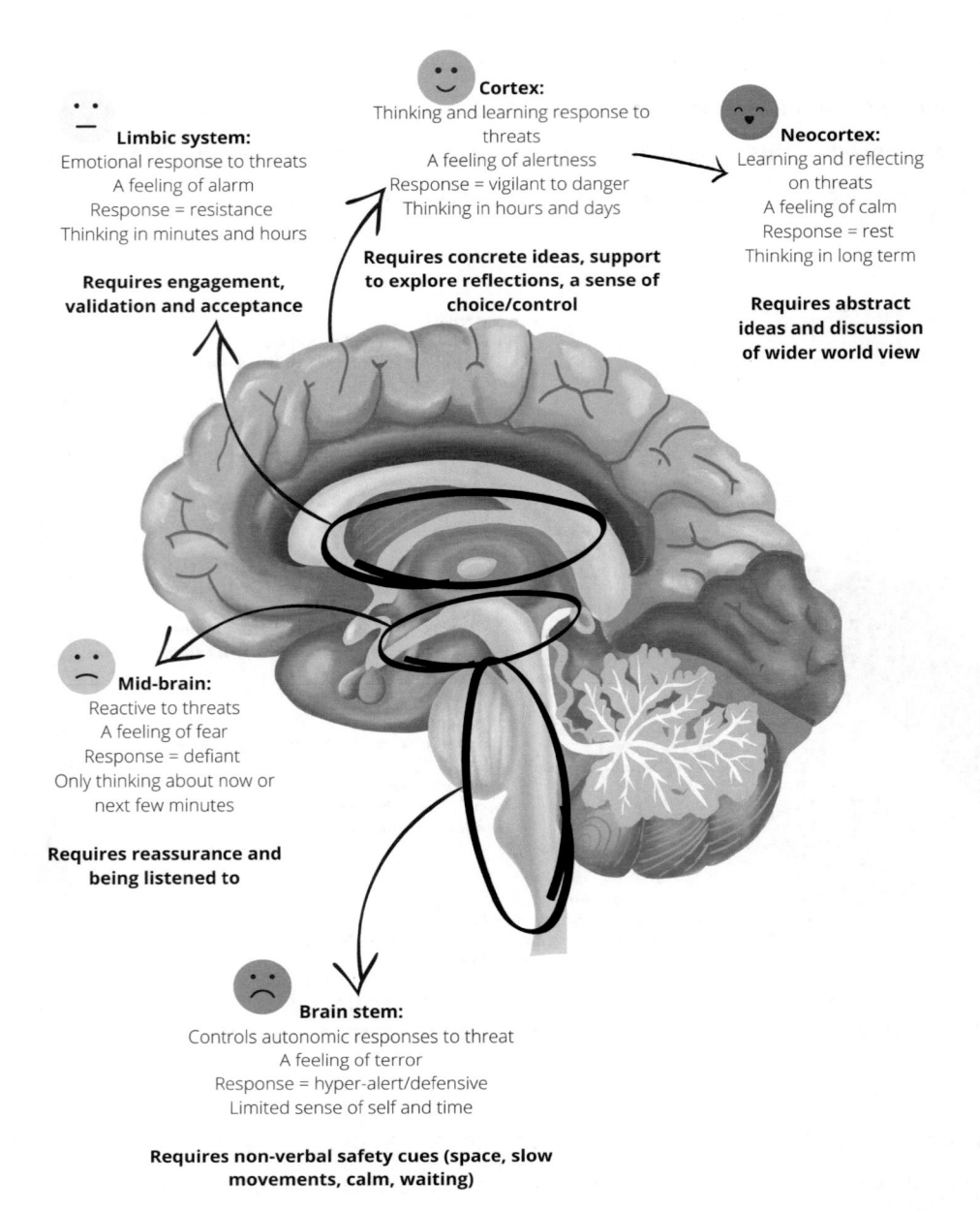

FIGURE 5.16 A visual showing neuroanatomy, trauma responses, the individual's psychological response and basic communication advice

Ideas for trauma-informed communication, listening to a disclosure and resolution are included at Appendix 28 in a form which can be copied and used for discussion of trauma-focused interactions with colleagues, such as communication training or within supervision.

Case example

Tom was in prison on drug-related offences. He was chaotic in his daily life in prison – gaining and losing employment, feeling distressed and using self-harm as a tool to cope, taking illicit substances when feeling low in mood and getting into debt to peers for these substances, which only added to his emotional burdens. After an episode of self-harm, Tom was being supported via the prison Assessment, Care in Custody and Teamwork (ACCT). The ACCT document captures his current emotional state and seeks to find solutions that will help. The ACCT process includes meetings where the individual is encouraged to discuss their emotional state. In one such meeting, Tom was asked to 'open up' and disclosed trauma in a way that was distressing for him. After the meeting, Tom returned to his prison cell. There followed several weeks of Tom feeling unsafe, getting into fights, using self-harm strategies to cope, damaging property and refusing to engage with people he would previously talk to. He was referred to SLT, and informal assessment showed that he required simple verbal communication forms plus reassurance. SLT consisted of:

- short visits at planned times with Tom's agreement
- visits located in his room with calm, slow and thoughtful pace of interaction
- talk about music preferences and quoting favourite songs
- gradual introduction of the SLT commenting on Tom's presentation (e.g. 'You look like you slept last night')
- gradual introduction of forced alternative choices of tasks which Tom might be able to complete (e.g. 'Do you want to help me do x or y?')
- gradual introduction of agenda setting (e.g. 'When I come and see you tomorrow, I want to ask you what your favourite animal is and why').

These strategies supported Tom to re-engage, regulate his trauma response and begin to re-establish relationships.

While trauma-informed practice can be time-consuming and labour-intensive for the clinician, the outcomes for the service users and service are as follows:

- improved engagement in interventions (Cocozza et al., 2005)
- increased clinical effectiveness in the domains of empowering the individual to make meaningful changes based on learning in clinic (Chandler, 2008)
- increased responsivity to risk-reduction interventions (Miller and Najavits, 2012)
- reduced length of time in treatment or hospital (Greenwald et al., 2012)
- decreased need to use physical restraint and seclusion or segregation (Azeem et al., 2011)
- decreased use of illicit substances to self-medicate against emotions (Chung, Domino and Morrissey, 2009)
- decreased intensity and duration of trauma symptoms (Gatz et al., 2007).

Forensic setting considerations

When an SLT is working in a forensic setting, there will be added requirements around resources which relate to local restrictions and the need to avoid materials that may be perceived to link to crime or criminal intent.

- Avoid resources that might be perceived as 'childlike'; if possible, use resources such as technical Lego or playing cards.
- Some SLT formal assessment resources used in forensic settings were created for the paediatric client group and are needed in order to acquire quantitative data. In these circumstances, using a 'childlike' resource is necessary and can often be overcome with an apology to the individual.
- Avoid images of children or references to children. SLTs need to be particularly vigilant around vocabulary lists which include items such as toys, nappies, cot, school, etc.
- Any images must be appropriate for the setting (e.g. adults, pro-social, non-triggering of trauma, not associated with crime or gangs or weapons).
- Avoid using maps of the local area which may assist in absconding.
- Avoid using timetables of local buses or trains which may assist in absconding.
- Avoid any items which can be moulded or take impressions such as playdough or clay.
- Avoid any items which can be used to plug locks such as chewing gum or blue tack.
- Avoid any items which contain tools such as Meccano, or glue such as in modelling kits.
- Avoid items which can be secreted and used for other purposes such as sewing equipment, knitting equipment, tin foil, etc.
- Avoid items which can be used as weapons such as scissors or metal cutlery. This includes less obvious items with the potential to be used as weapons such as pen tops and paperclips.
- Audio-visual or computer equipment of any kind should not be used.
- Check whether spiral-bound notebooks or assessments are allowed in a specific setting as the metal spiral may be misused.
- Be aware of local restrictions and issues which may change as incidents occur.
- Take particular care not to leave anything behind such as paperclips or pen caps; working in and out of a sealed folder may be helpful.

Conclusion

This chapter has advocated for a tiered approach to SLT provision in CJS settings so that the needs of a range of individuals are met by professionals who have the appropriate knowledge and skills. The tiered approach offers a structure for assessment and intervention which becomes more rigorous as the needs of the individual become more complex. For the most complex people, formulation and MDT working are essential for effective outcomes.

The assessment of individuals is recommended to be completed via a range of means, both formal and informal, and via a trauma-focused lens. The rationale for this is articulated at each stage in the text.

Throughout the chapter, suggested tools and strategies are proposed to support effective clinical practice. This includes resources within the appendices, information pertaining to accessible materials and factsheets that can be employed by SLTs and appropriately qualified professionals of a related discipline working in the setting.

References

Ace Aware Wales (2022) A short guide to understanding Adverse Childhood Experiences and a Trauma and ACE (TrACE) informed approach. Available at https://acehubwales.com/resources /a-short-guide-to-understanding-adverse-childhood-experiences-and-a-trauma-and-ace-trace -informed-approach [accessed 7th March 2021]

Auty, K.M., Liebling, A., Schliehe, A. and Crewe, B. (2022) What is trauma-informed practice? Towards operationalisation of the concept in two prisons for women. *Criminology & Criminal Justice.* https://doi.org/10.1177/17488958221094980

Azeem, M., Aujla, A., Rammerth, M., Binsfeld, G. and Jones, R. (2011) Effectiveness of six core strategies based on trauma-informed care in reducing seclusions and restraints at a child and adolescent psychiatric hospital. *Journal of Child & Adolescent Psychiatric Nursing*, 24(1), 11-15.

Baddeley, A.D., Emslie, H. and Nimmo-Smith, I. (1994) *The Doors and People Test: A test of visual and verbal recall and recognition*. Bury St Edmunds: Thames Valley Test Company.

Benedetti, F., Bollettini, I., Radaelli, D., Poletti, S., Locatelli, C., Falini, A., Smeraldi, E. and Colombo, C. (2014) Adverse childhood experiences influence white matter microstructure in patients with bipolar disorder. *Psychological Medicine*, 44(14), 3069-3082.

Bishop, D. (2003) *Test for Reception of Grammar*, Version 2 (TROG-2). London: Pearson Assessment.

Boardman, L., Crichton, C. and Butterworth, S. (2016) When you can't talk about it: Using Talking Mats to enable an offender with communication difficulties to express his thoughts and beliefs. *Probation Journal*, 63(1), 72-79.

Botha, M., Hanlon, J. and Williams, G.L. (2023) Does language matter? Identity-first versus person-first language use in autism research: A response to Vivanti. *Journal of Autism and Developmental Disorders*, 53(2), 870-878.

Bradshaw, J. and Pringle, J. (2019) The use of communication passports in services for adults with intellectual and developmental disabilities. *Journal of Intellectual Disability Research*, 63(7), 702-702.

Brown, P., Bakolis, I., Appiah-Kusi, E., Hallett, N., Hotopf, M. and Blackwood, N. (2022) Prevalence of mental disorders in defendants at criminal court. *BJPsych Open*, 8(3), e92.

Brown, S. and Völlm, B. (2016) The implementation of case formulation by probation officers: Service user and carer views. *The Journal of Forensic Psychiatry & Psychology*, 27(2), 215-231.

Buijsman, R., Begeer, S. and Scheeren, A.M. (2022) 'Autistic person' or 'person with autism'? Person-first language preference in Dutch adults with autism and parents. *Autism*. https://doi .org/10.1177/13623613221117914

Chandler, G. (2008) From traditional inpatient to trauma-informed treatment: Transferring control from staff to patient. *Journal of the American Psychiatric Nurses Association*, 14(5), 363-371.

Chaudhri, S., Zweig, K.C., Hebbar, P., Angell, S. and Vasan, A. (2019) Trauma-informed care: A strategy to improve primary healthcare engagement for persons with criminal justice system involvement. *Journal of General Internal Medicine*, 34(6), 1048-1052.

Christie, J., Clark, W. and Mortensen, L. (1986) *Mount Wilga High Level Language Test*. Speech Pathology Department, Mount Wilga Rehabilitation Centre.

Chung, S., Domino, M. and Morrissey, J. (2009) Changes in treatment content of services during trauma-informed integrated services for women with co-occurring disorders. *Community Mental Health Journal*, 45(5), 375-384.

Cocozza, J., Jackson, E., Hennigan, K., Morrissey, J., Reed, B., Fallot, R. and Banks, S. (2005) Outcomes for women with co-occurring disorders and trauma: program-level effects. *Journal of Substance Abuse Treatment*, 28(2), 109-119.

Combalbert, N., Pennequin, V., Ferrand, C., Vandevyvère, R., Armand, M. and Geffray, B. (2016) Mental disorders and cognitive impairment in ageing offenders. *The Journal of Forensic Psychiatry & Psychology*, 27(6), 853-866.

Communication Matters (2022) Communication passports. Available at www.communicationmatters.org.uk/what-is-aac/types-of-aac/communication-passports [accessed 7th January 2023]

Crew, M. and Gregory, J. (2008) *Communication Screen*. Leeds Community Healthcare Trust.

Department of Health (2015) *Reference Guide to the Mental Health Act 1983*. Available at https://assets.publishing.service.gov.uk/government/uploads/system/uploads/attachment_data/file/417412/Reference_Guide.pdf [accessed 7th March 2023]

Dunn, L.M. and Dunn, D.M. (2009) *The British Picture Vocabulary Scale*. GL Assessment.

Fowler, A., Phillips, J. and Westaby, C. (2017) Understanding emotions as effective practice in English probation: The performance of emotional labour in building relationships. In P. Ugwudike, P. Raynor and J. Annison (eds) *Evidence-Based Skills in Criminal Justice* (pp.243-262). Bristol: Policy Press.

Gatz, M., Brown, V., Hennigan, K., Rechberger, E., O'Keefe, M., Rose, T. and Bjelajac, P. (2007) Effectiveness of an integrated, trauma-informed approach to treating women with co-occurring disorders and histories of trauma: The Los Angeles site experience. *Journal of Community Psychology*, 35(7), 863-878.

Greenwald, R., Siradas, L., Schmitt, T., Reslan, S., Fierle, J. and Sande, B. (2012) Implementing trauma-informed treatment for youth in a residential facility: First-year outcomes. *Residential Treatment for Children and Youth*, 29(2), 141-153.

Hall, T.A. (2005) The Everyday Memory Survey: Development and Psychometric Analysis. George Fox University. Faculty Publications – Doctor of Psychology (PsyD) Program. https://digitalcommons.georgefox.edu/gscp_fac/68

Hammill, D.D., Brown, V.L., Larsen, S.C. and Wiederholt, J.L. (2007) *TOAL-4: Test of Adolescent and Adult Language*. Wood Dale, IL: Stoelting Co.

Health and Safety Executive (2014) *Health and Safety Toolbox: How to Control Risks at Work, HSG268*. London: HSE Books.

Helm-Estabrooks, N. (2001-2017) *CLQT: Cognitive Linguistic Quick Test*. Hove: Psychological Corporation.

Ireland, C.A. (2012) Brief Cognitive Status Exam. *The British Journal of Forensic Practice*, 14(3). https://doi.org/10.1108/bjfp.2012.54314caa.002

King, E.A. (2017) Outcomes of trauma-informed interventions for incarcerated women: A review. *International Journal of Offender Therapy and Comparative Criminology*, 61(6), 667-688.

Logan, C. (2017) Formulation for forensic practitioners. In R. Roesch and A.N. Cook (eds) *Handbook of Forensic Mental Health Services* (pp.153-178). New York: Routledge.

Lovett, E., Jr. (2018) What It Means To Be Healthy: Adverse Childhood Events and Their Influence on Neuroanatomy and Behavior. *Honors Theses*, 1585. https://digitalworks.union.edu/theses/1585

Marshall-Tate, K., Chaplin, E., McCarthy, J. and Grealish, A. (2020) A literature review about the prevalence and identification of people with an intellectual disability within Court Liaison and Diversion Services. *Journal of Intellectual Disabilities and Offending Behaviour*. http://dx.doi.org/10.1108/JIDOB-10-2019-0023

McKeown, A., Martin, A., Kennedy, P.J. and Wilson, A. (2020) 'Understanding my story': Young person involvement in formulation. *Journal of Criminological Research, Policy and Practice*. http://dx.doi.org/10.1108/JCRPP-02-2020-0020

McNamara, N. (2012) Speech and language therapy within a forensic support service. *Journal of Learning Disabilities and Offending Behaviour*, 3(2), 111-117.

Miller, N. and Najavits, L. (2012) Creating trauma-informed correctional care: A balance of goals and environment. *European Journal of Psychotraumatology*, 3. doi:10.3402/ejpt.v3i0.17246

Modecki, K.L., Zimmer-Gembeck, M.J. and Guerra, N. (2017) Emotion regulation, coping, and decision making: Three linked skills for preventing externalizing problems in adolescence. *Child Development*, 88(2), 417–426.

Morken, F., Jones, L.Ø. and Helland, W.A. (2021) Disorders of language and literacy in the prison population: A scoping review. *Education Sciences*, 11(2), 77.

National Autistic Society (2019) Help in Meetings Tools, NAS: Offenders with an Intellectual and/or Developmental Disability, 18th International Conference, Birmingham, 10th–11th April 2019.

Paterson, B. (2014) Mainstreaming Trauma. Presented at the Psychological Trauma-Informed Care Conference, Stirling University.

Prison Reform Trust (2008) No One Knows: Police responses to suspects learning disabilities and learning difficulties: A review of policy and practice. Available at https://prisonreformtrust.org.uk/publication/no-one-knows-police-responses-to-suspects-with-learning-disabilities-and-learning-difficulties [accessed 7th March 2023]

Randall, M. and Haskell, L. (2013) Trauma-informed approaches to law: Why restorative justice must understand trauma and psychological coping. *Dalhousie Law Journal*, 501. https://ssrn.com/abstract=2424597

Robertson, I. H., Ward, T., Ridgeway, V. et al. (1994) *The Test of Everyday Attention*. Bury St Edmunds: Thames Valley Test Company.

Soloff, N. (2011) The Impact of Speech and Language Therapy Service Delivery on Milton Keynes BESD and YOT settings. Available at www.the-futures-group.com/fg/files/Impact-of-Speech-and-Language-Therapy.pdf [accessed 18th March 2023]

Simpson, F., Christie, J., Mortensen, L. and Clark, W. (2006) *Mount Wilga High Level Language Test: Administration & Scoring Manual Plus Test Form with UK Adaptations and Large Print Additions*. Fiona Simpson.

Stans, S.E.A., Dalemans, R.J.P., de Witte, L.P. and Beurskens, A.J.H.M.(2019) Using Talking Mats to support conversations with communication vulnerable people: A scoping review. *Technology and Disability*, 30(4), 153–176.

Starkweather, C.W. and Gottwald, S.R. (1990) The demands and capacities model II: Clinical applications. *Journal of Fluency Disorders*, 15(3), 143–157.

Starkweather, C.W. and Gottwald, S.R. (2000) The demands and capacities model: Response to Siegel. *Journal of Fluency Disorders*, 25(4), 369–375.

Substance Abuse and Mental Health Services Administration (SAMHSA) (2014) SAMHSA's *Concept of Trauma and Guidance for a Trauma-Informed Approach*. Rockville, MD: Substance Abuse and Mental Health Services Administration.

Swinburn, K., Porter, G. and Howard, D. (2023) *Comprehensive Aphasia Test* (2nd edn). Routledge.

Turner, K. (2019) The speech, language and communication profiles of young people in custody, in England. Evaluating models of service delivery to meet their needs. A mixed-methods study (Doctoral dissertation, University of Sheffield).

Vaswani, N. and Paul, S. (2019) 'It's knowing the right things to say and do': Challenges and opportunities for trauma-informed practice in the prison context. *The Howard Journal of Crime and Justice*, 58(4), 513–534.

Whitehouse, A.J.O. and Bishop, D.V.M. (2009) *Communication Checklist – Adult*. London: Pearson.

Wiig, E.H., Semel, E. and Secord, W.A. (2013) *Clinical Evaluation of Language Fundamentals–Fifth Edition* (CELF-5). Bloomington, MN: NCS Pearson

Williams K.T. (2019) *Expressive Vocabulary Test* [Measurement Instrument], 3rd edn. Bloomington, MN: NCS Pearson.

Wilson, S.M., Eriksson, D.K., Schneck, S.M. and Lucanie, J.M. (2018) A quick aphasia battery for efficient, reliable, and multidimensional assessment of language function. *PloS One*, 13(2), e0192773.

Xie, H., Huffman, N., Shih, C.H., Cotton, A.S., Buehler, M., Brickman, K.R., Wall, J.T. and Wang, X. (2022) Adverse childhood experiences associate with early post-trauma thalamus and thalamic nuclei volumes and PTSD development in adulthood. *Psychiatry Research: Neuroimaging*, 319, 111421.

Zsolnai, A. (2015) Social and emotional competence. *HERJ Hungarian Educational Research Journal*, 5(1), 1–10.

SPEECH AND LANGUAGE THERAPY INTERVENTION

DOI: 10.4324/9781003288701-7

This chapter discusses speech and language therapy (SLT) intervention within the criminal justice system (CJS).

It is well known and understood that while people who are within the CJS have forensic SLT intervention needs, they are also subject to other physical and developmental conditions that impact on their speech, language and communication needs (SLCN). SLT intervention advice on topics such as (but not limited to) developmental language disorder, dysfluency, learning disabilities, autism spectrum conditions, aphasia, dementia, head and neck cancer, plus many more aetiologies which may be present, would be relevant and is not repeated here. SLT intervention would proceed as for the disorder but adapted to the conditions of the prison or mental health facility.

This chapter aims to accompany the published body of evidence-based practice with intervention advice that is aimed at the specific needs of people within the CJS. The intervention advice in this chapter is developed via clinical practice and what limited published evidence base exists in this field. The intervention advice does not claim to have been tested via any research methods. SLT within CJS is a field in its infancy, and, undoubtedly, an evidence base will emerge in time. For now, SLTs in this clinical area are pioneers, so please feel free to take some of these emerging therapeutic areas and adapt them to meet the needs of service users.

It is also important to reiterate that while we have divided material into separate chapters to assist the reader, the journey through investigations, interviews and court may have involved assessment, collation of relevant information and even therapeutic intervention (see Chapter 3). Similarly, assessment of communication (see Chapter 5) is integral to SLT intervention, and throughout the process of detention and progress through the prison system, SLT intervention may be present (see Chapter 4).

This chapter will offer information relating to:

- the communication environment
- SLCN goal setting and outcome measures
- linking SLT intervention to change
- positive behaviour support
- communicative competence with suggested interventions to develop communicative competence
- linking SLCN to risk
- neurological development
- health literacy.

A note about SLT intervention with this client group

Within the CJS, there are individuals who have led complex and often distressing lives. People have often had some or all of the following experiences:

- may have had poor care as children for various reasons
- may have spent time in the care of the local authority and moved locations many times
- may have been exposed to abuse or exploitation
- may have had poor access to formal education
- may have used substances from a young age
- may have developmental conditions which were not diagnosed or treated
- may have acquired conditions which were not diagnosed or treated.

For these reasons, it can be very hard to consider the biopsychosocial profile of any individual and make definitive declarations of an SLT diagnosis due to complex overshadowing of potential needs. It may be possible in some cases to diagnose, for example, a stammer of developmental origin that still manifests in an adult affecting verbal communication with associated avoidance behaviours. Previous SLT intervention may, or may not, have occurred, and the experience of that may be positive or profoundly negative. For other people in prison, there may be potential differential diagnoses being tested, or it may be that the SLT agrees to work with the person on their speech, language and communication goals without a formal SLT diagnostic label. Wherever possible, the multi-disciplinary team (MDT) or the referring agent (see Chapter 8) would agree the course of action with the SLT.

The communication environment

The communication environment was introduced as a consideration in Chapter 5, and a Communication Environment Tool is provided at Appendix 15. The Communication Environment Tool asks the non-SLT professional to consider the communication environment under the domains of the built environment, the interaction environment, the values environment and individual needs. If there are deficits in any of these four domains, the communication environment can be improved and SLT intervention may be sought so that any changes are efficient and effective.

In this section, the communication environment is considered via three domains which impact on communication: the built environment which is made up of the building, lighting, seating, etc.; the interaction environment which focuses on how information flow is created and how successful information exchange is; and the values environment – the willingness of conversation partners to engage and the ethos of respect. Each of these domains is considered in turn in this section.

Please note that, throughout this section, any changes to the communication environment are dependent on the individual, their risk assessment and the level of security within the setting. For example, more environmental changes may be feasible in a low-secure hospital compared to a high-secure hospital; more may be possible in a category C or D prison compared to a category A or B prison; more may be achievable in a community forensic team than an inpatient environment.

The built environment in a forensic setting is one of the harder domains of a communication-friendly environment to improve, as often items such as lighting, noise, surfaces and privacy have been designed at construction stage to meet alternative goals such as safety, surveillance or robustness. Ideally, the following would be in place to support communication and social interaction (Awofeso, 2011):

- adjustable lighting including access to daylight
- interiors and exteriors which invite well-being such as access to soft furnishing, nature, art and spiritual objects
- spaces or opportunities where people who are residing in a secure setting can mix socially both with peers and staff, but also with people from outside of the secure setting such as family, friends, the local community, work and exercise.

In terms of what an SLT can bring to the built environment, the focus would be based on supporting the individual to have choice, to be an active participant and to form connections (Davies and Gray, 2009). SLT intervention could include:

- negotiating ways in which individuals can make informed choices facilitated by information presented in ways that support their understanding and cognition, such as picture menus and visual timetables
- application of environmental aids to support orientation to person, place and time, such as calendars, wayfinding signage, personal photographs in private spaces
- implementing the formation of community groups so that decisions about the environment can be made via active participation such as whether to build a community garden, or buy a pool table, or have joint cooking sessions
- provision of seating, tables and grouped resources such as magazines or games to enable people to come together for personal enjoyment
- provision of shared spaces to eat so that there is a shared social eating experience

- finding solutions to issues in the built environment which cause distress, such as noise-sensitive people having access to ear plugs or noise-cancelling ear defenders, photo-sensitive people having access to tinted spectacles; negotiating the use of cleaning materials which are chemical-free for people who are intolerant of strong chemical smells.

The interaction environment is separate from the built environment in that it is the style of communication that is facilitated in order to give the individual autonomy, competence and relatedness in order to advance personal motivation. The underpinning ethos is to support the individual to have a sense of agency so that they can be confident in their own capacity to meet their personal goals in the future (Alper and McGregor, 2015). Such interpersonal skills are thought to be associated with reducing reoffending (Bouman, Schene and de Ruiter, 2009). The SLT would influence the interaction environment in the following ways:

- finding ways to support individuals to understand information and events around them, such as via accessible materials, clear explanations and the opportunity to ask questions and obtain meaningful answers
- training non-SLT professionals in adapting communication style to allow for increased choice making and negotiation
- supporting non-SLT professionals to have meaningful interactions with individuals while maintaining appropriate relational security (Department of Health, 2010)
- intervention that helps the individual understand their strengths and needs, and empowers them to ask questions at times when they need further information or clarification
- providing group opportunities where people can come together and collaborate on tasks that are motivating and which increase a sense of achievement. This can be a low-level intervention such as a games club, or more challenging such as sports events, longer-term projects such as creating a garden or ongoing projects such as producing an accessible in-house newsletter.

The overall aim is to maximise safe and appropriate communication flow so that communication competence is increased.

The values environment is located within the communication culture of the setting. This refers to treating people as individuals with respect, taking time to listen and understand, being engaged with communication exchanges and appreciating the different lived experiences of others. The SLT would impact on this domain in the following ways, via:

- communication and values training for non-SLT professionals (Back, Fromme and Meier, 2019)
- modelling values and communication approaches during daily interactions
- constructive challenge when poor communication values are seen
- contribution to peer supervision and event debrief
- supporting non-SLT professionals to understand the importance of terminology and appropriate use of vocabulary in all interactions.

The individual's needs within the communication environment include the use of spectacles or hearing aids to support communication flow; the use of visual aids, ramps and accessible materials; the provision of communication plans so that conversation partners are aware of strategies to support; the planning of a conversation so that it is at the best time and in the best location for the individual; plus any other adaptations required for the person to participate. The most effective way to support the individual's communication needs is to ask them what helps and to advocate for any reasonable adjustments. Following the interaction, it is vital to ask the individual for feedback so that there is an ongoing process of improvement within the communication environment.

Goal setting

Following SLT assessment and reporting which was discussed in Chapter 5, there is a need to discuss what the assessment results mean for the individual and whether any SLCN impact on their participation in activities of daily living. A useful framework is the World Health Organization International Classification of Functioning, Disability and Health (ICF) (Threats, 2006) which supports holistic understanding of the person, and engenders multidisciplinary working across teams (Scholten, Ross and Bickford, 2019). Figure 6.1 overleaf provides a visualisation of the ICF framework:

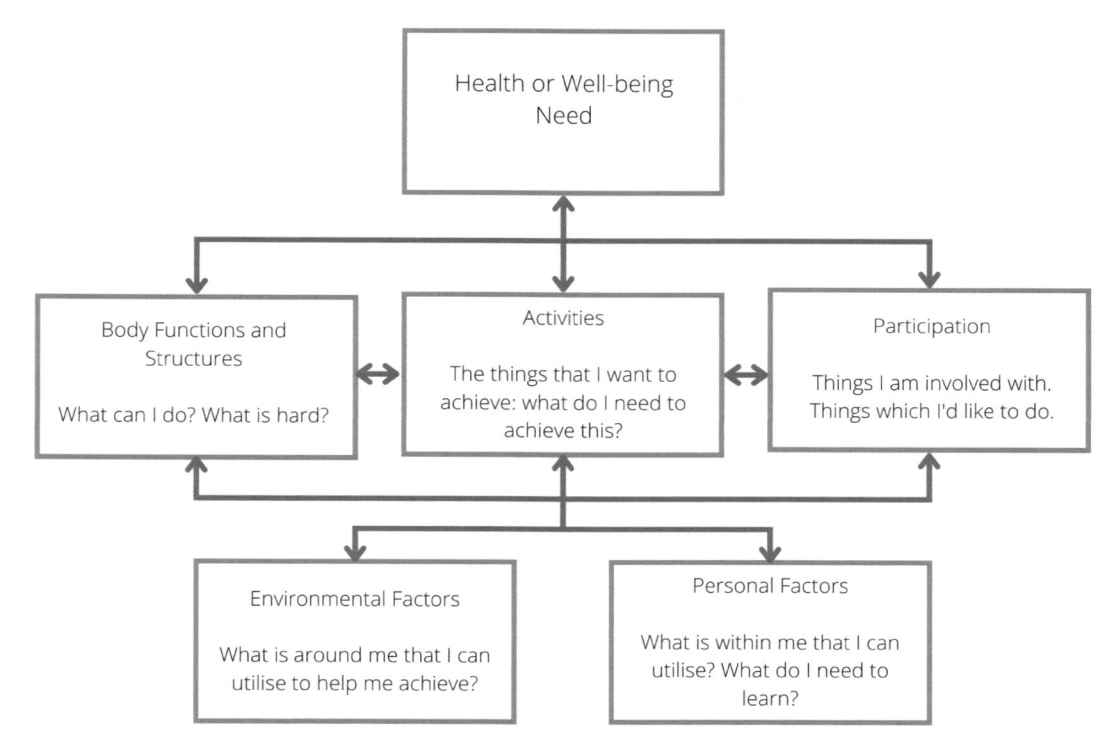

FIGURE 6.1 A visualisation of the World Health Organization International Classification of Functioning, Disability and Health

This framework can be used to help the SLT and the client to think about their speech, language and communication skills, what they are good at, what they find harder, what they want to achieve and things they would like to do. It also enables a conversation about what the individual may need in terms of skills or support. Figure 6.2 (overleaf) provides a worked example for a person in a low-secure hospital who would like to access a college course as part of their Section 17 leave. The individual – whom we shall call Liam – has a diagnosis of autism and finds it hard to judge how much to say in social situations especially when meeting new people. Liam has worked with the SLT to develop insight into his difficulties with judging how much to say. This work has focused on psychoeducation on quantity of information, such as why the listener might want to leave the conversation if Liam is not taking conversational turns. Liam has a communication passport which explains his communication skills and challenges. He has been working with the SLT on how he might use the communication passport to explain his needs to a new person.

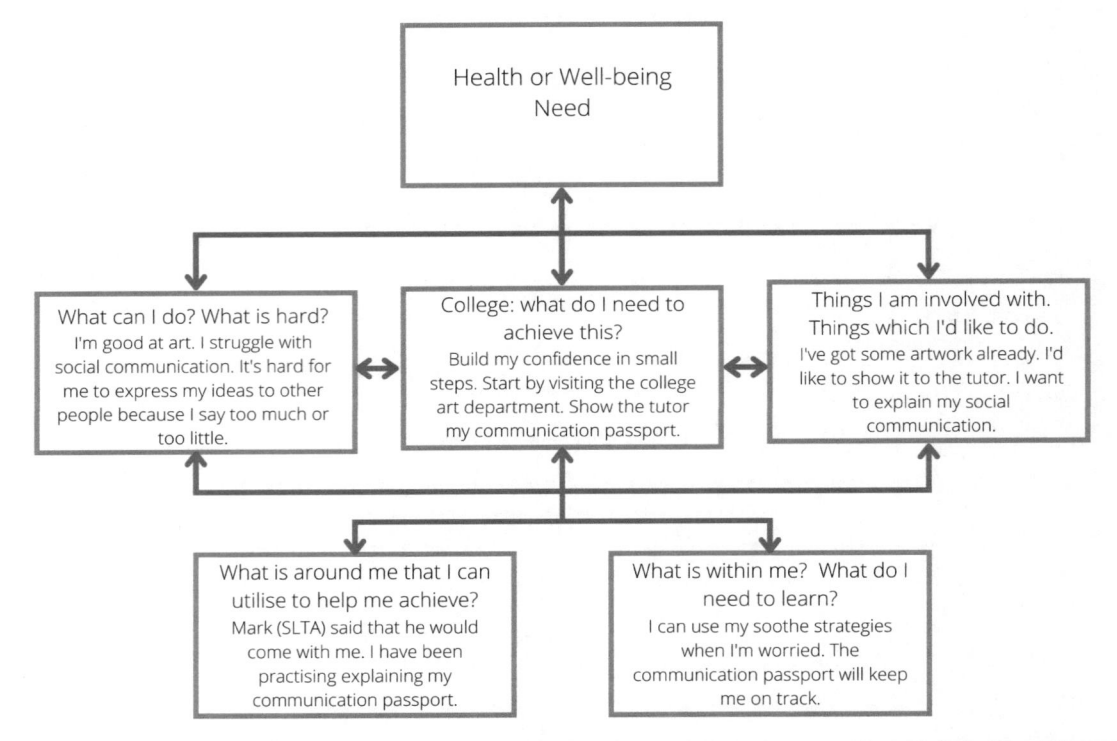

FIGURE 6.2 A worked example of the World Health Organization International Classification of Functioning, Disability and Health for a person with SLCN in a low-secure hospital who would like to access a college course

In order to help an individual think about what is hard, what they may want to do and what they may need in order to achieve, a set of symbol cards is provided at Appendix 29 for the SLT to use with the client in order to facilitate cognitive scaffolding of goal setting (Hodgetts and Park, 2017).

As the SLT and the individual discuss the things that the individual would like to achieve, it is important to remain rooted in setting functional meaningful goals. This is because the individual will remain engaged and motivated if the goal of intervention makes sense to them and is relevant to their life (Priniski, Hecht and Harackiewicz, 2018). It is also vital to consider how the conversation about future achievements is supported by the SLT.

A solution-focused approach concentrates on helping people move towards the future that they want and to learn what can be done differently by using their existing skills, strategies and ideas – rather than focusing on the problem. This approach treats the individual as the expert on their own life. The clinician asks questions to help the individual think about their future goals and help to make incremental steps in achievable chunks towards the future goal.

A solution-focused approach is helpful in this situation because the SLT is more focused on collaboration with the client to build communication skills rather than necessarily to find evidence of diagnostic thresholds or identification of deficits that would be addressed via impairment-based therapeutic ethos (De Shazer et al., 2021). Burns and Northcott (2022) guide the thoughts of allied health professionals (AHPs) by outlining the core assumptions which influence solution-focused intervention goals:

- Allow the client to decide. The client may have noticed a barrier to success in their daily life and found a way to overcome this barrier. It may not be the SLT's first choice of a strategy to overcome a barrier, but as long as there is no risk to themselves or others, it is OK to accept the client's problem solving in the knowledge that the client has the self-awareness and autonomy to decide what is a problem for them.

- Notice successes. If the individual has succeeded in using a strategy which has been co-produced in therapy, the role of the SLT is to notice this and help the individual reflect and identify their own next steps.

- Flexibility. A strategy may have seemed suitable in the clinical appointment, but may not work well in practice. In this situation, changing the strategy values the client feedback and promotes cognitive flexibility in problem solving and cooperation.

- Small steps. Valuing small changes which lead to bigger changes while increasing the person's self-esteem and sense of agency.

- Focus on present and future. This enables the SLT to facilitate the client to think about where they are located in the moment, and how they see their future and what is required in terms of communication skills to be future oriented.

- The words used. The AHP has a role in modelling the words used within the setting. For example, a prison officer colleague might refer to a person with SLCN as 'attention seeking' because they have asked the same question many times of different people. The SLT should support the officer to understand that the person is asking the question several times because they did not understand the reply, so are seeking clarity. The SLT will support the use of vocabulary across the milieu which is accessible, appropriate to the client's vocabulary level, positive, future oriented and proactive about the client. This will be informed by the assessment that the SLT has undertaken with the client on a one-to-one basis in clinic (see Chapter 5) and the values in the communication environment (see section in this chapter). Changes to the words used in the context of the service user enables him or her to experience improved self-esteem.

Case example

Bill is a man in a low-secure hospital. Bill has a diagnosis of learning disability. He is very keen to have social interaction alongside having receptive and expressive language needs that make it hard for him to understand information and have conversations with people if the conversation is fast-paced with complex sentences and vocabulary that is outside of his skill set.

As a result, Bill has developed a strategy of 'inventing' some conversational content which he can offer to the nursing staff in order to have a conversation. Within his hearing, team members laugh at Bill and call him a liar because his conversational content is implausible.

The SLT has completed assessment in one-to-one sessions and reported to the team on the severity of the SLCN, but this one facet of Bill's interaction style (inventing conversational content) has not been addressed via one-to-one session before because it was not stated in the reason for referral or seen within the clinic appointments. Discovering this communication need was dependent on the nursing staff reporting the issue.

The SLT was able to explain to the team that the 'inventing' was a conversation starter and offer advice to the team to accept the conversation starter and then move the topic to something that both parties can discuss such as the ward gardening project.

Conversations became more equal between Bill and the staff team. Bill was no longer being called a liar in his earshot which improved his self-esteem. The SLT supported Bill to think about the time when he was thought of as a liar and the time when he was not via stick-man pictures with thinking bubbles. Bill was able to consider that 'inventing' conversational content did not help him in the longer term, and he was motivated not to repeat this strategy in the future.

- Sustainability. The SLT acting as a reflection point for when a client has had a period of 'reduced barriers' or successes so that the person's ability to use their communication resources to solve problems is reinforced and promoted.
- Hope. The belief that people with SLCN who have offending histories can change and that there is choice about future outcomes which can be influenced by the individual with the SLT scaffolding communication so that the person's views are heard. In this scenario, the SLT uses skills in communication to increase participation and choice,

such as employing total communication strategies in a meeting to help the individual express their wishes.

Case example

Mr C is a man in prison with SLCN secondary to his mental ill-health. He has a diagnosis of paranoid schizophrenia which he is medicated for. While the medication reduces his distress, it does not resolve his communication needs. His communication profile is:

- Poor theory of mind so that he assumes that others know what he is thinking or expressing, which results in him using short utterances with limited explanation for the listener. This impacts on his expressive output which is abrupt and results in communication breakdown when the listener does not understand what is being said. The communication breakdown causes frustration in Mr C.

- Issues with social interactions and pragmatics in that Mr C offers too little quantity of information, presents his expressive output in a manner that others find aggressive, topic changes are often rapid and out of context, information is offered which does not seem relevant to the listener due to theory-of-mind deficits, turn taking is uneven and often use of gesture is incongruent.

- Misreading of gestures or facial expressions so that Mr C misinterprets the gestures or facial expressions of others and this impacts on his understanding of the intentions or meaning of information offered to him.

- Perceived as argumentative, assertive, or aggressive to others based on his rate of speech, volume of speech, use of gestures when talking and taking more conversational turns than the listener.

- Poor inferencing skills so that he is unable to notice and use visual or environmental cues to inform his understanding of spoken information.

- Socially isolated, with limited people tolerating his interaction style, which results in him trying to make 'new friends' but being rejected because of poor pragmatic language skills.

- Reduced social confidence associated with insight into the rejection that he faces from peers.

- Poor self-esteem.

- Unable to work well in a group or team associated with lack of social and pragmatic skills.

- Limited access to emotions vocabulary due to the lexical access barriers which are commonly seen in paranoid schizophrenia (Bryan, 2013) and which can be detected using the Comprehensive Aphasia Test semantic subtests (Swinburn, Porter and

Howard, 2023) or the Psycholinguistic Assessments of Language Processing in Aphasia (PALPA) selected subtests (Kay, Lesser and Coltheart, 1992).

Part of his daily life is tolerating intense and unwanted feelings of anxiety that he finds hard to express. He started using his toothbrush to scratch his inner arm when feeling anxious and this was accepted by the SLT because Mr C did not think that this was a problem for him.

Mr C wanted to use SLT sessions to improve his relationships with his family. Via discussion, it was decided to utilise the telephone as the tool for this goal and that the intervention would be building communication skills and strategies in successful phone conversations. Following the co-production of strategies for phone calls, which included a visual aid, visual rating scales and sand timer, the SLT and Mr C could notice successes in the application of the strategies.

The visual aid was an A4 document which was pinned to the wall next to the phone. It was to support Mr C in offering conversational turns which included adequate detail to support the listener to understand his meaning on the first attempt. The visual aid addressed Mr C's poor theory of mind and encouraged him to offer detail in his expressive output which he often omitted. It included prompts to disclose topic, place, people, antecedent information, the main message and any consequential information.

The sand timer was to raise Mr C's awareness that he had successfully chatted on the phone for a set amount of time (ten minutes in this case). Mr C had perceived his phone calls to be very short. Part of the concept of improving relationships was to help Mr C identify that he was having daily phone calls of ten minutes without communication breakdown.

Mr C could self-rate his successes and confidence, and this helped him to monitor the small steps to success. The valuing of the small steps helped Mr C have hope and positivity about future relationships, and to change his personal narrative about his role within the family.

Motivational interviewing (MI) is another style of engaging people to support goal setting for intervention. MI is (Miller and Rollnick, 2013):

- a communication style which involves listening to the person and working jointly so that the SLT gives advice and information for the person to use
- a communication style which empowers the person to own their goals via defining their own capacity for change and what change would mean for them

- a communication style which engenders partnership working and client autonomy within the partnership.

The MI evidence base indicates that it is a tool which is especially beneficial for people who are unsure about change or who have low confidence in their ability to change. People who are in the CJS are often ambivalent to change with mixed motivations and low confidence. The findings of Simourd, Olver and Brandenburg (2016) would suggest that MI is an engagement style which should be considered as a useful tool for the SLT when working with this client group. MI has been successfully employed by AHPs in various clinical settings to improve patient outcomes (Rollnick, Miller and Butler, 2008). In order to fully employ MI techniques, the SLT would need to access training via continued professional development.

While solution-focused and MI approaches help the identification of client-led goals, it remains necessary for the SLT to be able to articulate goals into an intervention outcome which can be measured in order to evidence the effectiveness of treatment. For example, the patient may have a client-led goal of using their Section 17 leave to buy a pair of shoes with minimal help. The same patient may have expressive language needs which make it hard for them to find words, create sentences and make requests to meet their needs. The SLT will need to break down the goal into stages and enact speech, language and communication intervention at the relevant stages in order to help the person achieve the goal. The SLT will also need to consider how to measure when each stage is achieved so that the effectiveness of treatment can be recorded both for the patient and for the service. This example can be broken down as follows:

1. The client needs to budget for the shoes. This is work being completed by OT.
2. The client needs Section 17 leave to the local shops. This is work being completed by the named nurse or care coordinator.
3. The client needs the vocabulary within their semantic system and strategies in order to self-cue word finding of the vocabulary in order to be able to use the vocabulary functionally. This is work being undertaken with the SLT who may measure the effectiveness by counting how many words the person knows that are related to shoe shopping before and after the intervention.
4. After the vocabulary has been primed, the client needs to be able to use this in basic sentences. This is work being undertaken by the SLT via a role-playing exercise. The effectiveness is measured via the SLT noting sentences being used in the role play. This may be measured on a Therapy Outcome Measures scale (Enderby and John, 2015).
5. The client using the sentences to make requests is being supported by the SLT and OT jointly via the client accessing Section 17 leave in the hospital grounds. The SLT and

OT escort the client to the onsite shop where they are prompted to use the sentences to request small purchases. The SLT models prompting for the OT to ensure consistency of strategy. The sub-goal is for the client to request five times. This is operationalised via counting the number of successful requests made during the leave.

6. Once the client has achieved Section 17 leave to go to the shops, they are escorted by the named nurse and OT to the shoe shop. The OT has noted the strategies that will be used to prompt requesting. The named nurse and OT allow the client to browse the shoes while they wait within the line of sight. The client follows the process which was practised in the role play with SLT. Once they select some shoes to try on, the OT approaches to see if the client needs support or prompting. Prompting is offered as needed with the OT standing back when not required in order to promote client autonomy. The effectiveness is measured via the named nurse and OT report of the success of the shopping trip, and potentially by the purchasing of shoes. The client self-rates their opinion on the effectiveness of the intervention using a self-rating scale.

SLCN outcome measures

An outcome measure is a statement that captures the impact that the SLT intervention has had on the individual (or their health) relating to the communication goal which was set. When the goal was identified, the client and the SLT worked together to identify the meaningful change for the person. The next steps are to consider what to measure to capture the expected meaningful change.

Case example

Mr C – the gentleman with paranoid schizophrenia and communication needs described in an earlier case example – wanted to improve his relationships with his family. This goal was operationalised by the SLT so that a way to measure the improvement in his relationship was specified. The decided measures of improvement were:

- Mr C self-rating his satisfaction pertaining to his relationship with his family. This is a subjective measure in that it can be impacted by factors such as Mr C's anxiety at the time of rating. This rating was completed weekly in clinic at the beginning of the appointment.
- Mr C rating the quality of the phone call based on his performance of giving adequate information to allow the listener to understand, based on the number of communication breakdowns, and based on whether he felt frustrated. This is another subjective measure which Mr C completed immediately after each call. The rating was reviewed weekly in clinic.

- The amount of time spent on a phone call which was noted immediately after each call and reviewed in clinic weekly. This objective measure assumes that a longer call equals an improved relationship, or more time spent on the phone in one week equals an improved relationship.

In this example, the measure is capturing Mr C's participation in communication activity, which, in this case, aims to lead to gains in his perception of his well-being.

The AHP Outcome Measures UK Working Group (2019) offered the following suggestions of outcome measures for the SLT to consider:

- Experience and satisfaction with care or intervention. This type of information can be gathered from the service user with accessible feedback questionnaires or satisfaction measures such as a traffic light system or focus groups to support communication. An example is asking a patient to complete an accessible patient-reported outcome measure with their named nurse, or asking the patient to place a thumbs up or thumbs down on a wall display as they leave the clinic room. At HMP Berwyn, the service-user engagement officer conducts focus groups with patients to ask them about their experience.
- Perception of health and well-being which can be a self-reported measure or a measure administered by the SLT such as Therapy Outcome Measures (TOMs) (Enderby and John, 2015).
- The individual's activity, communication function or participation which can be reported by the individual or by other key people in the environment. Within the secure hospital, the patient record is useful for gathering information in this domain because it is a detailed record of the patient's activity for the day – for example, the team can audit the patient record to note how many times the person accesses Section 17 leave or attends group sessions. Within the prison setting, the record keeping is different in that it is not as detailed due to the officer-to-prisoner ratio. In the prison setting, it may be necessary to rely on patient self-report. Within the community forensic team, record keeping will be different again depending on the team around the patient. Each setting will have its own sources of information to exploit for information gathering.
- How safe or effective the intervention was, which can be measured via TOMs score aggregate gains. The Royal College of Speech and Language Therapists Online Outcome Tool (Royal College of Speech and Language Therapists, 2016) is a web-based tool where SLTs can complete TOMs during an episode of care. Once the episode is concluded, the online tool can deliver data on effectiveness of intervention with aggregate gains for the individual client or for the service as a whole. Other ways to operationalise effectiveness are to count client dropout rates, clients failing to attend appointment

rates, or an outcome which can be counted pre and post intervention such as the number of times a person in prison is restrained. At HMP Berwyn, people who are subject to restraint are routinely referred to SLT in order to consider if communication breakdown is part of the reason for restraint. The SLT counts the number of times restraint occurs before and after SLT intervention. This data aims to demonstrate that SLT is successful in enabling the individual to explain why they are angry rather than to lash out.

- Service-level outcomes which are captured via service data such as length of time from referral to treatment, number of times that the person is seen or aggregate of TOMs scores across a caseload as explained above.

The challenge for the SLT is to present an intervention in clinic which supports the desired change (goal) and to articulate ways to measure the change. It may be helpful to consider this using the SMART framework (Bowman et al., 2015) as detailed in Figure 6.3 (below) and using the example of Mr C:

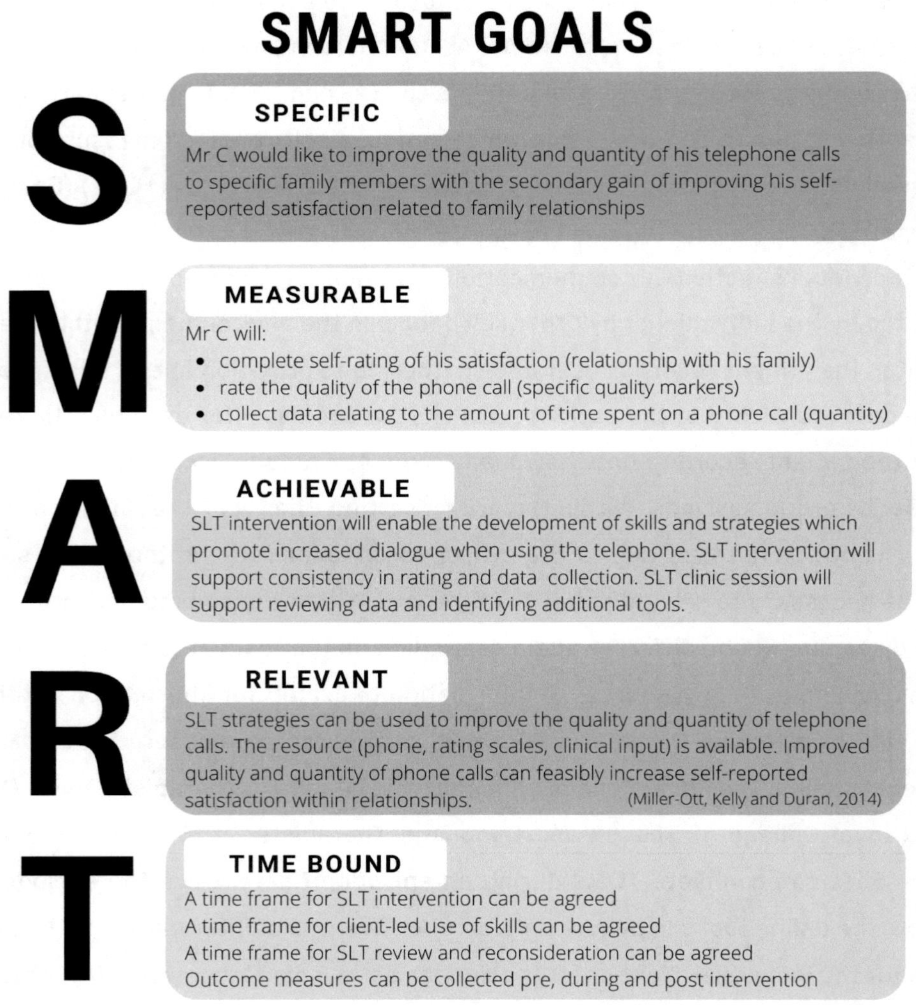

SMART GOALS

S

SPECIFIC

Mr C would like to improve the quality and quantity of his telephone calls to specific family members with the secondary gain of improving his self-reported satisfaction related to family relationships

M

MEASURABLE

Mr C will:
- complete self-rating of his satisfaction (relationship with his family)
- rate the quality of the phone call (specific quality markers)
- collect data relating to the amount of time spent on a phone call (quantity)

A

ACHIEVABLE

SLT intervention will enable the development of skills and strategies which promote increased dialogue when using the telephone. SLT intervention will support consistency in rating and data collection. SLT clinic session will support reviewing data and identifying additional tools.

R

RELEVANT

SLT strategies can be used to improve the quality and quantity of telephone calls. The resource (phone, rating scales, clinical input) is available. Improved quality and quantity of phone calls can feasibly increase self-reported satisfaction within relationships.   (Miller-Ott, Kelly and Duran, 2014)

T

TIME BOUND

A time frame for SLT intervention can be agreed
A time frame for client-led use of skills can be agreed
A time frame for SLT review and reconsideration can be agreed
Outcome measures can be collected pre, during and post intervention

FIGURE 6.3 A worked example of SLT goals using the SMART framework

Linking intervention to change

In order to evaluate the effect of the SLT intervention for Mr C, the clinician must understand how the intervention links to the desired change. In the worked example, SLT intervention included:

- Understanding how telephone calls are different to face-to-face interactions (e.g. lack of visual feedback and lack of visual shared references).
- Consideration of theory of mind using barrier tasks to demonstrate what communication is needed to allow the listener to know what the speaker knows when visual cues are reduced. A barrier task is a specific form of information gap activity. Information gap activities are communicative activities for two or more people, where person A has information that person B needs. In a barrier task, person A and person B sit with a barrier between them and are required to convey information to each other.
- Consideration of what needs to be included within verbal information to support the listener to understand.
- Planning conversational content in advance so that potential information gaps are identified and reduced.

These skills and strategies are planned in order to achieve the desired goal. If Mr C can employ these strategies, his self-rating and time spent on the phone could reasonably be expected to increase to reach a threshold that has been agreed with the client as the indicator of success (such as a ten-minute phone call with no communication breakdown).

As discussed in the section on outcome measures, the SLT is attempting to identify the client-led goal and to find a way to measure change which contributes to achieving that goal. The next part of the process is linking what the SLT and client did in clinic to the change that has occurred.

Telephone call example

In order to have a successful telephone call, each party must use the cooperative principle (Murray, 2010) and address information gaps which are not filled by visual cues. Skilled communicators will use devices such as:

- consideration of the types of questions asked and linking this to expectations of the persons daily activity (e.g. asking questions which the conversation partner can offer a response to)

- consideration of discussion of daily activities when one conversation partner has more options than the other, and what feelings this can engender (e.g. talking about a family meal when the conversation partner does not have the option to attend)
- skills in conversational openers which allow both parties to offer equal contributions such as reminiscence, national events or future plans
- awareness of types of questions used in a conversation (e.g. open versus closed questions) and how each question type might be employed
- using phrases or jokes which are personal to the family to create emotional closeness
- introducing topics which promote positive feelings such as holidays, pets, family events or amusing anecdotes from the past.

If the SLT were going to focus on some or all of these devices, it would be desirable to know which are being used prior to intervention and which are used post intervention. If targeted devices were used more post intervention, this would strengthen the case that any clinical gains are as a result of SLT input. This information could be gathered via observation of phone call conversational turns pre and post intervention.

Neurogenic stammer example

A man is referred to SLT with neurogenic stammer following a head injury which resulted from a violent assault. Assessment showed that his verbal expression difficulties are:

- repetitions, prolongations and blocks occur in all positions of words
- dysfluencies occur on grammatical words at a similar rate of occurrence as content words
- consistency in stuttering behaviour across speech tasks
- secondary symptoms such as facial grimacing, fist clenching and eye blinking are observed.

In agreement with the patient, the SLT focuses on slowing the rate of speech, breath support and breathing patterns, soft onset to words which begin with problematic consonants and acceptance of features of stammering. Prior to intervention, the patient is not accessing any of these strategies to support his speech. Post intervention, naturalistic observation of the patient shows him using the strategies and reducing the impact of his dysfluency. The observation data can be used to demonstrate that SLT input resulted in the change.

Finally, it is helpful in the early days of SLT goal setting to ask the client to consider how much can be changed in respect of the desired goal. For example:

- In Mr Cs case, he rated his relationship with his family as very poor but with open lines of communication in that he was in touch with them and they attempted phone calls several times per week. SLT assessment of communication needs identified tangible skills to acquire relating to telephone interactions, and the evidence base for input with people who have schizophrenia and impaired theory of mind is encouraging, so we could hypothesise that a positive change would occur as a result of SLT input (Ng, Fish and Granholm, 2015).
- In the case of a person in prison who has an SLT goal to change their mild dysarthria, which is secondary to an historic stroke, the potential for change may be less because the evidence base for this type of impairment-based intervention has not demonstrated effectiveness (Mitchell et al., 2017). In such a case, the SLT might explore with the person whether using a card to identify their impairment might be acceptable.
- In the case of a learning-disabled person in a medium-secure hospital who wants to be able to self-advocate in relation to SLCN, there is a potential for positive change via assessment of SLCN, understanding of strengths and challenges, being supported to learn how to successfully explain your own needs and via communication passports as a conversational ramp. Such interventions have been shown to create opportunities for people with learning disability to change the way that they perceive themselves and thus increase self-advocacy (Anderson and Bigby, 2017).

Once a potential for change has been discussed and agreed upon, the measurement of change should be considered. Table 6.1 overleaf offers suggestions on how to measure change with positive and negative considerations identified.

TABLE 6.1 Suggestions on how to measure SLT client progress with positive and negative considerations identified

Tool to measure change	Positive considerations	Negative considerations
Formal assessment before, during and after intervention	Standardised Objective Valid Reliable	Not all therapy interventions have a formal assessment to measure the proposed change Usually aimed at impairment-based interventions (Coppens, 2016)
Pre and post audit of activities (e.g. reports from colleagues, attendance registers, incidence of distress in clinical record, etc.)	Naturalistic data Functional ability in context Can be operationalised into numeric data	Time-consuming Dependent on accurate data entry by third party Poor interrater reliability Need to ensure validity (Santana et al., 2018)
Self-rating of SLCN pre, during and post	Patient-centred method Time efficient Increases patient self-monitoring, insight and reflection	Subjective and influenced by unconscious factors No control for patient bias such as inflating rating to 'please' the SLT (Harpe, 2015)
Informal assessment and/or observation by SLT in function	Patient-centred method Naturalistic data Time efficient Functional ability in context	Subjective and influenced by SLT bias Difficult to operationalise into numeric data The patient-reported 'problem' may not occur during the observation period (Shipley and McAfee, 2019)
Report from third party	Functional ability in context Patient-centred method	Subjective and influenced by unconscious factors No control for third-party bias such as inflating rating to 'please' the client or SLT Dependent on the third party being aware of SLCN and intervention goals (McConachie et al., 2015)
Patient-reported outcome measure tools	Patient-centred method Time efficient Increases patient self-monitoring, insight and reflection Useful for service audit Can be operationalised into numeric data	Measures patient satisfaction with care, not change in patient skill Subjective and influenced by unconscious factors No control for patient bias such as inflating rating to 'please' the SLT Tends to be during or post intervention measure not pre intervention (Marshall, Haywood and Fitzpatrick, 2006)

(Continued)

TABLE 6.1 Continued

Tool to measure change	Positive considerations	Negative considerations
Therapy outcome measure tools	Valid Reliable Useful for service audit Can be operationalised into numeric data Functional ability in context and impairment based Considers views of family and carers Close links with WHO ICF Can be completed by the clinician or the clinician and patient together Online RCSLT tool ROOT supports data analysis	There is a requirement for interrater reliability testing within teams (Moyse et al., 2020)
Goal attainment scale	An adaptable measurement tool which can be personalised to the individual or setting Allows for partial completion of goals Close links with WHO ICF Useful for service audit Sensitive to smaller changes in goal attainment	Requires the SLT to have been trained to use the tool appropriately Reliability and validity remains contentious (Schlosser, 2004)
Health Equalities Framework	Focus on the needs of one specific client group – people with learning disability Helps prioritise care and treatment for individuals Meaningful to the individual Useful for service audit Can be operationalised into numeric data Supports MDT working	Requires the SLT to have been trained to use the tool appropriately Focus on the needs of one specific client group – people with learning disability SLCN section of the framework is broad so lacks specificity (Atkinson and Moulster, 2019)
Care aims	Patient-centred method Supports MDT working Focus on clinical decision making Functional ability in context	Requires the SLT to have been trained to use the tool appropriately (Stansfield and Matthews, 2014)

Theory of change

The theory of change methodology (De Silva et al., 2014) can be useful for supporting the location of SLT activities into the wider context of an individual's lived experience. The model allows for intervention to be located in a logical sequence of wider change (Maini, Mounier-Jack and Borghi, 2018).

The model allows the SLT to state their activity, which contributes to change at the level of an interim outcome, which in turn contributes to change at the level of an ultimate outcome (Newbould, Tucker and Wilberforce, 2022). A theory of change model for Mr C may look like this:

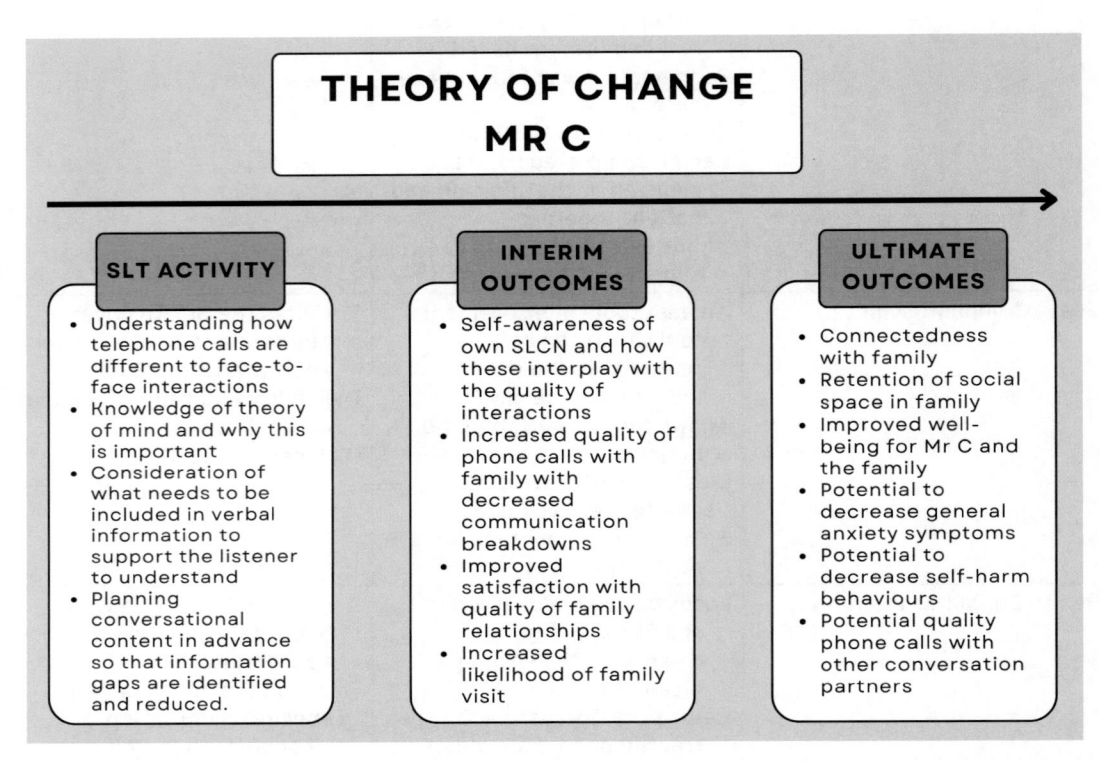

FIGURE 6.4 The theory of change methodology allows for SLT intervention to be located in a logical sequence of wider change

Theory of change models offer:

- the opportunity to identify causal pathways (e.g. between the work that an SLT completes in the clinic room to a wider level of well-being and participation for the individual)
- a visual model demonstrating the value of an intervention in a larger context
- a framework to help the clinician decide what communication outcomes to measure and how, while the identification of interim and ultimate outcomes supports colleagues and stakeholders to understand the value of an intervention.

The same model can be applied to SLT services as a whole, as shown in Table 6.2 overleaf which is an example of an inpatient low-secure setting for people with learning disability.

TABLE 6.2 The theory of change methodology applied to SLT services in the broadest sense

What SLTs do	Interim outcome	Ultimate outcome
What speech and language therapy does	*Because we do...staff or service users are able to do...*	*Staff and service users can now do...which matters because...*
Training and environmental needs Awareness training in SLCN Awareness training in dysphagia Bespoke training and support for key workers including writing easy-read materials Modelling effective communication Explain impact of communication and risks of not using strategies Provide training to students from a variety of health and social care backgrounds	Staff, family and individual are able to recognise signs of aspiration and choking risk and when an individual is having difficulties related to eating, drinking and swallowing Staff or family are confident in supporting a person with eating and drinking difficulties Staff, family and individual aware of speech, language and communication difficulties related to learning disability and are able to understand and recognise communication difficulties	**Diagnosis** Prevention of inappropriate interventions Decreased need for hospital admission or re-admission Access to appropriate healthcare Reduced health inequalities **Better awareness and understanding** Provide a supportive and welcoming communicative environment so that people who have learning disability can take part
SLT tasks 100% compliance with the Royal College of Speech and Language Therapy '5 Good Communication Standards' document	Stakeholders are aware of need to make reasonable adjustments and how to do this Prevented or reduced placement breakdown Staff are able to de-escalate difficulties which are associated with communication	Carers empowered and able to support service-user decisions Safe care and environments Dignity and respect Reduced need for NHS interventions including medication
Assessment and diagnosis Assessments of SLCN including risk assessment Informs differential diagnosis Assess for suitability of communication strategies and intervention Detailed reports, advice and recommendations Intervention case formulation	Staff, family and individual aware of the person's speech, language and communication difficulties Staff and family confidently able to support an individual to communicate appropriately and how to be a good communication partner Increased awareness of opportunities to communicate	**Life course benefits** Reduction of vulnerability to abuse Reduced social inequality Reduced or prevented ill-health including mental health Life opportunities maximised Participation in normal everyday life
Intervention/therapy Therapy including risk management Support to MDT and others related to communication and dysphagia Monitoring impact of intervention and recording outcomes Input into care plans and management plans Therapists and other colleagues and staff following national policy, standards and guidelines	Individual engaging successfully with others Gaining and maintaining positive relationships Decreased risk of aspiration or choking MDT informed about an individual's needs and how this relates to their own interaction, engagement and intervention	Maximum level of freedom and responsibility Optimal physical and emotional well-being Individuals empowered and able to influence decisions Individuals living in appropriate setting Individuals able to actively participate in their care Enjoyment of life (e.g. eating and drinking, socialising) Preventing relationship breakdown

(Continued)

TABLE 6.2 Continued

What SLTs do	Interim outcome	Ultimate outcome
Assist in determining capacity and advising on approaches to maximise comprehension for consent, etc.	Prevented or reduced placement breakdown Reduced risk of self-injury, injury or threats to others and damage to property	**Service development** Leaflets and written information is in easy-read format
Service-user gains and satisfaction Explain impact of communication and/or swallowing and the risks of not using strategies suggested by SLT Help the service user understand the 'whys' and 'hows' of their communication and/or swallowing Ethical decision making and service-user involvement in decisions	Inpatient and community settings share effective strategies to support transition and discharge Individual able to advocate for themselves or have an advocate to support them Advocate knows the best way to support the service user Gaining and maintaining positive relationships Individual able to make choices Individual able to swallow as safely as possible	Service-user-directed service development Effective and efficient use of specialist services Lower level of complaints and litigation Leave specialist or secure hospital, to return to community settings Access to and engagement with services Raised awareness in society about communication and swallowing difficulties Evidence-based safe practice
Other Involvement in multi-agency and partnership working Promotions related to new or current guidance and legislation Campaigns related to profession, communication and dysphagia, learning disability and related impact Research and audit CPD	Enjoyment in eating and drinking Improved self-esteem Service-user reporting on levels of satisfaction Patient able to access activities Individual and/or carers able to understand health issues and treatments	

Ultimate outcomes linked to SLT intervention

The ultimate outcome for most people within the CJS is to leave prison or hospital in order to live full lives within their communities. Often, this ultimate outcome cannot be achieved until risk-reduction work has been undertaken. Risk-reduction work is usually led by psychology teams who follow predetermined manualised programmes.

Within the theory of change model, SLT activity links into the interim outcome, which links to the ultimate outcome.

In order to inform the SLT activity, it is desirable for the SLT to know what psychological interventions are offered in their workplace to reduce risks of offending. The ultimate outcome for rehabilitation is to enable the person to progress in their incarceration (or hospital stay). In the prison setting, people can be expected to complete courses which relate to sex offending, violent offending, intimate partner violence, fire setting, problem solving, relationship building and thinking skills. In the hospital or community setting, people may be expected to complete adapted versions of similar courses.

These courses are verbally mediated group interventions, so the SLT's role is to inform the MDT whether the person has sufficient skills to cope with such an intervention, whether the necessary communication skills for group work can be taught, which might alter the timing of an intervention, or whether alternative sources of interventions are indicated. Examples of the ways in which SLTs and forensic psychologists work would include forensic psychologists noting when they meet a person who does not seem to understand, and referring them for SLT assessment. SLT might make clinical psychologists aware of communication needs and offer strategies to help the verbally mediated interventions. Psychological risk-reduction work often has specific vocabulary which can be hard to decode because it is low frequency, of low imageability and unlike other terms within the lexicon of the average person, so SLT support with vocabulary priming and acquisition would be desirable for improved outcomes (Hansen, 2017). In a low-secure hospital in central England, the SLT activity supports the psychological intervention via production of bespoke accessible materials for use in risk-reduction programmes.

Case example

K is a learning-disabled person who is residing in a medium-secure hospital. His offending history is one of violence against family or friends including the use of weapons. The MDT around him has identified the need for him to complete an adapted violent offender programme in order to progress to conditions of low security.

K has been assessed by SLT and found to have deficits with understanding verbal information, and to have a working vocabulary well below the expected range for his age. When the Test for Reception of Grammar (TROG-2) (Bishop, 2003) was administered, he scored on the first percentile with errors that indicated a deficit in processing verbal information. The first percentile is the age equivalent of a primary school child. When the British Picture Vocabulary Scale (BPVS3) (Dunn and Dunn, 2009) was administered, he scored in the extremely low range, also on the first percentile and also at the age equivalency of a primary school child. These SLT assessment results were consistent with his Intelligence Quotient (IQ) results as provided by the Wechsler Adult Intelligence Scale (WAIS) (Wechsler, 2008). IQ results placed him in the learning-disabled range of below 70.

The SLT meets with the clinical psychologist to discuss which words will be used as part of the group intervention and how to best support K. It is agreed that the SLT will use phonemic and semantic mapping of a core set of vocabulary in clinical sessions with K before he starts the violent offender programme in order to support his success in the programme (Meteyard et al., 2015).

Phonemic and semantic mapping is a tool whereby a target word is explored with the individual using a mind-map diagram. The target word is located at the centre of the mind map. The left-hand side is used to consider the characteristics of the word such as word initial phoneme, number of syllables, rhyming, spelling and word shape. The right-hand side is used to consider what the semantic features of the word are. Semantic features vary based on whether the word is a noun or a verb. The aim is to help the individual learn the word and to help the word become embedded in the lexicon with primed lexical access (Meteyard et al., 2015). Example phonemic and semantic mapping resources are located at Appendix 30.

In this way, SLT activity to address SLCN, as part of the theory of change model, can be vital to enabling people in the CJS to reduce their risk of recidivism. Hodgkinson et al. (2021) conducted a systematic review which found that improved emotion recognition, positive decision making and reduced defiance led to the development of psychological resilience and desistance in criminality. Acquisition of such complex skills would be compromised in an individual with a specific language disorder or an individual with a low level of language functioning.

Hart, Blincow and Thomas (2012) offer a resilience framework which can usefully be applied to the SLT activity for people with SLCN, which offers a contribution to psychological resilience and ultimate outcomes. The framework includes five key areas of need in respect of resilience and is represented in Table 6.3 overleaf.

TABLE 6.3 A resilience framework which can usefully be applied to SLT activity for people with SLCN

Resilience framework				
Basics	**Belonging**	**Learning**	**Coping**	**Core self**
Adequate housing	Feeling as though you belong to a set/group/culture	Make daily life operate as well as possible	Understand boundaries and keep within them	Sense of hope
	Feeling as if you have a place in the world		Being brave	
Feeling safe	Experiencing good influences	Create a plan	Solving problems	Know about yourself – strengths and barriers
	Sustain relationships			
Healthy diet	Build number of healthy positive relationships	Notice achievements, and when you are doing well, congratulate yourself	Keeping interests active	
Exercise and fresh air	Recognise which relationships give you hope		Calming skills/self-soothing	If you have a specific problem, seek help If you have skills which you have learned in treatment, use them
Adequate sleep	Build relationships which are reliable	Engage with a range of people/services/activities	Seeking support when needed	Understanding other people's feelings
	Responsibilities and obligations			
Being free from prejudice and discrimination	Able to focus on positives at some point each day	Be organised	Balance between work, learning, social opportunities and leisure	Take responsibility
Access to amenities	Have a sense of where you have come from		Notice emotions and how they feel	
Access to leisure	Feel positive about trying something new/meeting someone new	Continue to build more life skills	Remembering that tomorrow is another day/recognising that a situation can always be built on	Encourage yourself/notice and foster your talents
Adequate financial resources	Mix with other people		Finding positives to hold on to	

Table 6.3 offers numerous ultimate outcomes for resilience which could be used within the theory of change model to link recidivism with SLT intervention. A worked example is presented in Figure 6.5 below:

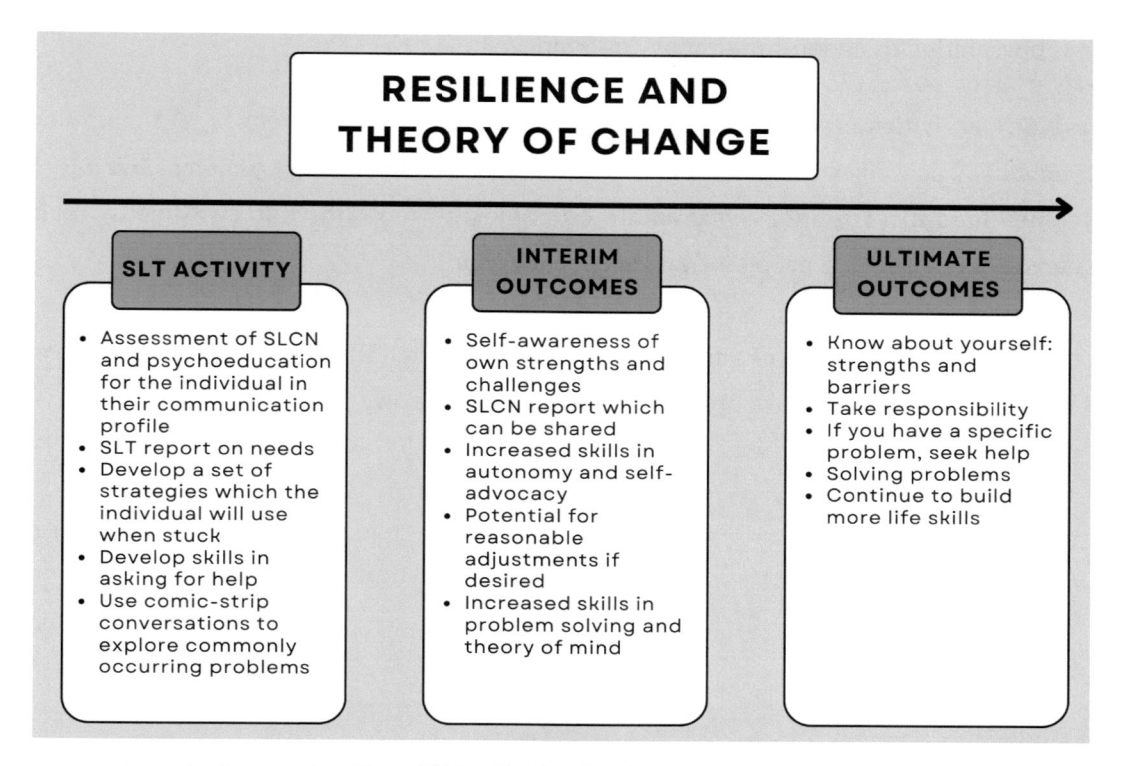

FIGURE 6.5 A worked example of how SLT activities link to the resilience framework and the theory of change methodology

In Figure 6.5, five ultimate outcomes for resilience are linked to SLT activities from the key areas of learning, coping and core self. In this non-specific general example, the SLT provides:

- Assessment of SLCN via appropriately selected formal or informal assessment tools.
- A report with explanations of the individual's communication profile.
- Discussion with the individual resulting in a co-produced set of set of strategies, which the person will use if they do not understand something or cannot resolve a problem. The strategies include items such as 'stop and think', asking a trusted person or phoning the helpline, and are produced as a set of pocket prompt cards.
- These are provided alongside clinical sessions which focus on skill-building work relating to how to ask for help (when, who, where, how) so that autonomy is promoted. The content of the clinical session is psychoeducation to notice the communication

environment when planning how to ask for help (see section on the communication environment in this chapter for details of the three components to be considered).

- Lastly, the clinical intervention offers exploration of frequently occurring problems via comic-strip conversations so that there is structured reflection on problems and opportunities to understand theory of mind.

These SLT activities create interim outcomes relating to self-awareness, autonomy and self-advocacy as well as tangible skills in asking for help and solving problems. The interim outcomes feed directly into the ultimate outcomes of knowing your own needs, taking responsibility, managing problems and skill acquisition.

Further to this, the Ministry of Justice (2019) have identified the needs of people who commit offences. These needs are presented in Figure 6.6 below:

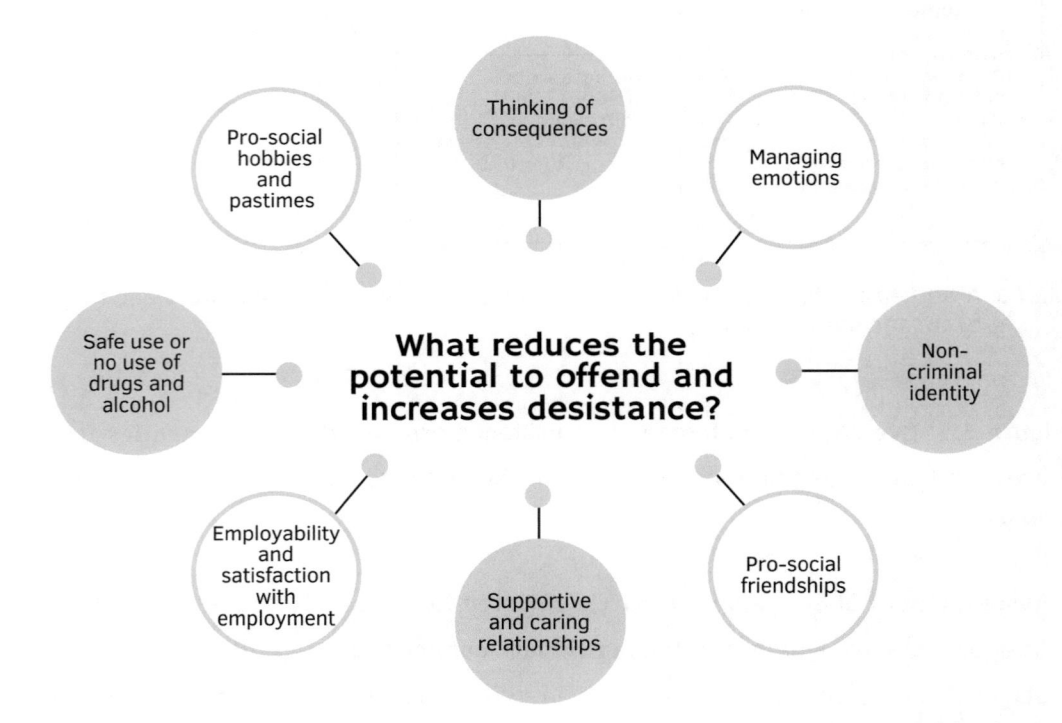

FIGURE 6.6 Factors that relate to resilience and ultimate outcomes, and reduce the potential of an individual to commit further crimes

In the same way that Hart et al.'s (2012) resilience needs can be used in the theory of change model to inform SLT activity that contributes to the interim and ultimate outcomes, the Ministry of Justice (2019) needs of offenders can also be applied to this model this model as shown in Figure 6.7 overleaf.

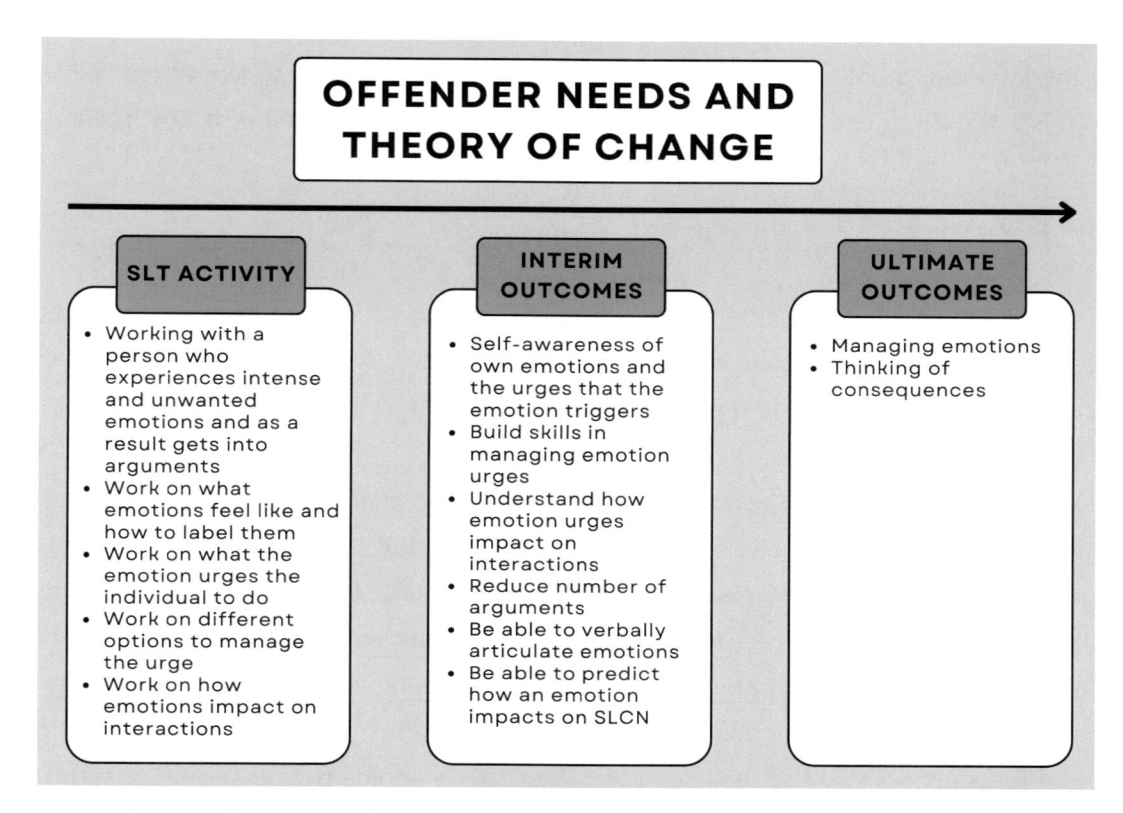

FIGURE 6.7 A worked example of how SLT activities link to the resilience framework, the theory of change methodology and the factors that reduce the potential of an individual to commit further crimes

In this example, the SLT offers intervention to the person with pre-identified SLCN focusing on:

- Emotion recognition using body maps to allow consideration of what happens in the body, how it might be described and which emotion descriptor should be attributed, and building a set of emotion words in the lexicon for use outside of SLT intervention.

- Emotion labelling and how emotions impact on interactions with others. Once the emotion vocabulary is established in the lexicon, it must be supported to be applied to real-life examples via comic-strip conversations and accessible root cause analysis of interactions with other people that were successful or unsuccessful, and how this correlates to the emotion being experienced with the aim to support the individual to gain insight into learning such as 'When I feel angry, I am more likely to shout, use angry facial gestures, not explain myself as clearly and slam doors', 'When I interact in this way, I am less likely to experience a successful interaction'.

- The interim outcome is skills in emotion regulation and a decrease in the frequency and duration of arguments. This work may be undertaken by the psychologist, occupational therapist or named nurse.

- The ultimate outcome is managing emotions and thinking of consequences, which reduces the individual's potential to offend and increases their potential to live within the law. This work will be undertaken as part of a risk-reduction programme with a psychologist.

Therapeutic alliance

When individuals are engaged and motivated with therapeutic input, their progress and potential to generalise skills increases (Kinney et al., 2020). Conversely, the individual can become demotivated and disinterested in attending an offered intervention.

Therapeutic theory addresses these matters, explaining that the therapist and the client both bring ideas, goals and agendas to the session, and that there is a continuum of negotiation between the two stakeholders so that both are satisfied (Muran and Barber, 2011). Therapeutic theory asks for the intervention to be purposeful, collaborative and with shared values, and once this is achieved, a therapeutic alliance is said to have been created. This is the optimal condition for clinical effectiveness as this is where the clinical theory becomes activity that enables the patient to be an agent of change (Constantino et al., 2017).

Indeed, this concept has become increasingly influential as a clinical change process, so that in some situations the therapeutic alliance could be the therapy goal (Muran and Barber, 2011) – for example, to develop an alliance with an individual such that the individual is supported to make a change that would enhance their lived experiences and which may not occur without the alliance.

Case example

A man with schizophrenia and dysarthria is residing in a community specialist mental health hospital, which offers older person and psychiatric intensive care services, following a placement breakdown that was associated with making inappropriate sexual comments to female staff. He is socially isolated with no next of kin or friends. The hospital refer the man to SLT, asking for help to improve the clarity of his speech so that 'ward-based staff can understand him'. The SLT attempts a formal assessment of dysarthria early in the clinical journey and the man does not feel motivated or engaged – it is possible that he is unaware of the referral to SLT or his own intelligibility.

From the small amount of formal assessment that was completed and informal observation of him making comments, the man has a slow rate of speech which is hypernasal. Consonants are imprecisely articulated and voice is breathy. There is very little use of intonation so that it is hard to distinguish a comment from a question. His intelligibility was estimated at 25% in spontaneous speech. Careful listening was required, and he did not use any environmental cues, gestures or strategies to augment his speech to support the listener in their comprehension.

It is likely that the man does not want to engage with the SLT assessment based on his presentation of low motivation. Eventually, he makes sexual comments, and the session is drawn to a close. Staff report that they always withdraw when sexual comments are made. It is noted by the SLT that the man may have developed this mechanism as a way to close interactions rapidly when he no longer wishes to engage. This is a successful strategy for the man in that it works consistently to obtain an end to interactions.

Little is known about the man, his past or his life. The SLT returns with some maps and photographs of the local area and engages the man in a conversation where the aim is to find out more about him. The maps and photographs are more motivating and support the beginning of a therapeutic alliance between the two parties. The SLT supports the man in the following ways:

- The SLT speaks slowly and clearly to model clear speech for him.
- The SLT comments on their own breathing pattern which supports their own speech, and encourages the man to improve his breath support.
- The SLT uses gesture to point to communication ramps and to augment their own expressive language. The SLT encourages the man to do the same by asking 'show me'.
- The SLT asks open questions first, but if the answer is unintelligible, they switch to closed questions to help the man succeed.
- To support the man's breathy voice, the SLT selects a quiet location with no other people around.
- The SLT explains that the conversation will end when the man feels ready and that he can indicate this at any time via pointing to a 'stop' sign which is placed on the table.
- The SLT is honest about the man's intelligibility via feedback such as 'I'm sorry, I did not understand, can you show me?' or 'Because I did not understand, can we try again with you taking a long breath to start the sentence?'

As a result of these supports, the conversation is being switched from SLT-led assessment to discussing the man and his experiences, which is engaging for him. The change to a supported conversation approach enables the SLT to model some useful strategies for the man via functional application.

As the process of the alliance develops, it supports an active bond whereby the individual's self-esteem increases, which in itself increases the potential for change as the person feels more confident to 'be brave' and try a new approach to situations (Muran and Barber, 2011). At all times, that 'bond' would not stray beyond professional boundaries or beyond any security restrictions (see Chapter 8). The SLT activity in this case example would build to identifying a set of support strategies that are acceptable to the man, and which the SLT can train the staff to employ. The strategies identified in the SLT activity could be around breath support, use of open and closed questions, ways to give the man more control via the stop sign, use of low- or high-tech augmentative and alternative communication aids, or use of total communication to reduce the burden placed on verbal output. The staff using the strategies may be an interim outcome in this man's progression towards leaving hospital for residential placement. A hypothesis is that if the staff used the strategies, the man would stop making inappropriate sexual comments to close interactions because he would no longer need to. If this mechanism to end interactions was no longer used as a result of SLT activity, it would also support his ultimate outcome.

The therapeutic alliance is defined as having the following three features (Bordin, 1979):

- agreement of goals
- a task or series of tasks that will support the person to achieve the goals
- the development of an alliance between the clinician and the patient whereby progress in the tasks is discussed and supported.

Ackerman and Hilsenroth (2003) conducted research to identify the characteristics of the clinician and the intervention in order to achieve the alliance and noted the following as important:

- Ability of the clinician to connect with the patient socially and emotionally so that confidence, trust and competence are communicated. Non-verbal gestures are important in achieving this, such as leaning forward and non-verbally indicating attentive listening and non-judgement.
- Dependable and person-centred responsive presentation of the intervention so that sessions occur with a predictable pattern which is changed only by the patient if needed (e.g. a session is moved if the patient has another commitment). This is vital for people with SLCN who may find it harder to tolerate unpredictable patterns if they

have a diagnosis of a condition such as autism or learning disability. This bullet point also applies to responding to the person's SLCN and interests by creating bespoke resources or adapting content to be engaging for them.

- Collaborative goals and tasks within the session so that the clinician is demonstrating responsiveness to the individual and their opinions.
- Clinical confidence in theory, evidence and practice demonstrated by the clinician.
- The clinician holding the patient in positive regard, which helps to promote understanding of the patient's lived experience, as well as offering the support required by the patient for them to reach their communication potential.
- Acceptance of the patient by the clinician in terms of their situation, mental health needs or offending history. An example might be when working in a medium-secure hospital with a person who has been convicted of a sexual offence. It is vital to accept the patient as an individual who needs clinical care rather than have an emotional response to their offending history. When working in the CJS, the SLT would expect to meet people who have been convicted of offences that are socially unpalatable.
- The clinician's ability to confidently engage in tasks that build towards achieving the intervention goals.

Therefore, for the SLT in the CJS setting, the following guidelines apply:

- being approachable and friendly alongside adapting communication to meet the needs of the client
- holding non-judgemental values such as being able to contain any emotional responses to the person's offence via awareness of own body language, and being able to distance oneself from the offence so that SLCN evidence-based intervention is offered regardless of offending history
- offering consistent patient-centred care which is rooted in co-production.

Positive behaviour support

Positive behaviour support (PBS) is the application of applied behaviour analysis (ABA). ABA seeks to understand (O'Reilly et al., 2016):

- Actions of the individual that are important to their success in their context, such as being able to communicate their requests.
- Whether the actions of the individual are effective in obtaining desired outcomes, such as feeling overwhelmed by too much verbal information and ending the interaction via hitting or spitting.

- The causal relationships between actions and outcomes, such as how positive non-verbal gestures such as pointing to request might be reinforced if the person obtains the item following the non-verbal request.
- The actions and outcomes being reinforced within the context due to the responses within the environment, such as a person who enjoys swimming alone in the swimming pool and shouts so that other people leave the pool, thus reinforcing the action of shouting in order to swim alone.
- The actions being seen more frequently and in more situations, such as the person who prefers to swim alone using shouting in the supermarket to cause other people to leave so that they can shop alone.

The goal of PBS is to create a client-centred plan which can be used to support the person to have activity and participation (see the ICF framework discussed earlier in this chapter). PBS is usually considered when the barrier to activity and participation is behaviours that make it hard for the person to access a range of places. These behaviours are generally considered to be difficult to manage and might include hitting, biting, self-harm or disinhibition. PBS is recognised as a social supports model of intervention because it enhances quality of life as the person is supported to access meaningful opportunities for activity and participation (Grey, Lydon and Healy, 2016).

PBS is a clinical intervention which has an evidence base for effective use with people with learning disability (Bowring et al., 2020). In recent years, the application of PBS to other diagnostic labels such as dementia (O'Connor et al., 2021) and brain injury (Carmichael et al., 2020) has been explored with positive results. PBS has also been successfully applied in forensic settings with beneficial outcomes seen (Davies et al., 2015).

PBS plans are usually developed with the client and their important stakeholders such as family, friends and carers. The PBS plan is usually a multi-disciplinary piece of work so that it includes SLCN, sensory needs, physical health needs and meaningful occupation.

Case example

Jim is a young man in prison. He has found being in prison difficult because of the amount of time he is expected to spend engaged in tasks that are not his preferred activity. His preferred activity is physical – riding dirt bikes, extreme sports and rock climbing. He is a very spontaneous person who tends to follow his own agenda when he is not incarcerated.

Jim has a diagnosis of attention deficit hyperactivity disorder (ADHD). ADHD is associated with SLCN of pragmatic language difficulties (social communication disorder) and developmental language disorder (Hawkins et al., 2016; Redmond, 2016). Jim completed SLT assessments and was found to have the following communication profile which is consistent with pragmatic language disorder and developmental language disorder:

- reduced attention and listening skills with a maximum 20 minutes of focused attention being possible in an environment with minimal distractions and motivating tasks presented
- below expected spoken language comprehension of sentences, locating him on the 10th percentile and indicating difficulties with decoding sentences of different types
- below expected vocabulary which resulted in functional limitations in his expressive output so that his expressive language was repetitive (vocabulary scores located Jim on the 12th percentile for vocabulary)
- issues with lexical access which impacted on semantic processing and presented as word-finding difficulties, circumlocution and use of non-specific terms which placed the burden of interaction on the conversation partner
- poor skills in discursive processing.

Jim had the following SLT needs:

- problems learning new words and generalising these outside the clinic environment, which is likely to be associated with semantic processing deficits

- problems modifying vocabulary to the situation (code switching), which resulted in inappropriate expressive offerings

- problems inferring information from non-verbal sources or the environment

- problems with offering too much information, breaching the pragmatic maxim of quantity and poor topic maintenance

- literal interpretations of phrases

- lack of skills to repair when communication breakdowns occur.

One day when Jim was in work, he became involved in an altercation with a peer which escalated to physical blows being exchanged. A general alarm was called and prison officers attended to make the situation safe. Jim was lawfully restrained because de-escalation strategies had failed on this occasion. During the restraint, Jim wrestled with the officers.

Afterwards, in the post-restraint debrief, which was conducted by the SLT because of Jim's communication needs, Jim reflected that he felt good after the restraint because he had had the same feelings as when he engaged with physical activities such as extreme sports.

During the next few months, Jim became involved in more occasions of restraint. Each time, the restraint escalated more quickly and each time Jim resisted and wrestled the officers with increased intensity. Each time, Jim would talk about the release of physical energy during and after the restraint, how he felt 'better' afterwards and how he enjoyed the feeling of physical pressure during the restraint. Jim also talked about planning restraint situations and the challenge of keeping the restraint active for longer periods via preparation (e.g. by covering himself in shower gel so that he was slippery to hold on to).

Applied behaviour analysis suggests that the causal relationship between Jim's actions and outcomes will become so embedded that there will be an automatic activation of this pattern of behaviour which will generalise to outside of prison (Vlaev and Dolan, 2015). Therefore, if this causal relationship is allowed to continue, it increases Jim's risk of violence after he is released from prison (Mooney and Daffern, 2015). A theory of change model for this scenario may look like this:

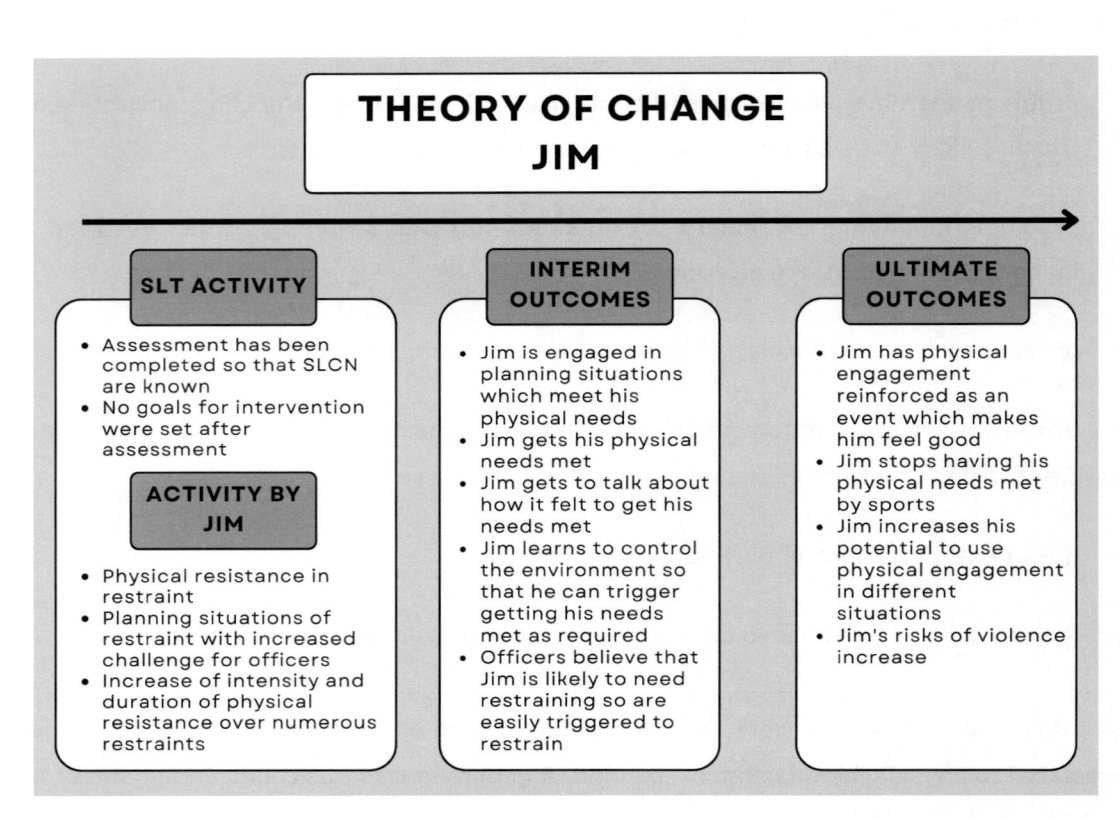

FIGURE 6.8 An example of the theory of change methodology applied to a situation where outcomes increase a risk of violence

PBS aims to understand what the individual's actions and outcomes tell us so that the person's needs can be met in alternative ways (Brown, Shawe-Taylor and Swan, 2017). PBS also provides a framework to understand the causal relationship and offer choices in how needs are met so that the individual has options when considering choice (Student author(s), 2021). In order to allow this to happen, the PBS assessment should consider:

- Whether the individual has a learned negative response – that is, they have learned that if an action results in their avoidance of something they dislike, then the action is reinforced. For example, a man in prison is being compelled to attend a maths class which he dislikes – he discovers that if he swears, the teacher sends him out of class – swearing is reinforced and he has a learned negative response.
- Whether the individual has a learned positive response – that is, they have learned that if an actions result in their needs being met, then the action is reinforced. This is the response seen in the case example of Jim.
- Where the locus of causality is located – was the action and outcome created by the individual (such as the case example of Jim) or by other people in the environment, or by the environment itself? For example, a female in a secure hospital was supervised by staff on a 1:1 basis due to risks that she may harm herself. She discovers that having this high level of staff support is useful as she can access more ward-based activities compared to her peers, and she then makes threats to self-harm in order to retain the staff support. In this example, the locus of causality is either the staff who enable more activity or the environment that allows this outcome.
- Whether the person has internal control over their emotions, actions and decision making so that they are making an informed choice to continue the causal relationship (such as the case example of Jim), or whether they require external support to control emotions, actions and decision making via scaffolding from staff members or via environmental supports such as visual aids.

PBS is a person-centred approach to change, so that the individual is aware of the concern relating to their actions and outcomes and is actively involved in making a plan that might change causality and reduce risk (Moreno and Bullock, 2011; Davies et al., 2022).

Principles of PBS are applicable in the case example of Jim because the ethos of PBS is to restructure and change the environment so that pro-social actions are reinforced. The aim is that the individual will exhibit pro-social actions which will be reinforced via pro-social outcomes, which in turn enhance quality of life (and reduce risks). Recent work by Davies et al. (2015, 2019) has demonstrated how PBS can be applied in forensic settings with outcomes relating to staff confidence in situations that have potential to escalate, and effectiveness in reducing the frequency, management difficulty and severity of aggression of individuals who are supported via individualised PBS plans. Indeed, Pont et al. (2015) advocate for increased input from healthcare professionals when working with people who would benefit from a PBS plan by saying:

> Health care professionals who care for prisoners are in a unique position to help identify and prevent violence, given their knowledge about health and violence, and because of the impartial position they must sustain in the prison environment in upholding professional ethics. Thus, health care professionals working in prisons should be charged with leading violence prevention efforts in custodial settings.
>
> *(Pont et al., 2015, p.1)*

A PBS assessment of Jim's situation could include noting the following observations of the situation (Jim has considerable SLCN but not all of these are impacting on the situation with restraint):

- Physical activity is important to Jim and helps his emotion regulation, but he has limited access to this due to the prison day. He lacks the expressive language skills to articulate this to people around him or negotiate a change to help him. He is frustrated because he cannot explain this, and feeling intense emotions because he has limited physical activity outlets. This creates a situation where Jim is primed to react to a trigger.
- Jim is working within the prison in an employment role. He finds it hard to give attention and listening because the role is not motivating for him. When Jim is demotivated, his workplace supervisor tries to talk to him about his motivation. The supervisor uses long and complex sentences with vocabulary that Jim does not understand. Jim cannot express his lack of understanding to the supervisor due to word-finding problems and poor self-advocacy. This makes Jim feel as though he is failing at work, which causes feelings of shame. Jim is further primed to react to a trigger such as communication breakdown.
- Jim is impulsive so does not think about cause and effect in his decision making. This interacts with his difficulties with code switching such that Jim swears and is perceived as rude by staff who challenge him on this. Because of poor discursive processing, Jim cannot function as an equal partner in this conversation which fuels communication breakdown. Jim cannot repair communication and seeks strategies to leave the situation (i.e. triggering restraint).
- The restraint itself is an outlet for emotions and triggers which have not been able to be managed via communication or other strategies.

- Jim may have sensory needs which are not being met within the environment. He has not been assessed for this by an appropriately qualified SLT or OT.
- The post-restraint debrief offers Jim an opportunity to talk about his experiences in a conversation which follows his lead with attentive listening and slower pace. This is an interaction that Jim can participate in as an equal. His triggers are already eliminated by the restraint episode.

A co-produced multi-disciplinary PBS plan could include the following in negotiation with Jim:

- Regular opportunities for physical activity such as attending the gym or joining the football team, which would be facilitated by prison officers.
- Psychoeducation relating to environmental triggers that are commonly associated with emotions or communication needs and which urge him to seek restraint. This can be undertaken by the SLT or the clinical psychologist following discussion with the SLT.
- A timetable so that Jim knows when he will access physical activity and can begin to self-manage the environmental triggers and the urge for restraint when he knows that a physical activity is happening soon and that this will help his emotion regulation. This can be completed by SLT, occupational therapist (OT) or clinical psychology assistants.
- Consideration of Jim's job role in the prison and whether the job is a good fit with Jim. Jim may be more engaged and motivated by a different job role such as working as a gym orderly or landscape gardening where there is more physical movement and autonomy in tasks. Consideration of this can be undertaken by Jim's case worker or offender manager.
- Sensory assessment with SLT or occupational therapy (OT) so that other ways to meet sensory needs are identified and put in place giving Jim more options than just physical exercise and increasing his meaningful occupation.
- OT training with Jim's workplace supervisors on how to break his work tasks into smaller chunks and offer him variation so that he is able to focus for longer periods.
- SLT training with Jim's workplace supervisors on communication needs and modifying information which is offered to Jim into forms that are easier for him (e.g. simple vocabulary, shorter utterances, slower pace with increased time to process), support for word finding and how to give Jim meaningful choices so that he feels a sense of control in communication.
- SLT work with Jim to help him develop strategies to leave a conversation as soon as he begins to feel triggered. This will include body map work to help Jim understand what the trigger feels like, how to label it verbally and negotiating how he will leave the conversation (e.g. walk away, ask to leave, use an emoji symbol card to indicate how he is feeling).

- SLT work with Jim to produce some communication advice tips that can be used by professionals with him. This would include ideas such as slowing down and using simple sentences. Following production of the communication tips, the SLT can spend some time with Jim helping him to develop a script which he can use to explain the tips to other people.

A multi-disciplinary PBS plan such as this offers Jim the development of new skills and strategies to replace his former ways of thinking and behaving, and this reduces his offending risks which are related to violence and fighting (Olver, 2016; Ministry of Justice, 2019; Hart et al., 2012; Gore et al., 2013). The plan also offers training for conversation partners who Jim interacts with. An updated theory of change model for Jim is illustrated at Figure 6.9:

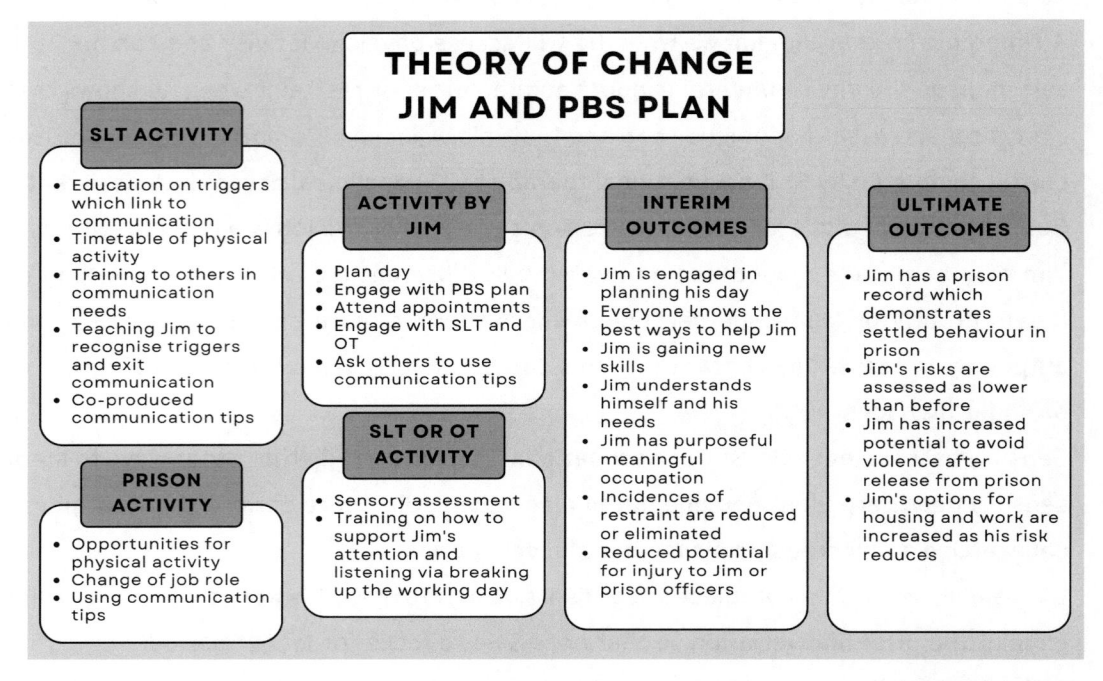

FIGURE 6.9 An example of the theory of change methodology with SLT activities which reduce a risk of violence

At the time of writing, some universities offer PBS as part of the SLT degree programme, but this is not universal across the UK. The British Institute of Learning Disabilities (BILD) offer free PBS training via their website, which can be located via any popular search engine. Workplaces that expect SLTs to employ PBS planning offer continued professional development in order to address any training needs.

PBS has also become the subject of some concern due to insufficient high-quality empirical evidence to suggest that PBS is effective with some client groups, specifically autism

(Simler, 2019; Knestrict, 2015), gender and ethnicity gaps in the evidence base (Reveley, 2016), and criticism from neurodivergent communities that the framework is ableist and traumatising for neurodivergent people (Milton, 2018). While these concerns are valid, there is also tacit knowledge that PBS can work well for some individuals because it enables the articulation of what is known and understood about best practice for supporting people (Gore et al., 2013). Hassiotis et al. (2018) advocate that professionals using PBS with individuals should be sufficiently trained in the intervention and have enough resources to complete the clinical process effectively – and if this was in place, perhaps some of the concerns would be allayed.

Communicative competence

In 1966, Dell Hymes coined the term 'communicative competence' to describe an individual's grammatical knowledge of syntax, morphology and phonology, social knowledge and when to use expressive output appropriately (Hymes, 1966). This term was later built upon by Celce-Murcia, Dörnyei and Thurrell (1995) to be defined in four domains. The definition of communicative competence was further expanded and applied directly to SLT interventions as an individual's ability to freely express ideas, thoughts and feelings to a variety of listeners across contexts providing the means to achieve personal, educational, vocational and social goals including emotional competence relating to self-advocacy (Blackstone and Wilkins, 2009; Light and McNaughton, 2014; Ahern, 2014). This definition is illustrated in Figure 6.10 (below):

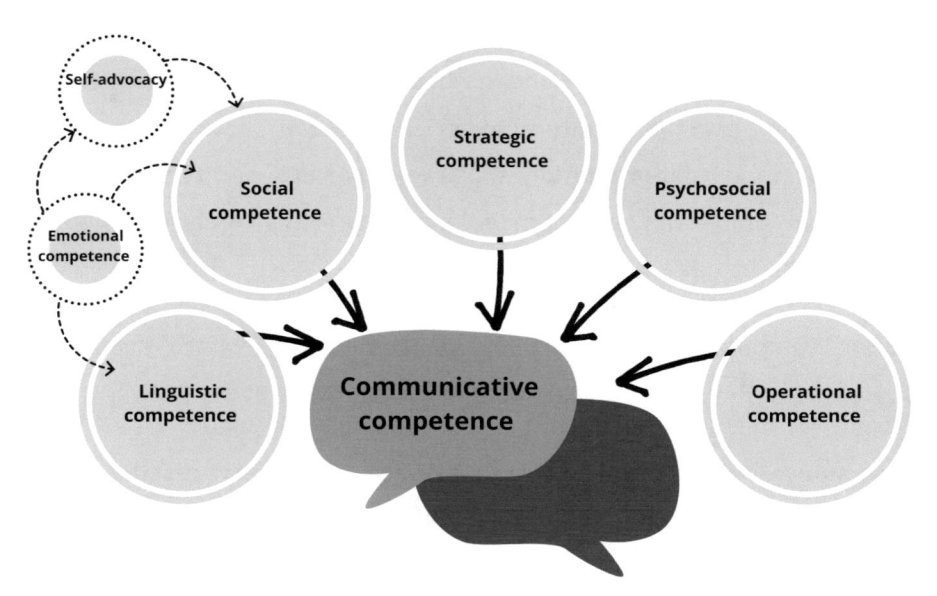

FIGURE 6.10 Communicative competence is the ability to express ideas, thoughts and feelings, providing the means to achieve personal, educational, vocational and social goals including self-advocacy

In Figure 6.10, the terminology can be understood as:

- Linguistic competence: the knowledge, use and judgement of vocabulary, grammar, syntax, morphology, written language, signs and pictures.
- Social competence: the who, what, when, where, why and how of communicating, including how suitable or successful communication attempts are made, as well as communication that supports making and keeping relationships.
- Strategic competence: having skills and strategies to fix communication errors, breakdowns or problems, including tactics to increase the effectiveness of communication. This can include skills in being persuasive or charismatic and code switching based on the conversation partner or context.
- Psychosocial competence: being able to manage the communication demands of daily life while maintaining well-being and being adaptive during communication so that communication goals are achieved in a pro-social manner. This domain links to motivation, resilience and self-confidence, and has clear links to topics covered earlier in this chapter associated with recidivism (Ministry of Justice, 2019; Hart et al., 2012).
- Operational competence: includes creating verbal and non-verbal communication such as speech or body language, cognition such as managing attention to task and perceptual abilities such as judging where to stand and volume of speech.
- Self-advocacy competence: being able to gather information which informs making decisions and expressing the decision, knowing rights and responsibilities; problem solving including eliciting help if needed. Self-advocacy links with resilience and recidivism (Ministry of Justice, 2019; Hart et al., 2012).
- Emotional competence: being able to identify, respond to and manage emotions within personal social and cultural experiences while recognising that other people will have differing emotions, social and cultural experiences. Emotional competence is required for self-advocacy, self-determination, social relationships, self-regulation and community integration. Emotional competence links with resilience and recidivism (Ministry of Justice, 2019; Hart et al., 2012).

Communicative competence is important, as language skills are acquired, because (Hitchcock, Harel and Byun, 2015; Bambini et al., 2016; Snow et al., 2016):

- Poor communicative competence increases parental anxiety, resulting in more difficulties forming a nurturing parent–child relationship and negative impacts on sibling relationships.
- Lack of communicative competence is a barrier to participation in both academic and social settings lasting into adulthood and affecting long-term employment

opportunities and earning potential – workplace difficulties, job termination, harass-
ment and discriminatory hiring practices are cited as negative outcomes of poor communicative competence.

- People with reduced communicative competence are judged more negatively than their peers in relation to intelligence and personality.
- Communicative competence is used socially as a measure of peer popularity, and therefore those lacking communicative competence find it more difficult to join social groups as these form.
- Lack of communicative competence results in negative consequences for the speaker in the domain of social interactions, which can lead to vulnerability.
- Poor communicative competence in respect of pragmatics, cognition and socio-cogni-tion correlates with poor quality-of-life outcomes.
- Poor communicative competence appears to be co-morbid with compromised ability to identify and name one's own affective states (alexithymia) and mental health problems such as depression and anxiety.

From reading earlier chapters of this book, the reader will be aware that many of the points listed here are risk factors for entering the CJS, such as poor attainment in school and social issues. For this reason, it is plausible to link lack of communicative competence to reduced life opportunities and the possibility of coming into contact with the CJS.

As a result, intervention offered by SLTs should address communicative competence. SLT intervention to increase or enhance communicative competence is supporting the indi-vidual to (Kiessling and Fabry, 2021):

- understand and skilfully use verbal and non-verbal conversational turns so that the individual is judged to be socially appropriate by their conversation partner in the immediate context of interaction
- select and apply communication skills that are appropriate and effective in the respective context such as the ability to code-switch
- judge appropriate timing of interactions and control of specific behaviour, which is a consequence of emotions and which may trigger communication breakdown
- be willing to communicate
- have motivational, volitional and social readiness alongside the ability to use problem solving in variable communication situations.

While these are very overarching skills, the SLT will identify which of the above are relevant to an individual client from the assessment process. The SLT will then make a judgement on where to focus intervention and goal setting in discussion with the client and wider MDT.

In order to achieve any of these goals, Auty, Cope and Liebling (2017) advocate for highly structured interventions as they are more effective in creating meaningful change. One such intervention is a modified version of Lego therapy (Levy and Dunsmuir, 2020) where three people work together to complete a Lego model and discuss the emotional responses to this task, which may impact on communication skills in an interaction.

Lego therapy is an intervention for SLCN which links with communicative competence via using conversational turns that are appropriate to the task, via supporting the individual to practise thinking of vocabulary to describe their intention and use this vocabulary in a sentence, via practising how emotions might place an increased demand on the production of expressive output and via negotiating resolution if there is a problem such as the Lego model having a component in the wrong place.

The job roles are modified in terms of job title so that there is a 'planner', a 'finder' and a 'builder', each with their own written job description. It is important to note that this modified version of Lego therapy is not aimed at any cohort with a specific diagnostic label (e.g. 'all people with autism in a forensic setting should engage with Lego therapy'), and it is only entered into with individuals who would like to participate, and who have sufficient language competence.

The job descriptions are located at Appendix 31. Table 6.4 overleaf offers a sample care plan for this modified version of Lego therapy intervention.

When this intervention is considered in the context of Hart et al.'s (2012) resilience framework, the following outcomes may see Table 6.5 on page 288.

TABLE 6.4 A sample care plan for modified SLT Lego therapy intervention

'Where am I now?' (current situation – service user's own view)	'Where am I now?' (current situation – MDT view)	'Where do I want to get to?' (Goal)	'How do I get there? Who is going to support me?' Milestone dates? (Actions and Timelines)	What progress am I making and how will I know?
I am developing communicative competence. I want to build my self-advocacy and emotional competence so that I can ask questions when I am stuck, get help if needed and manage my emotions while doing this.	We know that sometimes you can find group work hard. We want to help you to continue to build your communicative competence in a group that feels 'safe' and which has a set goal (building Lego). The skills that we want you to build are: being able to gather information that informs making decisions and expressing the decision, problem solving including eliciting help if needed, being able to identify, respond to and manage emotions while recognising that other people will have differing emotions.	I want to feel braver in social situations. For me this means: Saying what I want and need Telling someone if I do not understand Asking for help Feeling more confident in my social relationships Being better at managing my emotions when I am struggling	Lego therapy each week for 12 weeks for one hour per week I will take turns being the planner, the finder or the builder. If I am the planner, I will read the instructions, give verbal information to others, listen to their questions, answer questions, think about the words I need, and express to others what I know using supportive words and actions. If I am the builder, I will listen to the planner and follow the instructions from the planner. I will ask questions, say if I need information and concentrate on the words used. If I am the finder, I will listen to the planner, find the bricks based on the information and pay attention to words used. I will ask if I need more information and express any needs/if I am stuck. I will build Lego sets with my group colleagues which will involve cooperation skills – sharing, listening, asking, helping, waiting, thinking, supporting. At the end of the session, we will talk about how we felt, what was good and what was hard.	Jacqui will measure my progress in the group in the following ways: Noting when I say what I want or need Noting when I tell someone that I do not understand Noting when I ask for help Jacqui will look at my record and see if I have struggled with my emotions and try to understand why, when or how. Jacqui will meet with me on a 1:1 basis to chat to me about this. We will complete the emotions Talking Mat. I will self-rate my confidence in my social relationship during my keyworker sessions using a visual scale. I will be able to tell other people about the Lego therapy and how it makes me feel. My feelings about my progress are very important to me. I can talk to Jacqui or my keyworker about the group if I need help or have questions.

TABLE 6.5 SLT Lego therapy intervention located on the resilience framework

Resilience Framework

Basics	Belonging	Learning	Coping	Core Self
Adequate housing	**Feeling like you belong to a set/group/culture** Feeling like you have a place in the world	Make daily life operate as well as possible	**Understand boundaries and keep within them** **Being brave**	Sense of hope
Feeling safe	Experiencing good influences Sustain relationships	**Create a plan**	**Solving problems**	**Know about yourself – strengths and barriers**
Healthy diet	**Build number of healthy positive relationships**	Notice achievements, and when you are doing well, congratulate yourself	Keeping interests active	
Exercise and fresh air	Recognise which relationships give you hope		**Calming skills/self-soothing**	**If you have a specific problem, seek help** **If you have skills which you have learned in treatment, use them**
Adequate sleep	Build relationships which are reliable **Responsibilities and obligations**	**Engage with a range of people/services/activities**	**Seeking support when needed**	**Understanding other people's feelings**
Being free from prejudice and discrimination	Able to focus on positives at some point each day	Be organised	Balance between work, learning, social opportunities and leisure	**Take responsibility**
Access to amenities	Have a sense of where you have come from		Notice emotions and how they feel	
Access to leisure	**Feel positive about trying something new/meeting someone new**	**Continue to build more life skills**	Remembering that tomorrow is another day/recognising that a situation can always be built on	**Encourage yourself/notice and foster your talents**
Adequate financial resources	**Mix with other people**		Finding positives to hold on to	

A one-to-one clinical intervention by SLT that supports communicative competence in the psychosocial domain links with the SLT evidence base for narrative intervention (Spencer and Petersen, 2020). Traditionally, narrative has been used in SLT to help the development of academic and socially meaningful stills in casting, and recasting, accounts. Within the evidence base for offender rehabilitation, narrative is also valued as it provides 'the opportunity to reconsider and verbalise a description of one's life, re-writing the script from a hopeless one to an optimistic one, and can be instrumental in the choice to desist from crime' (Ansbro, 2008, p.2). Kirkwood (2016) advocated for the use of narrative to help individuals make meaning of identity – supporting motivation, resilience and self-confidence – and noted that quality interactions increase positive change for people in the CJS.

SLT narrative work can include:

- Talking Mats to support people with SLCN to report on their views and feelings with reduced potential to acquiesce (Boardman, Crichton and Butterworth, 2016).
- Using timelines of situations to create a visual scaffold of a narrative with key words (Schauer, Neuner and Elbert, 2017). This helps people with SLCN to consider who the agents in a narrative are and what they did, in what order. While timelines are used by a variety of professionals as a reflective tool, in this scenario the SLT is using the timeline as a communication aid to support cognition, receptive language and expression.
- Using comic-strip conversations to explore what happened, why and how with the process of drawing the comic strip as part of the reflection and casting the account (Reichow, 2021).
- Drawing a picture of a perfect situation and then using post-it notes to explore thoughts and feelings with written emotion cards to support the use of emotions vocabulary and future-oriented cognitive linguistics (Petrich, Liu and Nedelec, 2020).
- Mind maps, stick-men pictures or box-and-arrow sketches to explore cause and effect within narratives helping the individual to process agency and identity (Adshead, 2011).
- Using body maps, emotions stones or symbols to consider emotions and communicative interactions in situations that were challenging for the individual, which could include a before, during and after card-sorting element (Day, 2009).
- Using visual aids or prompts to help the individual consider what to include in their narrative and in what order (Fabry, 2021; Noel and Westby, 2014).

While this work may be perceived as overlapping with the role of a clinical psychologist, it differs in that clinical psychology is interested in considering the past and ways of thinking that have developed as a result of past experience, the role of agency and sense of identity (Ansbro, 2008). SLT in interested in communication, the future and building skills to improve communication. SLT narrative work includes using visual aids, adapted language and content, support of cognitive linguistic processing and the development of expressive skills in order to enhance future possibilities for the individual.

Case example

Mr V is a man with dementia in a medium-secure hospital. The age range of people in his hospital ward varies and he is the eldest person residing there. He is the only one with a diagnosis of dementia.

Mr V's dementia has impacted on his communication in the following ways:

- word-finding difficulties especially proper nouns and nouns
- semantic paraphasias
- decayed ability to use syntax in expression, leading to fragmented sentences
- reduced use of prepositional phrases in tasks
- reduced motivation to repair communication breakdowns or meet the needs of the conversation partner.

The hospital team have started using a whole-ward approach called 'Narrative Care' (Berendonk et al, 2020). Narrative Care aims to support the individual's self-identity by enabling them to create narratives that foster understanding of past experiences and self-identity. It is an intervention for people who reside in a long-term placement and where the staff team would like to focus clients on future-oriented goals instead of daily life or past transgressions.

Mr V is expected to need help to engage in Narrative Care so a request is made to the SLT to support. The SLT uses the following tools and strategies:

- Talking Mats to allow Mr V to comment on what hobbies he enjoyed in the past, and which he may like to try again as part of future planning.
- Photographs of people in Mr V's family in order to create a family tree, including names of people and important facts about them. This included discussion on who Mr V might live with if he were able to choose.
- Photographs and maps of Mr V's home town which were used with Mr V to sequence his life events into the story of him growing up and obtaining his first job. Mr V was supported to share this sequence in the coffee and chat group so that he could participate equally with peers who were sharing information.

While using these tools, Mr V required speech, language and communication support in order to allow him to express himself on the background of his communication difficulties.

Ideas for narrative development

It is well documented that people who are at high risk of coming into contact with the CJS are likely to have poor skills in casting a narrative (Snow and Powell, 2005) and that this impacts on their ability to explain what happened, when and why during the legal process (Kippin et al., 2021). In order to provide intervention for narrative skills, it is recommended that the following cognitive processes are developed initially (Noel and Westby, 2014):

1. Recognising what narrative is required to be told based on the situation and conversation partners. This may be a narrative about a problem that exists within the custodial setting or a narrative about a past sequence of events which is being asked about. These are cognitive linguistic decisions about topic, how much to say, what the other person already understands, and processing of cause and effect.
2. Defining the problem or the sequence of events so that all conversation partners have a shared reference or understanding and so that the person casting the narrative has used skills associated with theory of mind.
3. Identifying the goals of the narrative – for example, whether it is to use the conversation partner as a tool for reflection in problem solving or to enable everyone present to understand specifics of a sequence of events so skills in clarity or detail are required.
4. Generating multiple ways of responding to or casting the narrative alongside weighing the possible consequences of each option. This requires high-level cognition and linguistic skills applied in the moment.
5. Deciding on responses using knowledge of pragmatics so that the manner, quantity, quality and relevance of the information is a good fit to the context alongside use of word finding, grammar, syntax and code switching.
6. Acting on the decisions made at each stage alongside self-monitoring of how emotional states may be impacting on performance of each of the above.

Such a detailed framework may be beyond the understanding of many people in the CJS. Noel (2013) suggests using the SPACE acronym to help the individual to develop a framework which supports the cognitive load of narrative generation in relation to past events:

S. Setting the scene: who is involved, when and where does the subject of the narrative happen, what is going on for participants in this narrative?

P. Problem or Past: what is or was the situation, how do the participants feel, what do the participants need or want?

A. Actions: what did participants do?

C. Consequence: what was the result of the actions?

E. End or Evaluation: how did the situation end, what lessons were learned, what messages do you want the listener to understand, how do you feel as a result of this narrative, do the listeners need to ask questions to check anything, do you want to ask questions?

Case example

Sam is a man with learning disability who is remanded in custody. Prior to being in prison, he was residing in a group home for people with learning disability and had 24-hour support to maintain his daily routine and access the town he lived in. While Sam was in the town centre with a support worker, he went to the toilet independently and was subsequently accused of a crime.

Sam is very distressed in prison and has not been able to engage with formal SLT assessment due to being tearful. SLT informal assessment has found the following:

- Sam can follow verbal instructions with three information-carrying words. He is inconsistent with four information-carrying words.
- Sam has problems decoding sentences if the information is not presented in the order in which it is required to be processed.
- Sam has immature phonology including cluster reduction, consonant deletion and misarticulation of plosives which makes him very hard to understand.
- Sam has hyponasal speech.
- Sam has underdeveloped syntax so that sentences are not grammatical.
- Sam switches topic readily which compounds the listener's barriers to understanding him.

Sam is required to talk to legal professionals about what happened, when and how. The SLT introduces him to the SPACE framework with a visual aid and symbol to represent each part of the framework. The SLT cannot discuss events with him in relation to his criminal charge, so the SLT selects other situations to explore with Sam and encourage him to use the SPACE framework:

- The SLT and Sam watch some short excerpts from movies that Sam knows well and then applies the movie storyline to the framework while cuing Sam to stay on topic and offer a piece of information in each heading.
- In order to increase the challenge offered to Sam, the SLT and Sam watch some short excerpts from TV programmes that Sam has not seen before. He is required to think about how to explain people and places whose names he does not know, and events

that he does not know the conclusion of. Sam is prompted to include information in each heading of the SPACE framework.

- To increase the challenge again, the SLT and Sam sit together in a communal area of the prison and watch people passing by and any small events that occur. They retire to a clinic room and Sam is supported to explain what has been seen to include information in each heading of the SPACE framework.
- Lastly, Sam is asked to remember a happy event that occurred in his past with clear instructions that it cannot relate to the criminal charge. Sam is asked to cast a narrative of the happy event to include information in each heading of the SPACE framework. The SLT asks questions to help Sam notice if there are information gaps. This activity is repeated so that information gaps reduce.
- Sam is provided with the visual aid to keep and use when he is in meetings with legal professionals.
- The SLT provides a report explaining Sam's communication needs, the SPACE framework and recommendations relating to Sam accessing communication support as he progresses through his legal action.

While the SPACE framework thinks about generation of past narrative, Noel (2013) suggests alterations to make the framework future focused:

S. Setting: being aware of the setting, what all listeners know and understand of the setting, what needs clarifying first so that the listener can best understand next steps of this narrative

P. Problem: being aware of upcoming problems based on what is known from the past, the participants, how participants feel or what is known about participants' skills in communication or emotion regulation, what different participants want to achieve as a result of this narrative (e.g. a shared understanding, a solution to a problem, an appraisal of skills)

E. End goal: what is the best or preferred outcome for this narrative (e.g. a shared understanding, a solution to a problem, an appraisal of skills)?

A. Action mind: thinking about options and choices and consider which is best based on analysis of the problem and the end goal

C. Consequence prediction: predicting what might happen based on analysis of the problem and the end goal. Does the consequence prediction change the narrative in any way?

A. Action mind: what is the decision, what will be included in the narrative, what words will be used, how much will be said, how will the participants know that the narrative has been received as intended?

A. Action behaviour: completing the actions as decided

C. Consequence actual: what was the result for each of the participants once the narrative was presented?

E. Evaluation: did the narrative achieve the end goal?

This becomes a much more complex set of considerations for narrative generation and should only be used with people who have adequate residual skills to tolerate this level of complexity. The individual SLT may feel that some of these considerations are useful for their client, and so may adapt this framework for the individual and offer it with a visual cue such as pocket cards to enable generalisation of the methodology to outside of the clinic room.

Case example

Kyle is a man with ADHD and a long history of substance misuse. He is leaving prison on licence. This means that he has a set of conditions (or rules) that he must adhere to. He must also meet with his probation officer each week and explain to the officer what he has been doing and what he hopes to do.

Kyle has the following SLCN needs:

- Poor attention and listening associated with ADHD.
- Difficulty with topic maintenance so that he goes off topic and forgets what he wanted to say, often not answering the question asked and being perceived as evasive by professionals.
- Problems judging how much to say and being verbose.
- Semantic errors in his word finding, which can be associated with substance misuse. This results in Kyle misrepresenting himself to others because he has made a semantic error which he is not aware of.
- Problems casting a narrative because he leaves out information, loses focus on topic or provides too much information about a detail that seems small and irrelevant to the listener.

The result is that Kyle can seem an unreliable reporter when he talks to his probation officer. The probation officer has met with Kyle and the SLT jointly to discuss his communication profile, so there is awareness that Kyle may be misunderstood by the listener.

In preparation for leaving prison and being supervised by probation, the SLT and Kyle have been working on narrative skills using the future-focused SPACE framework. This work was similar to the previous case study of Sam with the SPACE framework, but also included the use of basic root cause analysis.

Root cause analysis can be used alongside the SPACE framework to support deeper consideration of the end goal, the action and consequence prediction. Using root cause analysis with people with SLCN lends itself to timelines or comic-strip conversations or decision trees. While these tools can be used by any professional, the SLT is using them to help maintain attention and topic, to offer feedback on topic maintenance to increase insight and to help the person judge how much to say. Because Kyle has semantic errors in his narrative, the act of producing a written analysis afforded him the opportunity to 'check for errors'. This became one of the greatest learning points for Kyle as he worked on these skills – the fact that if the narrative was constructed on paper, it became possible to 'check for errors' and then express the information to the listener with the paper-based preparation as a scaffold.

The SLT can conduct this type of work via the following method:

- Use pen and paper and ask questions as per the SPACE framework.
- Begin to capture the answers and information on the paper either in the form of a time line, a comic strip, boxes-and-arrows chart or mind map.
- Write in key words, especially nouns or verbs which may be most commonly subject to semantic errors.
- Ask for predictions of what might happen and add these to the paper working from left to right.
- If the individual is moving off topic, offer feedback or ask a question to refocus attention on the sequence being created.
- Once all of the information is captured, ask the person to check the written information for accuracy. Ask what needs to be added, what can be removed, what needs to be changed and if there are any words that are not the best choice.
- Once any corrections are made, support the person to cast their narrative where they are in the role of teller and the SLT is listener only.
- When the narrative is concluded, the SLT can offer feedback or suggestions for improvement.
- This type of task can be repeated many times as the skills develop with repetition.

Work on emotions and interactions

The interplay of emotions and interactions should also be considered when addressing communicative competence. This is because the emotional state of the conversation partners impacts on the success (or not) of the interaction (Marinetti et al., 2011). It is likely that most people will have had times when they have felt a strong emotion that has impacted on how an interaction has played out.

Barlow et al. (2010) suggest a method for working with individuals who find that emotions impact on their interactions regardless of diagnostic label or diagnostic overshadowing. Their work is based on the idea that the emotional state influences what a person thinks, senses in their body and does as an action. The emotional state and thoughts may happen automatically without the individual having attended to these factors prior to entering into an interaction. The emotional state and thoughts will also be influencing the actions of the individual such that they experience an 'action urge'. For example, a person who is feeling angry and who is thinking 'I am really annoyed' will have an action urge to be confrontational, which will spill into their interaction style as illustrated in Figure 6.11 below:

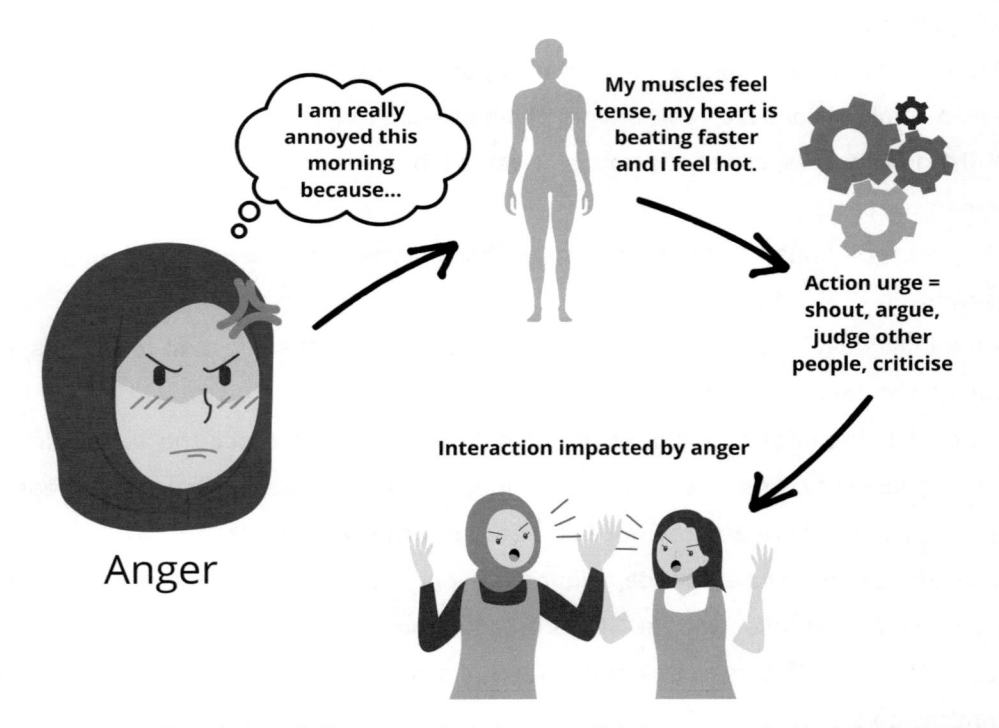

FIGURE 6.11 An emotional state influences what a person thinks, senses in their body and does as an action, which impacts on interaction style

In order to address this, the SLT can offer intervention that focuses on:

- being aware of what emotion you are feeling, what the emotion does to your body and how you might label the emotion
- being aware of the emotion and the associated action urge
- making a decision about whether to have an interaction while experiencing this action urge
- having awareness to contain emotions if an interaction occurs during the action urge
- having autonomy to ask the conversation partner to delay an interaction if the timing coincides with an action urge.

Linehan (2014) offers an outline of the ten emotions that are recognised within dialectical behaviour therapy, and which action urges are present. This information is represented in Table 6.6 (overleaf).

The SLT could use comic-strip conversations or chain analysis (see Figure 6.12 below) of patient self-report to explore what emotion may have been being experienced and whether the interaction suffered as a result. Over time, this will build increased emotional awareness. which will support the person to modify their interaction so that they are resisting the action urge. Additional clinic tasks could include matching the emotion to the action urge via sorting cards, watching TV clips from soap operas and noting the emotions, action urges and interaction results, or role-playing interactions and seeing if the individual can identify the emotion based on the role-play content.

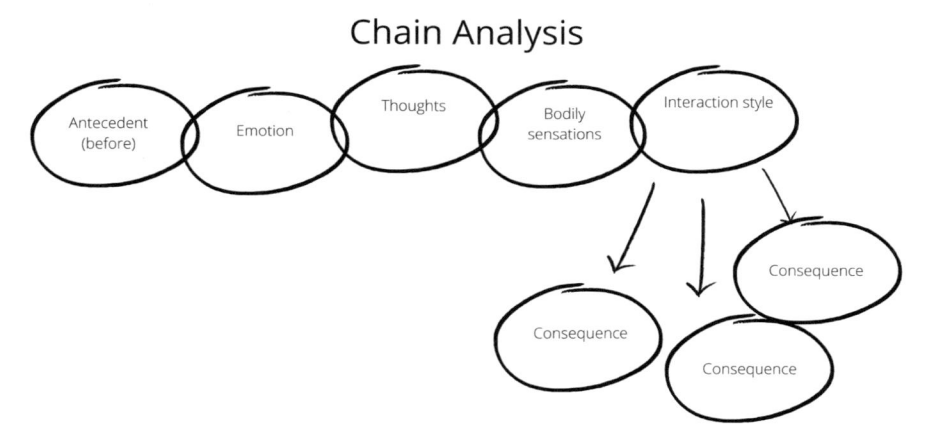

FIGURE 6.12 SLT chain analysis of interaction breakdown for use with people with SLCN

Again, this work can be undertaken by various members of the MDT such as OT, clinical psychologist or named nurse. This work is undertaken by the SLT when the individual has a confirmed or suspected speech, language or communication need such that they require the enhanced communication skills of the SLT.

TABLE 6.6 Ten emotions and their action urges, which impact on interaction style

Emotion	What the emotion is trying to signal to the individual	The action urge felt by the individual	Impact on interaction style
Fear	There is a threat present to physical health or emotional well-being	Flight – run away Fight – stay and fight the threat Freeze – overwhelmed and do not move	Avoid social situations Avoid certain people Avoid certain topics Enter into interaction but be overtly assertive or argumentative Speak more loudly and with increased gesture Say nothing, do nothing Rigid body language and flat facial expression
Anger	There is a threat present to physical health or emotional well-being	Fight – defend self and attack the threat	Enter into interaction but be overtly assertive or argumentative Speak more loudly and with increased gesture Assertive or aggressive body language or facial expression
Sadness	Something is missing or lost	Replace Isolate Withdraw Ruminate	Seek out social situations that might replace the loss (e.g. making new friends quickly, entering into new relationships, joining clubs or going to new places) Isolate self from social situation and avoid people, places or social events Ruminate on the loss which may affect social confidence or self-esteem
Disgust	Something is toxic to health or happiness	Avoid	Avoid social situations Avoid certain people Avoid certain topics Isolate self from social situation and avoid people, places or social events
Guilt	I betrayed my own values or moral code	Repair Isolate Compensate	Seeking to repair via apologies, compliments, praise Offering to do or give something in order to repair Isolate self from social situation and avoid people, places or social events Compensate with overt social gestures, be more outgoing, undertake acts that demonstrate values to others such as giving away possessions
Shame	I betrayed my social groups values and should be judged or excluded	Hide/withdraw Repair	Isolate self from social situation and avoid people, places or social events Seeking to repair via apologies, compliments, praise Offering to do or give something in order to repair

(Continued)

TABLE 6.6 Continued

Emotion	What the emotion is trying to signal to the individual	The action urge felt by the individual	Impact on interaction style
Joy	Good for health and happiness	Continue and find more	Be socially more engaged but talk about self/own joy more May show decreased awareness of the emotions of others
Love	A relationship that is good for health and happiness	Pursue Maintain Spend increased time with the focus of the relationship	Be socially more engaged but talk about self/own experience more May show decreased awareness of the emotions of others Neglect some relationships in favour of new relationship
Jealousy	Fear of losing something that you have to another person or group	Protect Control	Guarded and distrustful in interactions to protect object of jealousy Controlling in interactions to influence the object of jealousy Controlling in interactions to influence other people away from the object of jealousy More likely to give false or misleading information More likely to be watchful in interactions and to judge communication of others as suspicious
Envy	Another person or group has something that you do not have, but which you need or want or feel entitled to	Motivation to obtain the object of the envy	More likely to give false or misleading information to obtain the object of envy More likely to be watchful in interactions and to judge communication of others as suspicious Potential to be charismatic in order to obtain object or as a face-saving act

Case example

Shaun is a man in low-secure hospital who sustained a head injury when he was a teenager. As a result, he had the following cognitive linguistic impairment:

- poor emotional literacy so that he found it hard to express his emotions via speech
- poor emotion regulation such that once he felt an emotion, he found it hard to problem-solve how to self-soothe or resolve the emotional situation
- problems understanding the facial expressions and body language of others so that he would misread the intentions of others and be reactive to this, often reacting with aggression
- problems with reasoning such that he found it hard to think about social situations in a logical way using a range of information
- difficulties understanding situations from the standpoint of other people.

As such, his relationship with his family had suffered and he had moved out of home to a bedsit. He found it hard to make friends outside of the family home and misunderstood the intentions of others – for example, if a female smiled at him, he would take that to mean that she wanted to date him.

Within hospital, Shaun was noted to be emotionally triggered very rapidly, and as a result he would often 'go on to have an argument'. The argument was often prone to escalation such as throwing objects or damaging property. The ward team were concerned that Shaun would hurt himself or others and experience placement breakdown which would disrupt his rehabilitation. The SLT was asked to spend time with Shaun to address his 'getting into arguments'.

The SLT used chain analysis (see Figure 6.12 on page 297) and emotion action urges (see Table 6.6 on page 298) with Shaun in the following ways:

- helping Shaun focus on the before, what he was thinking and feeling
- helping Shaun identify the trigger and what the trigger made him feel while offering vocabulary options on written cards to support his expression
- using the vocabulary cards to create sample 'feelings' cards which Shaun could reflect on and start to practise using an augmentation to his spoken output
- looking with Shaun at his emotion cards and what action urges could be associated
- adding the action urges on to the reverse of the card

- asking Shaun to notice what he is thinking and verbally express his thoughts as an expressive language task in clinic
- asking Shaun to notice when he was thinking outside of clinic and report the thoughts within SLT sessions with SLT scaffolding his expressive language
- using body maps to draw Shaun's thought bubbles and note physical body sensations with the aim for Shaun to connect thoughts such as 'that's annoying' to sensations such as muscle tension, increased heart rate, faster breathing
- using mind maps to link the physical sensations to interaction style (e.g. 'When you have increased muscle tension, you find it harder to get words out so you might communicate via actions')
- finally, linking communication and interaction choices to consequences (e.g. 'When you communicated via actions and threw the chair, the consequence was...').

The visual resources should be collected and co-produced with Shaun into a workbook which he can review with his named nurse after incidents when his interaction style has resulted in communication breakdown end of case study.

The use of such sessions and the repetition of similar tasks with novel patient examples complement the evidence published by Kiessling and Fabry (2021) which states:

- People with little experience of a new area of knowledge or skill must first get an overview and then build up a knowledge base (e.g. by discussion, via explanation, via observation or by meaningful worked examples). This asks the SLT to offer sessions which offer knowledge or strategies with the understanding that the patient is a novice and will require repetition (using a process similar to examples offered in this chapter). The SLT is in the role of expert.
- At an intermediate level of knowledge or skill, the person benefits from increased personalised worked examples and reflection on their own application of skill, and can focus more on specific or complex problem solving. This allows the SLT to continue to offer the same knowledge and strategies but with greater emphasis on the patient's own examples and on patient reports of using the knowledge or strategies. The SLT and the client become joint explorers of the communication and interaction examples.
- Once the individual develops skills in transfer, they can recognise that the current situation has similarities with a previous situation such that knowledge or skill can be generalised. The SLT becomes a guide to using the knowledge and strategies as the patient becomes more proficient and self-directed.

The benefit to the clinician is that the patient can bring the situation or example to each session, and the clinician can use processes as detailed in examples in this chapter with repetition over several sessions.

Transactional analysis

Another tool that is useful for the consideration of communicative competence and self-advocacy in communication is transactional analysis, which has been demonstrated to have positive results in offender populations (Torkaman et al., 2020).

Transactional analysis considers the communication exchanges between people based on three potential states that a person can be located in before, during or after an interaction. The people engaged in the interaction can switch between states based on their internal drivers (feeling, thoughts and action urges) or external drivers such as the state that the conversation partner is occupying. The three states are:

- Parent: this is an interaction style that the individual has acquired from authority figures during their lived experience. This interaction style is subconsciously adopted when the communication environment is one in which the individual is reacting to the situation by providing authority. The individual either wants to control what is happening or voice their disapproval. When a person uses the parent state, those around them can be forced into a child state.
- Adult: this is the interaction style that enables the person to be in the present conversation without judgement. Features of this state are respect, compromise, listening and solution-focused outcomes. This interaction style enables the conversation partner to be in an adult state also, and offers the best potential for meaningful interactions.
- Child: this state is similar to how children might engage – either agreeing with an authority figure in order to be 'good' or entering into playful interactions, spontaneity, jokes or emotion-driven interactions in order to get their needs met. A person presenting in a child state will often trigger the conversation partner to enter the parent state.

Once an individual has been taught about the three states, they can self-monitor which state they occupy and can identify states in others around them.

Case example

J is a life-sentenced prisoner who has been incarcerated since his teenage years. He is now a middle-aged man who was referred to SLT by prison offers because they are finding him difficult to work with. The officers feel 'at the end of their tether' and he has been labelled a 'problem prisoner' because he disrupts the good order and discipline of the establishment several times per week.

J disrupts the prison day by refusing to do what is asked of him, by climbing on fences to protest at height and by instigating dirty protests.

On meeting with SLT, J stated that he thought that he might have autism. A detailed case history was taken, including linking with his parents with his permission. The case history indicated that J was unlikely to have autism.

In conversation, J was articulate and capable, so formal SLT assessment was not initially indicated. Informal assessment was conducted by offering some sessions to consider J's life story as a person in prison. It became apparent that J had developed the following social discourse adaptations as a result of his environment and experiences:

- distrust in all other people and no empathy for others
- a tendency to respond to other people by taking more conversational turns, dominating the interaction and being overtly assertive to the point of aggression
- being rigid in his conversational style
- being unable to express anything personal such as his needs or opinions in functional situations
- fast rate of speech
- poor skills at 'personal space' with a tendency to stand too close to the conversation partner
- overuse of large bodily gestures with arms including getting out of his seat and making grand gestures
- making longer and more intense eye contact.

J had a lived experience of adverse childhood experiences prior to prison and had experienced trauma within prison. His attachments to his family had been damaged by coming to prison at a young age and he had found it hard to maintain close relationships from within prison.

Once the SLT had identified the social discourse adaptations, very honest feedback was given to J about the way he conducts tasks, which included a challenge to J to ask himself if this social discourse style was meeting his needs. J was asked to reflect on this in his own time over the period of two weeks.

When J met with the SLT again, he had reflected on his social discourse style and he had discussed this with his sister. He had reached the conclusion that if he wanted to progress in prison, obtain release on licence and be successful in the community, he would need some help to address the adaptations that had become habit for him.

SLT intervention focused on:

- Teaching J transactional analysis states including very specific focus on the interaction style of each state with attention to conversational turns, flexibility of thought in interactions, slowing his pace of speech, being aware of personal space and reducing use of large gestures with arms.
- After the psychoeducation sessions were complete and J had an understanding of transactional analysis, he was set the task to watch others in their interactions and identify which states they were occupying at any given time.
- J would return to clinic with his observations and was able to make connections to people being in an adult state and this being more successful in terms of gaining help or goods.
- Drawings of interactions were created jointly with SLT and J to help embed learning. J was asked to self-monitor his own interaction states and keep an interactions diary for two weeks.
- SLT sessions included reviewing the diary and discussing which social discourse detail could be employed in the future.
- J attended a session and said, 'I was on the exercise yard and I wanted to return to my cell early. The officer went into parent – telling me the rules and the time – and I felt myself wanting to go into child and argue with him. But I caught myself and went into adult. I talked to him politely and asked if I could negotiate when I could return to my cell and why. He went into adult mode and let me go inside. Before, I would have argued, stormed off and immediately climbed on the fencing to inconvenience that officer who would have had to wait in the cold until I was ready.'

SLT sessions reduced in frequency to once per month in order to scaffold J while new skills and ways of thinking embedded. Over the period of 12 months, J was able to avoid any reports of poor behaviour and re-established his relationship with his offender manager.

After a further six months, J was successful in reducing his risks such that he could move to a lower level of security. He moved to a category D prison.

The SLT intervention with J enabled him to:

- modify his interaction state to be in adult mode
- influence his conversation partner to be in adult also
- exit interactions where the conversation partner is trying to force him into parent or child state
- resist interactions where the conversation partner is in parent state, which has previously resulted in J entering child state and being subject to action urges that have caused communication breakdown.

Appendix 32 offers some resources that can be used by SLTs to help in various situations, reflections or sessions relating to the development of communicative competence such as narrative and transactional analysis.

Communication needs relating to risk

Risk is a very poorly defined term which can be overused in the CJS. In order to discuss 'risk', it would be helpful to quantify what we mean by risk in this book.

Risk used in this text is a term for:

- a subjective construct which can be seen differently by different individuals
- a possibility of both reward and costs to the individual or others
- a possibility of harm to self or others
- the existence of a perceived threat in a situation
- uncertainty about an outcome
- an outcome that may be associated with numerous events such as a risk to health, a risk to self or others, a risk to society.

SLCN interplay with the risks that an individual may be perceived as having, and this is expanded upon in this section.

When reviewing guidance on what interventions help people within the CJS who have attracted diagnostic labels that are commonly associated with SLCN, the following recommendations are recurrent (Young et al., 2018a, 2018b; Young and Cocallis, 2019, 2021; McCarthy et al., 2019; Chaplin et al., 2017):

- structure and routine to the day which is consistently followed
- predictable application of rules
- staff who are consistent and predictable
- any changes to the structure and routine being planned in advance
- explanations being provided for any changes to the structure and routine
- having breaks or extra time to think
- visual aids
- intervention that is engaging and interesting
- intervention that is rooted in co-production
- asking the individual what helps them
- healthy habits such as food, exercise and sleep patterns.

The same body of work recommends that the following is taken into account to address risk reduction:

- improve self-esteem
- develop communication skills
- improve identification of emotions and the management of intense and unwanted emotions
- improve awareness that there is a link between emotions and communication skills
- improve skills in problem solving
- improve social communication skills so that relationships are fostered
- address assumption forming such as assuming what other people are thinking or feeling.

Finally, the following is suggested as additional strategies that help reduce risk:

- an opportunity to talk about thoughts and feelings
- mindfulness skills
- relaxation skills.

While not all of these interventions and strategies fall within the remit of SLT, many of them do. Table 6.7 overleaf illustrates this.

TABLE 6.7 Interventions that reduce risk linked to SLT input

Interventions or strategies to reduce risk	SLT contribution to risk reduction
Structure and routine to the day which is consistently followed	Provision of staff training so that structure and routine is valued and understood Support with visual timetables either in paper form or via computer technology Referral to OT for support with development of a meaningful routine
Predictable application of rules Staff who are consistent and predictable	Provision of staff training so that consistency and predictability in communication is valued and understood
Any changes to the structure and routine being planned in advance	Provision of staff training that helps the wider team understand how to manage change to routine and enact a transition
Explanations being provided for any changes to the structure and routine	Support with transition planning, co-production and communication needs in transition Provision of visual aids as needed
Having breaks or extra time to think	Provision of staff training addressing demands and capacities in communication, communication processing loads and how to support the individual
Visual aids	Provision of staff training in the use of visual aids (e.g. as an object of reference, as a choice-making tool, to support planning the day, as a timetable tool) Provision of appropriate and co-produced visual aids for use by individual and setting
Intervention that is engaging and interesting	Creation of bespoke materials
Intervention that is rooted in co-production	Creation of bespoke materials
Asking the individual what helps them	Provision of staff training to address SLCN and client autonomy Joint goal setting Co-production Creation of bespoke materials
Healthy habits such as food, exercise and sleep patterns	Referral to OT for support with development of a meaningful routine
Improve self-esteem	Referral to mental health groups for skill building Referral to OT for skill building Referral to clinical psychology for support with mentalisation SLT intervention that is rooted in a therapeutic alliance
Develop communication skills	Assessment and goal setting SLT intervention Scaffolding of skills Provision of staff training in how to develop communication needs for specific individuals
Improve identification of emotions and the management of intense and unwanted emotions	Assessment and goal setting SLT intervention Scaffolding of skills Referral to clinical psychology for support with development of emotion regulation skills

(Continued)

TABLE 6.7 Continued

Interventions or strategies to reduce risk	SLT contribution to risk reduction
Improve awareness that there is a link between emotions and communication skills	Provision of staff training on the topic of emotions and interactions, de-escalation skills and the impact of SLCN on non-verbal interactions MDT working with colleagues Co-production and joint goal setting with individual SLT intervention
Improve skills in problem solving	Assessment and goal setting SLT intervention Scaffolding of skills
Improve social communication skills so that relationships are fostered	Assessment and goal setting SLT intervention Scaffolding of skills
Address assumption forming such as assuming what other people are thinking or feeling	Assessment and goal setting SLT intervention Scaffolding of skills
An opportunity to talk about thoughts and feelings	SLT intervention Referral to mental health groups to create opportunities Provision of staff training addressing how to support people with SLCN to talk about their thoughts and feelings including the use of ramps Referral to clinical psychology for support with mentalisation
Mindfulness skills	Referral to mental health groups for skill building
Relaxation skills	Referral to OT for skill building

Mehay, Meek and Ogden (2019) explored how to mitigate risks for people in secure environments. Two of the risks that they identified fit with SLT provision were:

- perception of chronological time and how to effectively use time so that the day in a secure setting parallels the individual's concept of a 'normal' day
- socialising, building relationships, reclaiming a sense of normality as an adult with tactics to stay connected to events that are occurring outside of the secure setting in order to remain connected to friends and family.

The work on understanding and employing chronological time may fit with interventions from SLT or OT. Pembery, Doran and Dutt (2015) have created a comprehensive resource manual that supports work with adults who have learned some of the key concepts of time but need more in-depth knowledge, further practice or opportunities to practise skills in a functional way. The Pembery et al. (2015) text should be accessed for interventions in this domain.

SLT involvement in the areas of socialising, building relationships and maintaining connectedness should be considered as part of the communicative competence work and client-centred goal setting as previously described.

HM Prison and Probation Service collaborated with NHS England in 2020 to produce a practitioner's guide to working with people in the criminal justice system showing personality difficulties (HM Prison and Probation Service and NHS England, 2020) which also considers risk reduction. This useful document is available online and gives information on managing risk that is congruent with SLT intervention, such as:

- considering the symptoms and behaviours associated with difficulties of self-expression in certain situations, which is located in the territory of SLT work on emotions and interactions
- working with the individual in relation to impulsivity in their interactions, which includes work on communicative competence and increased self-awareness
- consideration of aggression as part of interaction, and problem solving why the person is seen as aggressive and how this could be addressed via PBS
- working towards developing greater autonomy and assertiveness over time via the person understanding their own needs and having strategies in explaining their needs to others.

In addition, the SLT can support engagement for the wider MDT via reassurance of the individual, contact outside planned appointments to help maintain motivation, help with attending and managing appointments with others via communication supports or memory aids and explanations of information in communication-friendly ways such as accessible documents and total communication.

The SLT also has a role within the MDT to help understanding of:

- How the individual's understanding and processing of 'rules' impact on their interactions (e.g. beliefs that 'the rules don't apply to me'), which should be addressed by cutting down the rules to a minimum and then enforcing them with consistency in a communication-friendly way such as with pocket prompt cards.
- Implementing PBS, which allows all involved to experience success and a sense of progress in situations where a risk may be present. The PBS goals and progress measures should be clear, consistent, easy to understand and easy to achieve.
- Targeting the risk factor most likely to lead to serious failure such as communication breakdowns or misreading social cues.

While considering communication and risk, it is important to recognise three risk situations that may present to the SLT as part of the clinical setting: self-harm by patients to themselves, aggression by clients to self or any other person, and individuals being hyper-vigilant, which can result in them being hard to engage or aggressive. Figure 6.13 (below) supports the SLT with some basic dos and don'ts for communication around risks:

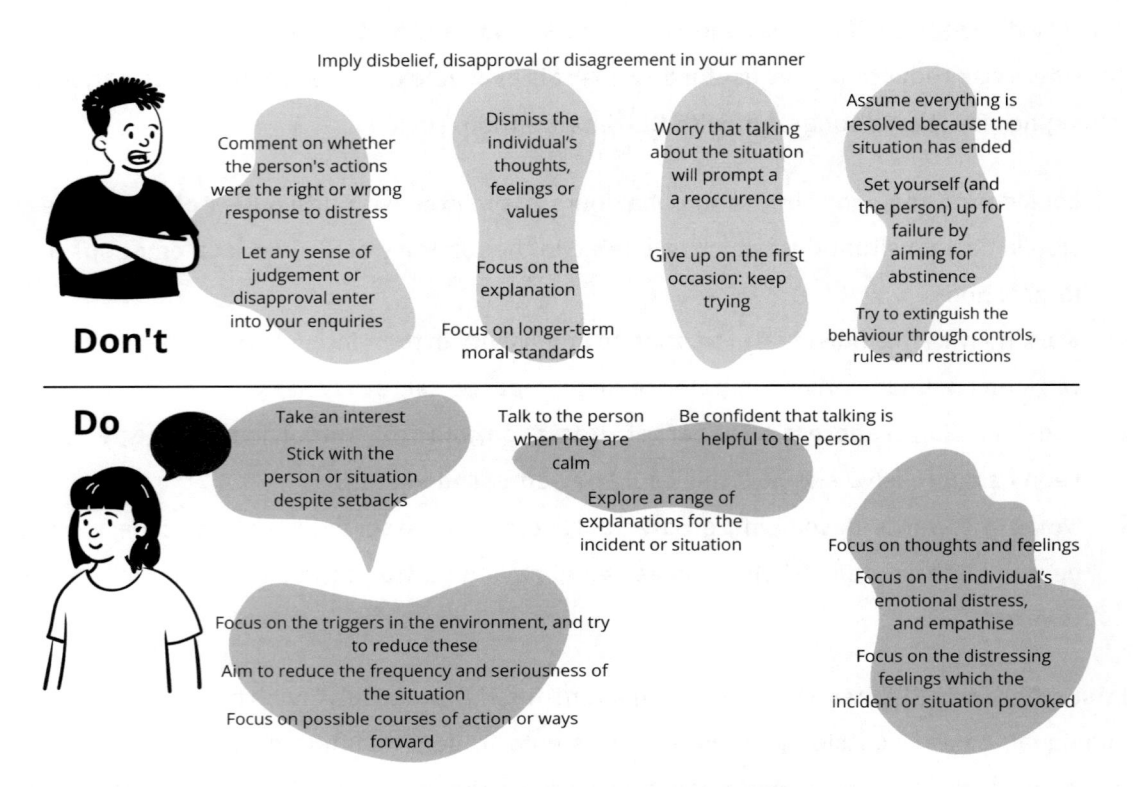

FIGURE 6.13 Basic dos and don'ts for communication around risk situations

Positive risk taking

Having considered risks as a subjective construct with a possibility of both reward or costs and with an uncertain consequence, it is important to acknowledge that risk taking exists on a continuum – with either positive or undesirable results (Duell and Steinberg, 2019). Examples of positive risk taking could include:

- allowing a person to use the bus independently for the first time to go to the swimming pool
- attending an audition for a role in a play
- showing another person a poem that you have written.

Positive risk taking is beneficial in offender rehabilitation because it increases the individual's well-being; helps the individual to build skills in weighing the pros and cons of a decision in context; assists developing ownership of decisions relating to self; and develops personal negotiation skills – all skills that the SLT seeks to nurture via intervention (Seale, Nind and Simmons, 2013). SLTs are experienced in supporting positive risk taking as this is a feature of Mental Capacity Assessments. However, it has to be accepted that it is possible for a person to use SLT support to express themselves and clearly make an unwise decision – an example might be to allow another prisoner to give them a prison tattoo despite the risk of blood-borne infection. Within dysphagia management, there might be positive and undesirable results associated with aspiration or choking that need to be managed based on the level of risk taken around continuing to experience oral feeding or particular foods.

Figure 6.14 (below) provides a framework for positive risk taking which is developed from work by Morgan and Andrews (2016):

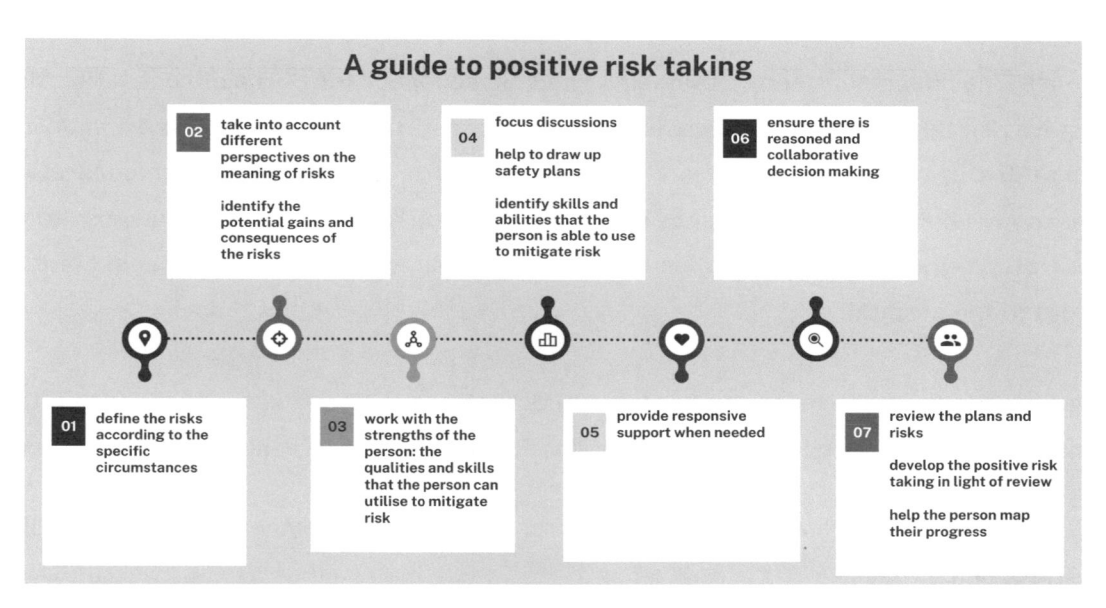

FIGURE 6.14 A framework for positive risk taking

The framework scaffolds the initial identification of the risk, the meaning of the risk to all stakeholders and the consequence. SLT skills in making complex information accessible to all involved come into play here (see Appendix 25), as well as visual aids to support the person to process information and state their view. The next stage requires working with the individual to explore their strengths, qualities and skills, which could be explored via tools such as a Talking Mat (Boardman et al., 2016) or via a visual card-sorting activity (see Appendix 29). It is likely at this point that the SLT would link with the forensic psychology team for direction on production of resources or on specific communication needs linked to risk.

Case example

Harry is a man in low-secure hospital who is close to being permitted unescorted Section 17 community leave as part of his progression plan. He has a diagnosis of autism and his communication profile is as follows:

- slower than average verbal processing, which impacts on comprehension especially if verbal information is presented quickly and in larger quantities
- difficulties with inferring meaning from idioms and metaphors
- difficulties with humour and understanding jokes or irony
- flat affect and reduced use of gesture in social interaction
- can easily be distracted from an agreed plan by special interests
- has good insight into his communication needs and is able to tell the interlocutor what he needs to improve his interaction success.

The MDT has been considering the gains and consequences for Harry of completing this positive risk-taking step. Gains include independence for Harry and testing his communication skills when he is in the community on his own. Consequences include communication breakdowns if Harry misunderstands or is exposed to idioms, metaphors, humour or irony, and Harry being distracted from his agreed plan, which would result in him being late to return to the hospital.

The SLT discussed the gains and consequences with the MDT and agreed to focus on the consequence of Harry being distracted via the following SLT intervention:

- A bespoke Talking Mat created for Harry to allow him to comment on what might distract him.
- Creating a visual aid for Harry to help him plan his Section 17 leave in specific time slots and to link these to his digital watch which he can program with alarms to cue him to refer to the visual aid. The visual aid was via an application on Harry's smartphone so is transportable and subtle to use in public. The visual aid included time to walk to town, visits to three different shops including one which might distract him, time to phone his mum using his mobile phone to speak to her for five minutes and time to return to the hospital.
- The provision of pocket prompt cards for Harry with suggestions of what to do if he is distracted – for example, check his visual aid on his phone, phone the hospital and explain what has happened, use calming strategies to manage the anxiety he will feel if he thinks that he will be late returning to hospital.

- A Talking Mat to use with his named nurse after unescorted community leave to enable Harry to feedback how he felt using the visual aid, his phone, his watch and the pocket prompt cards.

The positive risk taking continues on a cycle of test, review and consider next steps. Such a cycle is important so that the MDT has evidence of Harry's gains and consequences. The evidence would form part of a more official risk assessment which would be completed by forensic psychology colleagues.

Impulsivity, social and emotional needs

There is a body of evidence suggesting that social and emotional capability is important for long-term positive life outcomes (Early Intervention Foundation, 2015; Youth Endowment Fund, 2022). The published literature includes data that states:

- Impulse control, self-esteem, the belief that one's own actions can make a difference and self-regulation of emotions are all strongly associated with improved mental well-being, good physical health and better socio-economic outcomes.
- The ability to engage socially with others is important for mental well-being and having significant relationships that enrich well-being.
- Emotional health in childhood matters for mental well-being as an adult.
- Social and emotional capabilities matter because there is a direct correlation between these skills and positive life outcomes relating to mental health and life satisfaction, socio-economic potential, labour market progression, health experience and health-related outcomes.

The quoted research was longitudinal and focused on the development of social and emotional capability in neurotypical children linked to their longer-term experiences across a range of determiners (Youth Endowment Fund, 2022). The finding was that if an individual has the skills to 'think before they act, understand other people's perspectives, communicate effectively, and use strategies for managing impulsiveness or aggression [via] social skills and self-control [they] are less likely to become involved in crime and violence' (Youth Endowment Fund, 2022).

The SLT can contribute with knowledge of activities that allow the person to view situations from the perspective of different people (such as comic-strip conversations), developing strategies for resolving conflict and improving negotiation such as active listening, use of questions and support with creating accessible resources to be used by ward-based staff (Gaffney, Farrington and White, 2021). The SLT role here can be to train members of the MDT to use these resources and strategies in timely and responsive ways so that situations can be discussed in communication-friendly ways immediately after an occasion of impulsivity has occurred. SLT training of MDT members could include:

- use of total communication (see Appendix 12)
- using visual scales (see Appendix 13)
- using conversation ground rules (see Appendix 14)
- using Help in Meetings resources during a 1:1 impulsivity debrief (see Appendix 18)
- use of trauma-informed communication (see Appendix 28)
- general SLCN training that covers using simple short sentences with time to process, supporting expression via open and closed questions and supporting processing needs via reduced pace of interaction.

Case example

Jonny is a gentleman in a low-secure hospital who has learning disability. His assessment with OT indicated that he has problems with executive functioning that include working memory deficits, problems planning his day, problems with organising what he needs and when, difficulties solving problems that relate to planning and organising, and issues with behavioural regulation so that he might damage property when he is feeling upset.

The results of the OT assessment indicated a referral to SLT because of the known evidence that reduced working memory is often associated with reduced language ability, problems with semantics and issues with syntax. SLT assessment with the Clinical Evaluation of Language Fundamentals-Fifth Edition (CELF 5) (Wiig, Semel and Secord, 2013) showed low scores across all subtests.

Because Jonny has learning disability, it is impractical to offer impairment-based SLT to increase his speech, language and communication skills to the levels of the general population. The SLT discussed Jonny's needs with the MDT, and it was agreed that impulsivity remained one of Jonny's significant barriers to progression. This is thought to be because people with poor language skills struggle with the ability to use language skills internally to facilitate accomplishing goal-directed behaviour (Friedman and Sterling, 2019). It was decided that SLT would train Jonny's named nurse in using total communication skills with

Jonny in situations where his impulsivity had caused him to make decisions that were in disagreement with his OT therapy plan.

The OT therapy plan includes Jonny accessing Section 17 leave, working on budgeting and having more access to the telephone. He has been doing well with his OT therapy plan. However, last week he used the phone to order expensive items and has used all his savings. He revisits this situation using strategies that the SLT has taught his named nurse. The visual strategy supports Jonny to express himself and use his language skills to consider his goal-directed choices – see Figure 6.15 below:

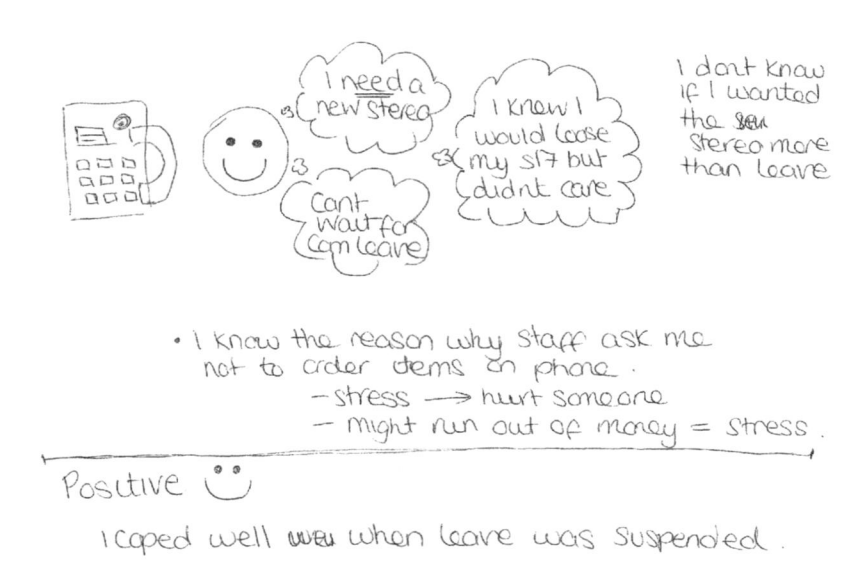

FIGURE 6.15 Visual strategies that support comprehension and expression used by registered nurse with a person with SLCN in a low-secure hospital setting

This example considers Jonny's skills in:

- articulating his OT plan via expressive language to demonstrate that he has internalised the information
- linking impulsive decision making to a framework that uses expressive language to consider what happened, why and how, and linking this with emotions vocabulary
- practising expressive language in order to work towards internalised language skills
- completing these tasks with his named nurse in a timely fashion after the event.

Appendix 33 offers sample resources for discussing emotions, including the intensity of the emotion and what impulsive response may be triggered. This type of resource would be suitable for a person such as Jonny who would benefit from a very structured approach to considering his impulsive emotional responses.

Adolescent brain development and neurological maturity

It is important to comment at this stage on brain development and maturity, as this has an impact on the presentation of people in contact with the CJS and their needs, which is relevant to SLT.

Neurologically, brain development begins before birth, and in the early years of life, the human brain proliferates synaptic connections within the grey matter. The synaptic connections are made rapidly to allow the child to learn basic new functions quickly, but as the child reaches adolescence, the neurological development changes.

At this stage, the synaptic connections are 'reviewed' by the brain. The basic ones, which are no longer needed, are 'pruned', creating more space for complex neural circuits to be established and brain efficiency to be improved in order to meet the necessities of the growing human. This allows for higher-level cognitive function, which is required for functioning as an adult to be established.

The frontal cortex of the brain is located in the anterior part of the brain behind the forehead area. This area of the brain controls expression of emotions, reasoning, the ability to predict consequences that may result from current actions (understanding of cause and effect), suppression of socially unacceptable responses to situations or people (inhibition), the modification of emotional expression to fit societal and cultural norms, and the processing of chemicals from the limbic system that could be described as 'emotional memories'. As such, the frontal cortex is involved with cognition and emotional impulse control, which is relevant to actions that are potentially going to attract the attention of the CJS.

The synaptic pruning that improves function and effectiveness of the brain in preparation for adult decision making starts from the posterior region at the base of the skull and travels in a back-to-front direction, so that the frontal cortex is the last part of the brain to achieve maturation.

Brain maturation is not complete until the individual is in their mid to late 20s, which is why many teenagers and young adults struggle with decision making, reasoning and emotional impulses. This is correspondingly the time when the individual is at risk of trying illicit substances or alcohol, which similarly impacts on frontal lobe function, and is at risk of experiencing symptoms of mental ill-health associated with neurological development.

Teens and young adults are likely to experience stress, anxiety and depression as part of their brain maturation.

Adverse childhood experiences (ACEs) result in toxic stress being placed on the maturing brain, which increases the possibility of developing any of the following co-morbid conditions:

- Gene methylation, which results in the regulation of stress responses being impaired so that the person is in a state of high stress often. This impairment can be life-long following childhood adversity and can be experienced as an ongoing problem over many years of adulthood. It is easy to link a feeling of high stress to the potential to abuse substances or commit a violent act.
- Shrinkage of the parts of the brain that are responsible for processing emotion and managing stress responses. This results in impaired decision making, reduced ability to self-regulate emotions and actions, and the part of the brain that perceives threat being hyper-sensitive. As a consequence, an individual may feel threat where none exists, with heightened emotional responses that they cannot resolve via decision making. The individual is likely to be impulsive and overreact in situations.
- Microglial cells, which are involved in neural pruning, can become overactive during periods of toxic stress. This can create conditions where the neural pruning develops deficits that influence the complex synaptic connections which are in the process of being formed. Thus, the individual can find themselves with poor executive functioning and decision-making skills, and increased risk of mood disorders.
- Our brains have a default mode network which functions in the background of our cognition to allow us to consider new and relevant information as it enters our consciousness. This is required to process information at the edge of our perception and integrate it into thoughts. Toxic stress damages the development of this region during neural pruning such that the individual is in a perpetual state of 'fight or flight' and finds it hard to react appropriately to the world around them.

Rocque (2015) outlines components of maturation and the possible links with desistence from crime, and his work has been adapted into Figure 6.16 overleaf which details four of the components and the features of each.

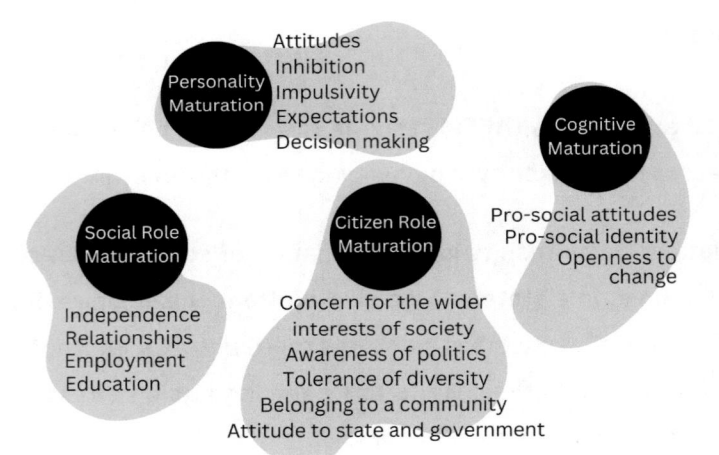

FIGURE 6.16 Components of brain maturation and the possible links between desistence from crime, elements of which overlap with potential SLT activity in the theory of change model

The relevance of this to SLT and SLCN is that elements of the components of maturation and desistence overlap with potential SLT activity in the theory of change model discussed earlier in this chapter. For example:

- Personality maturation links to executive functioning. Executive functioning and language impairment such as developmental language disorder have a bi-directional relationship, which means that difficulties in one area will suggest difficulties in the other (Kapa and Plante, 2015). People presenting with personality maturation needs should be considered for assessment of language skills.
- Social role maturation links to theory of mind and executive functioning. Theory of mind is a required skill for developing and maintaining social relationships, and deficits in this area result in social communication disorders (Bosco et al., 2017).
- Cognitive maturation, which has been linked to language use and processing, semantic skills and pragmatics (Brauer, 2011; McDonald et al., 2013; Fengler, Meyer and Friederici, 2016).

Therefore, people within the CJS who score poorly on assessment of maturation by psychologists or offender managers should be referred to SLT for consideration of SLCN. The SLT role here starts with education of fellow professionals on the identification of red flags for communication impairment (see Chapter 5).

Health and well-being literacy

The final area to be discussed in this chapter is health and well-being literacy. Published literature has long recognised the causal link between poor health literacy and long-term chronic health conditions (Poureslami et al., 2017). It is also known that people who are incarcerated have poor health literacy and high rates of chronic illness with eight out of ten people leaving prison with a long-term condition (Hadden et al., 2018).

Health literacy is defined as the 'degree to which individuals have the capacity to obtain, process, and understand basic health information and services needed to make appropriate health decisions' (Hasnain-Wynia and Wolf, 2010).

Health literacy relates to physical health, mental health, medication compliance and self-management of conditions. Research has demonstrated that if the individual within the CJS understands their own health and medication, their longer-term outcomes are improved (Carroll, Kinner and Heffernan, 2014; Wynn, 2021; Mehay, Meek and Ogden, 2021; Crossan, 2021).

The SLT has a role in health literacy for people within the CJS who have SLCN via use of total communication and visual aids to support comprehension of how the body works, what the condition is and what treatment options are available. The SLT also has a role in empowering the individual to tell other healthcare professionals if they have not understood, and to train colleagues in adapting their communication and explanations to those with SLCN.

Case examples

H is a man in prison with a long-term chronic condition which requires medication and iron infusion. H was very concerned about the iron infusion, what this would be and why his body required iron. H was able to explain to the SLT that he understands iron to be a strong piece of metal used in manufacturing. The SLT was able to use pictures and diagrams to explain to H what iron is, how it is linked to his condition and how his body uses iron in his blood. H was able to consent to the treatment and feel confident in understanding the rationale. He was also able to explain to his family so that they felt reassured also.

J is a man with learning disability in low-secure hospital. He has a heart condition. He had attended hospital and seen a consultant cardiologist, but had found it hard to understand the information given to him. He reported feeling scared and, as a result, declined to take his medication. The SLT was able to make him an accessible information booklet about his heart condition which he could keep in his room and refer to as needed. J was often most anxious about his heart condition before he went to sleep, so this intervention was the most appropriate to support him in self-soothing.

Conclusion

This chapter has covered a wide range of material relating to the communication environment, goal setting, outcome measures, SLT intervention linking to change, positive behaviour support, communicative competence, risk, neurological development and health literacy. Information and research has been offered, and this has been supported with resources within the appendices of this book.

The chapter should be read and understood alongside other works that address specific needs or conditions.

It is hoped that this chapter inspires the SLT to use a biopsychosocial model of care that locates the individual at the centre of the intervention – with co-production and joint working being the most important values utilised to enact change. The use of a biopsychosocial model requires the SLT to remember their core skills in simplifying information, helping people to process, scaffolding expression and building skills for success in interactions, but also to apply these skills in novel ways to help unique people with their specific requirements. It is hard to provide an 'off the shelf' set of resources for SLTs in CJS when this book advocates for bespoke care, so the reader should see this chapter as inspiration, ideas, resources to adjust and the licence to be empowered to work in evidence-based ways that can be adapted to suit the needs of the client.

It is hoped that the take-home messages relate to person-centred care, collaboration, empowerment and the importance of meeting the person via therapeutic alliance to support change.

References

Ackerman, S.J. and Hilsenroth, M.J. (2003) A review of therapist characteristics and techniques positively impacting the therapeutic alliance. Clinical Psychology Review, 23(1), 1–33.
Adshead, G. (2011) The life sentence: Using a narrative approach in group psychotherapy with offenders. *Group Analysis*, 44(2), 175–195.

Ahern, K. (2014) Meaningful and Evidence-Based Goals – Part One AAC. Teaching Learners with Multiple Special Needs. Available at http://teachinglearnerswithmultipleneeds.blogspot.com /2014/04/meaningful-and-evidence-based-goals.html [accessed 10th March 2023]

Anderson, S. and Bigby, C. (2017) Self-advocacy as a means to positive identities for people with intellectual disability:'We just help them, be them really'. *Journal of Applied Research in Intellectual Disabilities*, 30(1), 109–120.

Atkinson, D. and Moulster, G. (2019) Using the Health Equality Framework (HEF): Measuring Outcomes and Prioritising Person-Centred Practice Interventions. In G. Moulster, J. Iorizzo, S. Ames and J. Kernohan (eds) *The Moulster and Griffiths Learning Disability Nursing Model: A Framework for Practice* (pp.83–94). London: Jessica Kingsley Publishers.

Allied Health Professions (AHP) Outcome Measures UK Working Group (2019) Key questions to ask when selecting outcome measures: A checklist for allied health professionals. Available at www .rcslt.org/wp-content/uploads/media/docs/selecting-outcome-measures.pdf[accessed10thMarch 2023]

Alper, R.M. and McGregor, K.K. (2015) Agency as a construct for guiding the establishment of communication-friendly classrooms. *Child Language Teaching and Therapy*, 31(3), 337–346.

Ansbro, M. (2008) Using attachment theory with offenders. *Probation Journal*, 55(3), 231–244.

Auty, K.M., Cope, A. and Liebling, A. (2017) Psychoeducational programs for reducing prison violence: A systematic review. *Aggression and Violent Behavior*, 33, 126–143.

Awofeso, N. (2011) Disciplinary architecture: Prison design and prisoners' health. *Hektoen International: A Journal of Medical Humanities*, 3(1).

Back, A.L., Fromme, E.K. and Meier, D.E. (2019) Training clinicians with communication skills needed to match medical treatments to patient values. *Journal of the American Geriatrics Society*, 67(S2), S435–S441.

Barlow, D.H., Farchione, T.J., Fairholme, C.P., Ellard, K.K., Boisseau, C.L., Allen, L.B. and May, J.T.E. (2010) *Unified Protocol for Transdiagnostic Treatment of Emotional Disorders: Therapist Guide*. Oxford University Press.

Bambini, V., Arcara, G., Bechi, M., Buonocore, M., Cavallaro, R. and Bosia, M. (2016) The communicative impairment as a core feature of schizophrenia: Frequency of pragmatic deficit, cognitive substrates, and relation with quality of life. *Comprehensive Psychiatry*, 71, 106–120.

Berendonk, C., Blix, B.H., Hoben, M., Clandinin, D.J., Roach, P.M., Compton, R.M., Cave, M.T. and Caine, V. (2020) A Narrative Care approach for persons living with dementia in institutional care settings. *International Journal of Older People Nursing*, 15(1), e12278.

Bishop, D. (2003) *Test for Reception of Grammar*, Version 2 (TROG-2). London: Pearson Assessment.

Blackstone, S.W. and Wilkins, D.P. (2009) Exploring the importance of emotional competence in children with complex communication needs. *Perspectives on Augmentative and Alternative Communication*. https://doi.org/10.1044/AAC18.3.78

Boardman, L., Crichton, C. and Butterworth, S. (2016) When you can't talk about it: Using Talking Mats to enable an offender with communication difficulties to express his thoughts and beliefs. *Probation Journal*, 63(1), 72–79.

Bordin, E.S. (1979) The generalizability of the psychoanalytic concept of the working alliance. *Psychotherapy: Theory, Research, and Practice*, 16(3), 252–260.

Bosco, F.M., Parola, A., Sacco, K., Zettin, M. and Angeleri, R. (2017) Communicative-pragmatic disorders in traumatic brain injury: The role of theory of mind and executive functions. *Brain and Language*, 168, 73–83.

Bouman, Y.H., Schene, A.H. and de Ruiter, C. (2009) Subjective well-being and recidivism in forensic psychiatric outpatients. *International Journal of Forensic Mental Health*, 8(4), 225–234.

Bowman, J., Mogensen, L., Marsland, E. and Lannin, N. (2015) The development, content validity and inter-rater reliability of the SMART-Goal Evaluation Method: A standardised method for evaluating clinical goals. *Australian Occupational Therapy Journal*, 62(6), 420–427.

Bowring, D.L., Totsika, V., Hastings, R.P. and Toogood, S. (2020) Outcomes from a community-based Positive Behavioural Support team for children and adults with developmental disabilities. *Journal of Applied Research in Intellectual Disabilities*, 33(2), 193–203.

Brauer, J. (2011) Anatomical and functional connectivity keystones in brain maturation and in language development. Conference Abstract: XI International Conference on Cognitive Neuroscience (ICON XI). doi:10.3389/conf.fnhum.2011.207.00565

Brown, D., Shawe-Taylor, M. and Swan, S. (2017) Positive behaviour support for people with a diagnosis of personality disorder. *Clinical Psychology Forum: Special Issue Positive Behaviour Support*, 290, 25–29.

Burns, K. and Northcott, S. (2022) *Working with Solution Focused Brief Therapy in Healthcare Settings: A Practical Guide*. Routledge

Bryan, K. (2013) Psychiatric Disorders and Communication. In L. Cummings (ed.) *Handbook of Communication Disorders* (pp.300–318) Cambridge: Cambridge University Press.

Carmichael, J.J., Gould, K.R., Hicks, A.J., Feeney, T.J. and Ponsford, J.L. (2020) Understanding Australian community ABI therapists' preferences for training in and implementing behaviour interventions: A focus on positive behaviour support. *Brain Impairment*, 21(2), 191–207.

Carroll, M., Kinner, S.A. and Heffernan, E.B. (2014) Medication use and knowledge in a sample of Indigenous and non-Indigenous prisoners. *Australian and New Zealand Journal of Public Health*, 38(2), 142–146.

Celce-Murcia, M., Dörnyei, Z. and Thurrell, S. (1995) Communicative competence: A pedagogically motivated model with content specifications. *Issues in Applied Linguistics*, 6(2), 5–35.

Chaplin, E., McCarthy, J., Underwood, L., Forrester, A., Hayward, H., Sabet, J., Mills, R., Young, S., Asherson, P. and Murphy, D. (2017) Characteristics of prisoners with intellectual disabilities. *Journal of Intellectual Disability Research*, 61(12), 1185–1195.

Constantino, M.J., Coyne, A.E., Luukko, E.K., Newkirk, K., Bernecker, S.L., Ravitz, P. and McBride, C. (2017) Therapeutic alliance, subsequent change, and moderators of the alliance–outcome association in interpersonal psychotherapy for depression. *Psychotherapy*, 54(2), 125.

Coppens, P. (2016) *Aphasia and Related Neurogenic Communication Disorders*. Jones & Bartlett Publishers.

Crossan, D. (2021). Health literacy can improve inequities. Kai Tiaki Nursing New Zealand, Available at https://kaitiaki.org.nz/article/health-literacy-can-improve-inequities [accessed 10th March 2023]

Day, A. (2009) Offender emotion and self-regulation: Implications for offender rehabilitation programming. *Psychology, Crime & Law*, 15(2–3), 119–130.

Davies, R. and Gray, C. (2009) Care pathways and designing the health-care built environment: An explanatory framework. *International Journal of Care Pathways*, 13(1), 7–16.

Davies, B., Griffiths, J., Liddiard, K., Lowe, K. and Stead, L. (2015) Changes in staff confidence and attributions for challenging behaviour after training in positive behavioural support within a forensic medium secure service. *The Journal of Forensic Psychiatry & Psychology*, 26(6), 847–861.

Davies, B.E., Lowe, K., Morgan, S., John-Evans, H. and Fitoussi, J. (2019) An evaluation of the effectiveness of positive behavioural support within a medium secure mental health forensic service. *The Journal of Forensic Psychiatry & Psychology*, 30(1), 38–52.

Davies, B., John-Evans, H., Francis, N., Lazarou, D., Morgan, S., Hughes, J. and Morris, B. (2022) Using functional assessments to involve service users in their positive behaviour support plan. *Learning Disability Practice*, 25(3). http://dx.doi.org/10.7748/ldp.2020.e2004

De Shazer, S., Dolan, Y., Korman, H., Trepper, T., McCollum, E. and Berg, I.K. (2021) *More than Miracles: The State of the Art of Solution-Focused Brief Therapy*. Routledge.

De Silva, M.J., Breuer, E., Lee, L., Asher, L., Chowdhary, N., Lund, C. and Patel, V. (2014) Theory of change: A theory-driven approach to enhance the Medical Research Council's framework for complex interventions. *Trials*, 15(1), 1–13.

Department of Health (2010) Your Guide to Relational Security: See, Think, Act. Available at https://assets.publishing.service.gov.uk/government/uploads/system/uploads/attachment_data/file/320249/See_Think_Act_2010.pdf [accessed 10th March 2023]

Duell, N. and Steinberg, L. (2019) Positive risk taking in adolescence. *Child Development Perspectives*, 13(1),48–52.

Dunn, L.M. and Dunn, D.M. (2009) *The British Picture Vocabulary Scale*. GL Assessment.

Early Intervention Foundation (2015) Social and emotional learning: Skills for life and work. Available at www.eif.org.uk/report/social-and-emotional-learning-skills-for-life-and-work [accessed 10th March 2023]

Enderby P. and John A. (2015) *Therapy Outcome Measures for Rehabilitation Professionals* (3rd edn). Croydon: J & R Press.

Fabry, R.E. (2021) Narrative scaffolding. *Review of Philosophy and Psychology*, 1–21.

Fengler, A., Meyer, L. and Friederici, A.D. (2016) How the brain attunes to sentence processing: Relating behavior, structure, and function. *NeuroImage*, 129, 268–278.

Friedman, L. and Sterling, A. (2019) A review of language, executive function, and intervention in autism spectrum disorder. *Seminars in Speech and Language*, 40(4), 291–304.

Gaffney, H., Farrington, D.P. and White, H (2021) Social Skills Training: Toolkit technical report. Available at https://youthendowmentfund.org.uk/wp-content/uploads/2021/06/Social-Skills-technical-report.pdf [accessed September 2022]

Gore, N.J., McGill, P., Toogood, S., Allen, D., Hughes, J.C., Baker, P., Hastings, R.P., Noone, S.J. and Denne, L.D. (2013) Definition and scope for positive behavioural support. *International Journal of Positive Behavioural Support*, 3(2), 14-23.

Grey, I., Lydon, H. and Healy, O. (2016) Positive behaviour support: What model of disability does it represent? *Journal of Intellectual & Developmental Disability*, 41(3), 255-266.

Hadden, K.B., Puglisi, L., Prince, L., Aminawung, J.A., Shavit, S., Pflaum, D., Calderon, J., Wang, E.A. and Zaller, N. (2018) Health literacy among a formerly incarcerated population using data from the transitions clinic network. *Journal of Urban Health*, 95(4), 547-555.

Hansen, P. (2017) What makes a word easy to acquire? The effects of word class, frequency, imageability and phonological neighbourhood density on lexical development. *First Language*, 37(2), 205-225.

Harpe, S.E. (2015) How to analyze Likert and other rating scale data. *Currents in Pharmacy Teaching and Learning*, 7(6), 836-850.

Hart, A., Blincow, D. and Thomas, H. (2012) Resilience Framework (Children and Young People). Available at www.boingboing.org.uk/resilience/resilient-therapy-resilience-framework [accessed 23rd March 2023]

Hasnain-Wynia, R. and Wolf, M.S. (2010) Promoting health care equity: Is health literacy a missing link? *Health Services Research*, 45(4), 897-903.

Hassiotis, A., Poppe, M., Strydom, A. et al. (2018) Clinical outcomes of staff training in positive behaviour support to reduce challenging behaviour in adults with intellectual disability: Cluster randomised controlled trial (PDF). *British Journal of Psychiatry*, 12(3), 161-168.

Hawkins, E., Gathercole, S., Astle, D., The Calm Team and Holmes, J. (2016) Language problems and ADHD symptoms: How specific are the links? *Brain Sciences*, 6(4), 50.

HM Prison and Probation Service and NHS England (2020) Practitioner guide: Working with people in the criminal justice system showing personality difficulties. Available at www.gov.uk /government/publications/working-with-offenders-with-personality-disorder-a-practitioners -guide [accessed 9th March 2023]

Hitchcock, E.R., Harel, D. and Byun, T.M. (2015) Social, emotional, and academic impact of residual speech errors in school-aged children: A survey study. *Seminars in Speech and Language*, 36(4), 283-294.

Hodgetts, S. and Park, E. (2017) Preparing for the future: A review of tools and strategies to support autonomous goal setting for children and youth with autism spectrum disorders. *Disability and Rehabilitation*, 39(6), 535-543.

Hodgkinson, R., Beattie, S., Roberts, R. and Hardy, L. (2021) Psychological resilience interventions to reduce recidivism in young people: A systematic review. *Adolescent Research Review*, 6(4), 333-357.

Hymes, D. (1966) Two types of linguistic relativity. In W. Bright, (ed.) *Sociolinguistics* (pp.114-158). The Hague: Mouton.

Kapa, L.L. and Plante, E. (2015) Executive function in SLI: Recent advances and future directions. *Current Developmental Disorders Reports*, 2(3), 245-252.

Kay J. Lesser R. & Coltheart M. (1992) *PALPA: Psycholinguistic Assessments of Language Processing in Aphasia*. Psychology Press.

Kinney, M., Seider, J., Beaty, A.F., Coughlin, K., Dyal, M. and Clewley, D. (2020) The impact of therapeutic alliance in physical therapy for chronic musculoskeletal pain: A systematic review of the literature. *Physiotherapy Theory and Practice*, 36(8), 886-898.

Kirkwood, S. (2016) Desistance in action: An interactional approach to criminal justice practice and desistance from offending. *Theoretical Criminology*, 20(2), 220-237.

Kiessling C. and Fabry G. (2021) What is communicative competence and how can it be acquired? *GMS Journal for Medical Education*, 38(3).

Kippin, N.R., Leitao, S., Finlay-Jones, A., Baker, J. and Watkins, R. (2021) The oral and written narrative language skills of adolescent students in youth detention and the impact of language disorder. *Journal of Communication Disorders*, 90, 106088.

Knestrict, T.D. (2015) Deconstructing the positive behavioral support model and replacing it with the neo-Montessori constructivist intervention model or how Montessori changed my cold data driven heart. *Electronic Journal for Inclusive Education*, 3(3).

Levy, J. and Dunsmuir, S. (2020) Lego therapy: Building social skills for adolescents with an autism spectrum disorder. *Educational and Child Psychology*, 37(1), 58-83.

Light, J. and McNaughton, D. (2014) Communicative competence for individuals who require augmentative and alternative communication: A new definition for a new era of communication? *Augmentative and Alternative Communication*, 30(1), 1-18.

Linehan, M. (2014) *DBT Skills Training Manual*. The Guilford Press.

Marshall, S., Haywood, K. and Fitzpatrick, R. (2006) Impact of patient-reported outcome measures on routine practice: A structured review. *Journal of Evaluation in Clinical Practice*, 12(5), 559–568.

Maini, R., Mounier-Jack, S. and Borghi, J. (2018) How to and how not to develop a theory of change to evaluate a complex intervention: Reflections on an experience in the Democratic Republic of Congo. *BMJ Global Health*, 3(1), e000617.

Marinetti, C., Moore, P., Lucas, P. and Parkinson, B. (2011) Emotions in social interactions: Unfolding emotional experience. In P. Petta, C. Pelachaud and R. Cowie (eds) *Emotion-Oriented Systems* (pp.31–46). Springer.

McCarthy, J., Chaplin, E., Forrester, A., Underwood, L., Hayward, H., Sabet, J., Young, S., Mills, R., Asherson, P. and Murphy, D. (2019) Prisoners with neurodevelopmental difficulties: Vulnerabilities for mental illness and self-harm. *Criminal Behaviour and Mental Health*, 29(5–6), 308–320.

McConachie, H., Parr, J.R., Glod, M., Hanratty, J., Livingstone, N., Oono, I.P., Robalino, S., Baird, G., Beresford, B., Charman, T. and Garland, D. (2015) Systematic review of tools to measure outcomes for young children with autism spectrum disorder. *Health Technology Assessment*, 19(41). https://doi.org/10.3310/hta19410

McDonald, S., English, T., Randall, R., Longman, T., Togher, L. and Tate, R.L. (2013) Assessing social cognition and pragmatic language in adolescents with traumatic brain injuries. *Journal of the International Neuropsychological Society*, 19(5), 528–538.

Mehay, A., Meek, R. and Ogden, J. (2019) 'I try and make my cell a positive place': Tactics for mitigating risks to health and wellbeing in a young offender institution. *Health & Place*, 57, 54–60.

Mehay, A., Meek, R. and Ogden, J. (2021) Understanding and supporting the health literacy of young men in prison: A mixed-methods study. *Health Education*, 121(1), 93–110.

Meteyard, L., Stoppard, E., Snudden, D., Cappa, S.F. and Vigliocco, G. (2015) When semantics aids phonology: A processing advantage for iconic word forms in aphasia. *Neuropsychologia*, 76, 264–275.

Miller, W.R. and Rollnick, S. (2013) *Motivational Interviewing: Helping People to Change* (3rd edn). Guilford Press.

Milton, D. (2018) A critique of the use of Applied Behavioural Analysis (ABA): On behalf of the Neurodiversity Manifesto Steering Group. Internet article for the Labour Party's Neurodiversity Manifesto. Available at https://kar.kent.ac.uk/69268/1/Applied%20behaviour%20analysis.pdf [accessed 9th March 2023]

Ministry of Justice (2019) Identified needs of offenders in custody and the community from the Offender Assessment System, 30 June 2018. Available at https://assets.publishing.service.gov.uk/government/uploads/system/uploads/attachment_data/file/815078/oasys-needs-adhoc-stats.pdf [accessed 9th March 2023]

Mitchell, C., Bowen, A., Tyson, S., Butterfint, Z. and Conroy, P. (2017) Interventions for dysarthria due to stroke and other adult-acquired, non-progressive brain injury. *Cochrane Database of Systematic Reviews*, 25(1), CD002088.

Mooney, J.L. and Daffern, M. (2015) The relationship between aggressive behaviour in prison and violent offending following release. *Psychology, Crime & Law*, 21(4), 314–329.

Moreno, G. and Bullock, L.M. (2011) Principles of positive behaviour supports: Using the FBA as a problem-solving approach to address challenging behaviours beyond special populations. *Emotional and Behavioural Difficulties*, 16(2), 117–127.

Morgan, S. and Andrews, N. (2016) Positive risk-taking: From rhetoric to reality. *The Journal of Mental Health Training, Education and Practice*, 11(2), 122–132.

Moyse, K., Enderby, P., Chadd, K., Gadhok, K., Bedwell, M. and Guest, P. (2020) Outcome measurement in speech and language therapy: A digital journey. *BMJ Health & Care Informatics*, 27(1), e100085.

Muran, J.C. and Barber, J.P. (eds) (2011) *The Therapeutic Alliance: An Evidence-Based Guide to Practice*. Guilford Press.

Murray, N. (2010) Pragmatics, awareness raising, and the cooperative principle. *ELT Journal*, 64(3), 293–301.

Newbould, L., Tucker, S. and Wilberforce, M. (2022) Enabling older people with mental health needs to engage with community social care: A scoping review to inform a theory of change. *Health & Social Care in the Community*, 30(4), 1286–1306.

Ng, R., Fish, S. and Granholm, E. (2015) Insight and theory of mind in schizophrenia. *Psychiatry Research*, 225(1–2), 169–174.

Noel, K. (2013) *Social Problem Solving: Making Best Plans*. Chippewa Falls, WI: The Cognitive Press.

Noel, K.K. and Westby, C. (2014) Applying theory of mind concepts when designing interventions targeting social cognition among youth offenders. *Topics in Language Disorders*, 34(4), 344–361.

O'Connor, C.M., Mioshi, E., Kaizik, C., Fisher, A., Hornberger, M. and Piguet, O. (2021) Positive behaviour support in frontotemporal dementia: A pilot study. *Neuropsychological Rehabilitation*, 31(4), 507–530.

Olver, M.E. (2016) Treatment of psychopathic offenders: Evidence, issues, and controversies. *Journal of Community Safety and Well-Being*, 1(3), 75–82.

O'Reilly, M., Gevarter, C., Falcomata, T., Sigafoos, J. and Lancioni, G.E. (2016) Applied behaviour analysis and positive behaviour supports. In A. Carr, C. Linehan, G. O'Reilly, P. Noonan Walsh and J. McEvoy (eds) *The Handbook of Intellectual Disability and Clinical Psychology Practice* (2nd edn, pp.241–263). Routledge.

Pembery, J., Doran, C. and Dutt, S. (2015) *Time Matters: A Practical Resource to Develop Time Concepts and Self-Organisation Skills in Older Children and Young People*. Routledge.

Petrich, D.M., Liu, H. and Nedelec, J.L. (2020) The longitudinal associations between motivation, self-regulatory capacities, and future-oriented cognition and behavior among serious young offenders. *Law and Human Behavior*, 44(5), 424–436.

Pont, J., Stöver, H., Gétaz, L., Casillas, A. and Wolff, H. (2015) Prevention of violence in prison: The role of health care professionals. *Journal of Forensic and Legal Medicine*, 34, 127–132.

Poureslami, I., Nimmon, L., Rootman, I. and Fitzgerald, M.J. (2017) Health literacy and chronic disease management: Drawing from expert knowledge to set an agenda. *Health Promotion International*, 32(4), 743–754.

Priniski, S.J., Hecht, C.A. and Harackiewicz, J.M. (2018) Making learning personally meaningful: A new framework for relevance research. *The Journal of Experimental Education*, 86(1), 11–29.

Redmond, S.M. (2016) Language impairment in the attention-deficit/hyperactivity disorder context. *Journal of Speech, Language, and Hearing Research*, 59(1), 133–142.

Reichow, B. (2021) Comic Strip Conversations. In F.R. Volkmar (ed.) *Encyclopedia of Autism Spectrum Disorders* (pp.1080–1082). Springer.

Reveley, E. (2016) Positive behaviour management: A critique of literature. *Journal of Initial Teacher Inquiry*, 2. http://hdl.handle.net/10092/12843

Rocque, M. (2015) The lost concept: The (re)emerging link between maturation and desistance from crime. *Criminology & Criminal Justice*, 15(3), 340–360.

Rollnick, S., Miller, W.R. and Butler, C.C. (2008) *Motivational Interviewing in Health Care: Helping Patients Change Behavior*. New York: The Guilford Press.

Royal College of Speech and Language Therapists (2016) Online Outcome Tool. Available at www .rcslt-root.org/Welcome [accessed 9th March 2023]

Santana, M.J., Manalili, K., Jolley, R.J., Zelinsky, S., Quan, H. and Lu, M. (2018) How to practice person-centred care: A conceptual framework. *Health Expectations*, 21(2), 429–440.

Schauer, M., Neuner, F. and Elbert, T. (2017) Narrative exposure therapy for children and adolescents (KIDNET). In M.A. Landolt, M. Cloitre and U. Schnyder (eds) *Evidence-Based Treatments for Trauma Related Disorders in Children and Adolescents* (pp.227–250). Cham: Springer.

Schlosser, R.W. (2004) Goal attainment scaling as a clinical measurement technique in communication disorders: A critical review. *Journal of Communication Disorders*, 37(3), 217–239.

Scholten, I., Ross, K. and Bickford, J. (2019) 'A way to think of the client holistically': Factors influencing students' ICF regard and uptake. *MedEdPublish*, 8(1). http://dx.doi.org/10.15694/mep .2019.000061.1

Seale, J., Nind, M. and Simmons, B. (2013) Transforming positive risk-taking practices: The possibilities of creativity and resilience in learning disability contexts. *Scandinavian Journal of Disability Research*, 15(3), 233–248.

Shipley, K.G. and McAfee, J.G. (2019) *Assessment in Speech-Language Pathology: A Resource Manual*. Plural Publishing.

Simler, A. (2019) An investigation into positive behavioural support and quality of life. Doctoral dissertation, Cardiff University.

Simourd, D.J., Olver, M.E. and Brandenburg, B. (2016) Changing criminal attitudes among incarcerated offenders: Initial examination of a structured treatment program. *International Journal of Offender Therapy and Comparative Criminology*, 60(12), 1425–1445.

Snow, P.C., Sanger, D.D., Caire, L.M., Eadie, P.A. and Dinslage, T. (2015) Improving communication outcomes for young offenders: A proposed response to intervention framework. *International Journal of Language & Communication Disorders*, 50(1), 1–13.

Snow, P.C., Woodward, M., Mathis, M. and Powell, M.B. (2016) Language functioning, mental health and alexithymia in incarcerated young offenders. International Journal of Speech-Language Pathology, 18(1), 20–31.

Spencer, T.D. and Petersen, D.B. (2020) Narrative intervention: Principles to practice. *Language, Speech, and Hearing Services in Schools*, 51(4), 1081-1096.

Stansfield, J. and Matthews, A. (2014) Introducing advanced clinical reasoning to an adult learning disability service. *Journal of Intellectual Disabilities*, 18(1), 20-34.

Student author(s) (2021) Positive Behaviour Support and Forensic Mental Health Care. Available at http://oxfordhealth-nhs.archive.knowledgearc.net:8080/bitstream/handle/123456789/830/PBS%20essay%202.pdf?sequence=1&isAllowed=y [accessed 21st March 2023]

Swinburn, K., Porter, G. and Howard, D. (2023) *Comprehensive Aphasia Test* (2nd edn). Routledge.

Torkaman, M., Farokhzadian, J., Miri, S. and Pouraboli, B. (2020) The effect of transactional analysis on the self-esteem of imprisoned women: A clinical trial. *BMC Psychology*, 8(1), 1-7.

Threats, T.T. (2006) Towards an international framework for communication disorders: Use of the ICF. *Journal of Communication Disorders*, 39(4), 251-265.

Vlaev, I. and Dolan, P. (2015) Action change theory: A reinforcement learning perspective on behavior change. *Review of General Psychology*, 19(1), 69-95.

Wechsler, D. (2008) *Wechsler Adult Intelligence Scale-Fourth Edition (WAIS-IV)*. Washington, DC: APA PsycTests.

Wiig, E.H., Semel, E. and Secord, W.A. (2013) *Clinical Evaluation of Language Fundamentals-Fifth Edition* (CELF-5). Bloomington, MN: NCS Pearson.

Wynn, R. (2021) Mental health literacy of prisoners in Norway. *International Journal of Integrated Care*, 21, 325. https://doi.org/10.5334/ijic.ICIC20230

Young, S. and Cocallis, K.M. (2019) Attention deficit hyperactivity disorder (ADHD) in the prison system. *Current Psychiatry Reports*, 21(6), 1-9.

Young, S. and Cocallis, K. (2021) ADHD and offending. *Journal of Neural Transmission*, 128(7), 1009-1019.

Young, S., González, R.A., Mullens, H., Mutch, L., Malet-Lambert, I. and Gudjonsson, G.H. (2018a) Neurodevelopmental disorders in prison inmates: Comorbidity and combined associations with psychiatric symptoms and behavioural disturbance. *Psychiatry Research*, 261, 109-115.

Young, S., Gudjonsson, G., Chitsabesan, P., Colley, B., Farrag, E., Forrester, A., Hollingdale, J., Kim, K., Lewis, A., Maginn, S., Mason, P., Ryan, S., Smith, J., Woodhouse, E. and Asherson, P. (2018b) Identification and treatment of offenders with attention-deficit/hyperactivity disorder in the prison population: A practical approach based upon expert consensus. *BMC Psychiatry*, 18(1), 281. https://doi.org/10.1186/s12888-018-1858-9

Youth Endowment Fund (2022) Social skills training: Aims to develop children's ability to regulate their behaviour and communicate effectively. Available at https://youthendowmentfund.org.uk/toolkit/social-skills-training [accessed 9th March 2023]

THE CHANGING NEEDS OF THE CRIMINAL JUSTICE SYSTEM POPULATION

DOI: 10.4324/9781003288701-8

Prison populations

In 2019, a House of Commons Select Committee published a report on the predicted prison population and the associated health needs for England and Wales (Justice Committee, 2019). The predictions in the report were that:

- The prison population in England and Wales will increase in the coming years secondary to increased conviction rates and increased use of custodial sentences which is driven by political policies.
- Those people in prison will be serving longer sentences.
- There will be more people aged over 50 years of age in prison.
- Social and economic factors will result in increased crime and increases in people being recalled to prison while under community supervision.
- There will be less spending per head on prisoner care due to budgetary changes.

The report articulated a picture of prisons in England and Wales as overcrowded, with poor physical conditions in some older prisons, and with a high incidence of substance misuse and violence. The report called for attention to be given to the following demographic groups:

- incarcerated older people aged over 50 years of age
- females facing custodial sentences
- people from Black, Asian and Minority Ethnic groups in prison, and,
- people who have an indeterminate sentence of Imprisonment for Public Protection (IPP) and remain incarcerated.

Note is made of the health characteristics of these populations who often have complex needs associated with health comorbidities, long-term conditions, neurodiversity, dependency on substances, reduced mental and emotional health, and exposure to trauma or abuse (Wahidin, 2007).

Likewise, the inpatient population in secure hospitals is also increasing in age and presenting with complex health needs (Visser et al., 2021). Most of the research on older prisoners investigates the largest population – that is, men. See Bryan (2021) regarding the needs of older female prisoners.

This chapter aims to consider the changing needs of the population who are in contact with the criminal justice system (CJS) in relation to the growing need for the provision of speech and language therapy (SLT) in the CJS. Information will be offered on the following topics:

- growing old in a CJS setting
- communication-friendly environments
- health literacy barriers
- communication group ideas
- dysphagia
- indeterminate sentence of Imprisonment for Public Protection (IPP)
- community-based services as an alternative to custody.

Growing old in a CJS setting – prison

Ministry of Justice (2021) projections estimate that the prison population will be in excess of 97,000 people by the summer of 2025. The vast majority of this figure is adult males. The number of people in prison who are over the age of 50 years will increase, and the age spread of people over 50 will increase so that there are more people aged over 60 and 70+ years respectively (Prison Reform Trust, 2022). Ageing of the population is partially driven by more people being sentenced to determinate sentences with no release date (Ministry of Justice, 2021), and partially by the work undertaken in recent years to convict historic sex offenders (Office for National Statistics, 2021). The *Inside Times* newspaper, written for prisoners and detainees, recently reported on the death of a prisoner aged 105 years in February 2022 (Inside Times, 2022).

Research provides the following overview of health data for older prisoners (Justice Committee, 2019; Public Health England, 2017):

- 60% of people in prison aged over 50 years have long-standing illness or disability.
- 50% of people in prison aged over 50 years have three or more moderate or severe health conditions.
- 34% of older people in prison require walking aids such as walking sticks, walking frames or wheelchairs.
- 46% were either 'not confident' or 'partially confident' getting around the prison.
- 50% of those aged 50–65 were over-weight and 26% of the same age group were obese.
- In 2015 to 2016, 84% of those aged over 60 years accessed treatment for alcohol dependency.
- 90% reported a physical health problem which made it harder for them to take care of themselves
- 84% of deaths in prison from natural causes occur in those aged 50 or over.

The most important risk factors for disease in the 50 years and older prisoner group are alcohol dependency, obesity and physical inactivity (Public Health England, 2017). As a result of these three risk factors, people in prison experienced chronic physical ill-health and this is strongly correlated to depression. Figure 7.1 (below) summarises the multiple and complex health and social care needs of older people in prison:

FIGURE 7.1 The multiple and complex health and social care needs of older people in prison

Types of chronic diseases

Chronic diseases are categorised as either non-communicable chronic disease (that which cannot be directly transmitted between people) or communicable chronic disease (that which can be transmitted between people). In the over-50 cohort, the non-communicable chronic disease profile is illustrated overleaf in Figure 7.2 (Public Health England, 2017).

It is also noted that some people in prison will enter the end-of-life phase as a result of ageing while incarcerated (Aday and Wahidin, 2016). This is a topic outside of the scope of this book, but it is important to note. The Dying Well in Custody Charter was published in 2018 and offers a framework to support professionals in this area (Ambitions for Palliative and End of Life Care Partnership, 2018).

Non-communicable chronic diseases in those aged 50 years and over

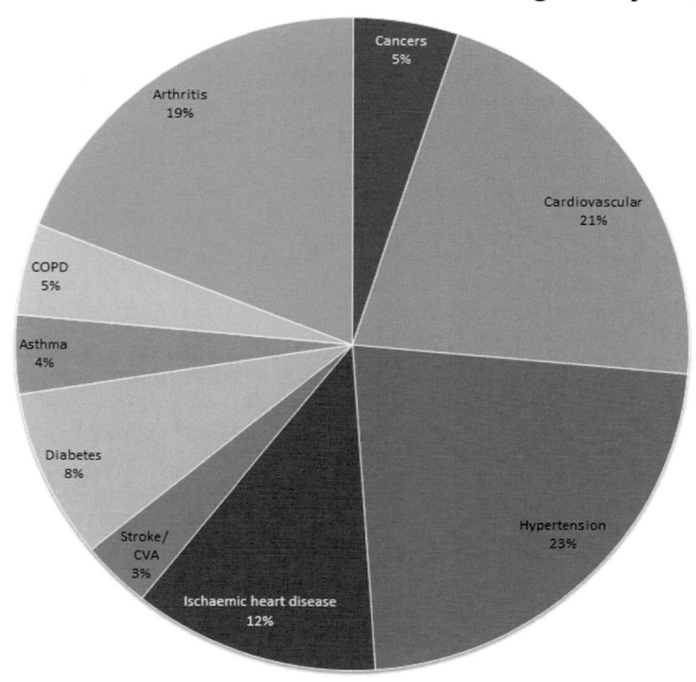

FIGURE 7.2 The non-communicable chronic disease profile of people over 50 years of age in prison

There is a clear professional role for SLT that should be offered to prisoners with non-communicable chronic disease exactly as it is offered outside of such environments. This is illustrated in Table 7.1 overleaf.

TABLE 7.1 Potential speech, language and communication needs and the SLT role with people over 50 years of age in prison

Disease	Potential needs	SLT role
Cancer	SLCN if associated with head or neck Dysphagia need if associated with head or neck Mental capacity concerns Advance care planning	Assessment and intervention for SLCN and/or dysphagia Mental capacity assessment and reporting Support with SLCN associated with advanced care planning
Stroke and dementia	SLCN Dysphagia Mental capacity concerns Advance care planning	
COPD	Dysphagia Mental capacity concerns Advance care planning	Assessment and intervention for dysphagia Mental capacity assessment and reporting Support with SLCN associated with advanced care planning
Cardiovascular disease	On a case-by-case basis	On a case-by-case basis
Hypertension		
Ischaemic heart disease		
Arthritis		
Diabetes		
Asthma		
Palliative care	Role within MDT Dysphagia Mental capacity assessment and reporting Support with SLCN associated with advanced care planning	MDT participation Assessment and intervention for dysphagia Mental capacity assessment and reporting Support with SLCN associated with advanced care planning

Information on speech, language and communication needs (SLCN), dysphagia, mental capacity assessment and advance care planning is available in a wide range of resources, which are applicable to people who find themselves within the CJS, including:

- *Using the Systems Approach for Aphasia* (Hayden, 2022)
- *Clinical Cases in Dysarthria* (Walshe and Miller, 2022)
- *Working with Communication and Swallowing Difficulties in Older Adults* (Allwood, 2022)
- *Language Case Files in Neurological Disorders* (Cummings, 2021)
- *Clinical Care and Rehabilitation in Head and Neck Cancer* (Doyle, 2019)
- *Speech and Language Therapists and Mental Capacity 2019: A Training Resource for Adult Services* (Jones and Volkmer, 2018)

- *Assessment and Therapy for Language and Cognitive Communication Difficulties in Dementia and Other Progressive Diseases* (Volkmer, 2013)
- *Working with Dysphagia* (Marks and Rainbow, 2001).

In order to meet the SLCN and swallowing needs of this population, the SLT service should aim to provide (Justice Committee, 2019):

- Training for other colleagues in identifying SLCN and swallowing needs
- A screening and assessment service to identify needs (see chapter 5)
- Goal setting and treatment to meet needs (see chapter 6)
- Trauma informed care (see chapter 5)
- Integrated multidisciplinary working which enables the coordination of treatment pathways
- Enabling environments (see Communication Friendly Environments in this chapter)
- Accessible communication tools (see chapter 6)
- Adequate resources to meet the needs of the patient group
- Data collection to inform understanding of the population (see Research Agenda in chapter 8).

Growing old in a CJS setting – secure hospitals

In terms of inpatient secure hospital settings in the UK, it is estimated that 20% of the population is over 50 years of age (Di Lorito, Dening and Völlm, 2018). Needs associated with this cohort are slightly different from the prison group as physical health needs are more proactively managed in this medical setting compared to the prison setting (Di Lorito et al., 2018). This results in degenerative or iatrogenic-associated impacts (Das et al., 2011; Ogloff et al., 2015; Fazel et al., 2016). These include:

- age-related changes to eyesight and hearing
- obesity related to physical inactivity, poor diet and medication side effects
- mental ill-health frequently managed by antipsychotic medication, polypharmacy and high doses of medication
- physical health conditions as side effects of antipsychotic medication such as dysphagia
- cognitive and memory decline
- social isolation
- substance dependency.

Outcomes for older people in secure hospital settings were correlated to their length of stay. Those with longer inpatient stays presented with needs associated with cognitive and memory decline such as apathy, lack of initiative, loss of interest, lack of individuality, submissiveness, reduced motor function and loss of ability for long-term planning (Bülow et al., 2022).

Older people in secure hospitals reported that their needs were related to social isolation and offender treatment programmes that did not respond to their age-related needs in respect of programme content or risk assessment (Di Lorito et al., 2018).

Staniszewska et al. (2019) conducted a systematic review of patient experiences of those in inpatient mental health hospitals and identified four themes that add further understanding to the changing needs of this patient cohort. These findings are illustrated in Figure 7.3 below:

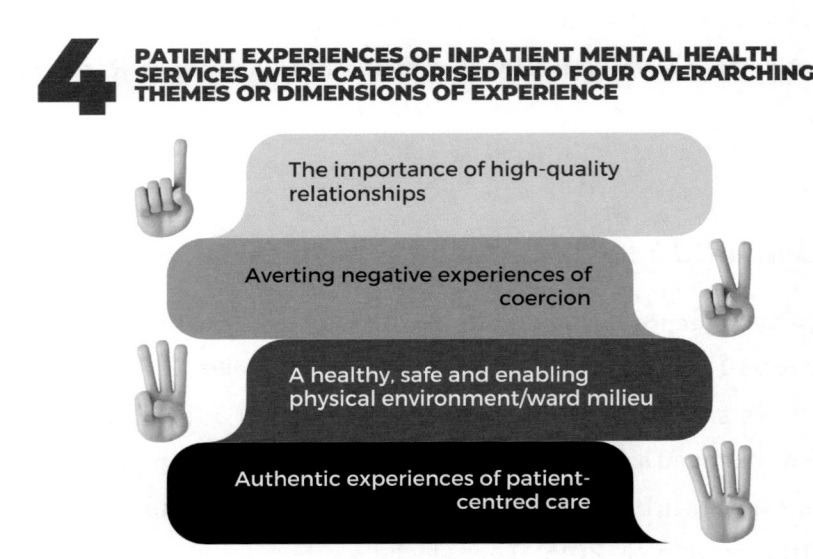

FIGURE 7.3 Four patient experience themes that were found to be important to people residing in secure hospitals

The importance of high-quality relationships included a specific focus on communication needs. Those residing in secure hospitals desired:

- meetings that included the patient at the centre of the decision making during which patients were listened to and treated as equal stakeholders (see Appendix 18 for help in meetings resources)
- communication that respected the individual's wishes and excluded perceived coercion as part of the agenda

- information presented in ways that excluded professional vocabulary or medical language which was a barrier to understanding
- interactions that were grounded in respect, positive affirmation and a desire by all conversation partners to listen with fascination
- information to flow to them from the staff caring for them and not from peers
- involvement of their family and friends in their care.

SLT has a role in supporting the above patient needs via training of staff and conversation partners, promoting inclusion at all stages, challenging perceived and actual coercion, and helping to establish a positive communication value base for the setting, which benefits all individuals not just those with SLCN (Tapp et al., 2013) (see Appendix 28).

People within the mental health setting wanted to feel safe in their daily activities, and the tension created by perceived coercion, potential sedation, seclusion or restraint impacted on this safety. Effective communication with an individual can help to achieve the above agenda as follows:

- promoting respectful interactions at all times – including when any party is feeling stressed or upset
- consideration of the individual's ability to consent, in the moment, in relation to the use of sedation, seclusion or restraint
- consideration of the individual's advance wishes relating to sedation, seclusion or restraint, and any advance wishes being included in decision making with the individual
- ensuring that individual reports of medication side effects are listened to and used to inform prescribing decisions (including any self-reports of feeling over-medicated)
- information and joint decision making about the use of seclusion and how long seclusion would continue for, including what conditions need to be in place to end seclusion
- individuals consistently reported restraint as a negative experience, which is also seen in other similar research (De Vries et al., 2016), so it is important that they fully understand why it was used and what will need to be different about their behaviour in future to prevent restraint.

The SLT role related to the above involves training staff so that they can achieve effective communication with an individual, or facilitating communication between the patient and another professional, leadership around communication values and continually advocating for the patient to be included in decision making. SLT also supports the establishment of a therapeutic or healing environment specifically by enabling effective and respectful communication within the setting (Goulet, Larue and Dumais, 2017; Oostermeijer et al., 2021).

A healthy, safe and enabling physical environment and ward milieu was the third identified need. As well as the built environment, which is outside of the scope of the SLT role, patients valued a communication environment where:

- staff and patients mixed together and had conversational interactions
- proactive management of disagreements was used to defuse tension and mitigate against arguments between individuals
- the communication conduct of staff 'set the tone' for interactions to be respectful
- they were able to have regular meaningful contact with family via phone, video calls and visits as well as family and friends' input into care where appropriate.

Work on the communication environment can be undertaken by SLT to address the patient needs above. See resources in Appendices 14, 15, 26, 27 and 28.

An authentic experience of patient-centred care is the last of the four needs identified as part of the systematic review (Staniszewska et al., 2019). The communication elements of this need are:

- the provision of information about diagnosis, treatment, choices and rights in a form that is understandable and includes two-way flow of information (see Appendix 25 and Chapter 5 Figure 5.9)
- patients being involved in decisions relating to their own care
- the timing of conversations so that the individual could participate at their optimal level (see Chapter 5 Figures 5.4–5.6).

In summary, people residing in secure hospitals are an ageing population as has also been shown in relation to the prison population. However, people in prison have increased physical health needs, while people in secure hospitals have increased degenerative or iatrogenic needs. Both cohorts have significant needs relating to their SLCN, which need to be met via a comprehensive SLT service across all custodial settings.

Communication-friendly environments

Communication-friendly environments are a setting or location where changes have intentionally been made to make communication easier for those located in that environment. Communication-friendly environments support cognition and independence for people with a wide range of needs such as learning disability, autism, aphasia or dementia (Davis et al., 2009; Simpson, 2016; Stans et al., 2017; Kristiansen, Olsen and Beck, 2022). A communication-friendly environment benefits everyone in that environment and should include:

- visual supports such as signage at eye level to help the individual to navigate the environment (e.g. find locations such as facilities)
- directions or maps to help navigation, which could include colour coding
- visual routines, timetables or planners to help people stay on task
- notice boards with information in accessible forms
- accessible letters and reports (see Chapter 5)
- communication that is adapted to be accessible, concrete and paced to allow for processing
- materials, resources or equipment stored in accessible places including communication ramps such as paper and pens
- quiet and private spaces
- adequate and appropriate lighting
- management of auditory or visual distractors
- orientation items such as clocks and calendars
- pictorial menus
- thoughtful use of colour, pattern and shiny surfaces to avoid cognitive confusion – for example, patterns can be distressing for people with dementia who see faces or forms within the pattern, and polished floor surfaces can be perceived as wet
- seating and tables that allow people to be alone or in groups depending on their chosen activity.

In addition to communication-friendly environments, the World Health Organization (WHO) has called for age-friendly environments that support the needs and well-being of all older people (Tiraphat et al., 2017).

While the WHO has identified eight domains within the age-friendly environment, not all of them are relatable to secure settings and SLT (World Health Organization, 2018). Those which are include:

- social participation such as involvement in a social life, joining in with planned activities and groups, being part of educational opportunities
- respect and social inclusion where all people – regardless of age, gender, social position, health or disability – are respected and have opportunities to participate and contribute
- civic participation by being involved in decision making, committees, employment roles within the establishment
- communication and information by accessing timely, reliable, relevant and understandable information about the setting, the community, ways to be involved, available services and health information.

Ridley (2022) outlines a project that was undertaken in a prison in England to meet the needs of men aged over 50 years within the prison setting. The project used HM Inspectorate of Prisons 'healthy prisons tests' which considers the four areas of safety, respect (which includes health), purposeful activity and resettlement. The project offered significant changes to the prison setting commensurate with the recommendations of communication-friendly and age-friendly environments as follows:

- Areas for people to gather and pursue hobbies such as gardening, games, reading, watching TV or socialising without feeling concerned for safety from younger peers and which addressed feelings of isolation.
- Changes to the built environment to improve independence and reduce falls such as grab rails, lighting and ramps.
- A prisoner information desk which was staffed by trained prisoners and offered information, problem solving, encouragement and support to engage.
- A weekly social group which offered 'quizzes, arts, crafts, music workshops, carpet bowls, darts and board games. Tea and coffee whilst background music played, reflecting the tastes of attendees. Sessions included presentations (including external speakers) about pensions, conviction disclosure, and the implications of a conviction when securing insurance, dementia-awareness, relaxation and diabetes. Healthcare representatives attended every two to three months to "meet and greet" and to allow prisoners to discuss any health issues that could be followed up. In the afternoon there was a gym session, supported by prison gym-staff, exclusively for older prisoners' Ridley (2022, p.8).
- Support in the time before and after release, which helped the older person transition from prison to living in their community.

The findings of this project were very positive and exemplify why communication-friendly and age-friendly environments are beneficial. These types of environments benefit from SLT input in respect of design, accessible information, staff training and support with medical conditions related to ageing which may impact on SLCN and dysphagia.

Health literacy needs of the population

Health literacy is a term used to describe how well a person understands their own health, including their skills in being able to recognise a change to their health and to seek information. The term also includes the application of the information so that the individual can make informed choices about their own health based on quality information (Mehay, Meek and Ogden, 2021). The skills of professionals to provide accessible information and the accessibility of services are also part of health literacy (Rudd, 2015). Health literacy is an issue for society and healthcare professionals as poor health literacy directly correlates with reduced health outcomes (Sørensen et al., 2015).

Health literacy is an issue for healthcare professionals working in the CJS because those in contact with the CJS have the following barriers to optimal health outcomes (Mehay et al., 2021):

- People within the CJS are marginalised, socially disadvantaged and socially excluded.
- As a cohort, they often have histories of social exclusions, low educational attainment, violence, bereavement, abuse, neglect and time spent in local authority care.
- As a cohort, they have often been excluded from valuable life experiences and learning opportunities such as formal education, positive peer learning and navigating health systems.
- They tend to have multiple and complex needs spanning physical and mental health domains.
- There are high rates of substance misuse or polypharmacy.
- There are high rates of communicable diseases when compared to the general population.
- The setting may offer poor environmental cleanliness, barriers to personal hygiene and close living conditions.
- The setting may also offer limited exposure to a variety of healthy food, physical activity and outdoor spaces.

Research undertaken by Mehay et al. (2021) suggests that the health literacy of younger people in prison is poor, with 72% of participants having poor health literacy. Health literacy correlated with the length of time the person had been incarcerated and their ability to engage with the prison regime – those with longer prison stays and poor ability to engage with the regime had reduced health literacy.

Lincoln et al. (2006) considered health literacy in a population of people with poor mental health and a lived experience of substance misuse. The findings indicated that there is a relationship between poor health literacy and increased feelings of depression.

Research by Brooks et al. (2013) stated that 'printed healthcare materials and patient-provider interaction is not always meeting the health literacy needs of individuals' (Brooks et al., 2013, p101). Marca-Frances et al. (2020) found similar evidence that people admitted to hospital often did not understand why they were admitted, information about their own health conditions or treatment, and what would happen with their health needs on discharge from hospital. There is an important role for SLT in ensuring that information is accessible, taking into account individual SLCN. SLT has a role within health promotion, in the CJS setting, in supporting doctors and other professionals to explain information effectively using a variety of carefully tailored resources. This might involve the SLT agreeing and monitoring how communication is to be achieved within an individual care plan. SLT can provide a library of communication and training in how to use resources for targeted groups of staff, joint sessions that address communication issues that arise in certain circumstances such as assessment of risk (see Chapter 5) and training within the MDT on how to make health information more accessible for those with low levels of health literacy.

Case example

At HMP Berwyn, each SLT session includes a time for patients to ask questions about their care. During this time, individuals have asked about medications, test results, referrals for imaging and confirmation of plans agreed with the GP. In one example, the SLT was able to explain information about puberty, which allayed fears relating to not being able to have children in the future. In some cases, the SLT has arranged a follow-up GP consultation so that information can be reviewed with the understanding that the person's health literacy is poor. Over time, this opportunity to ask questions has gained increased value for patients, and some have attended with peers because they had a question. As a result, SLT now offers some 'open door' time after each clinic where people can 'drop in' and ask health questions to support them in understanding their health issues and to ensure that their communication is facilitated to ask any questions or to explore any perceptions that concern them. The issues tend to be related to muscular aches and pains or weight. The SLT is able to provide accessible information and make onward connections within the team as needed to support the patient.

Group interventions to meet the changing needs of the population

As discussed in the section on communication-friendly and age-friendly environments, groups where people come together can have beneficial health impacts.

The World Health Organization (2007) recommends that all people who are residing in a CJS setting access advice on healthy lifestyles, support to have healthy routines, time to spend on social activities and opportunities for family ties. In addition, the WHO (2007) recommend that most people residing in a CJS setting access activities to improve their self-esteem and develop peer support for well-being.

Other research highlights the risks of loneliness, low mood and isolation in the CJS setting (Murphy, 2000; Yacoub and Hall, 2009; Esposito, 2015; Schliehe, Laursen and Crewe, 2021; Pageau et al., 2022). Such feelings could reasonably be addressed via more opportunities for social group interventions that increase participation.

The SLT role in this could be to facilitate groups that specifically address communication issues. Examples might be 'communication for groupwork', 'advanced communication skills' or 'talk to your baby' (a group run in a prison for new or expectant fathers, which addressed very basic communication skills under a heading that was acceptable to them). Tasks that the SLT might specifically plan into such groups to address particular aspects of communication might include:

- simplified Lego therapy to promote turn taking and cooperation with others (a modified approach as discussed in Chapter 6)
- a communication café for people with a particular SLCN, such as aphasia or dysfluency, where people come together for social participation and to build self-esteem in their own communication
- a conversation partner programme where people in prison or hospital are trained as conversation partners and are linked with people with SLCN to address social isolation (if appropriate within the setting based on levels of security and risk)
- a debating society where recent news, topical interests or popular ideas are discussed and explored, enabling the acquisition of specific conversational skills or acquisition of particular vocabulary
- parent–child interaction skills groups for parents to build skills in play and child interaction (Kennedy et al., 2016)
- a dementia group to support social interaction for people with cognitive changes related to ageing.

It is important to note that any form of group work in a custodial setting will require adherence to risk assessment and security clearance processes. Staff ratios may be prescribed so that the SLT works with other prison staff. There are usually ways to draw those staff into communication activities (as opposed to just being a security presence) that enable the group to be a learning experience for other staff. It is essential that the SLT is aware of any agreed requirements to ensure that certain patients do not have contact.

SLT input may also be desirable within groups offered by the MDT such as:

- healthy living groups
- thinking skills groups
- relaxation groups using mindfulness and sensory strategies
- recovery through activity (Brown, Stoffel and Munoz, 2019).

Here, the role of SLT is to facilitate communication generally or for group members who have specific SLCN. Again, the opportunity to model supported communication, scaffolding comprehension and the use of alternatives to verbal communication will provide a training opportunity for other staff as well as helping to facilitate communication within the group. The model of group interventions could be effective and efficient within the universal and targeted levels of service provision (see Chapter 5).

Dysphagia

As the population in contact with CJS ages and continues to present with a high incidence of mental ill-health, dysphagia (or swallowing) needs and choking risks will remain widespread. This is due to a range of causes:

- Dysphagia and choking incidence in the general population is predicted to be around 6%, but in those with mental ill-health, it is estimated to be between 9% and 46%. Medication and behaviours around eating and drinking are thought to be the most common causal factor (Aldridge and Taylor, 2012).
- Dysphagia and choking incidence is thought to be as high as 60% in institutionalised older people, such as those in forensic settings (Baijens et al., 2016).
- The highest prevalence of dysphagia has been observed in neurological patients: in up to 64% of those with stroke and over 80% of those with dementia (Baijens et al., 2016). Neurological conditions are more common in older adults, including those in prison.
- People with a lived experience of lower socio-economic status, poor oral health, malnutrition, less intake of fruits and vegetables, cigarette smoking and alcohol intake are at higher risk of developing dysphagia and are over-represented within the CJS (Gupta, Dall and Bansal, 2019).
- Between 13% and 16% of older adults in forensic settings have high frailty scores (Byard and Bellis, 2016). Sarcopenia – an age-related, involuntary loss of skeletal muscle mass and strength – is associated with increased risk of dysphagia in older adults (Cha et al., 2019).

- Dysphagia and choking can be sequelae of substance misuse and alcohol abuse, which has a high incidence within the CJS population (Dolezal, 2019).

Natarajan and Mulvana (2017) advocate for each secure setting to access SLT input for SLCN, dysphagia and choking.

Black, Asian and Minority Ethnic groups in prison

Black, Asian and Minority Ethnic (BAME) groups are a cohort that is part of the changing needs of the population within the CJS (Justice Committee, 2019). BAME individuals make up 26% of the prison population (Bignall et al., 2019) and are over-represented within the CJS in the following ways (Uhrig, 2016):

- BAME young males and adults were more likely than white peers to be arrested.
- The Crown Prosecution Service (CPS) charge black and mixed ethnic young males and mixed ethnic adult males at rates higher than white young males and adults.
- BAME males, both youth and adults, and BAME women were all more likely to be tried at the Crown Court compared to white peers.
- Asian women were greater than two times more likely to be committed to the Crown Court for trial compared to white women.
- BAME young people were more likely to receive custodial sentences compared to non-BAME young peers – for every white young male sentenced to custody, 1.2 black and about 1.4 mixed ethnic young males received custodial sentences.
- BAME adult males are more likely to be accommodated in higher levels of security compared to white adult males with similar offence histories.
- In prison, BAME individuals were more likely to be adjudicated (placed on report and facing disciplinary sanctions) than white peers, but also are more likely to have the adjudication dismissed. This may suggest that BAME individuals are subject to higher levels of scrutiny than white peers or may indicate institutional racism (see Chapter 1).

Uhrig (2016) made recommendations for further exploration of the needs of BAME groups in the areas of arrest, CPS decision making, entering a plea in court, referral to Crown Court, sentencing and the experience of BAME individuals in the CJS.

Research has also explored how people from BAME cohorts experience mental illness in conjunction with CJS (Bignall et al., 2019):

- BAME individuals are less likely to be identified with a mental health problem or learning disability at prison reception.

- BAME people on remand in prison are less likely to have their mental illness recognised than other prisoners. Chinese people were the least likely to have their mental health need identified.
- People from a BAME community who had psychosis had less favourable outcomes than white peers, and were more likely to be admitted to hospital as a compulsory admission with police presence.
- In addition, Gypsies and Travellers in custody reported the need for mental health practitioners to be mindful of how they spoke about mental health issues because of stigma within those communities related to mental health difficulties.

Martin and colleagues (2018) add to the picture of needs within the BAME CJS population by explaining how people from a BAME background in prison may be screened for mental ill-health, with the screen indicating that mental health support is needed, but they are still more likely to be overlooked for care and treatment when compared to white peers.

For further information on why BAME people are over-represented within the CJS, see Phillips, Bowling, Liebling and Maruna's book chapter entitled 'Ethnicities, racism, crime and criminal justice' (Phillips et al., 2017).

The SLT role in supporting BAME people within the CJS would include:

- supporting non-BAME clinicians to appreciate differences in communication style and cultural differences in the understanding of illness so that reduction of stigma is promoted (Aggarwal et al., 2016)
- raising awareness of the need for cultural competency in communication skills (Brown et al., 2016)
- promoting discussions on how individual choices can perpetuate racism and ableism in healthcare systems (Robinson and Norton, 2019)
- for the SLT to be knowledgeable about racial bias and to understand how culture interacts with communication style and to articulate this to the MDT (Robinson and Norton, 2019).

The interested reader is signposted to Hyter and Salas-Provance (2021) for detailed commentary on culturally responsive practices in SLT.

Imprisonment for Public Protection (IPP) sentence

The Imprisonment for Public Protection (IPP) sentence was introduced into the CJS in 2005 after being established in law by the Criminal Justice Act (2003). The sentence was conceived so that people who were considered by the court to be dangerous could be held in custody until such a time as the parole board considered them safe to release because they had successfully undertaken risk-reduction work while in custody. In addition, when released, the individual would be under the supervision of probation services for ten years so that they could be recalled to custody should there be any cause for concern. The sentence was designed to be applied to the most dangerous individuals but was overused by the courts (Cooper, 2007) such that between 2005 and 2012 almost 9,000 individuals were incarcerated for indeterminate periods of time (Taylor and Williams, 2014).

Details of the size of the IPP legacy are (Justice Committee, 2022):

- 8,711 individuals received an IPP sentence between 2005 and 2012.
- As of June 2022, there were 2,926 IPP prisoners remaining after the sentence was abolished in 2012.
- 1,492 of these individuals have never been released from custody and some of them have served more than ten years over their original sentence tariff.
- 1,434 individuals have been released on licence and then recalled to custody for breach of licence condition.
- The government expects more than 3,000 prisoners to still be serving IPP sentences by 2026 (Centre for Crime and Justice Studies, 2022).

Those who are serving IPP sentences illustrate part of the changing needs of the CJS population (Justice Committee, 2019). Research has indicated that IPP-sentenced individuals experience high levels of stress and anxiety, social isolation inside and outside of prison, and a high degree of hopelessness (Harris, Edgar and Webster, 2020). There is no research into the SLCN of IPP-sentenced prisoners, but tacit knowledge from clinical practice suggests that the SLCN of these individuals may be considerable, particularly where they are now also ageing.

Case example

At HMP Berwyn in 2018, 3.8% of the prison population were IPP-sentenced individuals. The SLT service at HMP Berwyn opened to referrals in summer 2017, and by summer of 2018, 40% of the SLT caseload was IPP-sentenced people who had significant problems with comprehension, processing and expression. The hypothesis was that:

- IPP-sentenced prisoners had communication problems when they were suspected, arrested and ongoing through the legal system so that they either acquiesced or disengaged, causing them to be judged as higher risk by the courts than peers who represented themselves differently. One IPP-sentenced man with a stammer stated that he did not speak at all after being charged because he knew that he would stammer and didn't want to be embarrassed about his communication in court.

- The IPP sentence itself, the amount of time spent in prison, the loss of hope, subsequent abuse of substances and becoming institutionalised all resulted in a reduction of speech, language and communication skills either due to neurological changes, motivational changes or isolation impacts.

It is interesting to note that in HMP Berwyn in spring 2019, there were ten men with a stammer on the SLT caseload. Nine of the ten were IPP-sentenced people.

Case example

An IPP-sentenced gentleman was transferred to low-secure hospital so that he could engage with adapted risk-reduction programmes because he had failed to complete prison-based modified programmes. The man was assessed with a Wechsler Adult Intelligence Scale (WAIS) (Wechsler, 2008) and found to have an IQ of below 70, thus indicating a learning disability. This need had not been identified before. He was moved to a low-secure hospital that specialised in the care of people with forensic needs and learning disability.

In the low-secure hospital for people with learning disability, the man was referred to SLT for assessment of his communication needs. On SLT formal assessment, he was found to have the following communication profile which would have impacted on his ability to complete a prison-based modified programme:

- receptive language on the 4th percentile on the Test for Reception of Grammar, Version 2 (TROG-2) (Bishop, 2003)
- vocabulary on the 1st percentile on the British Picture Vocabulary Test, 3rd edition (BPVS3) (Dunn and Dunn, 2009)
- reduced semantic memory identified via informal semantic sorting tasks
- repetitive expressive output with reliance on basic vocabulary and simple syntax
- tendency to confabulate in expressive output
- problems with concepts such as time
- problems with sequencing a narrative.

This assessment reinforces that it is unlikely that this individual would have understood the processes around arrest, being charged and attending court. His communication needs could well have influenced the judge's perceptions of his guilt and remorse around the offence.

Emerging tacit knowledge from SLT practice would suggest that every custodial setting should be considering the needs of IPP-sentenced people in relation to their communication. A setting that has commissioned SLT services should consider staff training in total communication as a tool to support people with unidentified communication needs to engage (see Appendix 12). Settings that do not have a commissioned SLT service should seek external continued professional development wherever possible. If there is an absence of appetite for training within a setting, any professional can participate in self-directed learning via the Royal College of Speech and Language Therapists online training 'The Box' which is available free of charge and can be found via any popular search engine.

Community-based services as an alternative to custody

The final part of the changing needs of the CJS population is in relation to increased custodial sentences which are of longer duration (Justice Committee, 2019).

Research has long found that (Killias et al., 2010; Baldwin and Epstein, 2017):

- Incarceration is not a deterrent to offending or reoffending.
- Custodial sentences increase the likelihood that an individual is involved in subsequent crime and the seriousness of the subsequent crime.
- People who have served custodial sentences find it harder to be in lawful employment after prison, which may contribute to the decision to commit further crime.
- The financial burden of custodial sentences is not just located in the cost to incarcerate a person, but also within the costs to society after incarceration such as unemployment benefits.
- Women are often sentenced to incarceration for non-violent crimes, and the impact on the women and their children is often significant and can be long-lasting.

The Justice Committee (2019) recommend consideration of community disposals instead of custodial sentences in the hope that this will negate some of the negative outcomes of custodial sentences.

This is outside of the scope of this book, except to say that if this recommendation becomes policy and is commissioned, there will be a requirement to include SLT provision in community-based services to ensure that the needs of these clients are met.

Conclusion

This chapter has sought to articulate the needs of the CJS population in the coming years. We expect the prison population to be increasing, with people staying in prison longer, we know that there will be more care necessary for ageing people across all CJS services, we know that there are issues relating to race and culture that must be addressed, and finally we know that the IPP-sentenced cohort is likely to have some very specific health and communication requirements.

This chapter illustrates that an adequately resourced SLT service needs to be an integral part of the MDT in every custodial environment. This is essential to ensure that SLCN is recognised and that staff are supported to achieve effective communication with prisoners who have SLCN and can therefore involve the person effectively in decisions about their care. It should also be noted that being unable to communicate with a person, whose care a member of staff is responsible for, is very stressful for that member of staff. SLT intervention therefore supports both the staff and the individual with SLCN. We hope that the information provided here and the supporting literature will assist service commissioners in securing the appropriate SLT workforce for prison populations.

References

Aday, R. and Wahidin, A. (2016) Older prisoners' experiences of death, dying and grief behind bars. *The Howard Journal of Crime and Justice*, 55(3), 312–327.

Aggarwal, N.K., Pieh, M.C., Dixon, L., Guarnaccia, P., Alegria, M. and Lewis-Fernandez, R. (2016) Clinician descriptions of communication strategies to improve treatment engagement by racial/ethnic minorities in mental health services: A systematic review. *Patient Education and Counseling*, 99(2), 198–209.

Aldridge, K.J. and Taylor, N.F. (2012) Dysphagia is a common and serious problem for adults with mental illness: A systematic review. *Dysphagia*, 27(1), 124–137.

Allwood, R. (2022) *Working with Communication and Swallowing Difficulties in Older Adults*. Routledge.

Ambitions for Palliative and End of Life Care Partnership (2018) Dying Well in Custody Charter. Available at www.england.nhs.uk/wp-content/uploads/2022/02/dying-well-in-custody-charter-apr-18.pdf [accessed 14th March 2023]

Baijens, L.W., Clavé, P., Cras, P., Ekberg, O., Forster, A., Kolb, G.F., Leners, J.C., Masiero, S., Mateos-Nozal, J., Ortega, O. and Smithard, D.G. (2016) European Society for Swallowing Disorders – European Union Geriatric Medicine Society white paper: Oropharyngeal dysphagia as a geriatric syndrome. *Clinical Interventions in Aging*, 11, 1403_1428.

Baldwin, L. and Epstein, R. (2017) Short but Not Sweet: A Study of the Impact of Short Custodial Sentences on Mothers & Their Children. De Montfort University. Available at www.nicco.org.uk/userfiles/downloads/5bc45012612b4-short-but-not-sweet.pdf [accessed 14th March 2023]

Bignall, T., Jeraj, S., Helsby, E. and Butt, J. (2019) Racial disparities in mental health. Race Equality Foundation. Available at https://raceequalityfoundation.org.uk/wp-content/uploads/2022/10/mental-health-report-v5-2.pdf [accessed 14th March 2023]

Bishop, D. (2003) *Test for Reception of Grammar*, Version 2 (TROG-2). London: Pearson Assessment.

Brooks, C., Ballinger, C., Adams, J., Russell, C. and Nutbeam, D. (2013) Using health literacy communication skills with service users. *British Journal of Occupational Therapy*, 76. www.researchgate.net/publication/313481964_Using_health_literacy_communication_skills_with_service_users

Brown, E.A., Bekker, H.L., Davison, S.N., Koffman, J. and Schell, J.O. (2016) Supportive care: Communication strategies to improve cultural competence in shared decision making. *Clinical Journal of the American Society of Nephrology*, 11(10), 1902–1908.

Brown, C., Stoffel, V.C. and Munoz, J. (2019) *Occupational Therapy in Mental Health: A Vision for Participation* (2nd edn). F.A. Davis.

Bryan, K. (2021) Adults in the Prison Population. In L. Cummings (ed.) *Pragmatic Language Disorders: Complex and Underserved Populations*. New York: Springer.

Bülow, P.H., Finkel, D., Allgurin, M., Torgé, C.J., Jegermalm, M., Ernsth-Bravell, M. and Bülow, P. (2022) Aging of severely mentally ill patients first admitted before or after the reorganization of psychiatric care in Sweden. *International Journal of Mental Health Systems*, 16, 35. https://doi.org/10.1186/s13033-022-00544-9

Byard, R.W. and Bellis, M. (2016) Incidence of low body mass index in the elderly in forensic cases – A possible marker for frailty syndrome? *Journal of Forensic Sciences*, 61(3), 676–678.

Centre for Crime and Justice Studies (2022) Call for the release of IPP prisoners 'without delay'. Available at www.crimeandjustice.org.uk/news/2022-09-06/call-release-ipp-prisoners-without-delay [accessed 14th March 2023]

Cha, S., Kim, W.S., Kim, K.W., Han, J.W., Jang, H.C., Lim, S. and Paik, N.J. (2019) Sarcopenia is an independent risk factor for dysphagia in community-dwelling older adults. *Dysphagia*, 34(5), 692–697.

Cooper, K. (2007) *Indeterminate Sentences for Public Protection: A Report on the Indeterminate Sentence for Public Protection (IPP)*. London: The Howard League for Penal Reform.

Criminal Justice Act (2003). Available at www.legislation.gov.uk/ukpga/2003/44/contents [accessed 14th March 2023]

Cummings, L (2021) *Language Case Files in Neurological Disorders*. Routledge.

Das, K., Murray, K., Driscoll, R. and Nimmagadda, S.R. (2011) A comparative study of healthcare and placement needs among older forensic patients in a high secure versus medium/low secure hospital setting. *International Psychogeriatrics*, 23(5), 847–848.

Davis, S., Byers, S., Nay, R. and Koch, S. (2009) Guiding design of dementia friendly environments in residential care settings: Considering the living experiences. *Dementia*, 8(2), 185–203.

De Vries, M.G., Brazil, I.A., Tonkin, M. and Bulten, B.H. (2016) Ward climate within a high secure forensic psychiatric hospital: Perceptions of patients and nursing staff and the role of patient characteristics. *Archives of Psychiatric Nursing*, 30(3), 342–349.

Di Lorito, C. Dening, T. and Völlm, B. (2018) Ageing in forensic psychiatric secure settings: The voice of older patients. *The Journal of Forensic Psychiatry & Psychology*, 29(6), 934–960.

Dolezal, O. (2019) 'Tongue Tied' Man with Opiate Addiction. In *Clinical Cases in Neurology* (pp.99–105). Springer Nature.

Doyle, P.C. (2019) *Clinical Care and Rehabilitation in Head and Neck Cancer*. Springer Nature.

Dunn, L.M. and Dunn, D.M. (2009) *The British Picture Vocabulary Scale*. GL Assessment.

Esposito, M. (2015) Women in prison: Unhealthy lives and denied well-being between loneliness and seclusion. *Crime, Law and Social Change*, 63(3), 137–158.

Fazel, S., Fimińska, Z., Cocks, C. and Coid, J. (2016) Patient outcomes following discharge from secure psychiatric hospitals: Systematic review and meta-analysis. *The British Journal of Psychiatry*, 208(1), 17–25.

Goulet, M.H., Larue, C. and Dumais, A. (2017) Evaluation of seclusion and restraint reduction programs in mental health: A systematic review. *Aggression and Violent Behavior*, 34, 139–146.

Gupta, A., Dall, T.S. and Bansal, D. (2019) Endoscopic evaluation of dysphagia. *International Surgery Journal*, 6(12), 4323–4326.

Hayden, S (2022) *Using the Systems Approach for Aphasia: An Introduction for Speech and Language Therapists*. Routledge

Harris, M., Edgar, K. and Webster, R. (2020) 'I'm always walking on eggshells, and there's no chance of me ever being free': The mental health implications of Imprisonment for Public Protection in the community and post-recall. *Criminal Behaviour and Mental Health*, 30(6), 331–340.

Hyter, Y.D. and Salas-Provance, M.B. (2021) *Culturally Responsive Practices in Speech, Language, and Hearing Sciences*. Plural Publishing.

Inside Times (2022) 105-year-old prisoner dies at Stafford. Available at https://insidetime.org/105-year-old-prisoner-dies-at-stafford [accessed 14th March 2023]

Jones, I. and Volkmer, A. (2018) *Speech and Language Therapists and Mental Capacity 2019: A Training Resource for Adult Services*. J & R Press.

Justice Committee (2019) Prison population 2022: Planning for the future. Available at https://publications.parliament.uk/pa/cm201719/cmselect/cmjust/483/full-report.html [accessed 14th March 2023]

Justice Committee (2022) Imprisonment for Public Protection (IPP) sentences. Available at https://publications.parliament.uk/pa/cm5803/cmselect/cmjust/266/summary.html[accessed14thMarch 2023]

Kennedy, S.C., Kim, J.S., Tripodi, S.J., Brown, S.M. and Gowdy, G. (2016) Does parent–child interaction therapy reduce future physical abuse? A meta-analysis. *Research on Social Work Practice*, 26(2), 147–156.

Killias, M., Gilliéron, G., Villard, F. and Poglia, C. (2010) How damaging is imprisonment in the long term? A controlled experiment comparing long-term effects of community service and short custodial sentences on re-offending and social integration. *Journal of Experimental Criminology*, 6(2), 115–130.

Kristiansen, S., Olsen, L.S. and Beck, M. (2022) Hospitality in dementia-friendly environments is significant to caregivers during hospitalisation of their loved ones. A qualitative study. *Journal of Clinical Nursing*. https://doi.org/10.1111/jocn.16400

Lincoln, A., Paasche-Orlow, M.K., Cheng, D.M., Lloyd-Travaglini, C., Caruso, C., Saitz, R. and Samet, J.H. (2006) Impact of health literacy on depressive symptoms and mental health-related: Quality of life among adults with addiction. *Journal of General Internal Medicine*, 21(8), 818–822.

Marca-Frances, G., Frigola-Reig, J., Menéndez-Signorini, J.A., Compte-Pujol, M. and Massana-Morera, E. (2020) Defining patient communication needs during hospitalization to improve patient experience and health literacy. *BMC Health Services Research*, 20(1), 1–9.

Marks, L. and Rainbow, D. (2001) *Working with Dysphagia*. Routledge.

Martin, M.S., Crocker, A.G., Potter, B.K., Wells, G.A., Grace, R.M. and Colman, I. (2018) Mental health screening and differences in access to care among prisoners. *The Canadian Journal of Psychiatry*, 63(10), 692–700.

Mehay, A., Meek, R. and Ogden, J. (2021) Understanding and supporting the health literacy of young men in prison: A mixed-methods study. *Health Education*, 121(1), 93–110.

Ministry of Justice (2021) Prison Population Projections 2021 to 2026, England and Wales. Available at https://assets.publishing.service.gov.uk/government/uploads/system/uploads/attachment_data/file/1035682/Prison_Population_Projections_2021_to_2026.pdf [accessed 14th March 2023]

Murphy, D. (2000) An exploration of the concept of loneliness in forensic psychiatry. *Medicine, Science and the Law*, 40(1), 33–38.

Natarajan, M. and Mulvana, S. (2017) New horizons: Forensic mental health services for older people. *BJPsych Advances*, 23(1), 44–53.

Office for National Statistics (2021) Historic sexual abuse convictions. Available at www.ons.gov.uk/aboutus/transparencyandgovernance/freedomofinformationfoi/historicsexualabuseconvictions [accessed 14th March 2023]

Ogloff, J.R., Talevski, D., Lemphers, A., Wood, M. and Simmons, M. (2015) Co-occurring mental illness, substance use disorders, and antisocial personality disorder among clients of forensic mental health services. *Psychiatric Rehabilitation Journal*, 38(1), 16–23.

Oostermeijer, S., Brasier, C., Harvey, C., Hamilton, B., Roper, C., Martel, A., Fletcher, J. and Brophy, L. (2021) Design features that reduce the use of seclusion and restraint in mental health facilities: A rapid systematic review. *BMJ Open*, 11(7), e046647.

Pageau, F., Seaward, H., Habermeyer, E., Elger, B. and Wangmo, T. (2022) Loneliness and social isolation among the older person in a Swiss secure institution: A qualitative study. *BMC Geriatrics*, 22(1), 1–11.

Phillips, C., Bowling, B., Liebling, A. and Maruna, S. (2017) Ethnicities, racism, crime and criminal justice. In A. Liebling, S. Maruna and L. McAra (eds) *The Oxford Handbook of Criminology* (pp.190–212). Oxford: Oxford University Press.

Prison Reform Trust (2022) Prison: The facts. Bromley Briefings Summer 2022. Available at https:// prisonreformtrust.org.uk/wp-content/uploads/2022/07/Prison-the-facts-2022.pdf [accessed 14th March 2023]

Public Health England (2017) Health and social care needs assessments of the older prison population: A guidance document. Available at https://assets.publishing.service.gov.uk/government/uploads/ system/uploads/attachment_data/file/662677/Health_and_social_care_needs_assessments_of _the_older_prison_population.pdf [accessed 14th March 2023]

Ridley, L. (2022) No place for old men? Meeting the needs of an ageing male prison population in England and Wales. *Social Policy and Society*, 21(4), 597–611.

Robinson, G.C. and Norton, P.C. (2019) A decade of disproportionality: A state-level analysis of African American students enrolled in the primary disability category of speech or language impairment. *Language, Speech, and Hearing Services in Schools*, 50(2), 267–282.

Rudd, R.E. (2015) The evolving concept of health literacy: New directions for health literacy studies. *Journal of Communication in Healthcare*, 8(1), 7–9.

Schliehe, A., Laursen, J. and Crewe, B. (2021) Loneliness in prison. *European Journal of Criminology*, 19(6). https://doi.org/10.1177/1477370820988836

Simpson, S. (2016) Checklist for autism-friendly environments. Available at https:// positiveaboutautism.co.uk/uploads/9/7/4/5/97454370/checklist_for_autism-friendly_ environments_-september_2016.pdf [accessed 14th March 2022]

Sørensen, K., Pelikan, J.M., R€othlin, F., Ganahl, K., Slonska, Z., Doyle, G., Fullam, J., Kondilis, B., Agrafiotis, D., Uiters, E. and Falcon, M. (2015) Health literacy in Europe: Comparative results of the European health literacy survey (HLS-EU). *European Journal of Public Health*, 25(6), 1053–1058.

Staniszewska, S., Mockford, C., Chadburn, G., Fenton, S.J., Bhui, K., Larkin, M., Newton, E., Crepaz-Keay, D., Griffiths, F. and Weich, S. (2019) Experiences of in-patient mental health services: Systematic review. *The British Journal of Psychiatry*, 214(6), 329–338.

Stans, S.E., Dalemans, R.J., de Witte, L.P., Smeets, H.W. and Beurskens, A.J. (2017) The role of the physical environment in conversations between people who are communication vulnerable and health-care professionals: A scoping review. *Disability and Rehabilitation*, 39(25), 2594–2605.

Taylor, P.J. and Williams, S. (2014) Sentencing reform and prisoner mental health. *Prison Service Journal*, 211, 43–49.

Tapp, J., Warren, F., Fife-Schaw, C., Perkins, D. and Moore, E. (2013) What do the experts by experience tell us about 'what works' in high secure forensic inpatient hospital services? *The Journal of Forensic Psychiatry & Psychology*, 24(2), 160–178.

Tiraphat, S., Peltzer, K., Thamma-Aphiphol, K. and Suthisukon, K. (2017) The role of age-friendly environments on quality of life among Thai older adults. *International Journal of Environmental Research and Public Health*, 14(3), 282.

Uhrig, N. (2016) *Black, Asian and Minority Ethnic Disproportionality in the Criminal Justice System in England and Wales*. London: Ministry of Justice.

Visser, R.C., MacInnes, D., Parrott, J. and Houben, F. (2021) Growing older in secure mental health care: The user experience. *Journal of Mental Health*, 30(1), 51–57.

Volkmer, A (2013) *Assessment and Therapy for Language and Cognitive Communication Difficulties in Dementia and Other Progressive Diseases*. J & R Press.

Wahidin, A. (2007) 'No problems – old and quiet': Imprisonment in later life. In A. Wahidin and M. Cain (eds) *Ageing, Crime and Society*. Routledge.

Walshe, M. and Miller, N. (2022) *Clinical Cases in Dysarthria*. Routledge

Wechsler, D. (2008) *Wechsler Adult Intelligence Scale-Fourth Edition (WAIS-IV)*. Washington, DC: APA PsycTests.

World Health Organization (2007) *Health in Prisons: A WHO Guide to the Essentials in Prison Health*. Available at www.euro.who.int/__data/assets/pdf_file/0009/99018/E90174.pdf [accessed 14th March 2022]

World Health Organization (2018) *Age-Friendly Environments in Europe: Indicators, Monitoring and Assessments*. Available at www.who.int/publications/i/item/9789289052122 [accessed 14th March 2023]

Yacoub, E. and Hall, I. (2009) The sexual lives of men with mild learning disability: A qualitative study. *British Journal of Learning Disabilities*, 37(1), 5–11.

FINAL THOUGHTS AND PRACTICAL INFORMATION

DOI: 10.4324/9781003288701-9

We conclude this book with a chapter that:

- reminds the speech and language therapist (SLT) about scope-of-practice considerations as part of their registration to practise
- provides information on two new topics – relational security and homelessness
- offers some useful information for individual SLTs in respect of their own health and well-being when working in a criminal justice system (CJS) setting.

Scope of practice

All health professionals offering clinical intervention are registered via a registering body such the General Medical Council (GMC) for doctors, the Nursing and Midwifery Council (NMC) for nurses and the Health and Care Professions Council (HCPC) for allied health professionals. SLTs will be registered with HCPC, and the aim of registration is to ensure that all SLTs operate within an agreed standard of proficiency to protect members of the public from harm (Health and Care Professions Council, 2022). The SLT standards of proficiency to register with HCPC are (Health and Care Professions Council, 2014):

- to be able to practise safely and effectively within the SLT scope of practice
- to be able to practise within the legal and ethical boundaries of the SLT profession
- to be able to maintain fitness to practise
- to be able to practise as an autonomous professional, exercising professional judgement
- to be aware of the impact of culture, equality and diversity on practice
- to be able to practise in a non-discriminatory manner
- to understand the importance of and be able to maintain confidentiality
- to be able to communicate effectively
- to be able to work appropriately with others
- to be able to maintain records appropriately
- to be able to reflect on and review practice
- to be able to assure the quality of practice
- to understand the key concepts of the knowledge base relevant to their profession
- to be able to draw on appropriate knowledge and skills to inform practice
- to understand the need to establish and maintain a safe practice environment.

The first standard of scope of practice is important to mention. Scope of practice refers to completing tasks or activities as part of the SLT role that the individual SLT has knowledge and skills in, so that the individual SLT is competent. The HCPC does not list a set of knowledge and skills that an SLT must demonstrate, so the knowledge and skills vary from clinician to clinician. It is the responsibility of the SLT to consider whether they have the knowledge and skills in order to offer an intervention within the CJS. Knowledge and skills can be gained via supervision, training or self-directed learning. The key questions to ask when considering scope of practice are:

- Do I have the skills and knowledge to carry out the activity safely and effectively?
- Can I complete training or receive other support (such as supervision) that will give me the skills and knowledge needed to carry out the activity safely and effectively?
- Is the activity restricted by law (e.g. prescribing) and, if so, can I legally do it?
- Does my professional indemnity insurance cover the activity?

The SLT within the CJS has an understanding of working within a restricted environment and may see a wide range of patients, making the SLT an expert generalist. However, the SLT may receive referrals that are outside the scope of practice if there is limited knowledge of the role of SLT within the wider setting. For this reason, wherever possible, the multi-disciplinary team or the referring agent would agree the requirements of any referral or the course of action within an intervention with the individual SLT.

Relational security in criminal justice system

It is vitally important in CJS settings that security and safety are embedded in all areas. This includes physical security such as locks, keys and doors; procedural security such as how activities are conducted through the day to ensure safety (e.g. arranging to see patients in advance, protocols for arrival on a residential ward or wing, ensuring that all equipment and materials are accounted for with nothing left behind); and, lastly, relational security.

Relational security is 'the knowledge and understanding the staff team has of a patient and of the environment, and the translation of that information into appropriate responses and care' (Department of Health, 2010, p.5). To unpack this important concept further, relational security includes (Markham, 2022):

- Having a working relationship with a person (patient, service user or client) that is professional, boundaried and purposeful where all parties understand the context and limits of the working relationship.
- Professionally, the clinician would be expected to have non-negotiable boundaries that are agreed across the whole staff group. These would be rules such as never discussing the staff group's families, never discussing where any person lives and not disclosing personal information such as birthdays (in some settings, no personal information can be given).

- Negotiable boundaries are rules that have caveats such as not touching the person. On a day-to-day basis, SLTs may be expected not to touch a patient, but there may be occasions where therapeutic touch is required such as a swallow assessment. (In some settings, additional arrangements would need to be in place to do this.) Negotiable boundaries may also include talking about feelings. There are times when it is clinically appropriate for the SLT to label their own feelings that are being experienced, but it would not be appropriate to do this outside a clinical rationale such as a care plan to address alexithymia.

- Noticing interactions between all parties so that all people support each other to remain focused on therapeutic aims. An important aspect of this is having an open forum where all staff can talk about their interactions. This would include supporting colleagues to maintain boundaries as well as noticing if there are any concerning interactions between patients such as coercion or bullying. In some settings, there may be requirements that certain clients do not have the opportunity to meet.

The clinician is expected to develop a therapeutic alliance with the individual so that there is knowledge of thoughts, feelings, triggers and motivations while maintaining the boundaries. The knowledge of the individual is an important part of the risk assessment associated with their care and treatment (Chester, Alexander and Morgan, 2017).

Case example

SLT Katie has been working with Tony for 18 months. She is aware that Tony gets upset in May each year because it is a significant anniversary for him. She is also aware that Tony struggles to manage his intense and unwanted emotions, finds it hard to express how he is feeling and can be unpredictable when he is emotionally aroused. As a result, Katie factors this into his short-term risk assessment. She thinks that Tony is at increased risk of being upset, getting into arguments or disengaging with his daily routine. In advance of the anniversary, Katie put in place an emotions board in Tony's room and uses it with him each day to talk about how he is feeling. Katie responds to Tony's self-report by helping him plan a day which scaffolds his mood e.g. engaging activities when Tony is feeling demotivated, relaxing activities when Tony is feeling stressed, activities with less communication such as a quiz book – when Tony is feeling sad. The planning of the day is captured on a visual timetable which includes a mood rating scale so that Tony can see if his activities are helping him to cope during a difficult time. Katie is able to feedback to the staff team whether Tony's risks are reducing, remaining the same or increasing. This can inform a conversation about next steps such as his planned Section 17 community leave.

Relational security contributes to a safer environment for staff and patients with high standards of relational security being linked to reduced security lapses (Chester et al., 2017) and high levels of relational security contributing to higher levels of patient satisfaction (Arsuffi, 2017).

A comprehensive staff induction to the setting is required to support the SLT in understanding and following local policies for relational security. The topic of relational security should be revisited regularly as part of clinical or managerial supervision to ensure that the SLT remains safe and supported. Where the SLT is visiting an establishment on a consultancy basis, they should expect a security briefing and to be accompanied at all times.

Homelessness

In recent years, there has been published evidence that explores the speech, language and communication needs (SLCN) of homeless people and rough sleepers (Pluck et al., 2020; Alexander, 2018; Andrews and Botting, 2020). The findings state the following important points:

- Adults with histories of homelessness may have lower language skills than would be expected based on their educational backgrounds and non-verbal cognitive abilities.
- Use of illicit substances or excess alcohol exacerbates communication problems.
- Homeless adults are disproportionately male, and disproportionately with childhood histories of living in poverty, which may be associated with a raised prevalence of developmental language disorder (DLD).
- A study of runaway and homeless young people found that a majority had severe deficits of phonological processing.
- Assessment of a group of homeless shelter residents demonstrated that 60% performed within the delayed or impaired range for auditory comprehension and oral expression.
- Language delays are significantly more common among children experiencing homelessness than their peers.
- In a study of persons experiencing homelessness, 45.8% of respondents reported deficits in their communication skills, and 41.7% felt their social skills were underdeveloped.
- SLCN are highly prevalent among rough sleepers and significantly greater than for the UK general population.
- Homelessness organisations should provide training for staff in SLCN.

The SLCN of homeless people and rough sleepers are in the domains of auditory comprehension, expressive language and social communication. These needs impact on the person via:

- impaired social functioning which had a bearing on social relationship maintenance
- the inability to access services which required skills in understanding, processing, expression or social engagement
- occupational potential not being met due to problems with job applications or interviews.

Hopkin et al. (2020) state that:

> people who are homeless are more likely to come into contact with the criminal justice system. There is some evidence of increased rates of offending but it has also been acknowledged that those living on the streets are disproportionately targeted by police with heavy handed responses for minor offences, such as public urination and begging. Once arrested, homeless people are often treated differently by police and courts and are less likely to be granted immediate bail, as community alternatives are thought to be less likely to succeed. Additionally, this group is likely to have histories of offending and to have already spent time in prison.
>
> *(Hopkin et al., 2020, p.3)*

Case example

Joe is a young person who has been in contact with the CJS. He is age 26 and was in and out of care as a teenager. Joe struggled in school and was labelled with a 'behavioural problem', resulting in him being excluded from school. After falling out of education, he left the children's home and started 'sofa surfing' (sleeping at different people's homes as a temporary measure). Joe ends up living rough at age 18 and gets involved in shoplifting in order to obtain basic living goods such as food or toothpaste. This escalates to breaking into business premises in order to steal items or money. Joe ends up in prison and is referred to SLT by his keyworker because he doesn't seem to be able to remember information that is given to him. Joe has very low self-esteem and, in prison, struggles to ask for help because he 'can't be seen to look weak'. Joe is assessed by SLT and diagnosed with developmental language disorder and has the following communication profile:

- difficulty paying attention scoring on the 1st percentile on the Test of Everyday Attention (Robertson et al., 1994)

- low scores on Clinical Evaluation of Language Fundamentals Fifth Edition CELF-5 (Wiig, Semel and Secord, 2013) across all administered subtests indicating problems with sentence comprehension, linguistic concepts, following directions and word classes
- problems with expressive language including word finding, semantic relationship and sentence assembly measured via low scores on CELF-5 (Wiig et al., 2013)
- barriers to organising sentences and retelling a story measured via the Expression, Reception and Recall of Narrative Instrument (ERRNI) (Bishop, 2004)
- problems with auditory memory and recall based on patient self-report.

When Joe was asked how he felt on coming to prison, he said that it was a relief – 'somewhere with a roof over your head, you don't have to think about where the next meal is coming from'.

Joe was released from prison with a set of licence conditions and some verbal instructions. He could not read and understand the vocabulary of the licence conditions. He could not recall the verbal information. Joe struggled to know where to go and what to do. He had his mobile phone from before he came to prison, but the battery was flat and he had no phone credit. Joe is at significant risk of his release on licence failing. He is at risk of returning to prison many times and becoming stuck in a cycle. Figure 8.1 (below) below illustrates that cycle:

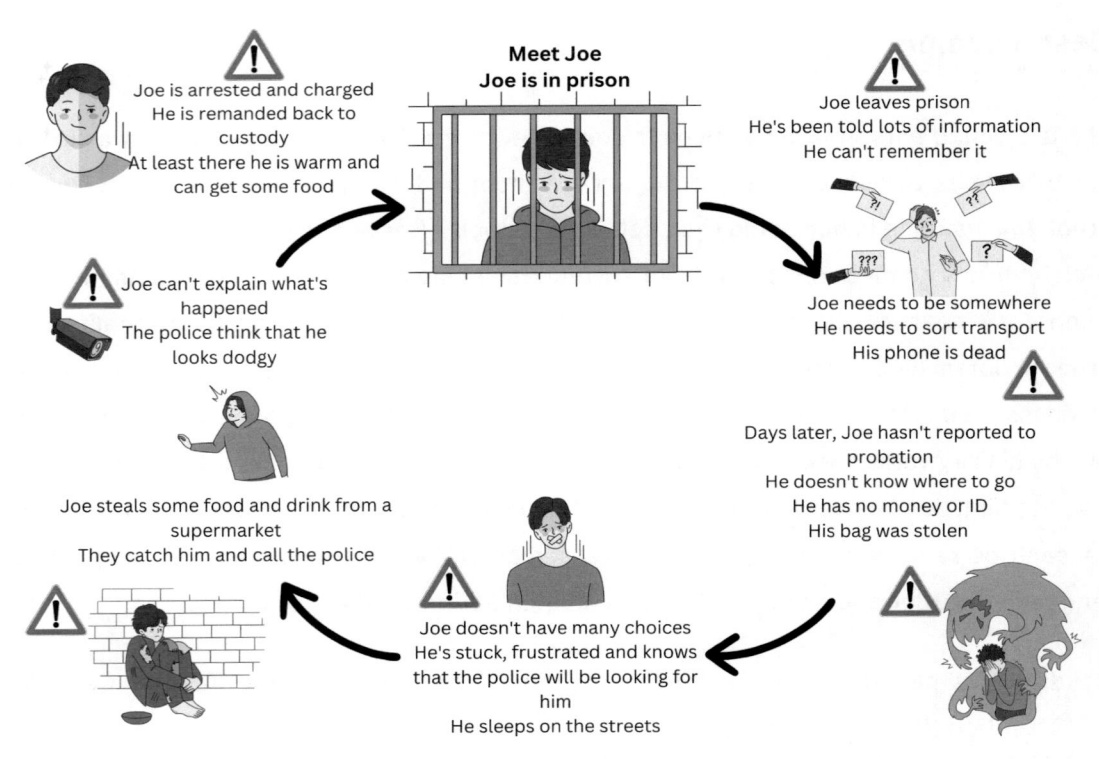

FIGURE 8.1 The cycle of leaving prison, SLCN and homelessness, which can result in returning to prison

What the research says about someone like Joe (Fitzpatrick, Johnsen and White, 2011; Lennox, 2014; Søndenaa, Wangsholm and Roos, 2016; Madoc-Jones et al., 2018, 2020; Dada, 2020; Morken, Jones and Helland, 2021):

- A person with this profile is likely to attract some court orders, which they breach, and end up with numerous short custodial sentences.
- Short sentences are very harmful to the potential for a stable living environment.
- Living rough, being involved in 'street activities', being in care and misusing substances are the four biggest risks for social exclusion. Social exclusion increases risks associated with homelessness and reoffending.
- People in prison have much higher rates of multiple and complex health and social problems compared with people in the general population. Many of these needs are unrecognised and unmet.
- Language is an essential part of social relations and serves several functions in social interactions. The failure to acquire and use developmentally appropriate language is known to contribute to non-verbal, aggressive behaviours.
- Joe may learn that antisocial behaviours are the most effective means of communicating his needs and achieving a desired outcome.
- Delinquent behaviour may represent an adaptation strategy for language-impaired people, providing an alternative way to obtain acceptance and maintain social position.
- All socially excluded groups are at increased risk of homelessness, but prison leavers are a distinctive and exceptionally vulnerable subgroup within the broader homeless population.

People who are homeless and at risk of contact with the CJS are a population group with particular needs. The SLT in the CJS should ask about homelessness as part of the case history and include support for leaving prison in discharge planning, particularly where the person is leaving to no fixed abode.

Training needs of self and others

The SLT will complete their qualification in speech and language therapy with the required skills to enable them to practise with a range of clients and a range of diagnostic labels. Beginning clinical work in SLT should always be supported with training specific to the role and supervision to support individual development.

Training needs will often be identified within the job description and person specification, and may include CJS-specific courses such as healing environment training, defensible documentation, personal safety and risk assessment. SLTs in the CJS may access training on positive behaviour support, Talking Mats, cognitive behaviour therapy, dialectical behaviour therapy, sensory integration, plus many more.

As the SLT progresses in their role, their training needs should be revisited annually via appraisal and throughout the year via management supervision. Other continued professional development opportunities include:

- Joining a clinical excellence network (CEN) (the Criminal Justice and Secure Settings CEN can be located via searching on Twitter).
- In-house peer working with colleagues such as occupational therapists, clinical psychologists and forensic psychologists.
- Attending conferences such as the National Autistic Society Offenders with an Intellectual and/or Developmental Disability conference or the Faculty of Forensic Psychiatry Conference. A wide range of conferences can be located via any popular search engine, and often interested parties can sign up for email alerts relating to lectures in specific areas of interest.
- Engaging with the evidence base via self-directed reading or joining a journal club.

Part of the SLT role will be to train other professionals and colleagues in understanding the SLT role, how to identify SLCN and how to contribute to the care of people within the CJS via intervention at the universal level (see Chapter 5). This is likely to include broad topics such as signs and symptoms of communication needs, total communication strategies and writing accessible materials, as well as setting specific topics such as how to support a person with SLCN to maximise their learning in group risk-reduction courses.

Lastly, the SLT has a role in training people with SLCN to understand their own needs and to acquire self-advocacy skills (see Chapter 6).

Different types of supervision and support

The SLT working in CJS should access supervision and support in the following ways:

- If newly qualified, complete newly qualified practitioner (NQP) competencies either with a professional supervisor, a workplace buddy or as part of a NQP peer support group. The NQP document can be found on the Royal College of Speech and Language Therapists (RCSLT) website.

- From the point of commencing in role, the SLT should access professional supervision from an appropriately experienced and qualified peer. Professional supervision provides the opportunity to discuss decision-making, clinical practice, the facilitation of learning via doing, professional development and the promotion of staff well-being. It is a useful forum to discuss clinical cases and it enhances staff well-being. Professional supervision can be from within the employing organisation or external to the organisation.
- Managerial supervision focuses on service delivery, working within scope of practice and clinical responsibilities, setting and reviewing performance targets and service development. Managerial supervision is usually offered by a senior colleague within the employing organisation and best practice suggests that the managerial supervisor should be separate from the professional supervisor.

In addition, SLTs can engage in professional support relationships via colleagues, Clinical Excellence Networks, informal peer support networks and buddy systems. Professional support can take the form of visiting a different setting to explore different service offerings, shadowing peers in their practice, sharing learning from small-scale in-house projects or forming a journal club.

Some workplaces offer a mentor scheme whereby SLTs who are developing new skills or increasing their scope of practice can have supportive meetings with a named mentor.

The goal of supervision is to have clarity about any activities which an SLT is entering into, and to feel supported or restored via the non-judgemental supportive experience of supervision.

For more detailed analysis of supervision, the RCSLT have published a comprehensive document which should be referred to (Royal College of Speech and Language Therapists, 2017).

Compassion and self-care

The SLT working in the CJS will encounter difficult cases which can cause upset or harm to their own or others' well-being. It is important to understand this and consider what it means and how to look after oneself.

Terminology for compassion and self-care:

- Compassion: a deep empathy for another's suffering, combined with a motivation to alleviate that suffering. Compassion can be experienced in multiple directions such as compassion for others, compassion from others and self-compassion. Compassion is recognised as being assembled of kindness (warmth and understanding), humanity (a shared connection to a fellow person) and recognition of the emotional state of the other person (Welford, 2012).

- Self-compassion: uses the same components as compassion, but with the components being directed to oneself. This is exemplified by being kind and understanding towards oneself in instances of pain or failure, rather than being self-critical; perceiving one's experiences of pain and failure as part of being human, rather than seeing these experiences as separating and isolating; holding painful thoughts and feelings in balanced awareness, rather than avoiding them or over-identifying with them (Walker, 2017).

- Burnout: a syndrome involving emotional exhaustion, depersonalisation and reduced personal accomplishment (Maslach, Jackson and Leiter, 1997). Emotional exhaustion includes feeling emotionally over-extended and exhausted by clinical work. People with high compassion levels are more at risk of emotional exhaustion due to over-empathy with patients.

- Depersonalisation is an unfeeling and impersonal response towards patients. Depersonalisation manifests as emotional distancing and reduction in empathy.

- Reduced personal accomplishment is feelings of incompetence and lack of successful achievement associated with feelings of self-doubt and negative self-evaluation, and it is particularly likely to occur in therapists whose self-esteem is contingent on their work performance (Walker, 2017).

- Self-care: various strategies of promoting or maintaining physical, psychological and spiritual health, as well ensuring that personal and family needs are met. Self-care requires self-reflection and sufficient awareness to identify both personal and professional stressors and supports (Walker, 2017).

The evidence base for therapists in relation to compassion and self-care suggests that the therapist should spend some time identifying their own stressors (unmet needs or triggers) either as a reflective exercise on their own or with a peer. After stressors are identified, the therapist should identify their personal self-care strategies, which can be used proactively but also reactively when a stressor is encountered. Self-care strategies should be across four domains: psychological, spiritual, physical and social (Walker, 2017).

In Chapter 1, the Good Lives model (Ward, 2002) was discussed in respect of people at risk of committing crimes having reduced risks if they have 'goods' in each domain of a circular diagram. A similar approach can be taken to the SLT having self-care strategies in each of the four domains of psychological, spiritual, physical and social.

Detail on each domain:

- Psychological: engaging with music; reading and writing; accessing good-quality supervision; spending time with activities or people who enhance your positivity; learning a new skill such as playing an instrument; peer support groups where compassion and burnout is discussed and normalised.
- Spiritual: spending time alone or in meditation; exercising mindfulness; practising a faith or religion; spiritual engagement with nature; journal writing.
- Physical: exercise; mindful walking; gardening; dance classes; eating a healthy diet; spending time outdoors.
- Social: seeing friends and family; engaging with peer support; being part of a social group or organisation.

Self-care is thought to be the main protective factor to prevent compassion fatigue and burnout, and should be applied to each of the stressors that were identified in reflective practice (Walker, 2017). SLTs are reminded that neglecting self-care is not helpful for the service user, the therapist themselves, the service that they work in or the organisation.

Lack of self-compassion has been found to contribute to feelings of depression, anxiety and overreaction to stress triggers in professionals (Teater and Ludgate, 2014). Ideas to improve self-compassion are:

- developing a daily routine which includes quality sleep, healthy food, rest and work
- spending time with friends and family following joint interests
- exercising, spending time outdoors and practising relaxation or mindfulness
- setting aside personal time for activities such as reading or soaking in the bath
- planning annual leave across the year so that there are regular breaks
- following hobbies, interests and leisure pastimes
- accepting compliments, reducing negative self-talk, increasing positive affirmations
- practising emotional awareness by noticing feelings and emotional expression via discussing feelings with trusted others
- engaging in time spent in spiritual or religious activities
- following a clearly defined work–life balance, including taking time off work if unwell

- accessing support, supervision, continued professional development, informal networks with colleagues
- structuring the working day so that tasks have adequate time allocated, work is paced, caseload sizes are achievable and work is prioritised.

Schwartz Rounds have been introduced within the NHS in the UK. These are regular multi-disciplinary meetings with the aim of discussing openly the challenges and demands of working with client groups that might stimulate distress in staff teams. The meeting allows people to be vulnerable about their own feelings, discuss shared values and reflect as a group. The evidence base for Schwartz Rounds indicates that the process increases team cohesion, reduces staff burnout and improves patient care (Flanagan et al., 2020; Farr and Barker, 2017; Adamson et al., 2018).

Compassionate supervision has been identified as protective against burnout and to be restorative for well-being (Beaumont and Martin, 2016). This is supervision where supervisors model compassion, inspire self-compassion in their supervisee via employing some of the strategies suggested in this section and encourage confidence in admitting vulnerabilities and increasing willingness to take on new challenges (Beaumont and Martin, 2016).

The role of managers and leaders in this area is to develop workplaces that have a culture of fairness, respect and social justice. This includes ensuring that workloads are manageable and sustainable, that there is fair and equal access to training opportunities, and that individuals feel seen, valued and heard (Heath, Sommerfield and von Ungern-Sternberg, 2020).

Case example

In Shropshire, the community learning disability team offered staff weekly guided mindfulness sessions as part of their working week for eight weeks. The sessions taught staff a range of mindfulness activities and encouraged staff to build these into their working week either individually or within a peer support framework. Outcomes via self-reported well-being questionnaires suggested that all staff had improved well-being and self-compassion.

Suggested reading:

- *The Therapist's Workbook* (Kottler, 2011)
- *Leaving it at the Office* (Norcross and Guy, 2007)

- *The Resilient Practitioner* (Skovholt and Trotter-Mathison, 2011)
- *Overcoming Compassion Fatigue* (Teater and Ludgate, 2014)
- *Transforming the Pain* (Saakvitne and Pearlman, 1996)
- *The Compassion Fatigue Workbook* (Mathieu, 2012).

Signposting to internet resources

The internet provides a wealth of resources and information. It is beyond the scope of this book to signpost the reader to all possible internet resources that may be useful within clinical areas that are associated with the CJS. However, a list of frequently used internet sites is included in Appendix 34.

Conclusion

This chapter has reminded SLTs about their scope of practice as defined by their registering body, HCPC. The chapter has introduced the topics of relational security and considered the importance of thinking about SLCN and homelessness. Lastly, the chapter has offered ideas relating to compassion and self-care.

References

Adamson, K., Searl, N., Sengsavang, S., Yardley, J., George, M., Rumney, P., Hunter, J. and Myers-Halbig, S. (2018) Caring for the healthcare professional: A description of the Schwartz Rounds™ implementation. *Journal of Health Organization and Management*, 32(3), 402–415.

Alexander, E. (2018) Communication Disorders among Persons Experiencing Homelessness (Doctoral dissertation, University of Kansas).

Andrews, L. and Botting, N. (2020) The speech, language and communication needs of rough sleepers in London. *International Journal of Language & Communication Disorders*, 55(6), 917–935.

Arsuffi, L. (2017) What is the Relationship between Relational Security, Attachment, Ward Incidents and Treatment Outcomes on Forensic Psychiatric Wards? (Doctoral dissertation, University of Birmingham).

Beaumont, E. and Martin, C.J.H. (2016) Heightening levels of compassion towards self and others through use of compassionate mind training. *British Journal of Midwifery*, 24(11), 777–786.

Bishop, D. (2004) *Expression, Reception and Recall of Narrative Instrument*. Pearson.

Chester, V., Alexander, R.T. and Morgan, W. (2017) Measuring relational security in forensic mental health services. *BJPsych Bulletin*, 41(6), 358–363.

Dada, T. (2020) 'Pupils excluded from school might as well be given a prison sentence' – Former Director-General. The Common Sense Network. Available at www.tcsnetwork.co.uk/young-people-excluded-from-school-might-as-well-be-given-a-prison-sentence-says-former-director-general [accessed 15th March 2023]

Department of Health (2010) See, Think, Act: Your guide to relational security. Available at https://assets.publishing.service.gov.uk/government/uploads/system/uploads/attachment_data/file/320249/See_Think_Act_2010.pdf [accessed 15th March 2023]

Farr, M. and Barker, R. (2017) Can staff be supported to deliver compassionate care through implementing Schwartz Rounds in community and mental health services? *Qualitative Health Research*, 27(11), 1652–1663.

Fitzpatrick, S., Johnsen, S. and White, M. (2011) Multiple exclusion homelessness in the UK: Key patterns and intersections. *Social Policy and Society*, 10(4), 501–512.

Flanagan, E., Chadwick, R., Goodrich, J., Ford, C. and Wickens, R. (2020) Reflection for all healthcare staff: A national evaluation of Schwartz rounds. *Journal of Interprofessional Care*, 34(1), 140–142.

Health and Care Professions Council (2014) Standards of proficiency – Speech and Language therapist. Available at www.hcpc-uk.org/resources/standards/standards-of-proficiency-speech-and-language-therapists [accessed 15th March 2023]

Health and Care Professions Council (2022) Why your registration matters. Available at www.hcpc-uk.org/registration/your-registration/why-your-registration-matters [accessed 15th March 2023]

Heath, C., Sommerfield, A. and von Ungern-Sternberg, B.S. (2020) Resilience strategies to manage psychological distress among healthcare workers during the COVID-19 pandemic: A narrative review. *Anaesthesia*, 75(10), 1364–1371.

Hopkin, G., Chaplin, L., Slade, K., Craster, L., Valmaggia, L., Samele, C. and Forrester, A. (2020) Differences between homeless and non-homeless people in a matched sample referred for mental health reasons in police custody. *International Journal of Social Psychiatry*, 66(6), 576–583.

Kottler, J.A. (2011) *The Therapist's Workbook: Self-Assessment, Self-Care, and Self-Improvement Exercises for Mental Health Professionals*. John Wiley & Sons.

Lennox, C. (2014) The health needs of young people in prison. *British Medical Bulletin*, 112(1), 17–25.

Madoc-Jones, I., Hughes, C., Gorden, C., Dubberley, S., Washington-Dyer, K., Ahmed, A., Lockwood, K. and Wilding, M. (2018) Rethinking preventing homelessness amongst prison leavers. *European Journal of Probation*, 10(3), 215–231.

Madoc-Jones, I., Ahmed, A., Hughes, C., Dubberley, S., Gorden, C., Washington-Dyer, K., Lockwood, K. and Wilding, M. (2020) Imaginary homelessness prevention with prison leavers in Wales. *Social Policy and Society*, 19(1), 145–155

Markham, S. (2022) See think act: The need to rethink and refocus on relational security. *The Journal of Forensic Psychiatry & Psychology*, 33(2), 200–230.

Maslach, C., Jackson, S.E. and Leiter, M.P. (1997) *Maslach Burnout Inventory*. Scarecrow Education.

Mathieu, F. (2012) *The Compassion Fatigue Workbook: Creative Tools for Transforming Compassion Fatigue and Vicarious Traumatization*. Routledge.

Morken, F., Jones, L.Ø. and Helland, W.A. (2021) Disorders of language and literacy in the prison population: A scoping review. *Education Sciences*, 11(2), 77.

Norcross, J.C. and Guy, J.D. (2007) *Leaving it at the Office: A Guide to Psychotherapist Self-Care*. The Guilford Press.

Pluck, G., Barajas, B.M., Hernandez-Rodriguez, J.L. and Martínez, M.A. (2020) Language ability and adult homelessness. *International Journal of Language & Communication Disorders*, 55(3), 332–344.

Robertson, I.H., Ward, T., Ridgeway, V. et al. (1994) *The Test of Everyday Attention*. Bury St Edmunds: Thames Valley Test Company.

Royal College of Speech and Language Therapists (2017) Information on Supervision. Available at www.rcslt.org/wp-content/uploads/media/docs/delivering-quality-services/infomation-on-supervision.pdf [accessed 15th March 2023]

Saakvitne, K.W. and Pearlman, L.A. (1996) *Transforming the Pain: A Workbook on Vicarious Traumatization*. W.W. Norton & Co.

Skovholt, T. and Trotter-Mathison, M. (2011) *The Resilient Practitioner: Counseling and Psychotherapy: Investigating Practice from Scientific, Historical, and Cultural Perspectives*. New York and London: Routledge.

Søndenaa, E., Wangsholm, M. and Roos, E. (2016) Case characteristics of prisoners with communication problems. *Open Journal of Social Sciences*, 4(4), 31–37.

Teater, M. and Ludgate, J. (2014) *Overcoming Compassion Fatigue: A Practical Resilience Workbook*. PESI Publishing & Media.

Walker, L. (2017) Compassion, Burn-out and Self-Care in NHS Staff Delivering Psycholgoical Interventions (Doctoral dissertation, University of East London).

Ward, T. (2002) Good lives and the rehabilitation of offenders: Promises and problems. *Aggression and Violent Behavior*, 7(5), 513–528.

Wiig, E.H., Semel, E. and Secord, W.A. (2013) *Clinical Evaluation of Language Fundamentals–Fifth Edition* (CELF-5). Bloomington, MN: NCS Pearson.

Welford, M. (2012) *The Compassionate Mind Approach to Building Self-Confidence*. London: Robinson.

Index